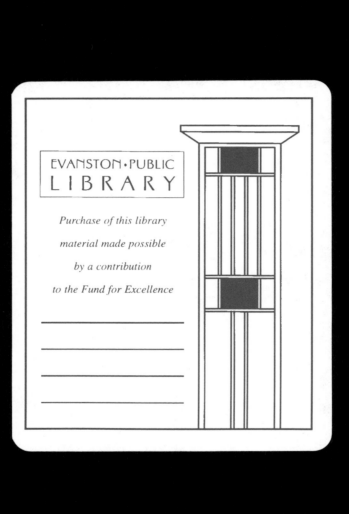

Surrealist Painters and Poets

Surrealist Painters and Poets
An Anthology

edited by Mary Ann Caws

The MIT Press

Cambridge, Massachusetts

London, England

This book was set in Bembo by Achorn Graphic Services, Inc., and was printed and bound in the United States of America.

Library of Congress Cataloging-in-Publication Data

Surrealist painters and poets: an anthology / edited by Mary Ann Caws.
   p. cm.
 Includes bibliographical references and index.
  ISBN 0-262-03275-9 (hc.: alk. paper)
  1. French poetry—20th century—Translations into English. 2. Surrealism—France.
3. Artists' writings. I. Caws, Mary Ann.

PQ1170.E6 S8 2001
700′.41163—dc21   00-032888

Source notes are found on p. 517.

*For my children
and in memory of René Char*

René Char as a child, with Emilienne, Lily, and Marthe Brun, in Lacoste, 1915. Gift of René Char to the author.

René Char with Matthew and Hilary Caws, at Les Busclats, L'Isle-sur-Sorgue, 1976.

Contents

Texts

Contents

Contents

Contents

Contents

Contents

Contents

Contents

SURREALIST GATHERING

Le champ de tous et celui de chacoun. (The field of each and everyone.)
—*René Char of Nicolas de Staël*

How do you know when an artist or a writer is part of a movement like surrealism? Is it by some set of criteria relating to the work of art or anti-art: strange imagery, apparently disconnected writing or thinking, an eccentric look, an odd subject matter, that is to say, something we judge to seem "Surrealist" by whatever criteria we accept? Or André Breton's stamp on the authentic Surrealism of such and such a writer, painter, thinker? Or is it the relation of the artist to a group considering itself "Surrealist" either in the past (or the present—despite the fact that Jean Schuster, on behalf of the Surrealist movement, declared its death in 1969)? All these are acceptable reasons for inclusion in a Surrealist anthology, and there are surely others; but, if pushed, I will find myself in agreement mainly with the last—the artist's own self-characterization.

In this grouping, I have chosen to include the artists and writers I think of as most interestingly surrealist, or dada-surrealist, as in the cases of Marcel Duchamp, Max Ernst, Tristan Tzara, Mina Loy, Francis Picabia. Let whatever gods and saints preside over creation and the great Surrealism-in-the-Sky pardon me, please, if I err in judgment: I have used my own and that of the creators most concerned here below. Wanting above all not to lose the spirit of excitement prevalent in the best of surrealist art and texts, I have found it advisable to maintain mine.

Hoping to represent as generously much as possible in this compilation, made over a long period of time and with great care, I have observed certain criteria and principles of organization. The grouping is triple, like a play in three acts: memoirs, texts, and various other writings. As for the selection, among the many possible forms of Surrealism, I have chosen according to three criteria: the most representative texts from among the great multiplicity of genres, the largest number of authors considering themselves, at least at one point, Surrealists, who could be accommodated in the space available, and the kinds of styles I have found to be the most lastingly persuasive. From the founders and writers of the movement, the choices are more plentiful, and lengthier. Selections from certain of Surrealism's epic texts are included here: Aragon's *Paris Peasant,* Breton's *Mad Love,* Tzara's *Approximate Man,* as from the celebrated Surrealist journals from the '20s through the '40s in diverse countries where the movement put down its hardiest roots, such as France, Belgium, Martinique, Senegal, and America: *La Revolution surréaliste, Minotaure, VVV, View, Tropiques.* The genres include memoirs, essays, poems, novels, film scenarios, dreams, trance events, collective stories, interviews, reworked proverbs, outlandish vignettes, manifestoes, and declarations.

The companion volume to this one, *The Surrealist Look: An Erotics of Encounter* (Cambridge: MIT Press, 1997), gives an idea of what surrealism looks like, how it looks outside and inside itself, and how it looks to us. The two books were conceived together, as a twin testimony to a movement of inestimable importance to the arts of the twentieth century, as a modern/post-modern phenomenon that has had an impact beyond its time and place. In a sense, it has represented us all, in one of our modes. It had many, as is apparent in these pages.

If Surrealism began as French, in 1923–24, after the Swiss-German impulse of Dada, in 1916–17, its spirit was present, and is present still in much of the creative world. So the reader will find included here writers and artists from England, France, Germany, Martinique, Mexico, Spain, Switzerland, Senegal, as well as North and South America.

Surrealist Painters and Poets is a deliberate followup to Robert Motherwell's great *Dada Painters and Poets*. He was to write the preface for this anthology, a task he had accepted with enthusiasm, as he did the table of contents I shared with him, not so very different from the present one. I was greatly looking forward to discussing it with him, and so I preface this volume in his memory, excerpting from my conversations with him some of his comments, in lieu of his own preface.

Motherwell's preface would have been at once simple and deep, practical and lyrical. I have chosen to reprint, quite simply, this interview in place of what he was going to write.

Interview with Robert Motherwell about Surrealism,
Provincetown, Massachusetts, 1990

MAC: Can you talk to me about your relation to the Surrealists, when they had come over here, during the war?

RM: It was an extraordinary experience, but it was not a big help for me in some ways, because I had a negative feeling about a lot of it. I guess I thought they weren't painterly

Robert Motherwell, *Caprice 34,* 1962; courtesy of Getty Archives. © VAGA.

Robert Motherwell, portrait by Renate Ponsold Motherwell, gift to the author.

enough. The painters were definitely secondary to the writers. The unexpressed opinion was the writers were good and the painters existed primarily to illustrate the writers' ideas. Of course, that was partly the problem with Surrealism in America, because Surrealism was identified partly with Dalí and several others, and because all the writing was in French. . . . I remember one of the crises. They were worried about being exiles, and all the rest of it. Breton was offered a position, to be regularly on the Voice of America, to broadcast to Europe in French, and was this giving in to capitalism and imperialism?, and so on. That kind of issue, and there were a couple of months of—I am sure on his part—tormented decisions, and so on. Whereas painters are much more peasants, one thing at a time. You know: what is the practical solution?[1]

Another thing that struck me was they would get into violent arguments, and there was one in particular: Max Ernst and Breton having a furious argument and standing face to face shouting at each other; it had something to do with their wives, and Breton saying at a certain moment, "If it weren't for me, your painting wouldn't exist." What struck me was the Frenchness—that at that point of emotion, Americans would have hit each other, but there was never any question of that. I remember once Breton had a meeting—there were occasional meetings—and it was to choose new saints for the calendar, the Bloody Nun, and so on. So everybody had to write about fifteen mythological personages that interested them. To Breton's rage, the three or four Americans present all put down the unicorn, whereas he preferred the Bloody Nun or the Black Mass. Finally, he wanted it to be part of the Surrealist document, this thing on the saints, and there was no consensus at all.

I remember [the journal] *VVV,* which also reminds me—they wanted a new letter, and I kept explaining that in French it makes perfect sense: "double-V, triple-V," but in English, "double-u," you can't say "triple-u." I remember another time Breton wanted a column called "The Conscience of Surrealism" in a magazine, and I asked if he means "consciousness" or "conscience," and he couldn't get the distinction with "conscience." He made it all quite ambiguous.

But basically I stayed on the sidelines, because what did interest me was the fraternity. All the American painters were basically rivals, and the collaborativeness of the Surrealists was something really amazing. Also I was particularly friendly with Matta, who was brilliant in his way, and generous, and my age. The Surrealists in general were a generation older.

It was the idea of poets sticking together—there was a real fraternity, with very high stakes, in the sense that if somebody was thrown out, it was almost like a family disinheriting a cousin or a son. And Matta was always a little sensitive to that, because he came from a wealthy background from which he had broken away, and was Spanish-speaking, and a young genius. The last young genius they had who was Spanish-speaking was Dalí, who was absolutely a traitor, and Matta instigated a palace revolt. He wanted to do abstract expression by creating a palace and getting Baziotes to go around and explain automatism to some other American artists, like Gorky, Hans Hofmann, De Kooning, and a more minor artist called Peter Busa. And the Americans were not very interested, maybe because I was just a beginning painter and didn't have any prestige, but mostly essential every man was on his own, and out for himself.

But Peggy Guggenheim, who was then married to Max Ernst, was interested in the project, and said if we did come up with a new visual idea of some sort, that she would give us an exhibition in her gallery, and that did interest especially De Kooning and Pollock. Then, a couple of months later, Matta fell in love with some very rich American girl and divorced his wife and twins and moved out of his poverty into more well-to-do circumstances, and into a crowd of more well-to-do people. He sort of abandoned us all, and so nothing came of it.

MAC: Did you gather over long dinners, or in cafes? How did that work?

RM: There used to be a restaurant in the mid-fifties, called Larre's, where Renate quite independently used to go. But I remember lunch was prix-fixe, for I think 85 cents, you had a three-course meal, and wine was fifteen cents a glass, and dinner was about a dollar and ten cents. I wasn't that intimate with them, but I certainly had many lunches there with them. Maybe I was there twice a week. And quite often in the evenings, sometimes at Breton's place, sometimes at Peggy Guggenheim's place, when she was married to Max Ernst.

Robert Motherwell, portrait by Renate Ponsold Motherwell, gift of Robert Motherwell.

MAC: Did you play Surrealist games?

RM: Yes, one game was "Penalty"—it was truth and consequences and you had to tell the truth or pay some devastating penalty. It was some question like "When did you first start masturbating?" and in front of fifteen people, it was awful. We played the "Exquisite Corpse" a lot, and in one sense there was a lot of childishness, from an American standpoint, I mean. Americans in an equivalent mood would be much more apt to horse-play, but the solemnity of these childish games was funny. And the other thing was that none of the Americans was Catholic-reared, and all of the Surrealists except Kurt Selig-mann were Catholic, so that one of the chief enemies was the Church and all the anti-

Catholicism that goes with it, which left all of us unmoved, because all the Americans were either Jews or Protestants, and there was none of the whole store of us who were Catholic. I always thought it extraordinary that one of the extraordinary things about that moment in painting is that there were no Roman Catholics, and I would have assumed that the French, Italians, Greeks, and Spaniards wou   naturally to painting.

I think it had a lot to do with American   , because Catholics grow up, after all, being surrounded by imagery. And I think it is why the French have always had great difficulty with abstract art, and why on the other hand, it blossoms in Holland. And the Italians have had difficulty with it. . . .

MAC: So if Mondrian had not been Dutch, the whole course of modern painting would have been different.

RM: He's a perfect Protestant painter, and his whole rationale for his painting—that the source of human anguish is conflict—so to make an art of harmony; and that the source of wars is every kind of conflict is what he calls the particular, that we would call the personal, you know, a husband and wife fighting, or Germany and France fighting. He would like to have made an art like Spinoza's sub-species *eternitatis*. It is ironic in some ways that his painting is the most dated of the period.

In short, I was very close to the Surrealists, but I had one tremendous advantage over them, since I was philosophically trained and had that kind of critical mind, and am not the kind of person who could be doctrinaire. For me, to put it in more vulgar terms, everybody has his own insanity. The best part of human reality and the part that is really crucial, you ignore, unless it comes to crucial issues. Also I liked abstract art, and in the 1930s, to really love Cubism, which I did, or Cézanne or Mondrian, was really very rare. And when I found them, I knew nobody who knew them or liked them. . . .

MAC: So you couldn't discuss them with anybody.

RM: No, they were my own private domain. One of the first pictures I ever made was in '43, all yellow and purple stripes. And I remember when Matta saw it, he said, "I don't know whether Breton would go for a painting of the flag." I knew it was a marvelous painting, that part of its impulse was the unconscious influence of Mondrian. He was the only one, and I fought against it, so I made the lines more handmade, more sensitive, more I don't know what. In another sense it wasn't abstract at all, in the Mondrian way of being an assertion of universal principles, and so on. It was done when I was in Mexico, or right after I got back, I don't remember. So in that particular sense, there was always a great gulf between me and the Surrealists. What attracted me was their Europeanness, their camaraderie, whatever I thought of their paintings, which I admired very much, but I remember the Surrealists asking me if I thought Miró was any good. He was too abstract for them, but I said "absolutely." Miró was also suspect in leading a perfectly ordinary, orderly bourgeois life. In fact, Matta told me that once, in a drunken studio party in Paris, somebody had seen Miró with his wife come out of church—it must have been a Sunday night— and somebody sober came in, maybe Giacometti—they had put a rope over the rafters, and they were about to hang Miró, and they cut the rope.

Robert Motherwell, *The Voyage,* 1949; oil and tempera on paper mounted on composition board, 48 in. × 7 ft., 10 in. Museum of Modern Art, New York. © VAGA.

MAC: Was there anyone else they disliked as much as that?

RM: Their bête noire was Dalí, whom they nicknamed Avida Dollars.

MAC: Did they talk about Tzara at all?

RM: No. The meetings I attended were always about some project, the next issue of *VVV,* the *First Papers of Surrealism,* that huge show at the Whitelaw Reid Mansion. There was always something specific. I think they tolerated me because one of their admirable qualities was to believe in young talent. Because after all, their heroes were Rimbaud and Lautréamont, Seurat, all of the great young people. For example, in the Whitelaw Reid Mansion show, there must have been a hundred pictures, including a Picasso, and the four youngest artists—I was one of them—were given the place of honor, and Picasso was given the worst place, as a beau geste.

There were lots of marvelous things. I would say in a way they were aware, and I guess in a way this is what attracted me to them. I never thought of it until this moment. The culture demanded responsibilities, and obligations, the way a citizen does, a citizen of a country, not somehow everybody for himself, who is going to be the first one to show a picture at the Museum of Modern Art, or get Knopf as a publisher, or whatever.

There was a real sense that culture entails responsibilities, but at the same time, because they were Marxists and anti-Stalinists, they were very free of the Stalinist cant which was all over the place in the '30s and the '40s. The *Partisan Review* in a way took the same position. . . . I think the strength of Marxism in the artistic and literary communities in the '30s and '40s is very underestimated. It was a very difficult problem for intellectuals.

MAC: Was there lots of talk about politics at those dinners and lunches?

RM: No, because I think they had already agreed in principle before they came to America, and most of their conversation was about more immediate problems: the fear that in America, if we entered the war, the mail would be censored, that this might become a totalitarian country. I spent a lot of my time reassuring them about that.

In fact, in those days I had a Mexican wife, and one day in Provincetown there was a knock on the door, and it was two FBI agents, with those anonymous pants and very serious, and finally they tore out a letter that my wife Maria—she was a very childlike actress—had written to her family in Mexico that a German submarine had been sunk off Provincetown, which was true, but rather childish gossip. As if a Ferris wheel had been turned over. The FBI guys were all upset about it and cut it all to pieces, so there was just "I love you," and a couple of other things left in it. And another time they came in and asked me about Max Ernst, who was technically a German citizen, though he had left Germany. In 1938, he had been in a huge show called "Masterpieces of French Art." They made him and Peggy Guggenheim leave the Cape, because it was against the law for an American citizen to live with an enemy alien within ten miles of the seacoast.

When I was living in East Hampton, they visited me and wanted to know, Who were all these naked swimmers? There were quite a few Surrealists out there who often went nude bathing on a secluded beach, so they were obviously in a deep political plot. The war was on everybody's mind. In the beginning, the *New York Times*—every day they would have the map of Europe, and every day it was blacker and blacker, and by the third year it seemed as though Germany was actually going to conquer all of Europe. . . . Everyone had relatives. I remember the French department at a women's college, Mt. Holyoke, arranged a conference like Pontigny.[2]

MAC: You went and spoke, I believe.

RM: Yes. André Masson was also there, and we went swimming, I think in the river, and when we were in our bathing shorts, I noticed he had a gaping hole in his chest, and I turned to his wife Rose, who is a lovely simple woman, and said, "My God, what's that cavity in André's chest?" and she said, "It's from a German machine gun in the First World War," and then she said: "André and Max Ernst both believed that they were in opposite trenches at the time it took pace, and that Max may have actually shot him in the chest."

Something that is not emphasized enough about the Dadaists is their involvement in World War I; I imagine if you have gone through something like that, then Dadaism and Surrealism would seem far more real, instead of parlor games and pure intellectualism.

That is the point of view of the American artist on the scene who was the closest to the French Surrealists. The viewpoint of the American writers on the scene is most amusingly expressed by William Carlos Williams, writing a letter to Charles Henri Ford's New York journal *View* (vol. 2, no. 2, 1942). Here Williams defines Surrealism as "don't try. An incentive to creation. . . . To me, Surrealism is to disclose without trying." But, four years later, he finds the opposite to be true of Breton's *Young Cherry Trees Secured against Hares* (published by View Editions, all the more ironic, since David Hare, the editor of the journal

VVV, was deeply involved with Breton's wife Jacqueline Lamba; she was later to marry Hare.) Reviewing the book for *View* in the Fall 1946 issue, Williams states categorically: "As with Catholicism and Sovietism everything is planned in Surrealism. . . ." He finds Breton's writing "simple and crystal clear."

> Everybody knows before hand everything that will be said. It is completely without invention in the American sense—this is its greatest achievement. . . .
> WE CAN EXPECT NOTHING NEW FROM FRANCE IN THE WORLD ANY MORE. This Breton recognizes and proves in his revolutionary work.

For Williams, Breton is hiding, under cover (*sub rosa*), his own appurtenance to the long tradition and convention of the great past of French thought starting with Descartes:

> It must be done without letting the others discover how quietly flows the great river of his genius beneath the false soil of the fields and skies he paints in his poems with the brushes used by miniaturists in making their copies of the portraits of Napoleon by David. . . . Oh, but this is difficult and onerous work. A man must labor under strange constraints to accomplish it. One could see Breton in New York for the past four years walking the streets or sitting drinking with his cronies at the Mont D'Or on E. 48th Street but never, never could one see beneath that pudgy surface the true son of France sleeping far from the dull gazes of the casual passerby. Thence emerges this magnificent and quieting book. . . . It is France redivivus. . . . It is a flight from abstraction to common sense. What is liberty? André Breton.

American poetry, smashing the line apart in its iconoclastic gesture should, says Williams, take notice of Breton's warning that such a procedure cannot work. This, by the Frenchman representing the great rationalism of French thought—which no one but he who in his heart is a Frenchman can fully know."

A word about poetry and genre may be in order. In the eyes of André Breton, a writer truly committed to surrealist principles was indeed a "poet," whatever the genre of writing. Surrealists were poets by definition. Surrealism was a lyric behavior, with all that it implied of moral principles, unbourgeois situations, and continuous creation. The surrealist poets as such rarely made any separation between their texts. Robert Desnos, for example, considered all his poems part of one great poem—just as the great symbolist poet Stéphane Mallarmé had considered all writing part of one book.

Surrealism connects. It celebrates the possibility of—in fact, it claims the existence of—a *capillary tissue* that enables a mental circulation between states of being, emotions, worlds, as between elements verbal and visual. "The role of this tissue is," says Breton, "to guarantee the constant exchange in thought that must exist between the exterior and interior worlds, an exchange that requires the continuous interpenetration of the activity of waking

Marcel Duchamp, *Young Cherry Trees Secured Against Hares;* cover of volume of André Breton's poems (face of Breton as the statue). New York: View Editions, 1946. © ARS.

and that of sleeping." For the "fundamental faculty" of sleep, he says, works the miracle of plunging the human consciousness into the unlimited connectedness of an "eternal being, falling with the stone, flying with the bird . . . in whom, far from annihilating themselves, all the adverse wills of all things are combined and marvelously limited."[3] And this consciousness, connected and connecting, is the one to which surrealism makes appeal. The basic distinctions between inner and outer states are overcome, and between kinds of thought and writing and creation.

Just as the separation between genres is blurred over, so is that between the arts, specifically between the visual and the verbal (including to some extent the musical, although, as is well known, André Breton's tone-deafness and his stricture: "Let the curtain fall on the orchestra" would seem to rule out certain kinds of music. Not, I would maintain, chamber music, which necessitates the kind of collective action that surrealism championed).

It was most of all important, said Breton, to attack the forms of conservatism: artistic, political, and ethical, and to take arms against what has already been done, thought, said yesterday, in honor of what is being done today. The question is now as to what remains valid of that attack now so many years ago, of that desire to recreate always the new forms that could "translate human desire in its continual fluctuation." How do we now see the surrealist struggle against "*simple* perception . . . ," that little pitcher so frequent in cubist still lives, together with "the little boat, the bouquet of flowers, and the woman posed there, clothed or naked"? The primary requirement, as Breton always claimed, is the spirit in which the work was conceived. It was, Breton would claim, of necessity visionary, bearing a new conception, belonging to a new order: *pace* William Carlos Williams. The artists he mentions are those we would expect: Ernst, Arp, Miró, early Chirico, Tanguy, Picasso. Here, in this collection, are others also, and among them, those banished from the Surrealist cenacle by Breton himself. For I have not wanted to put, at the heart of this collection, any strictures or separations. I have wanted to connect, to gather, to celebrate.

My view about Surrealism seen from here, in the new millennium, is that the division set up by Breton between European Surrealists and those of other countries—such as the United States, to take a case not really at random—has no longer any reason to hold. I have therefore selected from both sides of the Atlantic, the writing and art I find best benefitting that honorary term: Surrealist.

I can only hope for the reader at least a fraction of the delight in reading that the editor took in assembling this collection.

Notes

1. About the practical, Motherwell was often consulted. As he said to me, "I had to do little things . . . in those days, I was interested in cooking, and there were simple practical questions, for example, since

you couldn't get olive oil, which was the cooking oil that most resembled olive oil, and I happened to know it was peanut oil, which they didn't know about in those days. You couldn't get French wine, and I knew which American ones were the closest. I mean pretty simple practical things. . . ."

2. Meeting place in Normandy, founded by Paul Desjardins, where intellectuals held *décades,* or ten-day meetings around a topic: they were mostly French, like André Gide and Jean Wahl, but with others often participating, Lytton Strachey and Roger Fry from England, for example. These meetings continue at Cerisy-la-Salle, near St.-Lô.

3. André Breton, in *Communicating Vessels,* trans. Mary Ann Caws and Geoffrey T. Harris (Lincoln: University of Nebraska Press, 1990), 139.

ACKNOWLEDGMENTS

Over the years of preparation this volume has required, many have helped in its organization and realization. I would like to thank them all, and in particular the following: Yves Bonnefoy, François Chapon, Marie-Claude Char, René Char, Marie-Claire Dumas, Etienne-Alain Hubert, Tina Jolas, Judith Young Mallin, Robert Motherwell, Renate Ponsold Motherwell, Yves Peyré, Dorothea Tanning, Seth Young, Virginia Zabriskie. For his patience in helping me put this act together, my son Matthew Caws, and for their encouragement, Hilary and Jonathan Caws-Elwitt. I have had superb backing at the MIT Press, now and formerly: Roger Conover, Deborah Cantor-Adams, Julie Grimaldi, and all the highly skilled designers, in particular, Yasuyo Iguchi. For all the help with the archives from which many of these documents are taken, I am grateful to the librarians at the Bibliothèque de l'Arsenal, the Bibliothèque nationale, and the Bibliothèque littéraire Jacques Doucet in Paris; to the Scottish National Art Gallery in Edinburgh; to the Museum of Modern Art and the Columbia University Library in New York, as well as the archivists at Art Resource and the Artists Rights Society, VAGA, ADAGP, and the Bridgeman Art Library International. Many thanks also to the various persons and publishers who have granted permission to reproduce the texts included here. I have made every effort to trace the copyright holders, but if I have inadvertently overlooked any, I would be pleased to make the necessary arrangements at the first opportunity.

Memoirs of Surrealism

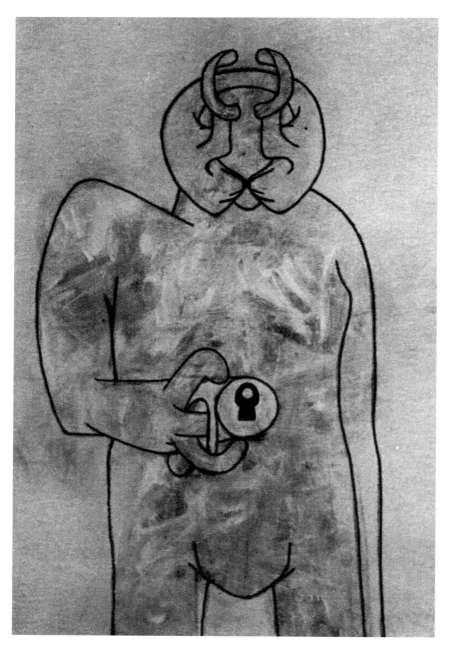

Matta (Echaurren), *Un Poète de notre connaissance (A Poet We Know),* 1944; Pierre Matisse
Gallery. © ARS.

Eileen Agar

Am I a Surrealist?

...n nature. I recall the account of Tanguy walking ...arine forms, studying the seaweed and the rocks. Then ...udio and create a painting which made references to what he would only be the starting point for his imagination. I adopt a similar app... ...ugh at the same time, abstraction would also be exerting its influence upon me, giving me the benefit of geometry and design to match and balance and strengthen the imaginative elements of a composition. Outer eye and inner eye, backward and forward, inside out and upside down, sideways, as a metaphysical airplane might go, no longer classical or romantic, medieval or gothic, but surreal, transcendent, a revelation of what is concealed in the hide-and-seek of life, a mixture of laughter, play and perseverance.

You see the shape of a tree, the way a pebble falls or is formed, and you are astounded to discover that dumb nature makes an effort to speak to you, to give you a sign, to warn you, to symbolize your innermost thoughts. Chance is not a neutral but a distinctly positive force, the surrealists believe that you can get on good terms with chance by adopting a lyrical mode of behavior and an open attitude.

My own method is to put myself in a state of receptivity during the day. I sit about sometimes for a quarter of an hour or more, wondering what on earth I am doing, and then suddenly I get an idea for something. Either it is the beginning of a title or just the germ of a visual image. Later on, if I am stuck with a half-finished painting, I might take a snooze and after that it comes together quite simply. It may well be that we hunt too much when we are completely on the alert. Too much awareness can be as inhibiting as too little.

One must have a hunger for new color, new shapes and new possibilities of discovery. The twentieth century has begun to realize that most of life's meaning is lost without the spirit of play. In play, all that is lovely and soaring in the human spirit strives to find expression. To play is to yield oneself to a kind of magic, and to give the lie to the inconvenient world

Eileen Agar, *The Angel of Mercy,* 1934; plaster, collage, and water color, Whitford & Hughes, London/ Bridgeman Art Library. © ARS.

of fact, and the hideous edifice of unrelieved utility. In play the mind is prepared to accept the unimagined and incredible, to enter a world where different laws apply, to be free, unfettered.

The earliest anecdote told of me, at the age of four (when my stature was of little account), was of me looking up at the ornate ceiling lavishly painted with naked ladies and flying cupids in the large restaurant where my parents were lunching. I said: "I see something but I mustn't tell." Was this a shocked awareness of what went on in the clouds? The second anecdote is of my constant and pressing request to all and sundry to buy me a balloon. I was obviously intent on exploring those clouds for myself.

MARY ANN CAWS

REMEMBERING JACQUELINE REMEMBERING ANDRÉ

for Aube, for Hilary, and for Matthew

I had been sent by Yves Bonnefoy that day so long ago in the 1970s, to see the former wife of André Breton, Jacqueline Lamba, to whose startling blonde beauty *L'Amour fou* (*Mad Love*) had been addressed. Bonnefoy had expected—and his expectation proved not to be wrong—that she would not mind, that she might indeed welcome, a talk with me. Not for my knowledge, especially, but for my receptive ear and general enthusiasm.

For years, I had been writing on surrealism, translating Breton's poetry, teaching and loving his prose, which I found more poetic by far than his poetry, and more sustained in its flow. My first, very brief book had concerned Breton. It was called *Surrealism and the Literary Imagination: Bachelard and Breton,*[1] and then I think I remember another subtitle along the lines of "A Poetics of the Possible" or the equally gooey equivalent. Printed in 600 copies, it sold out and sank instantly: dead on the spot, all ninety-two glittering pages. I have lost my only copy, and it seems unavailable even on the web. But that surrealizing imagination, or something like it, stuck in my mind. I was never to read contemporary poetry the same way.

It was, in the beginning, Breton's face I had loved, wherever I saw it.[2] In photographs, on the front and back covers of books, and, particular to my own love of Joseph Cornell, in boxes or not—his collage of Man Ray's most famous photograph of Breton, in his adaptation of that photograph—adding alchemical symbols around it, or then light curls, as in his *Laundry Boy's Charge.* Everyone else seemed to find that face leonine, massive, strong, impressive. I was no less impressed, but found it in the picture to be as vulnerable as it was striking; and so I loved it. I had no idea where his anguish came from, or what kinds of gestures it would have prompted, were I to have known him. He had always been presented as infinitely commanding, triumphant, a writer of manifestoes and statements. I saw something else.

André Breton, Diego Rivera, and Leon Trotsky, Mexico, 1928; photo: Fritz Bach.

Something troubled about his relation to himself. You may think me boring, he used to say; but Pierre Reverdy is still more so. Perhaps he was. Greatness can scarcely be thought to rule out self-denigration.

Jacqueline Lamba, Simiane-la-Rotonde

So, because of my friendship with a great poet, I went in 1973 to meet the ex-wife of a great poet. I returned from an expedition to Russia, left those domed cathedrals and my vain search for the Maiakovski museum, and for any trace of the Rayonists I had so loved—Natalia Goncharova? I asked at first; no such person, they told me. I was surely mistaken, they said.

I sought out Jacqueline in Simiane-la-Rotonde, carrying my first-ever tape recorder, wearing my best espadrilles, apprehensive. And I found, on the spot, someone I sensed to be quite as remarkable as her ex-husband had been. One look at her astonishingly sensitive countenance, and I hoped we would be friends—as indeed we always were to be. I turned the tape recorder to the bare white wall, just as her paintings were turned, in the high room in the house on a hill overlooking the plain.

Dora Maar, *Portrait of Jacqueline Lamba,* from *Minotaure* 8 (June 1936); courtesy of Aube Elléouët.

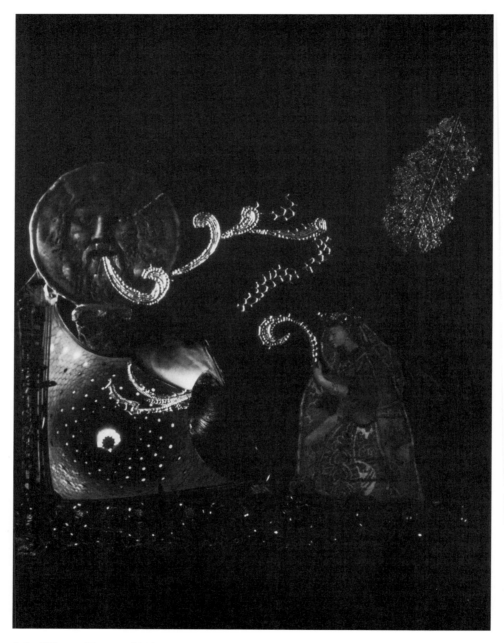

Aube Elléouët, *Hommage à Talisma Nasreen*, 1995; collage. Courtesy of Aube Elléouët.

Aube Elléouët, *La Goutte d'eau (The Drop of Water),* 1990; collage. Courtesy of Aube Elléouët.

The house seemed bare, and echoing. A sort of arcade near it, or under it, I cannot remember, but can sense its shape now. Simiane, on a hill, was like most of the towns I have loved in the South of France, and of America. On the days she was painting, she would hang out a red flag if the neighborhood children could come up and chat with her. Here, when a wasp would come, she would feed it, cherish it, as she did all animals, and her friends, among whom I was infinitely proud to be counted. When we were returning to Simiane from my cabanon, a small owl was perched atop the hood of the Deux Chevaux, looking at her hard. It was like that.

Nothing was surprising around Jacqueline. As the very long day went on, she turned a few of her works to face me, one at a time, slowly, as we talked.

Her voice was that of a painter, of the kind of painter she was. Skies she painted, or sometimes painted, sometimes trees, sometimes houses against a mountain. Her absolutist attitude to everything seemed marvelously in accord with what I had loved in surrealist writing and imagining, and also in two faces, first that of André Breton, and then hers— a beauty not so much physical as thoughtful. Everything about her was out of the ordinary:

Joseph Cornell, *Laundry Boy's Charge,* 1966 (photograph of André Breton by Man Ray, from 1931). © Joseph and Robert Cornell Memorial Foundation.

her masses of hair piled atop her narrow, aristocratic head; her way of walking, like a dancer; her long skirts she had worn ever since visiting Frida Kahlo in Mexico. When, years later, I found one of Kahlo's letters addressed to her in terms that could only be interpreted as those of love, it was instantly understandable. What Jacqueline cared about, the way she spoke, the way she looked at you—these were unforgettable.

When she spoke of Breton, it was almost always just "him"—"*lui.*" Sometimes, "André," but more often, just "*lui.*" This was not, or so it seemed to me, a love that had ever diminished. She had not wanted to be just Madame André Breton. Could André Breton

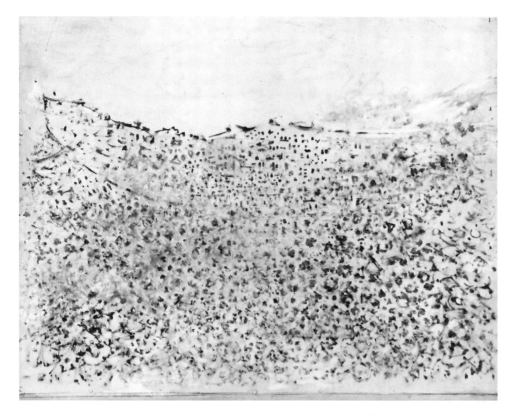

Jacqueline Lamba, *Landscape at Simiane-la-Rotonde,* n.d. Courtesy of Aube Elléouët.

have possibly wanted her to be just that? In any case, she was, and remained, Jacqueline Lamba. Difficult, exigent, in her friendships as in her love. She was the sort of person you did not want to let down.

The one thing she hated the most was the self-sufficiency that speaks in the bearing of some intellectuals, the good opinion about oneself that lies in wait for the unwary. When I saw this self-sufficiency and her swift reaction, it was like seeing the vengeance of a god, the nemesis of ancient myth. People should have been more wary of Jacqueline than they knew how to be. She never ceased being wary, of herself and others.

About André, she talked for four hours. There were other subjects, such as Antonin Artaud, to whom she had remained close, and others she had loved and cared about. But to this topic, this "him," she would always return. There were always new things to tell me. Some I would recall afterwards, some not. What concerned her most was that never

Jacqueline Lamba, *Untitled Black and White,* n.d. Courtesy of Aube Elléouët.

would she speak—or so she thought—as well as André. In any case, she spoke as no one else I remember has spoken, and the day could have gone on even longer.

I know André Breton married again; I spent time with Elisa also, and she was kind to me. I know Jacqueline married, and loved, David Hare. But none of that changed what was so instantly and so continually visible: André and Jacqueline shared something that leaps out of the magnificent photographs Claude Cahun took of them against a curtain, and is clearer still in Claude's photographs of Jacqueline alone—a radiance unlike any I had encountered before or have again, after her.

What did we talk about, talking about him? Of course, their meeting. How he had seen her in the club, how the poem "Sunflower Night" had predicted her, how poetry worked magic. What sorts of things Breton believed in, how he went about coordinating his group. His heroes: Duchamp in particular. Did I love Duchamp's face, as she had, and Breton's even more? Yes. And also the face of Atonin Artaud, as Breton had. What an odd friendship they had had. When Artaud returned, haunted, from Ireland, Jacqueline had continued walking with him, and remembered for me how he would place his blackthorn stick straight in the way of some oncomer, and demand a sum to remove it. How he had trusted her. His tragedy and his greatness. Their joint mental adventures. The time when the playwright Arthur Adamov had gotten him out of the asylum, hoping, and they had all gone to the Théatre du

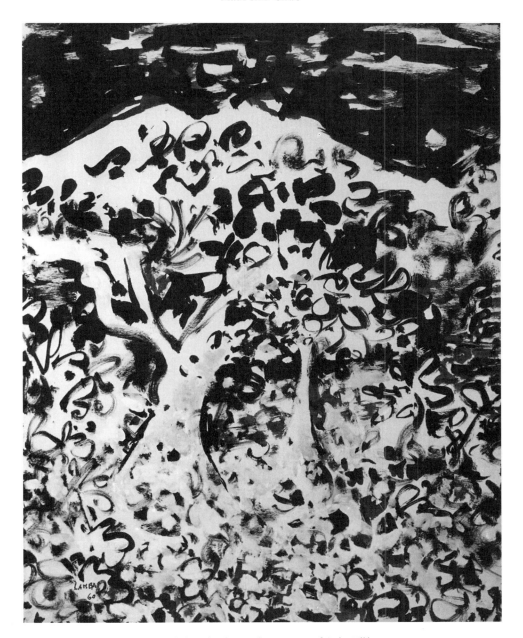

Jacqueline Lamba, *Landscape in Black and White,* n.d. Courtesy of Aube Elléouët.

Vieux-Colombier to hear him speak. What Jacqueline had most feared, had happened. Artaud, unable to put his papers or thoughts together, had swept them off the podium, and they all wept. Jacqueline, telling me about it, in her low voice, wept again.

She talked about things large and less so, about the André she had loved. Small things sometimes, like his not wanting to be seen without his shoes on—Jacqueline enjoyed going barefooted. The way he talked, and walked. His relation to others, to himself. Why was she trusting me? The question never arose. I suppose she knew she could.

On my wall in the south of France, where she would come to visit in her long skirt, to the utter delight of my children, hangs one of her drawings of a group of houses against a mountain. She did not drive, nor did I. I took the bus to meet her bus; it seemed right. And one day, she brought me a picture that hangs in my cabanon, arriving with it under her arm, immense and significant in its utter simplicity. If she arrived at noon, in the blaze and desperate heat of the midday sun, and the children wished to walk with her up the hill nearby to a chapel, she would set off with them instantly, against all prudence. Once, she fell down my stone step into the road, picked herself up, smoothed down her long skirt, gave me her most radiant smile, and started off, with a child on either side. That is what, among other things, André—her André—must have loved about her, that adventuresome spirit with which she was so marvelously endowed.

I gave her something too, just a piece of Provençal cloth, bright blue and red, as I remember, and she hung it out on her line, for the colors to fade. That was right too: everything, in those years, seemed right. About her, about our relationship.

Jacqueline Lamba, 8 blvd Bonne Nouvelle

When we had known each other a few years, I learned the way to telephone her. You let it ring four times, then you hung up; then you phoned again, and she, knowing it was you, picked it up. That quiver in her voice, that warmth, the way she would, whenever I came back through Paris, prepare me lunch, or tea, or both, with magical things in tiny wooden bowls. I loved to watch her gliding noiselessly about, taking care. I would climb up the five flights of stairs to her apartment, marked: "Jacqueline Lamba-Hare, artiste-peintre." Here too, the paintings were turned to the walls. My grandmother, a painter too, so long ago, had she turned her paintings to the walls of her studio? I did not think so, but perhaps in her gleaming still lifes and portraits there was less mystery. About Jacqueline, there hung an air of great reserve, through which shone a great passion.

She wanted to know about Jacques Lacan—could we go together to his lectures? She wanted to talk to me about Groddek and his notion of the "ça." She wanted me to tell

Jacqueline Lamba, *L'Atelier at 8, Boulevard Bonne Nouvelle*, n.d. Courtesy of Aube Elléouët.

her what René Char had turned out to be like, for she had known him so long ago. One day, she had finally gone to see him at L'Isle-sur-Sorgue, greatly moved as they both were by the idea and the reality. She had left there with him her roll of paintings that she had taken to show him. They were both surprised, it appeared, by their rediscovery of each other. He had preferred her to André Breton, had read me passages from his notes about them both. And he had found her, he told me later, after the first shock of sight, just the way he had known her. It had been a fine meeting.

Jacqueline had not always had an easy time. Once, about to be operated on, she had not mentioned that she was the wife of André Breton, through some reserve. She had, as an impecunious and anonymous nonperson, so she said, fallen prey to a surgeon with a knife more eager than his talent would support. Ever after, she had seen blood behind her eyes, had had difficulty painting, had had pain. Her beauty had almost caused her blindness.

Nor had she found the scene in America an easy one: she and Simone de Beauvoir had not exactly hit it off. Simone de Beauvoir had treated her, she said, like a maid, this story illustrated in a way I do not care to tell. To lose Jacqueline's confidence or trust was, I would have thought, to lose a great deal. But then, you can see how I loved her.

She was a staunch friend, frighteningly so. Hearing that I was once hesitating about how to publish a book on René Char, written in French, she drew herself up to her full height of five feet one or so, her head mightily lifted, and said with fearsome conviction: "I will go with you and sweep all their papers and their books off all their tables until they change their mind." She had determined, against every probability I could imagine, that I would turn out to be strong, and that with her by my side, it could happen. Now that I think back, I consider that perhaps it might have, for a while.

When, once, I was leaving for Spain the next night, alone, sad, and a little weary of it all, she slipped an envelope in my hand, requesting me not to open it until it was midnight, in Barcelona, and I needed a companion.

Now, like most impassioned readers of surrealism, I loved the love of André and Jacqueline. And I translated it: "Mad Love," I called it, finding *L'Amour fou* too close for comfort.[3] But then, of course, neither of them could be described as persons of comfort. "Le merveilleux" was something else, more like discomfort and the special elation that brings.

The next night on the train, I felt the envelope, thin and safe in my pocket. It was indeed midnight in Barcelona when I opened it. Within was a fragile sheet of blue paper, with the tiniest writing imaginable upon it, in Breton's hand I knew by then. It was, said her note included in the envelope, his first love letter to her. I like to think he would not have minded—love can be passed on. I have that letter still, just as I have my memory of Jacqueline. What was indelible, more than the ink on the letter now grown pale, was her memory of him, the one who never needed to be named, the one always present to her mind.

• • •

Jacqueline died, in a residence for the aged, in a small room she had chosen, because it gave her, instead of surrounding space, the sight of a tree just out the window.

That drawing she gave me, still on the wall of our cabanon, has weathered the storms and the many visitors. It is really just a few lines, black on the yellowed paper, suggesting more than could ever be told, here or anywhere. But it is a whole town, and makes the Mont Ventoux near which I have chosen to live my summers seem more human-sized. As do my memories of René Char, the original reason I came there with my family, and have returned each year since then, saving up my thirst for the light through the New York winters.

My letters from Jacqueline bear all the colors of her pencils: red, green, blue. Each color had its tone, each letter its special hue.

I won't be forgetting them, or her. Some presences mark a place and a lifetime: it must have been true of André, her André, as it was true of her.

Notes

1. The Hague: Mouton, 1966.

2. Of this face, read more in my *Surrealist Look: An Erotics of Encounter*. Cambridge: MIT Press, 1997.

3. *Mad Love*. Lincoln: University of Nebraska Press, 1984.

RENÉ CHAR

THE JOURNEY IS DONE

The marriage between the mind of a twenty year old and a violent phantom turns out to be disappointing as we ourselves are disappointing. It is no more than the deed created by a natural revolt and carried along by an accompanying fire or rather by a collective mirror. Only too soon is it burnt out by the divorce of its elements. Because what we were hunting after could not be discovered by several men at one time; because the mind's life—threaded, unlike the heart's, on a single strand—is fascinated, as it contemplates the temptation of poetry, only by a sovereign and unapproachable object which splinters into a million fragments once, having broken through the limits of distance, we are about to take hold of it. On the outskirts of the concrete that provides a style of existence beyond compare.

This shadowy going along of ours—which, stupidly, works itself out under little bursts of light—is without sparkle and has no stepping stones. Though those bursts of light are all alike, at least what they show us, each time they are caught in a ring of brightness on the retina, is different. Distress and hostility hold court there along with wonder. We cannot explain it, as I know only too well. A work which is integral at its roots, an undertaking as vast as Surrealism is speckled through with defects, pettiness and ungainliness in much the same way as a stone, a tree, or a man. It makes little difference what energy it had, what mass it possessed, what revolutionary faith it professed. We are all accountable for what was defective in it. And truth—we need not fear saying it anew—is personal, stupefying and personal. Surrealism's journey is done. History has offered it airports and railroad stations, while waiting to sort out, in some commonplace library, what was beautiful and what was dusty in it. Its childish noises will not escape the tally; but neither will its pageantry and its rightful imprecations. As young men we never thought ahead to that, and we were right!

It is not for me to look contradictorily into Surrealism's effects, whether the hateful or the others. Any basin that becomes a stream, flooding lands and muddying walls, is not

René Char in Struth, Alsace, in the winter of 1939–1940; gift of René Char to the author.

René Char, 1973; photo: Lutfi Ozkök. Gift of René Char and Lutfi Ozkök to the author.

defective. Isn't it true, after all, that man is no more than an offshoot of solar matter cast over with a gadfly shadow of free will? On a crater of horrors, under an imbecilic night, the stubborn, fertile flower suddenly blossoms out under a man's nostrils and in front of his eyes. Its pollen goes forth to mingle with his spirit, in a pure moment, a spirit unsatisfied with the quibbles of terrestrial intelligence and heaven's customs.

I write these remarks in haste, yet as evidence of faithful friendship.

GIORGIO DE CHIRICO

FROM *THE MEMOIRS OF GIORGIO DE CHIRICO*

I reached Paris in the autumn of 1925. The great orgy of modern painting was raging in the French capital. The dealers had instituted a real dictatorship. It was they who, with their hired art critics, created or destroyed a painter, and that independently of his value as an artist. In this way a dealer, or a group of dealers, could create extremely high prices for the canvases of a painter completely lacking in even the slightest genius, make his name famous in every continent, while they could also boycott, suppress and reduce to poverty an artist of great value. The dealers did all this by taking advantage of the confusion which reigned and unfortunately reigns more than ever in the art world, and by ignominiously exploiting the snobbery and imbecility of a certain category of people. Their clientele consisted especially of Anglo-Saxons, who were acutely snobbish, and especially of North Americans; their clients also included a few Scandinavians, a few Germans, several Swiss, a few Belgians and a few Japanese. French clients were fairly limited in number, while Spanish and Italians were even fewer. It must be said in our favour and to our credit that these Italians were taken in less than everyone else.

Between the dealers and those who surrounded them existed a real freemasonry with its rites, rules and procedures, which functioned wonderfully well. One famous trick consisted of false auction sales at the Hôtel Drouot. A dealer would decide, for example, that the works of a certain painter, whom he supported, were extremely expensive. He would put one of these paintings up for auction at the Hôtel Drouot, the painting in question usually belonging to a collector who was in league with the dealer. The dealer would send a few of his own men to the sale and they would push up the price of the painting, while the dealer would naturally sacrifice a certain sum to pay the commissions due to the auctioneers. In this way the impression was given that the picture had sold for a very high price, while in fact it had not been sold for any price. Then it would be left lying for a certain time in the back room of the dealer's shop or in the collector's cellars.

Luxury magazines were paid in order to support a particular painting or a particular type of painting, and in all this obscene manoeuvring the only thing never mentioned was

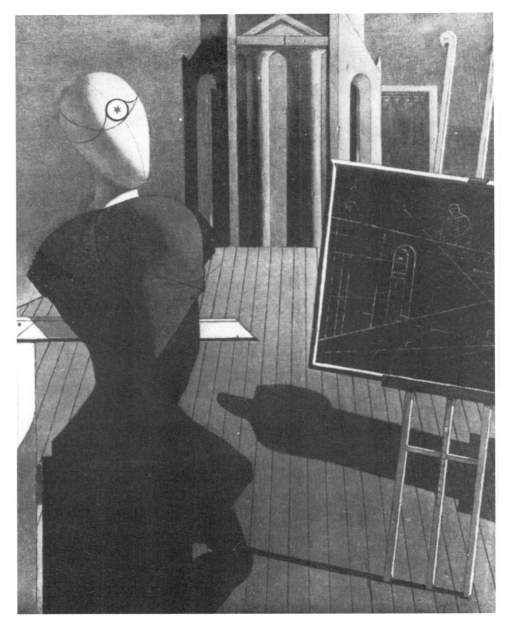

Giorgio de Chirico, *The Prophet (The Seer),* 1915; oil on canvas, 35 × 27 inches. Art Resource. © ARS.

the artistic value of a painting. Never, since the beginning of the world, since men have exerted themselves drawing, painting, modelling and sculpting, never, I say, have the highest values of the spirit and the highest aspirations of mankind, namely art and works of art, reached such a state and in this way been prostituted and dragged through the mud. There are two great scandals of our time: the encouragement given to what is bad in art and the fact that there is no opposition to this encouragement by any authority, either civil or ecclesiastical. At the same time there is speculation based on deceit, even on swindling, which takes advantage of the ignorance, vanity and stupidity of the men of today. All this had and still has one sole purpose, one sole motivation: money—to earn money at all costs, to earn it in any way, under the aegis of a false artistic ideal. I accuse openly and courageously all the shameful gang who have helped and are still helping to make painting decline to the point to which it has declined today. I accuse them today and tomorrow and assume full responsibility for such an accusation. I am sure that the efforts I am making and perhaps somebody else is making to restore painting to a level of nobility and dignity, will not be in vain. I am not a theoretician, nor someone who makes empty speeches; I am speaking like this because I have studied and examined the problem deeply. Other people, too, have spoken and written about the decadence of modern painting, but these are people who understand only up to a certain point and have not been able to put their finger on the trouble, as I have been able to. Also, before one really has the right to speak in such a way one must in the first place be a painter of great intelligence and one must have been capable of painting the paintings which only I have succeeded in painting in the first half of our century. The present method of dealing with art, the method used by fools, thieves and pimps has since spread throughout the entire world, but the origin and centre of it all were in Paris.

Now that I have written frankly what I think of modern painting and of those who have supported it and spread it abroad and are still doing so, I will return to my memories, observations, reflections and personal adventures.

Soon after reaching Paris I found strong opposition from that group of degenerates, hooligans, childish layabouts, onanists and spineless people who had pompously styled themselves *Surrealists* and also talked about the "Surrealist revolution" and the "Surrealist movement." This group of not very worthy individuals was led by a self-styled poet who answered to the name of André Breton and whose aide-de-camp was another pseudo-poet called Paul Eluard, a colourless and commonplace young man with a crooked nose and a face somewhere between that of an onanist and a mystical cretin. André Breton, therefore, was the classic type of pretentious ass and impotent *arriviste*. After the First World War, M. André Breton, together with a few Surrealists, had bought at auction sales, for low prices, a certain number of my paintings that I had left in a little studio in Montparnasse when I had gone to Italy. In order to earn the rent, which I had not succeeded in paying during the war, the owner of the studio had sold my paintings, together with a little furniture which had remained there. M. Breton and his acolytes hoped that I would remain in Italy, that I would die in the war, that in some way I would no longer appear on the banks of the Seine, and in this way they would have been able quietly and gradually to pick up all the paintings of mine in Paris, since later, in addition to those which were sent to the saleroom by the owner of the studio, the surrealists acquired paintings of mine even from private individuals, and especially from Paul Guillaume, the man in love with Derain, who stupidly sold them various paintings of mine which I had sold to him between 1913 and 1915. In this way the Surrealists had hoped to monopolise my metaphysical painting, which naturally they called Surrealist, and then, by means of publicity, articles and a whole system of skilfully organised bluff, they hoped to do what dealers had done earlier with Cézanne, Van Gogh, Gauguin, Douanier Rousseau and Modigliani, known as Modì, that is to sell my paintings at extremely high prices and pocket stacks of money.

My arrival in Paris with a collection of new paintings, my relationship with local dealers and my exhibitions of painting different in type from what they possessed and whose value they inflated, caused confusion in the Breton camp and made a mess of everything. For this reason the Surrealists decided to undertake a large-scale boycott of my new output; when, in 1926, I had an exhibition at the Léonce Rosenberg Gallery, they immediately organised, in a shop they had opened in the Rue Jacques Callot, an exhibition of metaphysical paintings of mine which they owned. The exhibition was arranged in the middle of a collection of Negro sculpture and so-called Surrealist objects; then they published a catalogue with an utterly silly preface by that same Aragon who now aspires to sit among the Immortals in the Academy. The preface was a kind of libel and consisted more of criticising the paintings I was showing at the Rosenberg Gallery than of praising those shown by the surrealists. They were so persistent, so hysterical in their envy—which resembled that of eunuchs and old maids—that they were not content with boycotting my work in Paris, but organised, through their representatives and agents abroad, large-scale boycotts of my work also in Belgium, Holland, Switzerland, Britain and the United States. Their silliness then reached the point of doing things of this type. When my exhibition at the Rosenberg Gallery and the exhibition of my metaphysical paintings arranged by the Surrealists at their gallery in the Rue Jacques Callot opened more or less at the same time, the Surrealists organised a kind of parody of the work I was showing at the Rosenberg Gallery in the window of the other one. For example, in order to represent my pictures showing horses by the sea, they had bought in a bazaar some of those little rubber horses which are given to children to play with and had placed them on a little heap of sand, with a few stones round them and a piece of blue paper, presumably the sea. Then, in order to parody the pictures which I called "furniture in the open," they had shown some of that dolls' furniture which is sold in toyshops. The result, however, was that this parody in the window of the Surrealists' gallery provided great publicity for my show at the Rosenberg and I sold many pictures, which gave the pseudo-poet André Breton a liver attack.

In spite of the hysterical envy of the surrealists and the other agitated failures living in the French capital, my new painting aroused great interest, but I cannot say that the intellectuals put themselves out to support it. The only intellectual who supported me at that time with a certain warmth was Jean Cocteau, but I think he did so more to spite the Surrealists than for any other reason; in fact, I realised later that even he was not worth much more than the Surrealists. At first the Surrealists had been full of envy because Jean had made something of a name for himself in snobbish Parisian circles, but when Cocteau supported my new painting they became absolutely hydrophobic and resorted to methods which could be called sordid and squalid in the worst possible way. For example, they would make anonymous telephone calls in the middle of the night to Cocteau's elderly mother, who was an extremely fine lady, full of good-hearted kindness, in order to tell her that her son had ended up under a motor-car.

Apart from behaving like hooligans and petty delinquents the Surrealists also did things which were incredibly funny and diverting. The meetings in Breton's house reached the heights of comedy. Soon after my arrival in Paris, before the Surrealists had realised the danger I represented for their dubious projects, that is before their hydrophobia had been fully released, I twice had occasion to attend their gatherings. The guests would arrive at Breton's place about nine in the evening. His place consisted of a vast studio overlooking the Boulevard de Clichy; there were a few bedrooms and every modern comfort. Although the Surrealists professed unadultered communist and anti-bourgeois feelings they always tried to live as comfortably as possible, dress very well and eat excellent meals washed down with excellent wines; they never gave so much as a centime to a poor man, never lifted a finger in favour of someone who needed material or moral support and above all they worked as little as possible, or not at all.

The gatherings took place in Breton's studio. Here is a description of one of these gatherings at which I was present. Breton's wife and the friends he had invited sat on huge divans in thoughtful, reflective attitudes. The atmosphere reminded me of that of Guillaume Apollinaire's Saturdays which I had attended about ten years earlier, and it was just as much like Balestrieri's famous *Beethoven* which is on show at the Revoltella Museum in Trieste, except that on the walls at Breton's place, instead of Beethoven's mask or *art nouveaux* paintings, hung cubist paintings by Picasso, some metaphysical paintings of mine, Negro masks and paintings and drawings by some obscure surrealist painter whom the owner of the house was trying to launch; in fact, the scene was more or less the same as that in

Apollinaire's house. In this atmosphere of false meditation and ostentatious concentration André Breton walked about the studio reading in a sepulchral voice extracts from Lautréamont. He declaimed the foolish remarks by Isidore Ducasse with a severe and inspired expression. On other occasions a new "turn," a new genius was presented at these gatherings. The evening when I was there two young men who appeared said they lived in the Latin Quarter and were medical students. One of them, the younger, declared that he could draw the portrait of anyone, even from memory, and even if he had never seen them; but his portraits consisted of one eye only, he drew only one eye. The older of the two, who seemed to be the other's manager, turned to those present and asked them to decide whose portrait it should be. A hysterical woman's voice shrilled out: "We want a portrait of Proust!" The young student immediately sat down at a table; paper, pencil and eraser were brought to him. The other, his friend, motioned to those present to remain silent and to move some distance away in order not to disturb the artist. They all retired respectfully and you could have heard a pin drop in Breton's studio. The young student became withdrawn for a moment and it looked exactly as though he had fallen into a trance; then, with the gestures of a somnambulist, watched over by his companion, he seized the pencil, looking into space, and began to draw. He drew for a few seconds, then put down the pencil and his companion said loudly, "The portrait is finished!" Everyone rushed forward and they all yelled together: "It's Proust! It's Proust's eye!" I also went up and saw a kind of eye, drawn from the side, rather like those attempts at drawing done by children; the eye could have belonged just as easily to the President of Nicaragua as to Proust.

The second time that I went to Breton's studio some spiritualist sessions were organised. There was a young man called Desnos who was considered the medium *par excellence* of the company. He would pretend to fall into a trance and would then begin to recite silly verses, of which this is a sample:

> Fertile migrations towards horrible seashores!
> I have seen the ants migrating!
> Come and remove from the faithless stirrup
> The evening's encounter with flesh that is rotting!

And so on, always in the same vein. Breton would give orders and issue instructions; scribes and stenographers would rush up with paper and shorthand pens so that they would not lose a single word of all the idiocies which the pseudo-medium rattled off.

I learnt later that in Breton's studio punitive expeditions were sometimes launched against the St-Sulpice district, which is the Catholic quarter of Paris, where there were many religious bookshops and many shops selling sacred images. In Paris there were two forms of snobbery, especially among certain literati. One consisted of *making Catholics,* and so for certain literati the so-called Catholic crisis was a classic event, and did not happen even on purpose, but always when the reputation of the writer in question was very low. The other form of snobbery, which was precisely that of the surrealists, consisted of making atheists and anti-clericals. In those days in Paris there lived a strange type of priest, probably slightly unbalanced, who from time to time went down from the St-Sulpice district to cause scandals on the Grands Boulevards and tear up magazines such as *La Vie Parisienne, Le Rire,* and others on sale at the kiosks, because he considered them dangerous for the morals of good Christians. Naturally, the owner of the kiosks would protest and wanted the priest to pay him for the magazines he had torn up, but instead of money he received only inspired speeches on the decadence and immorality of our times. In the end a policeman would come up and take the moralising priest and the owner of the kiosks to the nearest police station. Whenever one of these scandals caused by the above-mentioned priest came to the ears of André Breton he would immediately order the young Desnos, who was ready to do anything for the triumph of surrealism, to go to the St-Sulpice district and tear up religious reviews and newspapers in the kiosks.

Then there was a poet called Benjamin Péret whose complete works consisted of four lines only with the title "Asleep." Here are the four unique lines by this fertile poet: "What can you see?"/"Water."/"What colour is this water?"/"Water."

Jean Cocteau supported my painting and wrote a book about it called *Le mystère laïc* [The Lay Mystery]. I illustrated this book with a few drawings. I am very grateful to Jean Cocteau for the interest he has shown in me, but I must say that I do not in fact approve the kind of praise he accords me and the intepretation he likes to put on my pictures. Moreover, I have always found myself in the difficult position of having to side against even my friends, even those few who have said and still say nice things about my painting, not in a tendentious way and free of the innuendoes or maliciousness of many people in Italy and also outside it, especially in the United States. I must unfortunately and most regretfully say this, because even many people who are favourably disposed towards me do not understand anything about my painting.

The orgasmic saturnalia in the modern painting market in Paris reached its climax in the year of grace, 1929. The collectors seemed insatiable; galleries sprang up like mushrooms. Not a day passed without some new gallery being inaugurated and they all resembled each other like Siamese twins. It was always the same thing: a window draped with grey fabric; a room, or a small room, also draped with grey fabric; in the window and the rooms were the usual daubs by modern painters, fixed in stripped wooden frames with *passe-partout,* also covered with grey fabric, and in the case of the better paintings, with silk. The dealers paid painters in advance for pictures they had not yet begun to paint. Every device was utilised to launch new "geniuses." Diaghilev, the balletomane, invited the better-known painters to execute scenery and costumes. I too was invited to collaborate in a ballet entitled *Le Bal,* set to music by the composer Rietti. This ballet was put on in Monte Carlo in the spring of 1929 and in the summer at the Théâtre Sarah Bernhardt. It was very successful; at the end of the ballet the audience applauded and began to shout "Scirico! Scirico!" I had to come on stage to thank them, together with Rietti and the principal dancers. While leaving the theatre I met the industrialist Gualino, who was accompanied, I believe, by his wife. Professor Lionello Venturi was also with him. They had been present at the performance and I thought, logically, that Signor Gualino wished, as would have been natural, to congratulate me and rejoice with me over the success of my scenery and costumes. Instead, Signor Gualino said nothing whatever about my work but stood there and began to declaim in an emotional voice a dithyrambic poem of praise by Felice Casorati. I stood there for a time listening courteously, but seeing that the dithyrambic praise continued, and aware that my mother, my brother and my sister-in-law were waiting for me with a group of friends, I made my excuses, said good-bye to the Casorati eulogist and left. But in my mind, through the association of memories, I thought of Paul Guillaume and his crazy love for Derain.

But all these successes satisfied me only partially and my conscience as a painter was not very clear. I returned to the study of truth and at this period painted a whole series of nudes and still lifes. Through their plastic power some of these paintings are among the best of all my work. Many paintings of this period were acquired by the collector Albert Borel, brother-in-law of the Rosenberg brothers. M. Albert Borel, although he lived in Paris and was related to two dealers in modern painting, was totally devoid of any form of snobbery, he understood painting and loved it sincerely; in fact, he was one of the very few normal and interesting men whom I met in Paris.

At that time came the first warnings and first punishment that the Universal Genius sent to stupid men, who had profaned the sacred world of art (I admit here that I am imitating the grand style of Isabella Far). The collapse of the New York Stock Exchange had automatic repercussions in Paris; the dealers put up their shutters. No trickery, no freemasonry, no bluff, no secret society could maintain prices. The Americans, and foreigners in general, came no more and the legendary avarice of the French strongly asserted itself. "The crisis has come! And this is only a beginning! We shall have to tighten our belts!"

RENÉ MAGRITTE

LIFELINE

In my childhood I used to play with a little girl in the old crumbling cemetery of an out-of-the-way provincial town, where I always spent my vacations. We would lift the iron grates and descend to the underground passageways. Climbing back up to the light one day I happened upon a painter from the Capital, who amidst those scattered dead leaves and broken stone columns seemed to me to be up to something magical.

When, about 1915, I myself began to paint, the memory of that enchanting encounter with the painter bent my first steps in a direction having little to do with common sense. A singular fate willed that someone, probably to have some fun at my expense, should send me the illustrated catalogue of an exposition of futurist paintings. As a result of that joke I came to know of a new way of painting. In a state of intoxication I set about creating busy scenes of stations, festivities, or cities, in which the little girl bound up with my discovery of the world of painting lived out an exceptional adventure. I cannot doubt that a pure and powerful sentiment, namely, eroticism, saved me from slipping into the traditional chase after formal perfection. My interest lay entirely in provoking an emotional shock.

This painting as search for pleasure was followed next by a curious experience. Thinking it possible to possess the world I loved at my own good pleasure, once I should succeed in fixing its essence upon canvas, I undertook to find out what its plastic equivalents were.

The result was a series of highly evocative but abstract and inert images that were, in the last analysis, interesting only to the intelligence of the eye. This experience made it possible for me to view the world of the real in the same abstract manner. Despite the shifting richness of natural detail and shade, I grew able to look at a landscape as though it were but a curtain hanging in front of me. I had become sceptical of the dimension in depth of a countryside scene, of the remoteness of the line of the horizon.

In 1925 I made up my mind to break with so passive an attitude. This decision was the outcome of an intolerable interval of contemplation I went through in a working-class Brussels beerhall: I found the door moldings endowed with a mysterious life and I remained

René Magritte, *Le Poison (Poison);* Ex-Edward James Foundation. © ARS.

a long time in contact with their reality. A feeling bordering upon terror was the point of departure for a will to action upon the real, for a transformation of life itself.

When, moreover, I found that same will allied to a superior method and doctrine in the works of Karl Marx and Frederick Engels, and became acquainted about that time with the Surrealists, who were then violently demonstrating their loathing for all the bourgeois values, social and ideological, that have kept the world in its present ignoble state,—it was then that I became convinced that I must thenceforward live with danger, that life and the world might thereby come up in some measure to the level of thought and the affections.

I painted pictures in which objects were represented with the appearance they have in reality, in a style objective enough to ensure that their upsetting effect—which they would

René Magritte, *Icarus' Boyhood,* 1960. © ARS.

reveal themselves capable of provoking owing to certain means utilized—would be experienced in the real world whence the objects had been borrowed. This by a perfectly natural transposition.

In my pictures I showed objects situated where we never find them. *They represented the realization of the real if unconscious desire existing in most people.*

The lizards we usually see in our houses and on our faces, I found more eloquent in a sky habitat. Turned wood table legs lost the innocent existence ordinarily lent to them, when they appeared to dominate a forest. A woman's body floating above a city was an initiation for me into some of love's secrets. I found it very instructive to show the Virgin Mary as an undressed lover. The iron bells hanging from the necks of our splendid horses I caused to sprout like dangerous plants from the edge of a chasm.

The creation of new objects, the transformation of known objects, the change of matter for certain other objects, the association of words with images, the putting to work of ideas suggested by friends, the utilization of certain scenes from half-waking or dream states, were other means employed with a view to establishing contact between

René Magritte, *Eloge de la dialectique (In Praise of Dialectics),* 1935; photo: Lauros-Giraudon, Musée d'Ixcelles, Brussels. © ARS.

consciousness and the external world. The titles of the pictures were chosen in such a way as to inspire a justifiable mistrust of any tendency the spectator might have to over-ready self-assurance.

One night in 1936, I awoke in a room where a cage and the bird sleeping in it had been placed. A magnificent visual aberration caused me to see an egg, instead of the bird, in the cage. I had just fastened upon a new and astonishing poetic secret, for the shock experienced had been provoked by the affinity of two objects: cage and egg, *whereas before, I had provoked this shock by bringing together two unrelated objects.* From the moment of that revelation I sought to find out whether other objects besides the cage might not likewise show—by bringing to light some element that was characteristic and to which they had been rigorously predestined—the same evident poetry as the egg and cage had produced by their coming together. In the course of my investigations I came to a conviction that I had always known beforehand that element to be discovered, that certain thing above all others attached obscurely to each object; only, this knowledge had always lain as though hidden in the more inaccessible zones of my mind. Since this research could yield only one exact "tag" for each object, my investigations came to be a search *for the solution of a problem for which I had three data: the object, the thing attached to it in the shadow of my consciousness, and the light under which that thing would become apparent.*

The problem of the door called for an opening through which one could pass. I showed, in my *Réponse Imprévue,* a closed door in a room; in the door an irregular shaped opening reveals the night.

Woman was responsible for *Le Viol (The Rape).* In that picture a woman's face is made up of the essential details of her body. Her breasts have become eyes, her nose is represented by her navel, and the mouth is replaced by the sexual zone.

The problem of the window led to *La Condition humaine.* In front of a window, as seen from the interior of a room, I placed a picture that represented precisely the portion of landscape blotted out by the picture. For instance, the tree represented in the picture displaced the tree situated behind it, outside the room. For the spectator it was simultaneously inside the room; in the picture the outside, in the real landscape, in thought. Which is how we see the world, namely, outside of us, though having only one representation of it within us. Similarly, we sometimes situate in the past something going on in the present. Time and space then lose that unrefined meaning in which daily experience alone takes stock.

A problem to the solution of which I applied myself, over a long period, was that of the horse. In the course of my research I again had occasion to find that my unconscious knew beforehand the thing that had to be brought to light. In fact, the first glimmer of an idea was that of the final solution, however vaguely adumbrated. It was the idea of a horse carrying three shapeless masses. Their significance became clear only after a long series of trials and experiments. First I painted an object consisting of a jar and a label bearing the image of a horse, with the following printed letters: *HORSE PRESERVE (CONFITURE DE CHEVAL)*. I next thought of a horse whose head was replaced by a hand, with its index finger pointing the direction: "Forward." But I realized that this was merely the equivalent of a unicorn.

I lingered long over an intriguing combination. In a black room, I placed a horse-woman seated near a table; with her head resting on her hand, she was dreamily gazing at a landscape whose limits were the silhouette of a horse. The animal's lower body and forelegs were earthen-colored, while upward from a horizontal line at the level of the horsewoman's eyes, the horse's coat was painted in different sky and cloud hues. What finally put me on the right track was a horseman in the position assumed while riding a galloping horse. From the sleeve of the arm thrust forward emerged the head of a noble charger, and the other arm, thrown back, held a riding whip. Beside this horseman I placed an American Indian in an identical posture, and I suddenly divined the meaning of the three shapeless masses I had placed on the horse at the beginning of my experiment.

I knew that they were horsemen and I then put the finishing touches to *La Chaîne sans fin*. In a setting of desert land and dark sky, a plunging horse is mounted by a modern horseman, a knight of the dying Middle Ages, and a horseman of antiquity.

Nietzsche is of the opinion that without a burning sexual system Raphael could not have painted such a throng of Madonnas. This is at striking variance with motives usually attributed to that venerated painter: priestly influences, ardent Christian piety, esthetic ideals, search for pure beauty, etc., etc. . . . But Nietzsche's view of the matter makes possible a more sane interpretation of pictorial phenomena, and the violence with which that opinion is expressed is directly proportionate to the clarity of the thought underlying it.

Only the same mental freedom can make possible a salutary renewal in all the domains of human activity.

This disorderly world which is our world, swarming with contradictions, still hangs more or less together through explanations, by turns complex and ingenious, but apparently justifying it and excusing those who meanly take advantage of it. Such explanations are based on a certain experience, true.

But it is to be remarked that what is invoked is "ready-made" experience, and that if it does give rise to brilliant analysis, such experience is not itself an outcome of an analysis of its own real conditions.

Future society will develop an experience which will be the fruit of a profound analysis whose perspectives are being outlined under our very eyes. And it is under the favor of such a rigorous preliminary analysis that pictorial experience such as I understand it may be instituted.

That pictorial experience which puts the real world on trial inspired in me belief in an infinity of possibles now unknown to life. I know I am not alone in affirming that their conquest is the only valid end and reason for the existence of man.

MAN RAY

FROM *SELF-PORTRAIT*

When my old friend Roland Penrose, who ran the Institute of Contemporary Art in London, put the gallery at my disposal for an exhibition, I selected works from the earliest period to the present—a most comprehensive choice, quite austere, as some would say—and then composed the catalog carefully, including a transcription of an article by that delightful, profound and enigmatic composer, Erik Satie. I had come across it in a musical review of 1912, written by him in answer to attacks by critics. I changed a few words in the article, to suit my case: when he speaks of music, I speak of painting, when he says, sound, I say color. The title: *What I Am:*

> At the beginning of my career, I at once classed myself among the photo-metrographers. My works are purely photometric. Take *Revolving Doors* or *Seguidilla, Le Beau Temps* or the *Shakespearean Equations,* you will notice that no plastic idea entered into the creation of these works. It is scientific thought which dominates.
>
> Besides, I take greater pleasure in measuring a color than looking at it. Holding a photometer I work joyfully and surely.
>
> What have I not weighed or measured? All Uccello, all Leonardo, etc. It is very strange.
>
> The first time I used a photoscope I examined a pear of medium size. I assure you I have never seen anything more repulsive. I called my servant and showed it to her.
>
> On the photoscale a commom ordinary nude weighed two hundred pounds. She was sent by a very fat painter whom I weighed also.
>
> Are you familiar with the cleaning of colors? It is quite filthy.
>
> Spinning is cleaner. Knowing how to classify them is very delicate and requires good sight. Here we enter phototechnicology.
>
> As for color explosions so often disagreeable, cotton wool placed on the eyes will attenuate them suitably for one. Here we arrive at pyrophotology.
>
> To draw my *Mains Libres* I used a caleidophoto-recorder. This took seven minutes. I called my servant and showed it to her.

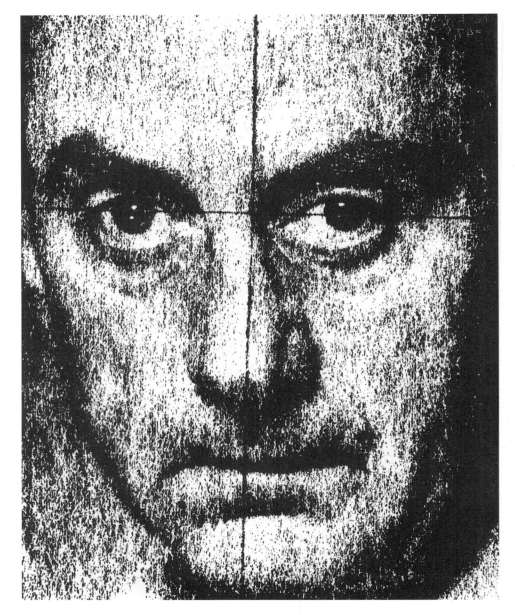

Man Ray, *Self-Portrait, Hollywood*, 1947; photoetching. The J. Paul Getty Museum. © ARS.

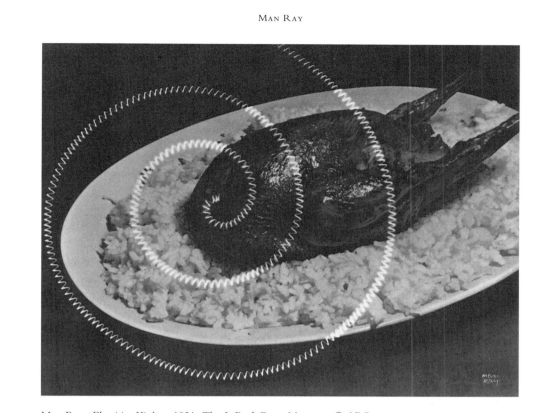

Man Ray, *Electricity-Kitchen,* 1931. The J. Paul Getty Museum. © ARS.

I think I may say that photology is superior to painting. It is more varied. The pecuniary yield is greater. I owe to it my fortune.

Anyhow, with a monodymanophote, a barely trained photo-measurer can record in the same time and with the same effort more colors than the most adept painter. It is thanks to this that I have painted so much.

The future belongs to philophotology.

• • •

Dadamade

Who made Dada? Nobody and everybody. I made Dada when I was a baby and I was roundly spanked by my mother. Now everyone claims to be the author of Dada. For the past thirty years. In Zurich, in Cologne, in Paris, in London, in Tokyo, in San Francisco, in New York. I might claim to be the author of Dada in New York. In 1912 before Dada.

Man Ray, *Portrait through Wire;* from *Le Surréalisme au service de la Révolution* 1 (July 1930). © ARS.

In 1919, with the permission and with the approval of other Dadaists I legalized Dada in New York. Just once. That was enough. The times did not deserve more. That was a Dadadate. The one issue of New York Dada did not even bear the names of the authors. How unusual for Dada. Of course, there were a certain number of collaborators. Both willing and unwilling. Both trusting and suspicious. What did it matter? Only one issue. Forgotten—not even seen by most Dadaists or anti-Dadaists. Now we are trying to revive Dada. Why? Who cares? Who does not care? Dada is dead. Or is Dada still alive?

We cannot revive something that is alive just as we cannot revive anything that is dead.

Is Dadadead? Is Dadalive? Dada is. Dadaism.

André Masson

Painting Is a Wager

For those of us who were young Surrealists in 1924 reason was the great "prostitute." We considered Cartesians, Voltairians and other functionaries of the intellect as men who had utilized it in order to conserve values which, though established, were moribund; their nonconformism was only an affected front. But the supreme indictment against them was that they had given intelligence the mercenary task of railing at "Love," and at "Poetry." Our group denounced that with the utmost vigor. It was a great temptation then to try operating magically on things, but first of all on ourselves. Our collective enthusiasm for that magic operation was so great that none of us could resist. As early as the end of the 1924 winter, a frantic surrender to automatism was the rule with us. The phrase has survived.

Objectively, I shall add that, to that immersion in the night (into what the Germans called the nocturnal face of things) and to the ever desirable appeal of the marvelous was added the game: and it was a serious game.

I see us in retrospect: it would have occurred to no one then, dizzied as we were by our vain or efficient magic, to ask if the "opposite of a mistake was not just another mistake." A century earlier Friedrich Schlegel had asked himself that question and illuminated the whole romantic irony with one query.

Certainly, as soon as the first Surrealist conquests had occurred, the question of whether surrender to the associating imagination should not be transcended ought to have been raised. Some of us have since answered it affirmatively. The danger of automatism is probably that it often associates only unessential relations, whose content, as Hegel puts it, "does not go beyond what is contained in the images." It is fair to add that if, in philosophical research the crucial law is to distrust the association of ideas, the same does not apply to artistic creation whose essence is in the intuition of the senses. The process of images, the sense of wonder or of anguish brought on with their encounter, open up a road rich in plastic metaphors: *a fire of snow*. From this stems its lure and its frailty: it may be too easily

André Masson, *La Nuit fertile (The Fertile Night),* 1960; photo: Lauros-Giraudon, private collection. © ARS.

satisfied with itself and lose touch both with numbers and with the tactile approach to the world.

Whatever the case may have been, there were several of us who feared "the other mistake:" that of making the summons to the unconscious into something as limited as the rationalism we were indicting, but in vain. Around 1930, five years after the founding of Surrealism, a frightening scourge appeared in its midst with the arrival of the demagogy of the irrational. For awhile it led pictorial Surrealism toward conventionality and a desire for mundane approval. It was a meager conquest indeed, that of the irrational for the sake of the irrational, and it was a sad day that saw the operations of an imagination which associated only those elements already worn out by reason's bleak activities. It took as its own materials tarnished by lazy habit, by memory—materials picked up arbitrarily from works of "popular physics," in old curiosity shops, or in the magazines favored by our grandfathers.

Thus in its turn Surrealism enclosed itself in a dualism which was incomparably more grave than that of cubism. In contrast with the latter, the Surrealist dualism consisted in:

1. freeing the psyche's menagerie, or at the very least simulating that liberation so as to utilize it as a theme;

2. expressing oneself with means that had encumbered the academies of the past century. The rediscovery of the old horizon, that of Meissonier, was the climax of this reactionary perversion. The back-tracking was accomplished with assured insolence. The admirable achievement of Seurat, Matisse and of the cubists was counted as nothing. Their exalting conception of space and their discovery of essentially pictorial means were treated as a burdensome legacy which had to be thrown overboard.

Should we have bowed to this new academism? Certainly not.

On the contrary, the lofty task which we felt was incumbent upon us was to get from the academism to a rigorous conception of the conditions of the imaginative work.

First of all, we had to propose this principle: since the imaginative artist can only make his work with elements already existing in reality, it is crucial that, with his eyes open on the exterior world (and sometimes they are!), he should not see things in their worn out generality, but in their revealed individuality. A whole world is contained in the drop of water which trembles on the edge of a leaf; but it is there only when an artist and a poet have the gift of seeing it in its immediacy.

However, and let no mistake be made about it, this revelation or inspired knowledge, this contact with nature, are profound only in so far as they have been prepared by the reflection and by the intense meditation of the artist. Only in this way can the revelation of the senses enrich knowledge. The tendency to allow oneself to be invaded by objects, of making the self into a vase to be filled by objects, indicates an absorption with things which represents a very low stage of consciousness. Similarly, the all too facile summons to subterranean powers, the superficial identification with the cosmos, as well as a false primitivism are little more than aspects of a none too estimable pantheism.

The true power of a work of the imagination, once the impact of surprise is gone, will result from the three following conditions:

1. The intensity of the meditation which preceded it.

2. The freshness of vision brought to looking upon the exterior world.

3. The need of knowing the pictorial means which are proper to the art of our time. Delacroix's observation that "a figurative work must be above all else a feast for the eyes" remains entirely true.

Does that mean one must give precedence to reflection over instinct, or to intelligence over what is commonly called "inspiration"? I think not. The fusion of the heterogeneous elements set up by the poet-painter will take place with the lightning speed of light. Intuition and understanding, the unconscious and the conscious, must work out their transmutation in the superconsciousness, in the exfoliating unity.

PHILIPPE SOUPAULT

HYMN TO LIBERTY

At the age of eight I was sent to a school run by priests. I worked absent-mindedly at my studies and have retained a memory of this school which is morose, disagreeable, and dust-covered. For it was a kind of huge barracks where the dust from the surrounding streets sought refuge. A long courtyard planted with broomsticks was given over during recess to authorized games. When I think of prisonyards it is always that yard I see. The schoolrooms, which were even gloomier, were painted a light brown and had black tables and dirty windows. Here we were taught catholicism, not severely, but also not brilliantly, and I don't remember having passed through a phase of mysticism. The sessions in the school chapel and those at church seemed equally long and monotonous to me. For eight years I remained shut in, watched over from seven in the morning till seven at night. The only means of escape was to think of something else; and that I certainly did. I read with keen interest the various anthologies and histories of literature, as well as certain interlinear translations, and a little later of *Lundis* of Sainte-Beauve. But I had little taste for Latin version and a holy horror of Latin composition and versification. Greek I found more amusing. And so, from the age of eight till fourteen, my life was one of exemplary monotony. Above all, I was exceedingly bored. During the classes at the Condorcet grammar school where the priests used to accompany us, I sought primarily to make the time pass more quickly. With one of my schoolmates, Robert Bourget, great-grandson of Buloz and grandson of Edouard Pailleron, I looked about for some sort of diversion. We carved the table with our knives, played ball, or talked of this and that. We also ate cakes and candies, and read *Nick Carter* . . . It was for these latter diversions, especially, that we were punished. Usually, however, we didn't care.

"Soupault, you're not listening."
"Soupault, answer."

One of my more solemn professors, grown weary of repeating "you're not listening," and observing bitterly that I had understood nothing of the aorist tense, said to me:

"Soupault, I will destroy your future like a twig," and suiting the gesture to the word, he broke in two a piece of chalk which was supposed to symbolize my destiny. But nothing was of any avail. I remained just as absent-minded, ferociously absent-minded, as ever.

"Two hours after school!"
"You'll be kept in on Sunday!"

Our chief thought was how to get away from school. My recollection of our conversations is rather vague, but I remember a little better the teasing and derision which we addressed especially to "good" pupils, or to those who memorized French verse.

In the schoolyard I caught a glimpse from time to time of my brothers, who were more intimate with each other than with me. At night I went home to my mother and sister. But of course I had to "go to bed early." Short as they were, however, I was at a loss to make these evenings pass. I wandered about the apartment, disgusted with everything, thinking bitterly that tomorrow would be like all the other days.

This childhood of mine seems to me to have been, above all, a series of little disappointments, a daily boredom; going to school and wanting perpetually to leave it in order to go and sleep, only to come back the next day to that "hole." It was a vicious circle, and I am sure that my great, imperious need of liberty, my horror of physical and moral restraint, my desire always to elude all outside suggestions or thoughts, even, date from this period.

Two days out of the week, Thursday and Sunday, I was free. But I was sick of everything, and enjoyed things only mildly. I was unaccustomed both to liberty and its uses, and hardly knew what to do with myself. Sometimes I was taken for a walk in the Bois de Boulogne. But this was the height of boredom. When it rained I was taken to a museum.

It was nevertheless on these free days that I acquired a taste for reading. Not knowing what to do, and tiring easily of playthings, I seized upon all printed matter. In fact, I read anything and everything: *My Diary,* the *Bible, Adventures of Captain Corcoran,* Andersen's *Fairy Tales,* the short stories of de Maupassant, Guisot's *History of England,* the works of Lenôtre. . . . Every week I devoured three or four books. Then, when I had none left, I would re-read those I had forgotten. It really became a vice. I remember my mother used to say: "If you want to keep him quiet, you have only to give him a book."

The summer vacations were pleasant, but I was really very apathetic. I think, too, that I must have been a child with rather frail health and a particularly inattentive mind. In any case, my recollections of this period are somewhat vague, the principal reason being, probably, that I accepted what was done to me without much resistance, and at the same time escaped all restraint, paid attention to nothing. It is natural that I should have retained so little now that I am grown.

When I think back on these small details that composed my childhood, I am surprised to see how dull it was. Nor can I blame anyone for it. When all is said, I suffered very little, learned very little, and was merely very much bored.

But I was alive, which was already a lot. And during this period I did acquire one thing: a passion for liberty. This passion, which was eight years taking hold of me, has developed to such an extent that it is now probably the most violent thing about me. Liberty of movement and of thought, which could easily reach a point of tyranny and even destruction, are essential to me. It is quite in earnest, and with all the seriousness of which I am capable, that I now pen this hymn to Liberty.

O longed-for Liberty, you who are the source of my malady, who torture and kill me like thirst, I wish that once in my life I might behold your face. Only once, and I should be happy.

Each time I feel your presence and something tells me simply: "she is here," I know that my heart begins to beat faster and that my legs are seized with a desire to run. A strange odor pervades the air, a purer sound, a calmer voice, and a light which is more wonderful than joy itself. It is enough for me to know that your life touches mine, O Liberty, for me to feel stronger and more sure of myself.

You are really mine, and I am really your slave, only when your presence weighs on me, causing me to gasp with anguish. I am a stricken being, I press my elbows close against my trembling body, I clench my fists, my back is bowed. You are not beside me.

When the whole world is sleeping and night, like the oldest of goddesses, turns her head away; when the moon utters its little owl-like cry, then, O Liberty, I know that you are approaching in your silken gown, which is more beautiful than nakedness, and I wait. My lips, my ears, my fingers grow redder than the spider on the wall, and my heart is a little bull in my breast. I have already thirty times watched the coming of a new year; I have already seen that the sun is the most faithful of lovers; I have already forgotten that I was born and that I must die. But Liberty, I am poorer than ever, more sincere than ever because you have not raped me.

Far off, in a mountain village, I see linen drying in a field where the sun is happily browsing. But nearby, walking along the highroad, men with bent backs are coming to gulp down their evening meal and then to sleep without protest. They have forgotten that the sky is like a great open hand, that the road which they wear down a little more each day leads to a mountain torrent, or to the steel-blue sea. They have forgotten that their sex organs might have some use, and that their feet have a shut-in odor; they have forgotten everything except eating and drinking. But they must be punished, Liberty, they must be punished, for they understand only possession.

A man whose nose is a dust bin and whose mouth is an old shed to keep teeth in, is bending over the earth. He would like to eat a piece of it spread on a crust of bread he has carefully saved for this moment. Here is a man who loves this earth of his, with its peculiar excremental taste, and he wants to keep it for his very own. If need be, he would have himself buried in it, in order better to watch over it! At his side, O Liberty, a frolicsome dog that cares not a rap for persons or things, is daintily wetting the flowers. O Liberty, with your starlike face, do not forget this man who licks the earth as though it were made of sugar. I well know that I am not the only one who calls and would like to follow you, that others too are your friends. But I am the most cowardly, the stupidest of all. So you must signal first to me, because I am the slowest and the dullest and because I really cannot live longer without you; because I am about to pass out with thirst, and the ink which I have taken to drinking really no longer suffices to quench this burning. I know well, beloved Liberty, that it would be enough for me to see one sign, one sign only, and with a bound I would stand ready. I am thinking of you, Liberty.

There are those who laugh and mock, and others who shrug their shoulders and thrust out their dung-yellow lips. I known that the best thing for them to do is to shut their traps up good and tight and watch what is going to happen. There are also those who know, the smart ones who made learned calculations with figures and statistics, but who are even duller than the others. These last are called men with a future. Liberty, I am nothing but a youngster enamored of Liberty, and I forget the rest without much effort, because I have a thirst, a wolf-like thirst which is sometimes a thirst for fresh blood, for your blood, Liberty. I have been told that there are men who will go to any lengths to bar your path and eliminate all those who seek to follow in your footsteps. The shaggy-headed idiots have not yet looked at themselves. It is possible, Liberty, that they don't know that this death, which they brandish like a bogey, is our friend and your sister, and that we shall learn to love her if you say so; that we love you more because we still have faith in you, but that we are not afraid and, in order to follow you, we wll not hesitate to take the path that leads direct to her? Then, O Liberty, let us have one sign, a grand sign, like dawn, or a gush of blood.

Joseph Cornell, *Letter to Parker Tyler*, 1940. Courtesy of Harry Ransom Humanities Research Center.

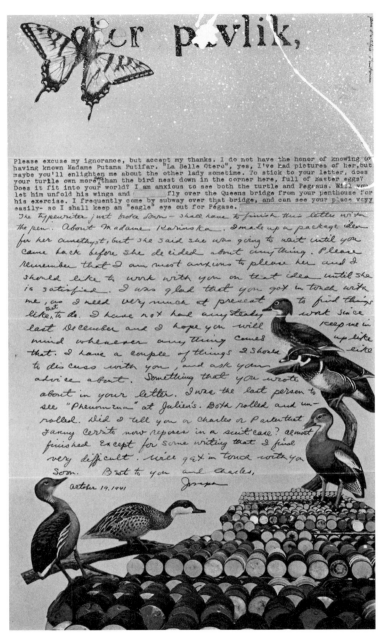

Joseph Cornell, *Letter to Pavel Tchelitchew,* 1941. Courtesy of Harry Ransom Humanities Research Center.

TEXTS

Joan Miró, *Untitled,* 1924; photo: Giraudon, 1929. © ARS.

ANONYMOUS [SCRUTATOR]

AUTOMATIC DRAWING

Anybody who has recollection of having learned to draw a straight line or a regular curve will be well assured that the act belongs to the order known as purposive or voluntary action. The experienced artist or draughtsman will know equally well that drawing of the line or curve very soon falls into the region of the automatic and involuntary. The fact is that every action tends to become habitual, involuntary, and automatic from the time of its first performance, whether it be merely the stroking of the moustache, the preening of the hair, the satisfaction of an appetite, or the recollecting of a name. Even a mental attitude or viewpoint tends to become habitual and to that extent beyond the control of the thinker.

What becomes of all these habitual memories by which our actions and thoughts are unconsciously controlled? They pass into the realm of the subconscious, and from time to time, as they are awakened by some suggestive stimulus from the normal or attentive consciousness, they spring into activity and induce to repetitive action. The stimulating agent, its action on the subconscious self, and the automatic response are equally unperceived by the mind that is actively engaged. Only when the attentive mind is temporarily drowsy and in relaxation such automatic effects will manifest in feelings of uneasiness, restlessness and desire. The subconscious or automatic part of us manifests most strongly when the attentive mind is most actively engaged and preoccupied. In the human brain there are two bodies, naturally adapted to the reception, memory, and expression of these two sets or orders of mental function. The cerebrum, or grey matter of the brain, is the depository of all conscious thought and feeling. It is from the cortex of this brain that all mental energy proceeds.

The interior of the brain receives impressions from the afferent centers of the sense-organs. These sense-impressions are then radiated as vibrations through the grey matter of the cerebrum, which responds and adjusts the person by means of the afferent centers of the nervous system acting upon the muscles.

But there is another brain called the *corpora striata,* or streaked body, which is in effect the lieutenant of the superior cerebrum. To this brain are delegated all those actions which, while automatic or habitual, are yet under the control of the thinking part of us. I decide to

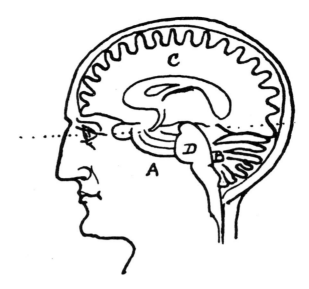

A. *Corpus Striatum.* Region of sub-conscious automatic action.
B. *Cerebellum.* Region of sub-conscious organic action.
C. *Cerebrum.* Region of attentive mind or normal consciousness.
D. *Medulla.* Centre of nervous radiation.

walk to a certain place. My first few steps are purposive and are directed to the fulfilling of my intention. Then, acting under some suggestion of things heard or seen *en passant,* I fall into a train of thought, or voluntarily pursue some subject of my own selection. But the trusty lieutenant of my brain, the *corpora striata,* keeps me going in the right direction. Not only that, but it also keeps me from colliding with passengers on the way or running my head against a lamp-post. Rather than that should happen it would bring me quickly to a halt.

Yet this is not the brain that tells me I am hungry or that I have exerted myself too much, or have eaten unwisely. That is another of my useful auxiliaries. It is the cerebellum, or leaf brain, the *arbor vitae.* Its function is to keep the animal part of me in orderly relations with my superior intelligence, to the end that the body may be regulated and nourished without my having to keep an eye continually on the clock. For this purpose it has a clock of its own—the heart, which tells it when food and rest are wanted.

It will thus be seen that there are parts of the encephalon adapted to purposive action, automatic action and organic action. It is to the second of these, to which automatic action is related, that I would refer the phenomenon known as automatic writing and drawing. But in doing so I would not wish to convey the idea that I negate the agency of extraneous intelligences. There are instances in which at least an extended consciousness in the medium

was necessary to cover the nature of the information thus received. The question of "spirit agency" in connection with such automata as the planchette, ouija, etc., is beset with many difficulties, and what is called "direct" writing tends rather to complicate than to elucidate matters. It is always presumed that a medium can write normally, but drawing with any degree of elaboration and finish is not a presumed accomplishment. Consequently, the production of complex drawings rapidly executed by one who, to use her husband's expression, "could not draw a three-legged stool to save her life," is a matter of no little psychological interest. However, I will here give my own idea of the elementary drawing of the article referred to, the process requiring eight strokes of the pen, together with the primitive hieroglyph employed by the Chinaman to represent a wooden thing to rest upon, and then leave my correspondent to tell the story in his own way.

He writes:—

It happened that early in 1895, while at Sydney, my wife and I with our son were inmates of a house where spiritualistic phenomena had obtained a grip. Some there were who took the matter seriously, others regarding it in the light of an amusement. I, who had previously investigated the subject, naturally approached it in more sober spirit. There were the usual rappings and table-turnings, but nothing of a satisfactory nature. Then automatic writing was tried. In this I took common part for a while, but not liking the general atmosphere of the company I subsequently decided to try alone. My first attempt was void of any results, but on the second evening I obtained a movement of the pencil which quickly developed into writing, which took the form of a message of rather startling import, sufficiently convincing to assure me of the presence of some intelligence transcending my normal self. Names of persons were given and also an address which was quite unknown to me, but which I was afterwards able to verify.

My wife, hitherto skeptical of the whole matter, was so far impressed by this experience as to be induced to make a private and serious effort to obtain similar results. She resolved to sit for one hour daily for a whole month and judge of the matter accordingly. It was decided that the hour from noon to one o'clock should be adhered to daily. She sat at a table holding a pencil over a sheet of notepaper.

During the first week the pencil never moved from the spot where it was first placed. A second week produced no better effect. My wife was getting disheartened, but I urged her to fulfil her purpose and see the trial through the month. In the third week a movement producing wavy lines and angles was obtained, but all very crude and meaningless, like a child's first attempts at writing. Yet these inchoate scribblings might well have spelled the word Hope!

One morning during the fourth week I returned to lunch, and my wife having finished her séance had gone to the dining-room. On the table of the room in which I stood were the sheets of paper she had been using, and on one of them I saw what appeared to be an Oriental drawing resembling the carving on some ancient Indian or Maori temple. I thought some visitor had been at work, for I knew my wife could not draw at all. At the luncheon-table I inquired who had done the drawing and was astonished to hear that she had herself been made to do it during the previous hour. She was elated with her success and now willingly extended her sittings to an additional hour in the evening. The drawings rapidly grew into remarkable designs and quaint-looking scroll-work. A drawing-book which I procured for her was rapidly filled with a number of strange subjects, all of a distinctly antique appearance, some looking like fossils, masses of heads, bones, and peculiar things buried in earth. All these drawings were accomplished with great celerity of action, and my wife now found that she could be "controlled" in company equally well and even hold conversation while the work was in progress. The drawings of heads were becoming so fine and small that I made an effort to obtain bolder effects, and on using a large sheet of paper and a Conté crayon, large and satisfactory drawings were procured. In twenty minutes by the clock my wife completed a most elaborate piece of work representing a male head surmounted by a huge Oriental-looking helmet, supported by handsome scroll-work, and each day one of these extraordinary figures was produced. The remarkable feature was that in every instance the heads were drawn either with the face turned downwards or upwards, as if the figure were lying on its face or back, and never upright as one would naturally draw them. Eight large drawings of this sort formed four distinct pairs of heads, being alternately a male and a female, set *vis-à-vis*.

No trance or abnormal condition occurred during these automatic drawings, but my wife's hand perspired very freely and she spoke of a "peculiar cold thrill" passing down her arm into her hand, while at the end of every séance she was in a state of great exhaustion. Failing health finally put an end to these experiments, but before terminating them we obtained the information that the control was named "Menthes," and this name was written several times in reply to our inquiries.

Here I must leave the subject with my readers. Menthes or the subconscious self? Spirit agency or latent faculty? These are questions which I am not competent, in the circumstances, to answer.

GUILLAUME APOLLINAIRE

ONEIROCRITICISM

The coals of the sky were so near that I was afraid of their heat. They were on the point of burning me. But I was conscious of the different eternities of man and woman. Two animals of different species were coupling, and rose-vines covered the trellises which moons weighed down with grapes. From the monkey's throat came flames which made the world blossom like a lily. In the myrtle an ermine was turning white. We asked it the reason for the unnatural winter. I gulped down the tawny herds. Orkenise appeared on the horizon. We went toward that city, regretting to leave the valleys where the apple trees used to sing and whistle and roar. But the song of the cultivated fields was marvellous:

> By the gates of Orkenise
> A ploughman wishes to come in.
> By the gates of Orkenise
> A vagabond wishes to go out.

> The city sentries straightaway
> Fall upon the vagabond:
> "What are you taking out with you?"
> "I left all of my heart behind."

> The city sentries straightaway
> Halt the ploughman in his tracks:
> "What are you bringing in with you?"
> "My heart, for I shall marry here".

> How many hearts in Orkenise!
> The sentries laughed and laughed.
> O vagabond, the road is dull,
> And ploughman, love is just as sad.

> The worthy sentries of the town
> Knitted on complacently;
> The heavy gates of Orkenise
> Then began closing gradually.

But I was conscious of the different eternities of man and woman. The sky suckled its young panthers. Then I noticed crimson spots on my hand. Toward morning some pirates carried off nine ships that were at anchor in the harbor. The kings were becoming cheerful. The women, as well, did not want to mourn anyone's death. They prefer old kings, stronger in their love than old dogs. A man making a sacrifice wished to be immolated himself in place of the victim. They cut his belly open. I saw there four I's, four O's, and four D's. We were served fresh meat, and I suddenly grew larger after having eaten it. Monkeys as big as their own trees violated ancient tombs. I called one of these beasts on which laurel leaves were growing. It brought me a head made out of a single pearl. I took it in my hands and questioned it after having threatened to throw it in the sea if it did not answer me. This pearl was ignorant and the sea swallowed it up.

But I was conscious of the different eternities of man and woman. Two animals of different species were making love to each other. However only the kings were not dying of laughter, and twenty blind tailors came to cut and sew a veil destined to cover the sardonyx. I directed them myself, backwards. Toward evening, the trees took flight, and monkeys became motionless, and I saw myself a hundred strong. This band which was I sat down beside the sea. Great ships of gold crossed the horizon. And when night had fallen, a hundred flames came to meet me. I procreated a hundred male children whose nurses were the moon and the hillside. They loved the flabby kings who were kept moving about on balconies. When I had come to the bank of a river, I took it in both hands and brandished it about. This sword refreshed me. The languid spring warned me that if I stopped the sun, I should see it as actually square. A hundred strong, I swam toward an archipelago. A hundred sailors received me and, having taken me to a palace, they killed me ninety-nine times. I burst out laughing at that moment and danced, whereas they were weeping. I danced on all fours. But the others no longer dared to move, for I had the frightening appearance of a lion.

On all fours, on all fours.

My arms and my legs were alike, and my eyes which had multiplied crowned me attentively. Then I rose up to dance like hands and like leaves.

I was gloved. The islanders took me to their orchards so that I might pick fruit like women. And the island, adrift, filled up a gulf where immediately red trees sprang up. A soft beast covered with white plumes was singing ineffably, and a whole population admired him without tiring. I found on the ground the head made out of a single pearl, which was crying. I brandished the river and the crowd dispersed. Some old men were eating smallage, and being immortal did not suffer more than the dead. I felt free, as free as a flower in its season. The sun was no freer than a ripe fruit. A flock of trees browsed among the invisible stars and the dawn gave its hand to the storm. In the myrtle one came under the influence of darkness. A whole people, heaped into a press, were bleeding and singing. Men were born from the liquid which flowed from the press. They brandished other rivers, which struck one another with a ringing sound. The shadows came out of the myrtle and went off to the gardens which a shoot watered with the eyes of men and animals. The handsomest of all the men seized me by the throat, but I succeeded in throwing him down. On his knees, he showed me his teeth. I touched them. Sounds came from them which changed into serpents the color of chestnuts, and their tongue was called Saint Fabeau. They dug up a transparent root and ate some of it. It was the size of a turnip.

And my quiet river covered them without drowning them.

The sky was full of feces and onions. I cursed the unworthy stars whose light flowed out over the earth. No living creature appeared any more. But songs arose on every side. I visited empty cities and abandoned cottages. I gathered up crowns of all the kings and made of them the immobile minister of the loquacious world. Ships of gold, unmanned, crossed the horizon. Gigantic shadows passed across the distant sails. Several centuries separated me from these shadows. I despaired. But I was conscious of the different eternities of men and women. Shadows of different kinds darkened with their love the scarlet of the sails, while my eyes multiplied in rivers, in cities, and on mountain snows.

LOUIS ARAGON

FROM *PARIS PEASANT*

At the level of the printer who prints cards while you wait, just beyond the little flight of steps leading down into the Rue Chaptal, at that point in the far north of the mystery where the grotto gapes deep back in a bay troubled by the comings and goings of removal men and errand boys, in the farthest reaches of the two kinds of daylight which pit the reality of the outside world against the subjectivism of the passage, let us pause a moment, like a man holding back from the edge of the place's depths, attracted equally by the current of objects and the whirlpools of his own being, let us pause in this strange zone where all is distraction, distraction of attention as well as of inattention, so as to experience this vertigo. The double illusion which holds us here is confronted with our desire for absolute knowledge. Here the two great movements of the spirit are equivalent and all interpretations of the world have lost their power over me. Two universes begin to fade at their point of contact; like a woman adorned with all the magic spells of love when daybreak has raised her skirt of curtains and penetrated the room gently. For a moment, the scales dip towards the weird gulf of appearances. Strange lure of these arbitrary arrangements: here is someone crossing a street, and the space around him is solid, and there is a piano on the pavement, and motorcars squatting under their drivers. Unequal height of passers-by, uneven temperament of matter, everything changes according to the laws of divergence, and I am greatly astonished at God's imagination: an imagination attuned to infinitesimal and discordant variations, as though the great question was to bring together, one day, an orange and a piece of string, a wall and a glance. It looks rather as though for God the world simply provides the occasion for a few attempts at still-lifes. He has two or three little stage props which he uses assiduously: the absurd, the trumpery, the banal . . . impossible to get him to change his script.

If, standing at this sentimental crossroads, I direct my eyes alternately towards this land of disorder and towards the great arcade illuminated by my instincts, I do not experience the tiniest stirring of hope at the spirit of either of these illusionistic landscapes. I feel the ground tremble beneath me and suddenly I feel like a sailor aboard a ruined castle. Every-

Dora Maar, *The Double (Specializing in Permanent Waves and Sets),* 1935. © ARS.

thing signifies havoc. Everything is crumbling under my gaze. The sense of uselessness is squatting beside me on the first step. He is dressed like me, but with an added touch of nobility. He does not carry a handkerchief. The infinite is reflected in his face, and he holds extended between his hands a blue accordion which he never plays, and upon which one can read: PESSIMISM. Pass me this little chunk of azure, my dear Sense of the useless, its song will please my ears. When I squeeze its bellows only the consonants can still be seen:

PSSMSM

As I stretch them again, the I's reappear:

PSSIMISM

followed by the E:

PESSIMISM

And the whole thing starts wailing from left to right:

ESSIMISM—PSSIMISM—PESIMISM
PESIMISM—PESSMISM—PESSIISM
PESSIMSM—pessimim—PESSIMIS

PESSIMISM

The wave reaches this shore with a barbaric explosion. And starts to recede again.

PESSIMISM—PESSIMIS—PESSIMI
PESSIM—PESSI—PESS
PES—PE—P—p . . . , nothing more.

Standing on one leg, the other foot cupped in his hand, a bit theatrical, a bit common, clay pipe, cap tilted over one eye, and singing I do believe: *Ah, if only you knew the details of the life of Burgundy snails* . . . at the top of the steps, in the dust and the fag ends, why if it isn't that charming boy: the Sense of the useless.

• • •

I know: one of the principal reproaches that has been made to me in the past, and that is about to be repeated now, is this gift for observation which you have to observe at work in me in order to confirm its existence and so hold a grudge against me for it. But honestly, I would never have thought of myself as an observer. I like to let the winds and the rain blow through me: chance is my only experience, hazard my sole experiment. I do not subscribe to the idea that the world can be had for the asking. This handkerchief saleswoman, this little sugar bowl which I will describe to you if you don't behave yourself, are interior boundaries of myself, ideal views I have of my laws, of my ways of thought, and may I be strung up by the neck if this passage is anything else but a method of freeing myself of certain inhibitions, a means of obtaining access to a hitherto forbidden realm that lies beyond my human energies. Let it assume its true name, then, and let Monsieur Oudin come and put up the plaque himself:

The stranger reading my little guide lifts his nose and says to himself: it's here. Then directs his steps mechanically towards the point where I have just abandoned him in favor of my oneiric placard, and, addressing the raspberry-and-pistachio lady politely, makes an enormous effort of the imagination and then asks for details of her tariff. The price seems very reasonable to him, and like a photographer in his studio the lady supervises the whole delicate operation personally. But what plunges the visitor over a precipice of conjecture is that instead of a standard rate being in operation there are three classes, as on the railway. He dreams of demanding "the whole works," as though he were at the hairdressers, and at the same time is scared to death of the idea. He thinks of the fantasies he created about love, his whole life flashes through his mind: his innocent childhood, his little sister and his parents gathered around the hearth, a painting on grey silk representing Paul and Virginia fleeing the storm, a heart pierced with an arrow, and two or three furnished rooms. Finally, he resigns himself to the least expensive simulacrum. But can I believe what I see in his eyes? This sacrifice of everything worthy of respect to an ardour that is welling up so powerfully in him at this moment, this base quest for the ephemeral lacking even the illusion of duration, this absence of pretext going as far as anonymity and the isolation of pleasure, all this excites him mightily, and he is in something of a hurry to disappear into the shadows where I can just make out the languid movements of a pair of hands. Follow your inclinations boldly, stranger. You have my blessing, and that is a great deal, believe me. He grows taut. He writhes. Oh, he certainly didn't take very long, did he!

What are these sentimental murmurings I begin to hear? Can the orchestra stalls be taking themselves for musicians? I endorse all of mankind's inclinations, and for example I endorse his liking for the ephemeral. The ephemeral is a polymorphous divinity, as is its name. My friend Robert Desnos, that remarkable sage, who keeps strange ships moored in each fold of his brain, has pored long over these syllables which ring out like a legend peopled with green eyes and goblins. He has descended philology's silk ladder in his search for the meaning concealed by this word at the heart of its fertile images:

ÉPHÉMÈRE

F. M. R.
(folie - mort - rêverie)

Les faits, m'errent

LES FAIX, MÈRES

Fernande aime Robert
pour la vie!

o   ÉPнéMÈRe   o
ÉPHÉMÈRES

Ephemeral, F.M.R.L. (frenzy-madness-reverie-love), a fame really, every merrily, Effie marry Lee: there are words that are mirrors, optical lakes towards which hands stretch out in vain. Prophetic syllables: my dear Desnos, beware of women whose name is Faenzette or Françoise, beware of those smouldering glances that could fatally ignite your passions, those women loved ephemerally, those Florences, those Ferminas, so easily inflamed to *affirm airily* an imaginary pregnancy. Desnos, steer clear of Fanchettes.

To your left, in a decor of trunks, attaché cases, chests, suitcases, hatboxes, cutlery boxes, wine cabinets, valises, portmanteaux, satchels, bags, baskets and the whole magic paraphernalia of voyages, Vodable, whom we have already met in the other arcade, occupies the ground floor of number 17, next door to the Certa. To your right, opposite, numbers 16 and 14 are shared, beyond the handkerchief shop, by black-painted premises which are the offices of the *Journal des Chambres de Commerce* and by a colourful boutique *Henriette, modes,* whose hats scarcely protrude above the level of the half-curtain running across the lower portion of the window. Woe betide any young people who get so carried away by the mysteries of this particular stretch of the arcade that they stand on tiptoe in front of the latter establishment, hoping for the revelation of some new and intoxicating irregularity: immediately the honest milliners will rush out, fluent with imprecations, calling heaven to witness to the purity of their hearts and castigating with operatic hyperbole the district's shameful transactions, and the consequent tendency to imagine a mythical ambiguity in the harmonious gestures of work and probity. The three disparate enterprises are capped, as though with a pediment, by the *Evenement politique et littéraire*. Forward, forward, let us clear the path on either side of us of its enigmas, or rather let us call forth these enigmas as the mood takes us, as temptation lures us: to the left, the doorway of number 17 and its shadowy staircase are framed by placards which immediately send me into a reverie.

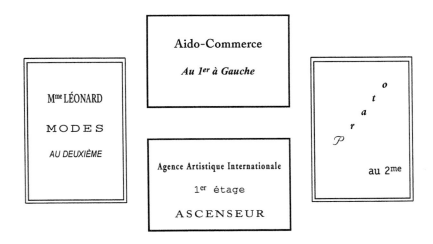

Demon of conjectures, fever of phantasmagoria, pass your sulphurous and nacreous fingers through your tow hair and answer me: who is Prato, and on the first floor with its paradoxical lift what is this agency which I am obstinately convinced must be a vast organization engaged in white-slave traffic. Turn round, and see, there right opposite is the little restaurant where, in our progress towards the depths of the imagination, I find the last traces of the Dada movement. When Saulnier seemed too expensive for us, we used to come here, appeasing our inopportune appetites as best we could with food cooked in rancid coconut oil and with their sharp, unpleasant wine, consumed in a stuffy, vulgar atmosphere. What memories, what revulsions linger around these hash houses: the man eating in this one has the impression he is chewing the table rather than a steak, and becomes irritated by his common, noisy table companions, ugly, stupid girls, and a gentleman flaunting his second-rate subconscious and the whole unedifying mess of his lamentable existence; while, in another one, a man wobbles on his chair's badly squared legs, and concentrates his impatience and his rancours upon the broken clock. Two rooms: a bar room with a zinc counter and a door opening on a low-ceilinged, smoke-filled kitchen, and a dining room extended at the end by an alcove just big enough to accommodate a table, a settee and three chairs, this being really a tiny courtyard covered over to provide the space for six extra customers. The chorus girls of the Théâtre Moderne, their lovers, their dogs, their children, plus a few commercial travellers, are the chief occupants, these days, of the restaurant's settees. The whole scene—sweaty walls, people, stodgy food—is like a smear of candle grease.

But who is this fat, surly old man stationed between the gunsmith and the hairdresser, and playing with a hoop? I am the only one to show any surprise. A strange, gaily coloured hoop, painted with scenes that link up in the manner of the stations of the Cross:

First station: The sea, three seashells, a forest and the department of Puy-de-Dôme.

Second station: A seed.

Third station: The wave, the fire, a green plant; a figure representing egosim, a sort of naked, tiger-striped god, emerges from a conch, brandishing a telegraph form on which someone has written: *It's me, it's me!* and forgotten to fill in the name and address of the sender.

Fourth station: A woman spitting flowers; in the distance, Eros, wearing a thornbush on his head, leans over the fountain's calmness. Title: "I forget."

Fifth station: The seed.

Sixth station: Breathings on the door of silence await the slave who does not return.

Seventh station: In ripping apart, the veil reveals a glimpse of desire in the form of a flamingo.

Eighth station: The flamingo flies away.

Ninth station: The flamingo loses its feathers in the open air.

Tenth station: The air.

Eleventh station: The seed blowing in the air.

Twelfth station: Egoism and Cupid, supporting the armorial bearings of an imaginary country, mingle their hair together just as the sun strikes midday above the Puy-de-Dôme.

The peculiar old man disappears in the direction of the boulevards, bowling the illustrated circle along with a magic wand. I ask the hairdresser, who is standing in his doorway, if he knows this dreadful apparition.

"Do I know him, my dear Sir!" this affable artist replies, "I do indeed! He is a regular customer of mine, name of Sch . . . , who spends his life playing at what he calls the wheel of Fluxion. Do come in."

• • •

Blah blah blah. I only have to imagine what you are thinking to know it doesn't matter, all of you, little ones clustered round my feet for the moment, and I in all my great splendour, the sky for crown, my kaleidoscope reversed, shipwrecks in my pocket, a patch of meadow between the teeth, the whole universe, the vast universe where the ponies run free and unbridled, the columns of smoke amuse themselves by forgetting straight lines, and the glances! The glances have no reason to stop roaming, yet they are firmly focused: look, a scene on the bridge of a ship, with some damn fool of an officer giving a command through a cardboard loudspeaker; farther on, there are stone-breakers at a crossroads in the mountain, and their vizors make me laugh; then, above the heads of frozen sentries the nightingales' messages cross the track along which the white rats are racing at full speed, while from the ledge of a casement-window a business letter which is not precisely a business letter but a pretext, well to put it bluntly a love letter, launches itself into space and flies away, away. Ah I have seen the soft step of burglars on the roof. The curious material of their jackets arrests my attention because of its resemblance to the check pattern of evergreens. O blue breath of ventilators.

Who is there? who is calling me? Darling, I am not mutinous, I hasten to you. Here are my lips. So steals away. And then afterwards. Me of course, not difficult. Damned, damned. Let me collapse, beat me, break me in. I am your creature, your victory, better still my defeat. That's all finished. You demand that I speak, me then. But what you want, what you love, this sonorous serpent, is a phrase in which the words enamoured of your whole self should be happily modulated and weighty as a kiss. What matter the iron filings lavished upon these scales, and the desperate sense assumed by every word in making the leap from heat to lips, what matter what I say if the sloughed sounds, transformed into agile hands, touch your lightly-clad body at last? Forbid me nothing any longer: look, I surrender. My whole thought process is yours to command, sun. Come down upon me from the hills. The air is redolent of a certain childish charm that you beget, it is almost as though your fingers were roaming in my hair. Am I really alone, in this grotto of rock salt, where miners carry their torches behind the darkness's transparent pendants, and go past pulling their snowy trucks. Am I alone, under these carefully pruned trees where in an azure heat the mules turn bucket-wheels, from habit; am I alone in this delivery van decorated with a faithful reproduction of the already outmoded sign of a lingerie shop. Am I alone at the brink of this man-made canyon in a garden to the south-west, where one can hear the clear laughter of women encrusted with emeralds. Am I alone no matter where, under any artificial lighting, heedless of what retains me, beyond the little isochronous oscillations of my love, but strong in this love which reverberates within what serves as the bedrock of delirium, strong in the lynchings of kisses, in the summary justice of my eyes, the heart well and truly hanged, while the carelessly tied-up horses trail their tethering ropes as they graze, shying at the shadows, following the barberry hedges, and shaking their bicoloured manes. Am I alone in any abyss whose splendours have just a moment since been veiled, above the heartsickness, the wrench of having to take leave suddenly of a happy company, above the fleeting perversities, and the other white skylarks already skimming the ground in a desire for rain and for omens in which a whole cloud of sweat was smoking. Alone from the ploughed lands and the swords. Alone from the bleedings and the sighs. Alone from the little urban bridges and the suburban solutions. Alone from the squalls, the bouquets of violets, the wasted evenings. Alone on my own sharp point, where in the winking lights of an unmasked ball a man lost in a brand-new and deserted district of a town seething with excitement, one divine summer night, lingers to piece together with the tip of his malacca cane the fragments, scattered at the foot of a wall, of a nostalgic postcard negligently torn up by an ungloved hand on which beside the rings there glittered the sharp bite, recently inflicted, of a tooth you do not know. More alone than stones, more alone than mussels in the dark, more alone than an empty pyrogen at midday on the table of a café terrace. More alone than everything. More alone than what is alone in an ermine coat, than what is alone on a ring of crystal, than what is alone in the heart of a buried city.

Climb down into your idea, inhabit your idea, well digger hanging from your rope. At first it was only an outline, a halo, and by now it has not got very far, and everywhere I touch upon things which are not that idea of yours, I touch that idea through everything that refutes it, the world expires along its shores. My idea, my idea clings to countless bonds. A long story and I am moved to pity by its scarred form, I kiss the imperfections of its foot.

 Fearsome, charming whores, let others take to generalizing in their arms. Let such people become intoxicated at rediscovering, beneath this shifting, and for me disconcerting, appearance, what unites them all, what nevertheless amounts to true love. I prefer their kisses. I prefer each kiss, I single it out, I shall dream about it for a long time, I shall never forget it. I have heard men complain that their mistresses lacked some pleasant womanly characteristic, while succumbing to some other foible that most women avoid: these men suffered because they never felt beneath the skin they caressed this frisson of general law, which would have sent them into raptures. Well, not me. I adore you for this adorable, peculiar quality, not an inch of the body, not a tremor in the air that would be valid for anyone else. No museum could ever reconstruct you on the basis of your little dimpled hand. You put laws to confusion while at the same time you give expression to them. A great freedom that laws neglect bursts out around your feet. What is marvellous is that I should have fled from womankind towards this woman. A vertiginous crossing: the incarnation of thought, and there I am, I cannot conceive of a greater mystery. Yesterday I clutched blindly at empty abstractions. Today a single person dominates me, and I love her, and her absence is an intolerable pain, and her presence . . . Her presence passes my understanding, for every aspect of her, her very power over me, springs from a source beyond nature. An attitude. A word. A single rustle of her dress. O, when the bracelet plays against the flesh.

I had paused at this point in my thoughts, like a man who no longer knows what has brought him to the place where he finds himself, and who looks vainly for a path by which to leave again. The unfortunate thing is that my way of thought governs my way of life. My friends, I know, were worried about the state of mind they saw me in; but they never suspected that it was a lack of metaphysical perspective that had put me to such confusion. I demeaned myself with the kind of petty literary activities that make me feel ashamed now when I think about them: the same sort of stirrings of shame that accompany one's recollection of stray episodes from childhood, of family existence. No logical step seemed capable of liberating me from this logical prison which showed itself in my melancholy. It was then that a total upheaval in my fortunes, a process in which I felt I played no part at all, so altered the direction of my thoughts that they in turn were overtaken by my new intentions. I fell in love, and what these four words leave to the imagination is unimaginable.

The question of when the idea of love, of this love, precisely of this love, arose in my mind is one that I cannot answer and yet at the same time can answer perfectly well. Every possible barrier existed between myself and this woman whom I at first determined to shun, and to shun in myself, above all. With women I tend to get carried away violently by a certain arrogance derived from various sour memories, from a long-held conviction that at the very best a woman could only hate me, from a horrible sense of failure that continually carries me to the farthest reaches of a mortal darkness. I had forbidden myself to love this woman and, in a sort of confession of terror, had refused her even the regrets of memory. Various feelings within me also helped to dictate my behaviour. It was no doubt at this point that I guessed, though not clearly enough to trace the outline of a phantom, that my heart was undergoing a profound modification: the strange filigree of love was already starting to impress its pattern there. I thought I was simply experiencing a change of temperament, and it was in this state of genuine confusion that I met another woman. Let me make this confession to her today, may all this lapse back into unconsciousness, and may she pardon me. I did love her in my fashion of those times, within my limitations, and without knowing that her image was already blended with another's, I loved her truly, without lying, with a love that faded only in the light of love itself, and she knows quite well that she made me unhappy. Even with all the obstacles which, sometimes half-heartedly, she placed in my way I never wore out this love, and certainly it drew its very life from her. But listen to me, my dear, I rediscovered in myself what I had denied. You had been my sole defence and already you were retreating from me. So then I became unhappy for the other woman, unable to believe that she could know nothing of all this. I carried on my existence without making the slightest effort to contact her. As I have said, other feelings held me at a distance from her at that time. Then I trembled at the thought of my weakness being put to the test. I feared that if she humiliated me even once, life would become unbearable for me. She did this extraordinary thing of calling me to her: and I came. Evening filled with confusion, evening of eclipse: then, in front of the fire that bathed us in its great glow, I acquiesced, seeing her eyes, her huge, calm eyes, I acquiesced to the idea of this love that had been no sooner conceived than denied, that suddenly compelled my recognition through its manifest existence, there within reach of my hand which thought it had gone crazy. I did not hurry. Hours and hours passed on the avowal's scarcely perceptible slope. There was no sharp break between indifference and love. A door finally yielded, and there before us stretched the marvellous landscape.

It is taken for granted too easily that passion befogs the mind: in fact, it baffles only that vulgar aspect of the mind, diligence. The amusements of lovers and the bemusements of savants remain equally diverting: they represent an identical process of adaptation to a very great objective. I discovered in love, through the very mechanism of love, what the absence of love had prevented me from perceiving. An emanation from this woman, beyond her image, re-formed itself into that same image which then blossomed into a particular world, that taste, that divine taste that I know so well in every vertigo, forewarning me yet again that I was entering this concrete universe which is closed to passers-by. For me, the metaphysical spirit was reborn from love. Love was its source, and I hope never to leave this enchanted forest.

FROM *THE FATE OF LA FONTAINE*

"To do" in French means to shit.
For example:
Let us not force our talent:
We would DO nothing with grace.

The postcard showed a little boy on a potty. A subject of endless jest, and yet half the population is grieving over all those *bons mots* that have been put to pasture since the commode went out of style. The improvements made on the bidet, however, warm the hearts of even our youngest generation. This is how we go through life, between two hedges of good, succulent shit stories. Open your ears in the train stations and at the dinner tables. Not even counting your hierarchical superiors—from the barracks to the boardrooms—in the majority of institutions newspaper is used as toilet paper. Our pleasure is thus twofold: we recover precious excremental matter as we read, nourishing both mind and heart.

Who would want to let this eminently French matter slip through our fingers? *Everything the nation produces belongs to us.* If this race of cesspit cleaners wants to brag about having the best paintings in the world, the best dirty oil, the best cuisine, the best hookers, the best manners *(After you. I DO insist),* so be it. Having stepped in a little Gallic salt with its left foot, it has an untainted history, one of the most valiant: it would be futile to seek therein the least trace of error or the memory of one cowardly deed. But elegance and gallantry do not preclude laughter. And so we laugh. From childhood on, the little Frenchman is in stitches whenever the word *caca* rings patriotically in his ear.

When Kant heard the news of revolution, he interrupted his walk. Goethe continued his. How pretentious of them both!

• • •

When a young man enters the art of writing like a little mouse tiptoeing into an attic bursting with eggplants and mandrakes for the first time without its mother, not even sure of the down on his cheeks, and asks himself, with his ink-stained fingers and a terrible cramp in his right shoulder, if the rhyming dictionary—whose pages, if not the cover, may very well be in tatters by this time and which perpetually crumples up under the blows of his anxiety—will be of use to him much longer, his self-doubt follows the indiscreet paths of distraction which abound in both big, silent houses and small, noisy rooms, and this self-doubt begins to giggle here and there, doing amazing magic tricks like breaking a pen, placing a charming specter in the blue shadow of a pair of shoes or a jousting tournament on a fingernail, changing the location of the sky, or peeling the earth and throwing away the pits, for example. Or perhaps a notary clamors for a treatise on style, and the water sings in the teapot where the joyous lime blossoms steep. An entire pale population is thrashing about in the depths of asylums. Larrive and Fleury's grammar books are snatched out of bookstore windows by a thirst for knowledge that will be disappointed long before it tires. But there are not enough of these little gems to meet the needs of the inquiring minds of the children of our century, who call in fright to Echo (whom they adore), since what they are in fact seeking is an echo, because Rhyme has been abandoned in our day like a little postdisestablishment country chapel, and they say stupid things. First a ballad in honor of Babylon. Next Acheron circles nine times around hell. The Muse of history then appears, holding in her hands a bottle of Chartreuse. From which the unicorn philosopher will drink in his turn. A little sip won't hurt, replies the cinema in the grass to the music hall. And the ink flows freely over the black days of the world.

But here allow me to make due apology to the journalists.

It must be pointed out that my previous masterpiece—it is to *Le Paysan de Paris* that I refer—did not receive from the press the kind of acclaim, applause, in a word, the encouragement, it had the right to expect, given its bright promise, my oratory precautions, and the perfect working order of the back-scratching mechanism. Nevertheless, some insults addressed to journalists having found their way, no doubt inadvertently, to the bottom of a page, and I dare say it was one of the best pages of the book, an explanation—satisfactory from a scientific point of view as well as from all others—was put forward by a German scientist. An explanation of what? Of what? Of this meteorological phenomenon. It would appear that journalists are termites nesting in the ear of fame or, according to other sources, that they are of the annulated species—ringworms who feed only on mustard and excrement, but so temperamentally touchy that they cannot hear themselves called bastards without grinding their teeth and stamping their feet. And *I* called them bastards. Had I been better acquainted with zoology, I would no doubt have chosen to call them curs. But my classes at the Sorbonne did me little good. This time, however, armed with the knowledge of the effect of my previous insults and eager to give the present work every possible chance to succeed (a work which is commendable, mind you, both for the quality of its writing and for the author's obliging intention to aid his readers, especially those who have received their baccalaureate degree, in the bitter study of their mother tongue), I am pleased to present, and not, this time, as a footnote, but in the most honorable of places, as exordium, a lovely bouquet of excuses to the Esteemed Editorial Staff. I take back everything I said. One may, if need be, shake the hand of a journalist. Has it in fact ever happened that a man who had shaken hands with a journalist, appalled by his dishonor, shot out his brains, or even so much as attempted to do so? Did his mother chase him away, saying: "Go, go, you are not of my flesh"? Did his chaste fiancée become a nun and, when he appeared at the gates of the convent where perhaps another insanity had compelled her, did he hear the nun in attendance say: "Get back! Get back! You have shaken the hand of a journalist!"? No. I would even go so far as to say: there are those who think it's to their credit to know an editor at the *Petit Var,* or even at the *Intransigeant.* Although this kind of judgment can be considered the result of aggravated perversion or, at the very least, of base imbecility, it would be extremely dishonest of me to skip over such an interesting peculiarity which has, by the way, been omitted from the Dictionary, where the entry under "journalist" above all attests to the loathsome manner in which the members of the Academy have been terrified by periodicals, as the post office calls them. I therefore declare that it is possible to shake hands with a journalist. Under certain conditions, of course. Wash immediately afterward. And not only the contaminated hand, but the entire body. Especially the genitals, for we still have little knowledge of how the journalist poisons his victims, and we cannot exclude the possibility that he emits from each and every pore or from his clothing a kind of volatile and particularly pernicious venom with an extraordinary aptitude for lodging itself in the folds of the body, even in those that are the most well-hidden by habit and decency. I am speaking now to those who have a place of residence. Should a journalist appear at your doorstep, my advice to you until now had been to throw him promptly out on the street, without listening to a word he had to say. I was wrong. I shall now make amends for this insult to the press by offering more moderate advice, agreeable to all. But beforehand, I beg the Honorable Press, and especially the Honorable Critical Press, to take into account that my previous works were written in my greenest youth, when I did not yet have the benefit of experience or reflection. Among the great beauties to be discerned in those works, certain hasty observations—more the results of thoughtlessness than finishing touches— should not be taken for the final expression of my thought. You'll see in this present work just how much I have mellowed. And shall continue to mellow. Who knows, perhaps in the end I shall say that a journalist is almost a human being. However, I have not yet reached that point; I was speaking to homeowners. So: do not throw the intruder out on the sidewalk. You might regret it, and the next day you could have a rude awakening upon reading your name written with slaver in the columns of *Le Matin*. Have the visitor come in, but only as far as the foyer. If you do not have a foyer, you must at least have a john. In any case, never invite him into the kitchen, it would be unsanitary. Put on gloves, cover your head with a black sheet such as the one the photographer dons to immortalize us, and then ask politely, but without platitudes, what you have done to deserve being disturbed in this way. Do not listen to the answer, and immediately say: "I shall see." Then, without heeding the remarks of the dangerous centipede, have him violently removed from the premises. Use the element of surprise to accomplish this, and do it once and for all. Then, wherever you perceive the glistening trace of the jellyfish, take steel wool to it, disinfect the air by burning sulfur, and spray some sweet-smelling scent to make yourself forget both the illness and its cure.

I hope journalists will now be able to view the products of my genius in a new light. I have abased myself so much in their presence that I have touched the ground; I cannot be expected to continue this little charade any longer. Besides, this work will be no less beneficial to said journalists than it will be to novelists and civil servants, both of whom from time to time have to take examinations in which it is not always knowledge that is rewarded, for at times the elegant turn of a sentence can distract the mind from the almost unblievable stupidity of its content. I am speaking to anyone who is capable of holding a pen, from the infant in the cradle to the old man in the coffin, anyone who has the debility necessary to hold between his fingers that squeaky, grinding machine, which, for all that, one would be wrong to compare to a mill, and that only a superficial observer insists on comparing to the cuttlefish; a machine eminently similar to the grasshopper, even though the grasshopper is limited in its leaps and bounds by the seasons of the year, and even more closely related to the cockroach found on ships, for a reason I shall not go into, since its analogies rely on the very habits of ships and writers, each one masturbating in a manner too long and too obscene to describe, the former by means of its parasites and the latter by means of his instrument of labor.

I pause here for the satisfaction of my pride. No one before me—and we see the significance of this: it is like those Before and After posters at the dry cleaners'—had dreamed, had dreamed of, how shall I put it, laying down in writing what he thinks, standing up, about writing. No, no. It is useless to remind me of the feeble attempts of my ridiculous predecessors. Bad choice of words, predecessor. In any event, you have but faint idea of my intentions, my little doves. No one. And even if, at the hour when the lamplight fades and the first tramways stretch themselves, trailing their old painted madams' faces through clusters of half-awakened suburbs, in the semiconsciousness of some night watchman who no longer relights his old cigarette, chewed up in the visions of a consumptive morning; even if in the dream of a young girl whose arm lies bared or in the sullenness of a shop assistant who slams open the shutters of the store; even if the shadow I have grasped has flitted by just once, it does not matter. No one. Before-After: all the mystery of my mastery can be found in this half-shaved face. I will first speak about syntax.

And what if it amuses me to speak about syntax? Does this mean that the reader's shoulders should shake convulsively? Take some bromide. I have for several years impressed upon your admiration pages and pages in which faults of syntax abound. Not errors, but faults. Still, you admire. Therefore I am lecturing you on syntax. Simpleminded like the ass and stupid like the thistle, you did not notice with what livid fearlessness I trample under foot the black foliage of all that is sacred. Syntax? Systematically. One might wonder what bizarre advantage I stand to gain by this incomprehensible trampling. One might wonder. Not a single answer arises from the gulf. The birds that circle above the abyss in which the previously mentioned stomping is perpetually perpetrated with portentous perseverance do not let a single cry drop into this abyss. They are used to it. I, however, trample. And syntax gets trampled. That is the difference between syntax and me. I do not trample syntax for the simple pleasure of trampling it or even for the simple pleasure of trampling in general. In the first place, I derive very little pleasure from my feet and the pleasure I do derive from them comes only rarely from trampling. I trample syntax because it must be trampled. Like grapes. You see my point. Faulty or defective sentences, misbehaving parts, forgetting what has been said and no foresight of what is to come, lack of agreement, disregarding rules, run-on sentences, inaccurate expressions, steering wheels out of kilter, clauses out of whack, confusion of tenses, figures of speech in which a preposition is replaced by a conjunction without shifting gears, any and all procedures similar and analogous to the old prank where you set fire to the newspaper your neighbor is reading without his realizing it, mistaking the intransitive for the transitive and vice versa, conjugating with *être* when the correct auxiliary verb is *avoir,* putting one's elbows on the table, making verbs reflexible at the drop of a hat and then breaking the mirror, not wiping one's feet, such is my character. If you take each of these phrases individually, beginning with the last and in reverse order, moving very slowly, you will be quick to note that the subject has not been exhausted. Yet at the same time you will realize that the sentence ending with the word "character," in less than no time, enables the person who has understood it as it should be understood, to use a system—lacking at most but one small cog—to dry up that well which was believed exhaustible only by means of a vast treatise. I have thus finished with the question of syntax.

• • •

Be aware that if I look both ways before I cross the street—even though *not* to do so would be more heroic in your eyes and even though you thought you could detect in my writing an idea of existence that is not compatible with prudence—it is because I have no desire to be run over, since I don't believe it is very wise to allow oneself to be run over; this, however, does not take away my right to say that I am not at all grateful to my mother and father for having brought me into the world, and that I also want to arrive on the other side of the street with my right hand—and preferably with my two feet—in order to slap someone more easily, perhaps even you, whom I have the avowed intention of slapping sooner or later. I live under the conditions I have been given. Did I choose the shape of my nose or the strength of my fist? When I write, I express myself outside of this arbitrariness. When you read what I write, do not forget that life is one language, and writing an entirely different one. Their grammars are not interchangeable. Irregular verbs.

Stupidity is in full force when you consider, I could not keep myself from using the previous comma because there is in intransitive consideration something that allows one to ridicule one's subject most agreeably, the famous dilemma between action and dream. More and more has been written on this subject since the first French Revolution. Rubbish, rubbish and more rubbish! Why? For a simple reason dear to elementary-school teachers: you cannot add apples and oranges, at least not without giving your audience fair warning. The bird, the pie, the leek soup, the poor devil who was the first to, oh well, I am calming down. History in fact has not retained his name. But who, who could have gotten the idea into his head that dream and action were opposites? The dream is the opposite of the absence of a dream, and action is the opposite of inaction. Obviously dream and action are not compatible, like vermicelli and caramel. The idea of hitching them to one another is one of those brilliant ideas of a nitwit. It responds to nothing in the reality whose door we have all gone through. Nonetheless it is the old story of dream versus action that gives us the melodramatic concept of the professional writer and the debates that take place between chimeras and livelihoods, not to mention Daily Disappointments, that symbolist motif. We have had painters hanging themselves in front of failed masterpieces; the horrible heartbreaks of Pygmalions coming out of the boudoir, abandoning several quite lovely ladies in order to throw themselves on Marble; we have had the Parnassus who had solved the problem by impassiveness; we have had the misunderstood who were tormented by the thought that they were not understood; the f-folks who wanted to c-commune with the c-crowd; people who made themselves a following, and those who did not; we have struck our breast so many times that it has lost its abstract form; we have shouted, whined, vomited, whined again, so much that it has become a Comédie Française; we have . . . but what was this all about? It was about, oh yes, the incompatibility of dream and action, my dear. I wonder where this incompatibility manifests itself and who the hell cares if it manifests itself or if it doesn't manifest itself here or there. Dream and action. Action and dream. The day will come when students will be taught this unbelievable cliché of recent times and they will be bored shitless by it. Dream and action. Try some, oh constipated ones. Dream and action. Brochure sent free upon request.

Besides, I refuse to make a distinction between those two fictive beings, the author and the guy who washes his hands of the matter. The man who has traced misspelled but precise words on this wall is the same iguanodon who is window-shopping here, and I insist on saying that if I write it is not out of sheer disinterestedness. Show me, if you will, a single disinterested person. Strange eunuch. And then, if I were disinterested, it would probably benefit someone who was not disinterested in the least. I write something as best I can, at times with great difficulty, and when it doesn't click, I start over again, and I care enormously about what I write and I claim full responsibility for it.

To speak in order to say nothing: the devil if this is what poets are all about. For one must compare this "nothing" to the "something" of people who aren't poets. The claim to substance is passed off as substance. Between true poetic expression—I am not saying the poem—and other kinds of expression lies the distance between thought and chatter.

Still, poetic emptiness is an idea which is so universally accepted that even poets have been known to grab on to it and adorn themselves with it. They have been the plaything of this mirage, and they have demanded the right to say nothing, with pride. But this was not possible, and even their silence took on *meaning*. One is therefore surprised to see some of them—ever victims of this optical illusion—scandalized if one of their kind, mixing genres, speaks of something close to his heart. You will notice, the day a woman overshadows everything in a man's life that is not love, how much this man, if he is a poet, becomes—in his words that betray the uniqueness of his passion—becomes suddenly suspect to those of his contemporaries who affect spotless reputations. The mixing of genres. Good God, haven't you ever seen a house on fire? There is nothing like a good fire to mix genres, when the poor devils in shirt-sleeves hightail it into the night and the flames, the beams collapsing on top of squalling babies, the bathrooms with their tissue paper ablaze, the gold watches tossed from windows, sparks in the jewel case, and the water of the rescuers in red drowning the plush sofas. What a man feels naturally seeks to express itself. The modesty of the daylight is offended, and disapproves of what it considers an application. And then, what a racket if it is not necessarily love but, using their vocabulary, "politics" that is heard booming in the voice that is raised. For I must be silent and not shout if the worms crush my toe.

Poet, take up your lute. But shut up if, while reading the morning paper, you find this nastiness and this stupidity intolerable in the end; don't say a word when you have the extraordinary nerve to feel moved, concerned, when somewhere people who simply protested against military training periods or the Moroccan war, and who apparently caused the reserves to disobey, are condemned to thirty, to ten years of prison. Well, there is no point in putting it off if I feel like saying what I think about this matter. I find—and although of course this no doubt does not have the seriousness desirable for a judge, it possesses a bit more future efficiency than a declaration in a newspaper swallowed by the trash basket, because this statement is expressed in a book that one can expect to find for a long time in the hands of very young and very easily angered people—I find the right that the French government and the law claim today to forbid those who despise the army from expressing in writing, with whatever commentary they desire, the disgust that they feel toward a revolting institution, against which all undertakings are humanly legitimate, and all criminal attempts recommended, I find this right to be a vile violation of the rights of man. And these Republicans respond to writing with physical constraint. I belong to the levy of 1917, so they say. Well, *I* am saying here—and perhaps I intend, and of course I intend to provoke with these words a violent emulation from those who are called to serve in the armed forces—I am saying here that never again shall I wear the French uniform, the livery that was thrown over my shoulders eleven years ago; I shall no longer be an officer's flunky; I refuse to salute these brutes and their badges, their tricolored Gessler hats. It seems that a certain Painlevé, a man who at one time, but if the tune has stayed the same, the words have certainly changed, a certain Painlevé, Minister of War, signed a monstrous decree the other day: any officer or noncom, any asshole paid to march, from now on has the right to arrest me in the street. The police were not enough. And like them, they are sworn in as of now. The word of this dung is law. Well, agriculture will no longer be lacking for cows. So: since looking at them cross-eyed in the street will get me time in the slammer, I have the honor, in my own home, in this book, here and now, very consciously, to say that I shit on the entire French army.

Hans Arp

Notes from a Diary

man is a beautiful dream. man lives in the sagalike country of utopia where the thing-in-itself tap-dances with the categorical imperative. today's representative of man is only a tiny button on a giant senseless machine. nothing in man is any longer substantial. the safe-deposit vault replaces the may night. how sweetly and plaintively the nightingale sings down there while man is studying the stock-market. what a heady scent the lilac gives forth down there. man's head and reason are gelded, and are trained only in a certain kind of trickery. man's goal is money and every means of getting money is alright with him. men hack at each other like fighting cocks without ever once looking into that bottomless pit into which one day they will dwindle along with their damned swindle. to run faster to step wider to jump higher to hit harder that is what man pays the highest price for. the little folk song of time and space has been wiped out by the cerebral sponge. was there ever a bigger swine than the man who invented the expression time is money. time and space no longer exist for modern man. with a can of gasoline under his behind man whizzes faster and faster around the earth so that soon he will be back again before he leaves. yesterday monsieur duval whizzed at three oclock from paris to berlin and was back again at four. today monsieur duval whizzed at three oclock from paris to berlin and was back again at half past three. tomorrow monsieur duval will whiz at three oclock from paris to berlin and will be back again at three oclock that is at the same time he leaves and day after tomorrow monsieur duval will be back before he leaves. nothing seems more ridiculous to present-day man than broad clear living.

spiders flee into the cracks in the earth in the face of man's ugliness and human thinking. from his eight curl-ringed holes he shoots off a lot of hot air. man wants what he can't do and despises what he can. the trick is his goal and its achievement. he feels himself a god when he roars up to heaven with a clockworks under his behind. when dada unveiled the deepest wisdom for man he smiled indulgently and continued to jaw. when man thinks and jaws even the rats have to vomit. jawing is to him the most important thing of all.

jawing is a healthy airing. after a beautiful speech we also have a huge appetite and a different point of view. man takes for red today what he thought was green yesterday and what in reality is black. every moment he emits final explanations about life man and art and knows no more than the stink-mushroom what life man and art are. he thinks that this blue fume this grey fog this black smoke which he gives forth is more important than the braying of a jackass. man thinks he is related to life. gladly this big-mouthed frog calls himself a son of light. but light dwells magnificently in the sky and chases man far from its path. only as a murderer is man creative. he covers with blood and mud everything within his reach. only the physically unfit among men compose poems pluck the lyre or swing the paintbrush.

in art too man loves a void. it is impossible for him to comprehend as art anything other than a landscape prepared with vinegar and oil or a lady's shanks cast in marble or bronze. every living transformation of art is as objectionable to him as the eternal transformation of life. straight lines and pure colours particularly excite his fury. man does not want to look at the origin of things. the purity of the world emphasizes too much his own degeneration. that is why man clings like a drowning creature to each graceful garland and out of sheer cowardice becomes a specialist in stocks and bonds.

man calls abstract that which is concrete. yet i find this a good deal in his favor since for the most part he mistakes with nose mouth and ears, in other words with six of his eight curl-framed holes the behind for the front. i understand that he should call a cubist picture abstract because parts have been abstracted from the object which served as a pretext for the picture. but a picture or a plastic for which no object was pretexted i find as concrete and as perceptible as a leaf or a stone.

art is a fruit growing out of man like the fruit out of a plant like the child out of the mother. while the fruit of the plant grows independent forms and never resembles a balloon or a president in a cutaway suit the artistic fruit of man shows for the most part a ridiculous resemblance to the appearance of other things. reason tells man to stand above nature and to be the measure of all things. thus man thinks he is able to live and to create against the laws of nature and he creates abortions. through reason man became a tragic and ugly figure. i dare say he would create even his children in the form of vases with umbilical cords if he could do so. reason has cut man off from nature.

i love nature but not its substitute. illusionistic art is a substitute for nature. in many points however i have to count myself among the ugly men who let reason tell them to put themselves above nature. gladly would I create children in the shape of vases with umbilical cords. we must smash the toys of these gentlemen said the dadaists in order that the lousy materialists can recognize on the ruins what is essential. data wanted to destroy the rationalist swindle for man and incorporate him again humbly in nature. data wanted to change the perceptible world of man today into a pious senseless world without reason.

that is why hugo ball furiously beat the dadaistic kettle-drum and trumpeted the praise of unreason. data washed out the venus of milo and made it possible for laocoon and sons after a struggle of a thousand years with the rattle snake to at last step out for a moment. their worn out tooth brushes were restituted to the great benefactors of the people and their vocabulary of wisdom was revealed as a hieroglyph for greed and murder. dada is a moral revolution. dada is for nonsense. which does not mean bunk. dada is as senseless as nature and life. dada is for nature and against art. dada is direct like nature and like nature wants to give its essential place to each thing. dada is moral the way nature is. dada represents an infinite sense and finite means.

the earth is not a fresh-air resort and the idyllic prospectuses of the earth tell lies. nature does not run along the little thread on which reason would like to see it run. the light of day is beautiful but poisonous and rustic life even creates hexameters and madness. we can of course insure our house against fire our cash register against burglary or our daughter against devirgination but heaven looks nevertheless down into the bottomless pots of our home countries and extracts the sweat of fear from our foreheads. every moment we shuffle off this mortal coil by a hair's breadth. from out of every plank seat a black claw grabs us by the back sides. all bosom friendship and love is a lot of apple sauce. like water off the duck's back so love runs off the human bacon. in loneliness man rides down the styx on his chamber pot. in the neighbourhood of karlsruhe he would like to get off because his name is karl and he would like to take a little rest. but chance would have it that here a thicket of laurel feet victory tripe and sabre rattling germanic spooning couples make it impossible for him to get off in that beautiful landscape and thus man damn it to hell contin-ues riding lonelily down the styx on his chamber pot. shamelessly nude clouds without fig leaves or decorations ride past the blue german eyes and lay their eggs in heraldic nests. from the springs beer flows in streams. water fire earth air have been gnawed at by man. but also from man to man the mannikin does what he can. no ha-ha-hallelujah can help him. in carl einstein's poems the design of a landscape there is no further mention that man the measure of all things gets away with a black eye. of man in these poems there remains less than of his lares and penates. einstein gives man a good drubbing and sends him home. the white buttocks of an aged narcissus emerge once but it is quickly ignored as fata morganata. aside from this encounter and a few parts of the human anatomy that flow through the black belly of this landscape concepts are the most corporeal vestige of man. you speaks with i about flight and fear of death. human qualities migrate through light and shadow.

carl einstein's design of a landscape is an ice-cold pit. no rabbit can live and sleep in this pit for these pits are bottomless. In order that the third dot on the i be not missing i

Jean (Hans) Arp playing chess. Photo: André Gomes.

would say further that this pit is as tenebrous as night. no perfumed columns, no fluted rump weals, no schwepperman's eggs architecturally beautify its entrance. with teeth chattering the reader asks this insomnia in persona can you give ghost knocks but not even a violet answers him so much as cuckoo. with staring eyes and mug hanging wide open this landscape roars through the void. only a handfull of snuff remains of the sphinx the olympus and Louis XV. the golden rule and other valuable rules have vanished without leaving a trace. a chair leg clings sea-sick with madness to a torture stake. shreds of sneezing skies jump over ruminating coffins. each of these poems is served on ice. the breasts of this landscape are made of cold storage meat. but nevertheless in the coldest abstractions of einstein there is very distinctly the unmodern question why has this garden party been arranged. einstein is not satisfied with the art pour art of the world. he is for the delusional ideas of the good old days and against reason. he does not want to see illusion used as a scare crow nor the reservation of the ghosts eliminated. it seems to him that people have not yet succeeded in unveiling the world through reason. a great deal in the new doctrine for him does not fit together like a meander in patent leather shoes who goes walking on the arm of a somnambulist box of sardines through the sooty hortus deliciarum. einstein's poems have nothing to do with modern alarm clocks. before them reason takes its tail between its legs and goes philandering somewhere else. einstein does not want to cover up the asphodel meadows. his apollo is not yet the hen-pecked mate of a hundred horse power mrs rolls royce. here an unhygienic polonaise is being danced against all the prohibitions of the concrete top-hat of the glass neck-tie and the nickel cutaway to the tune of the old snowman still lives. whether today people planted antennae instead of narcissi doesn't matter one way or the other. the main thing is to have here and there a lucida intervalla in order to be able to take a gulp from the saving whiskey bottle of illusion. the darkness which einstein distills from the smiling meads of the earth goes beyond jack and the bean stalk beyond the corner grocer and beyond all human endurance. yes yes the earth is not a valley of tears in the vest pocket.

the seven head lengths of beauty have been cut off one after the other but nevertheless man acts as if he were a being that vegetates outside of nature. industriously he adds seven to black in order to get thereby another hundred pounds of chatter. gentlemen who always stood for the dream and life are now making a loathsomely industrious effort to reach the goal of class and to deform hegel's dialectics into a popular song. i am justified in my theory that man is a pot the handles of which fell out of his own holes. poetry and the five year plan are now being busily stirred together but the attempt to stand up while lying down will not succeed. man will not let himself be made into a happy hygienic number which brays ee-on enthusiastically like a jackass before a certain picture. man will not let himself be standardized. in this ridiculous circus which stands without relation to life itself the books of hugo ball epitomize a gigantic act. hugo ball leads man out of his silly corporeality towards his true content dream and death. art and the dream represent the preliminary step to the true collectivity of the redemption from all reason. hugo ball's language is also a magic treasure and connects him with the language of light and darkness. through language too man can grow into real life.

FERNANDO ARRABAL

THE FOLLY STONE

The curé came to see my mother and told her I was a fool.

Then my mother bound me to my chair. The curé made a hole in the back of my neck with a lancet and extracted from me the folly stone.

Then they carried me, tied hand and foot, as far as the ship of fools.

Behind there is a nun and a big frying pan on the fire. I think she is making an omelette, for I see near her two gigantic eggs. I approach, she is looking at me intently and I glimpse beneath her habit two frog's thighs instead of legs.

In the frying pan there is a man who has an air of indifference. From time to time he puts a foot out—maybe he's hot—but the nun stops him. Now the man doesn't move any more and a sort of bouillon that smells of consommé covers him completely. The soup is getting very thick, I can't see him any more.

The nun tells me to come into a corner. I go with her. She begins to speak to me and to say dirty things to me. To understand her better, I come close to her. I feel her caressing my sex organ but I don't dare protest. Someone is laughing behind us. I look at the nun's hands and discover two frog's legs.

I am naked. I'm afraid I will be seen in this state. She tells me to get into the big frying pan so that no one will take me by surprise. I get in. The bouillon becomes more and more burning hot: I try to put a foot out of the frying pan but the nun stops me. Suddenly the consommé covers me completely and I feel the heat increasing incessantly.

Now I'm burning.

The naked little girl on horseback told me to go to the square.

I went. I saw the people playing with spheres that they would throw and catch again thanks to a strong elastic. When I crossed the square they all stopped playing and pointed a finger at me, laughing. Then I began to run and they threw some spheres at me which rolled on the ground near me without hitting me: These spheres were made of iron.

I plunged blindly into the first street I came to. I realized, afterward, that I'd chosen a dead end. I returned in the direction of the square.

A horse came charging after me; I hid behind a tree with several trunks, to escape from it. The horse threw itself on me but remained a prisoner of the tree, the branches of which closed about it. I was raising my eyes and I saw the naked little girl.

I tried to free the horse; it bit my hand, tearing off part of my wrist. It whinnied and seemed to laugh. The people began to throw iron spheres at me and the naked little girl on the horse was hiding her face so as not to show she was shaking with laughter.

"My child, my child."

At last she lit the tiny lamp and I was able to see her body but not her face, lost in the darkness.

I said to her, "Mamma."

She asked me to take her in my arms. I took her in my arms and felt her nails sink into my shoulders: soon the blood spurted, wet.

She said to me, "My child, my child, kiss me."

I came close and kissed her and I felt her teeth sink into my neck and the blood flowing.

Then I realized she was wearing, hanging from her belt, a little cage with a sparrow inside. He was injured but he was singing: his blood was my blood.

She gave me a bouquet of flowers, put a red vest on me and made me climb on her shoulders. She was saying: "As he is a dwarf he has a terrible inferiority complex" and the people were laughing.

She was walking very fast and I held tightly to her forehead so as not to fall. Around us there were many children and it made no difference that I had climbed up her, I hardly reached the level of their knees.

When I felt tired she gave me a cup to drink, full of a red liquid that had the taste of Coca-Cola. As soon as I'd finished she began to run again. And the people were laughing, you'd have thought they were cackling. She asked them not to laugh any more because I was very sensitive. And the people roared with laughter.

She was running faster and faster and I could see her uncovered breasts and her blouse that was flying in the wind. The people were laughing louder than ever.

Finally she put me down on the ground and disappeared. A group of enormous red hens came up to me, cackling. I was no bigger than the beaks that were approaching to peck at me.

Sometimes my right hand detaches itself from my arm at the level of my wrist and joins my left hand. I hold it tight, to prevent it from falling, for I could lose it. I have to keep watch on it constantly so as to avoid, in some absentminded moment when the time comes to replace it, putting it on backward, with the palm facing outward.

I placed the compass point on her belly and I traced several concentric circles than ran some through her knees and some through her navel or again over her heart.

So as not to forget her face, I imagined it full of numbers.

Then it began to rain, and she got onto a horse, standing, naked.

I was holding the reins. Fish fell from the sky and they were passing, laughing, between her legs.

A man dressed as a bishop, a whip in his hand, told me to go into the church. It seemed to me the porch was formed by the two thighs of a kneeling giantess.

In a corner, in front of me, danced a woman, completely hidden by veils, so that I could only guess at her shape. I wanted to look for the altar but I was watching the woman dance. She came up to me and asked me to touch her breasts; I was afraid someone would catch us but I obeyed. Then she removed one of her veils and under my hand, in place of the breast, I felt the head of a newborn baby. The head was laughing. I withdrew my hand and the baby fell to the ground. He began to cry, but when I bent down to pick him up, he had disappeared.

Then the woman took me in her arms. I was afraid of being seen. I tried to break loose, but without success. As I struggled, I tore off one of her veils, and I saw that her arms were big leafless branches, and her face seemed to me very pale and all wrinkled. She laughed, showing a toothless mouth.

I heard the child's voice shouting, "It's him." I turned around and caught sight of his head on the hand of the man dressed as a bishop, who was looking at me intently. I wanted to run away, but the woman's branches imprisoned me like pincers.

I hit the old man's head with an ax and she emerged from the hole, naked. She came toward me and I handed her a toad which she suckled.

The old man closed his split skull with the help of his hands. Then flames began to shoot from his feet. She came forward and swallowed up the fire.

She and I both went into a house, but we soon perceived it was a big transparent egg. We embraced, and, when I wanted to step away from her, I felt we formed one body with two heads.

The old man blew on the egg which flew away, carrying us both off.

We were both in a movie theater. Instead of watching the film, I was watching *her*. I touched her curls and smoothed her eyelashes. Then I kissed her knees and put on her stomach a paper bird I'd made out of the tickets.

She was watching the film and laughing. Then I fondled her bosom and each time I pressed one of her breasts a blue fish came out of it.

Gentlemen:

With reference to your 8763 BM/PR of November 27, ult. Kindly excuse my delay, but violent pains in the back of the neck are causing me a lot of suffering at the moment, and leave me prostrate for days at a time.

Indeed I did hang two big violet drapes over the front of my house. Please believe me when I assure you they are absolutely necessary to give me peace. I recently received certain visits likely to disturb my serenity, and I find myself obliged to avail myself of a method for discouraging these. You will readily understand that I cannot stand guard night and day on my balcony. As for the different signs on the wall, they were put there for the same purpose, as was the notice: "Keep away from me, vermin."

The solution you suggest (placing those drapes and the signs in the entrance hall of my apartment) can be of no assistance to me. The visitors always come in through the window (often passing through the wall), and everything leads me to believe they come to me flying through the air.

Reassure my fellow citizens, then, and tell them they must not see anything that can offend them in my modest means of protection.

I thank you for your kind attention to my most intimate problems and remain, Gentlemen, respectfully.

ANTONIN ARTAUD

THE SHELL AND THE CLERGYMAN
FILM SCENARIO

The cinema to-day seems to be at a parting of the ways, and both the avenues ahead of it may well prove to be blind alleys. On the one hand we have the "pure" or abstract cinema; the other way leads to a commonplace, hybrid art which depicts, more or less adequately, psychological situations which would be in place on the stage or in the pages of a book, but not on the screen where they exist only as the pale image of a world whose real existence and significance lie elsewhere.

All that the pure or abstract cinema has given us so far is obviously lacking in one of the essentials of cinematographic art. For, however great may be the aptitude of the human mind to find its way to the core of every abstraction, we remain insensible to pure geometrical shapes, which in themselves mean nothing and are devoid of that sensory quality which alone can be assimilated and realised by the optics of the screen. The deeper we dig down into the human mind, the clearer it is that every emotion, even an intellectual emotion, is based on an affective sensation, a nervous process, involving (even if only in a minor degree) a material basis of some kind or other, a vibration which is the reflex of certain experienced or imagined states, presented under aspects already apprehended in our dreams or waking hours. The significance of pure cinema, then, would depend on the reconstitution of images of this kind, governed by that rhythm and movement which are the specific qualities of the art of the cinema.

On the one hand, then, we have the purely linear abstraction (and an interplay of light and shade comes under this category) and, on the other, the psychological film which illustrates the development of a narrative, whether dramatic or otherwise. But, between these extremes, there is room for an art of the cinema, whose value and purport have been, so far, entirely overlooked by producers.

The emotion or humour of the adventure film depends wholly on the narrative, apart from the pictures; with some rare exceptions, all the meaning of such films is derived from the captions, and this is true even of those films which ostensibly dispense with sub-titles; the emotion is of a verbal order and calls for the aid of words or, anyhow, a verbal interpretation; for the action and images derive from an explicable situation. You will look in vain for a film which is based on purely visual situations, whose action springs from stimuli addressed to the eye only and is founded, so to speak, on the essential qualities of eyesight, untrammelled by psychological and irrelevant complications or by a verbal story expressed in visual terms. It is futile to look for an equivalent of written language in visual language—such a translation from one idiom to another is foredoomed to failure. The essence of the visual language should be so presented, and the action should be such, that any translation would be out of the question; the visual action should operate on the mind as an immediate intuition.

In the scenario which follows I have tried to realise this conception of a purely visual cinema, where action entirely ousts psychology. Though no doubt my scenario falls short of the acme of what can be done on these lines, it is yet a precursor. I do not suggest that psychology should be wholly banned; that is not the ideal I propose for the cinema—far from it. But such psychology should be presented under a living, dynamic aspect, exempt from glosses inserted to explain the so-called motives of our acts by a preposterous logic, instead of exhibiting such acts in all their primitive, indeed barbarous, inconsequence.

This scenario is not the story of a dream and does not profess to be such; and I shall not try to justify its incoherence by the simple device of labelling it a dream. Dreams have a logic of their own; more, they have a life of their own, infused with darkly rational truth. This scenario seeks to portray a dark truth of the mind by a series of pictures, self-engendered and owing nothing to the circumstances whence they spring, but governed by, so to speak, an inherent and ineluctable necessity of their own, which forces them out into the light.

The outer skin of things, the epidermis of reality, these are the raw material of the cinema. In glorifying the material it reveals the profound spirituality of matter and its relation to the mind of man whence it is derived. The pictures come to birth, each the offspring of its predecessor, qua picture, and the objective synthesis which they depict is more authentic than any abstraction. They create an autonomous world of their own. And from this interplay of images, a transsubstantiation of elements, there arises an inorganic language which works on our minds by an osmosis and demands no translation into words. Since the cinema handles matter itself, the action which it creates springs from the impact of objects, of shapes, attractions, repulsions. It does not cut itself off from life, but rediscovers things in their primitive arrangement. The most successful films are those where there is a marked element of humour—as, for instance, in the early Malec films and those of Charlie Chaplin where the 'human interest' is at its minimum. Humour at its wildest—that is the stuff of a cinema facetted with the glamour of dreams, a cinema full of the breath of life. A perpetual movement of objects, shapes and appearances is best realised in the grotesque convulsions, the death-throes, of reality, lacerated by an irony which is the cry of the human soul strained to breaking-point.

The first view shows us a man, dressed in black, mixing a liquid in glasses of different height and capacity. To decant the liquid from one glass to another he uses a sort of oyster-shell, and breaks each glass after he has employed it. There is an immense pile of phials beside him. Presently a door opens; an army officer enters. He is a prosperous-looking fellow, fat and debonair, and is plastered with medals. After him trails a gigantic sword. Like a spider he prowls around, now in a dark corner, now on the ceiling. As each phial is shattered the officer gives a jump. Now we see him stand behind the man in black and take the oyster-shell from his hands. The latter allows him to do this, with a quaint air of astonishment. The officer walks once or twice round the room, holding the shell; then he draws his sword from the scabbard and cleaves the shell with a swinging blow. The whole room quivers at the impact. The lamps flicker and on each of the flickering rings of light hovers the point of a sword. The officer strides out of the room, followed on all fours by the clergyman (for this the man in black seems to be).

We see the clergyman still on all fours, trotting along a street. A series of street-corners is now projected. Suddenly an open carriage, drawn by four horses, appears; in it is seated the officer, accompanied by a very beautiful woman with white hair. Crouching at a street-corner the clergyman watches the carriage go by and then runs after it at top speed. The carriage comes to a church. Officer and woman alight and, entering the church, move towards a confession box. Together they enter it. At this moment the clergyman springs up and throws himself on the officer. The officer's face swells, grows lined and pimpled; the clergyman is holding in his arms not an officer but a priest. It seems that the white-haired woman also is aware of the priest, but she sees him differently. In a series of close-ups we are shown the priest's face, amiable and complaisant as it appears to the woman's eyes; savage and menacing when it is turned to the clergyman. Night falls with strange swiftness. The clergyman lifts the priest in his arms and swings him to and fro; around him the air grows blank and now we see that he is on a mountain top. At his feet lies (in super-impression) a tangle of rivers and plains. The priest is hurled from the clergyman's arms like a bullet, a projectile which, exploding, falls dizzily through space.

The woman and the clergyman are in the confessional. The clergyman's head quivers like a leaf and of a sudden it seems as if some inner voice began to speak within him. He rolls up his sleeves and softly, ironically, taps thrice the panels of the confessional. The woman gets up. Then the clergyman crashes the door open with a mad blow of his fist. He eyes the woman before him. Then he throws himself on her and tears open her dress as though to lacerate her breasts. But these now appear covered with a carapace of shells. He tears off this breastplate and brandishes it flashing in the air. As he frantically waves it the scene suddenly changes to a ballroom. Couples enter, some treading stealthily on tiptoe, others in febrile haste. The candelabra seem to follow the movements of the dancers. The women have very short skirts displaying their legs, opulent breasts and bobbed hair.

A royal pair enter—the officer and woman whom we already know—and take their seats on a dais. The couples are closely linked together. In the corner there is a man alone, about him a wide empty space. He is holding an oyster-shell, peering down at it with a strangely rapt regard. We gradually recognize in him the clergyman. But suddenly this selfsame clergyman enters, upsetting everything in his way and holding the carapace or breastplate which he was wildly brandishing a moment ago. He raises it aloft as though he were going to belabour a couple of the dancers. But at this moment the couples are frozen into rigidity, the white-haired woman and officer are absorbed into the air and this same woman appears at the other end of the room in the archway of a door which has just opened.

This apparition seems to alarm the clergyman. He drops the breastplate which, as it is shattered, emits a column of flame. Then, as if he were struck by a sudden sense of shame, he makes the gesture of wrapping his garments tight about him. But as he clutches his coat-tails to draw them over his thighs, the coat-tails seem to lengthen out and form a vast avenue of darkness. Along the darkness clergyman and woman run like souls demented.

The scene of their flight is interspersed with images of the woman in various states: sometimes her cheek is hugely swollen, now she sticks out her tongue and, as it lengthens out into infinity, the clergyman clutches it as if it were a rope; sometimes her chest swells to fearful dimensions.

At the end of their course we see the clergyman entering a passage, while the woman seems to swim after him in a sort of sky-scape.

Appears a huge door, studded with iron. The door opens to some unseen pressure and the clergyman walks backwards, calling to someone in front of him who does not come. He enters a large room in which there is a great glass globe. Still walking backwards, he beckons an invisible person.

We feel that that person is near him. He raises his arms as if to embrace a woman's body. At the moment when he is sure he holds this phantom, this viewless double, he flings himself on it and strangles it, grimacing with sadistic glee. We grow aware that he is introducing the severed head into the glass bowl.

He is in the corridors again, he seems at a loss and is twiddling a big key in his hands. He scurries along a passage at the end of which is a door; he opens the door with the key. Beyond the door there is another passage and, at the end of this, two people—the same woman and the decorated officer.

A scene of flight and pursuit. From all sides fists batter on a door. The clergyman is in a ship's cabin. He gets up from his bunk and goes on deck. The officer is there, in chains. Now the clergyman seems to meditate and pray, but, when he raises his head, two mouths which touch each other, level with his eyes, reveal to him the officer beside the woman who a moment ago was not there. The body of the woman is suspended vertically in the air.

He is shaken with a paroxysm. It seems as if the fingers of his hands were twitching to throttle a neck. But between his hands there appear sky pictures, phosphorescent landscapes; ghostly white, he passes on his ship under domes of stalactites.

Distant view of the ship far away on a silver sea.

Close up of the clergyman's head, reclining, breathing.

From his parted lips, from between his eyelashes, stream glistening vapours which, condensing in a corner of the screen, reveal a city or landscapes of an intense luminosity. Finally, his head fades out and houses, landscapes and cities swirl together, tangled and disentangled, forming a fantastic firmament of celestial lagoons and incandescent stalactites. Beneath grottos and clouds and lagoons we see the outline of the ship, moving to and fro, black against the white background of cities, white against mirages which suddenly turn black.

On all sides doors and windows are flung open. Light floods the room. What room? The room which contains the glass globe. A troop of servants and housewives invade the room, carrying brooms and buckets, and rush to the windows. They scour the room with passion, with a frenetic zest. A woman who seems to be the housekeeper, dressed in black, enters with a bible in her hand and takes up her place near a window. When we see her face, we recognize the handsome woman we know. In the street outside we see a priest hurrying forward, and behind him a girl in a sports costume holding a tennis racquet. She is playing with an unknown boy.

The priest enters the house. Men-servants arrive from all directions and line up in an imposing retinue. But, to enable the cleaning to proceed, it is necessary to shift the glass globe, which turns out to be a sort of vase filled with water. It passes from hand to hand, and at moments it seems as if a human head were moving in it. The housekeeper calls in the boy and girl from the garden. The priest too is present. Once again we are confronted with the clergyman and the woman. It seems as if they were about to be married. But at this moment there crowd together from the edges of the screen the visions seen by the clergyman when he slept. A huge ship approaches, bisecting the screen. The ship vanishes and we see a staircase leading up the sky, down which comes the clergyman, headless now, carrying a parcel. When he enters the room where all the people are assembled he unfastens the parcel and produces the glass bowl. All watch him intently. Then he leans towards the ground and breaks the globe of glass, from which emerges a head, his own head.

The head makes a hideous grimace.

He is holding it in his hand as if it were a hat. The head is placed on an oyster-shell. As he raises the shell to his lips, the head melts and becomes a dark liquid which he drinks up, his eyes closed.

Antonin Artaud, *Auto-portrait (Self-Portrait),* ca. 1919; charcoal, 23.8 × 15.5 centimeters. Musée National d'Art Moderne—Centre de Création Industrielle, Centre Georges Pompidou, Paris. © ARS.

The Mountain of Signs

The land of the Tarahumara is full of signs, shapes, and natural effigies which do not seem to be mere products of accident, as if the gods, whose presence here is everywhere felt, had wished to signify their powers through these strange signatures in which the human form is hunted down from every side.

Indeed, there is no lack of places on earth where Nature, impelled by a kind of intelligent caprice, has carved human shapes. But here it is a different matter: for here it is on the entire *geographic area of a race* that Nature *has intentionally spoken.*

And the strange fact is that those who pass this way, as if stricken with an unconscious paralysis, seal their senses so as to know nothing of this. That Nature, by a strange caprice, should quite suddenly reveal a man's body being tortured on a rockface, one might at first suppose to be a mere caprice, a caprice signifying nothing. But when, day in and day out on horseback, this intelligent spell is cast repeatedly, and *Nature stubbornly manifests the same idea;* when the same pathetic shapes recur; when the heads of well-known gods appear on the rock-faces and a theme of death emerges of which man bears the burden—and in response to the drawn and quartered form of the human, there are, *becoming less obscure* and more freed from a petrifying substance, those forms of the gods who have forever tormented him,—when a whole country develops on stone a philosophy parallel to that of men; when one realizes that the original men used a sign language and that one rediscovers this language enormously magnified on the rocks, then indeed, one can no longer suppose this to be a caprice, a mere caprice signifying nothing.

If the major part of the Tarahumara race is indigenous, and if, as they claim, they fell out of the sky in the Sierra, one could say that they fell into a Nature already prepared. And this Nature wanted to think as man thinks. And as she *evolved* from men, likewise she also *evolved* from rocks.

I saw this naked man they were torturing, nailed to a rock, with certain forms at work over him even as the sun was evaporating them; but I don't know by what miracle of optics the man beneath them remained complete, though exposed to the same light.

Whether it was the mountain or myself which was haunted, I cannot say, but I saw similar optical miracles during this periplus across the mountain, and they confronted me at least once every day.

Maybe I was born with a body as tortured and counterfeited as that of the immense mountain; but it was a body whose obsessions might be useful: and it occurred to me in the mountain that it might be just useful to have an *obsession for counting*. There wasn't a shadow but I had it counted, when I sensed it turning, hovering around something or other;

and it frequently happened that in adding up these shadows I made my way back to some strange hearths.

I saw in the mountain a naked man leaning out of a huge window. His head was nothing but an enormous hole, a sort of circular cavity, where successively and according to the hour, the sun or moon appeared. He had his right arm outstretched like a bar, and the left was also like a bar but drowned in shadows and folded inward.

His ribs could be counted, there were seven on either side. In place of his navel, there gleamed a brilliant triangle, made of what? I could not really tell. It was as if Nature had chosen this mountainside to lay bare her imprisoned flints.

Now, though his head was empty, the indentations of the rock on every side imposed on him a definite expression, the nuances of which changed with the changes of hour and light.

This forward stretching right arm, edged with a ray of light, did not indeed point in any commonplace direction . . . And I questioned what it portended!

It was not quite noon when I encountered this vision; I was on horseback and rapidly advancing. However, I was instantly aware that I was not dealing with graven images, but with a predetermined play of light which had *superimposed itself* upon the stone relief.

This likeness was known to the Indians; to me, it appeared by its composition, its structure, to be governed by the same principle by which this fragmented mountain was governed. In the line that arm made, I saw a rock-girt village.

And I saw that the stones all had the shape of a woman's bosom with two breasts perfectly delineated.

Eight times I saw the repetition of a single rock, which cast two shadows on the ground; I twice saw the same animal head holding its own likeness in its jaws and devouring it; I saw, dominating the village, a sort of huge phallic tooth with three stones at its summit and four holes on its outer face; and I saw, according to their principle, all these forms pass little by little into reality.

I seemed to read everywhere a tale of childbirth amid war, a tale of genesis and chaos, with all these bodies of gods which were carved like men, and these truncated human statues. Not one shape that was intact, not one body that did not appear as if it came out of a recent massacre, not one group where I could avoid reading the struggle that divided it.

I found drowned men, half-nibbled away by the stones, and on the rocks higher up, other men engaged in driving them off. Elsewhere, a statue of Death loomed huge, holding in its hand a little child.

There is in the Kabbala a music of Numbers, and this music which reduces material chaos to its prime elements explains by a kind of grandiose mathematics how Nature orders and directs the birth of forms she brings forth out of chaos. And all I beheld seemed to be governed by a Number. The statues, the shapes, the shadows all yielded a number,—such as 3, 4, 7, or 8,—which kept recurring. The truncated female torsos were 8 in number; the phallic tooth had, as I have said, three stones and four holes; the evaporated forms were 12 in number, et cetera. I repeat, these forms may be assumed natural, granted, but their repetition is far from natural. And what is even less natural is that these forms of their land are repeated by the Tarahumara in their rituals and dance. And these dances result from no mere accident, but they are governed by the same secret mathematics, the same concern for a subtle play of Numbers which governs the entire Sierra.

Now this inhabited Sierra, which breathes a metaphysical system into its rocks, has been strewn by the Tarahumara with signs, signs which are perfectly conscious, intelligent, and concerted.

At every crossroads one sees trees *deliberately* burnt into the shape of crosses, or of beings, and often these beings are doubles, and confront each other, as if to express the essential *duality* of things; and I saw this duality reduced to its prime elements in a sign . . . enclosed in a ring, which struck me as having been branded on a tall pine tree with a red-hot iron; other trees bore spears, trefoils, acanthus leaves surrounded with crosses; here and there, in sunken places, corridors choked with rocks, rows of Egyptian ankhs deployed in files; and the doors of Tarahumara houses displayed the Maya world-symbol: two facing triangles whose points are joined by a bar; and this bar is the Tree of Life passing through the center of Reality.

Thus, as I was making my way across the mountain, these spears, these crosses, these trefoils, these leafy hearts, these composite crosses, these triangles, these beings which confront and oppose each other to signify their eternal war, their division, their duality, awakened in me strange memories. I recall suddenly that there were in History certain Sects which had incrusted the rockfaces with identical signs, and the members of these Sects wore these signs carved in jade, hammered in iron, or chased. And it occurs to me that this symbolism hides a Science. And it seems strange to me that the primitive Tarahumara people, whose rituals and thought are older than the Flood, could have already possessed this Science long before the first Legend of the Graal appeared, long before the Rosecrucian Sect was founded.

FROM "VAN GOGH: THE MAN SUICIDED BY SOCIETY"

• • •

Nothing but a painter, Van Gogh, and nothing more, no philosophy, no mysticism, no rite, no *physcurgy,* no liturgy.

no history, literature or poetry, those bronze-gold sunflowers are painted: they are painted like sunflowers and nothing more, but to understand a sunflower in nature, it's necessary now to go back to Van Gogh; just as to understand a storm in nature,

a stormy sky,

a plain in nature,

it will be forever impossible not to refer to Van Gogh.

It was stormy like that in Egypt or on the plains of Semitic Judaea,

perhaps it was dark like that in Chaldea, in Mongolia, or on the Mountains of Tibet, and no one has ever told me that they have been moved.

And yet, looking at that field of wheat or rocks as bleached as a heap of buried bones, over which that purplish sky broods, I can no longer believe in the Mountains of Tibet.

As a painter, and nothing else but a painter, Van Gogh adopted the methods of pure painting and never went beyond them.

I mean that in order to paint he used no other methods than those that painting afforded him.

A stormy sky,

a chalk-white plain,

canvasses, brushes, his own red hair, tubes, his yellow hand, his easel,

but all the lamas in Tibet can shake, under their robes, the apocalypse they will have prepared;

Van Gogh will have given us an inkling of the nitrogen peroxide in a canvas that depicts just enough sinister things to force us to get our bearings.

One fine day he decided not to surpass the motif,

but when Van Gogh's work has been seen, one can no longer believe that there is anything less surpassable than the motif.

The simple motif of a lighted candle on a straw armchair, with a purplish frame, tells a great deal more under Van Gogh's brush than the whole series of Greek tragedies, or the plays of Cyril Turner, Webster, or Ford, which, incidentally, have never been played.

Without being literary, I have seen Van Gogh's face, red with blood in the explosions of his landscapes, coming at me

    KOHAN

    TAVER

    TINSUR

    And yet,

in a burning,

in a bombardment,

in an explosion,

avengers of that millstone that Van Gogh the madman wore around his neck all his life.

The torture of painting without knowing why or where.

For it is not for this world that we have already worked,
struggled,
brayed against the horrors of hunger, misery, hatred, scandal, disgust
that we were all poisoned,
even though we were all enthralled by these things,
and because of which we finally committed suicide;
for are we not all like poor Van Gogh, men suicided by society!

Van Gogh refused to tell stories in his paintings, but the marvelous thing is that this painter was only a painter,

and more of a painter than other painters, as if he were a man for whom the material, and painting itself, held a place of prime importance,

with color seized as if just pressed out of the tube,

with the imprint of each hair of his brush in the color,

with the texture of the painted paint, distinct in its own sunlight,

with the I, the comma, the period of the point of the brush itself screwed right onto the hearty color that spurts forth in forks of fire which the painter tames and remixes everywhere,

the marvelous thing is, this painter who was nothing more than a painter but also, among all the existing painters, is the one who makes us forget that we are dealing with painting,

with painting to represent the subject he has distinguished,

evoking for us, in front of the fixed canvas, the enigma pure, the pure enigma of a tortured flower, of a landscape slashed, pressed and plowed on all sides by his drunken brush.

His landscapes are old sins that have not yet found their primitive apocalypses, but will not fail to do so.

Why do Van Gogh's paintings give me the impression of being seen from the other side of the tomb, from a world where finally his suns will have been the only things that spun around and lit up joyously?

For is it not the whole history of what was one day called the soul which lives and dies in his convulsive landscapes and flowers?

• • •

He who does not smell of a smouldering bomb and of compressed vertigo is not worthy to be alive.

This is the solace that poor Van Gogh took upon himself to reveal in a burst of flame.

But the evil that watched over him wounded him.

The Turk, with his honest face, approached Van Gogh delicately, to pluck the sugared almond from within him,

in order to detach the (natural) sugared almond that was forming.

And Van Gogh wasted a thousand summers there.

He died of this at 37,

before living,

for every monkey had lived before him with forces that he had assembled.

And that is what must now be restored in order to bring Van Gogh back to life.

Compared to a humanity of cowardly monkeys and wet dogs, Van Gogh's painting will prove to have belonged to a time when there was no soul, no mind, no consciousness, no thought, only raw elements alternately enchained and unchained.

Landscapes of strong convulsions, of insane traumas, as of a body that fever torments in order to restore it to perfect health.

Under the skin the body is an over-heated factory,

and outside,

the invalid shines,

glows,

from every burst pore;

such is a Van Gogh

landscape

at noon.

Only perpetual struggle explains a peace that is only transitory,

just as milk that is ready to be poured explains the kettle in which it has boiled.

Beware of Van Gogh's beautiful landscapes whirling and peaceful.

One day Van Gogh's painting, armed with fever and good health,

will return to toss the dust of a caged world into the air, a world that his heart could no longer bear.

Post-scriptum

To come back to the painting of the crows.

Who has ever seen, as in this canvas, land equal to the sea?

Van Gogh, of all painters, is the one who strips us down the furthest, and right down to the thread, just as one would delouse oneself of an obsession.

Of making objects look different, finally of risking the sin of the *alter-ego,* and the earth cannot take on the color of a liquid sea, and yet, with his hoe Van Gogh tosses his earth like a liquid sea.

And he infused his canvas with the color of the dregs of wine, and it is the earth that smells of wine, still splashing among the waves of wheat, rearing a somber cockscomb against the low clouds gathering in the sky on all sides.

But, as I have already said, the funereal part of the story is the opulence with which the crows are treated.

That color of musk, of rich nard, of truffles from a great banquet.

In the purplish waves of the sky, two or three heads of old men made of smoke venture an apocalyptic grimace, but Van Gogh's crows are there inciting them to be more decent, I mean inciting them to less spirituality,

that is what Van Gogh meant in this canvas with its underslung sky, painted at almost the exact moment that he was delivering himself of life, for on the other hand this work has the strange almost pompous aspect of birth, marriage, departure.

I hear the wings of the crows beating cymbals loudly above a world whose flood Van Gogh can apparently no longer contain.

Then, death.

The olive trees of Saint Rémy.

The solitary cypress.

The bedroom.

The promenades.

The Arles Café.

The bridge where one feels like plunging one's finger in the water, in a gesture of violent regression to a state of childhood forced upon one by Van Gogh's amazing grip.

The water is blue,

not a water-blue,

but a liquid paint blue.

The suicided madman has been there and given the water of paint back to nature,

but who will give it back to him?

Van Gogh, a madman?

let him who once knew how to look at a human face take a look at the self-portrait of Van Gogh, I am thinking of the one with the soft hat.

Painted by an extra-lucid Van Gogh, that face of a red-headed butcher, inspecting and watching us, scrutinizing us with a glowering eye.

I do not know of a single psychiatrist who would know how to scrutinize a man's face with such overpowering strength, dissecting its irrefutable psychology as if with a knife.

Van Gogh's eye belongs to a great genius, but from the way I see him dissecting me, surging forth from the depths of the canvas, it is no longer the genius of a painter that I feel living within him at this moment, but the genius of a certain philosopher never encountered by me in this life.

No, Socrates did not have this eye; perhaps the only one before Van Gogh was the unhappy Nietzsche who had the same power to undress the soul, to pluck the body from the soul, to lay the body of man bare, beyond the subterfuges of the mind.

Van Gogh's gaze is hanging, screwed, glazed behind his naked eyelids, his thin wrinkleless eyebrows.

It is a look that penetrates, pierces, in a face roughly-hewn like a well-squared tree.

But Van Gogh chose the moment when the pupil of the eye is going to spill into emptiness,

where this glance, aimed at us like the bomb of a meteor, takes on the atonal color of the void and inertia that fills it.

This is how Van Gogh located his illness, better than any psychiatrist in the world.

I pierce, I resume, I inspect, I cling to, I unseal, my dead life conceals nothing, and, after all, nothingness has never harmed anyone. What forces me to withdraw within myself is that disheartening absence that passes and overwhelms me at times, but I perceive it clearly, very clearly, I even know what nothingness is, and could even say what is inside it.

And Van Gogh was right, one can live for the infinite, and only be satisfied with infinite things, there is enough of the infinite on the earth and in the spheres to satisfy a thousand great geniuses, and if Van Gogh was unable to satisfy the desire to fill his life with it, it is simply that society forbade it.

Flatly and consciously forbade it.

One day Van Gogh's executioners arrived, as they did for Gérard de Nerval, Baudelaire, Edgar Allan Poe and Lautréamont.

Those who one day said to him:

And now, enough, Van Gogh, to your grave, we've had our fill of your genius, and as for the infinite, the infinite belongs to us.

For it is not because of his search for the infinite that Van Gogh died,

obliged to choke with misery and asphyxiation,

he died from seeing the infinite refused him by the rabble of all those who thought to withhold it from him during his own life;

and Van Gogh could have found enough infinite to live on for his whole life-span had not the bestial mind of the masses wanted to appropriate it to feed their own debaucheries, which have never had anything to do with painting or poetry.

Besides, one does not commit suicide alone.

No one was ever born alone.

Nor has anyone died alone.

But, in the case of suicide, a whole army of evil beings is needed to force the body to perform the unnatural act of depriving itself of its own life.

And I believe that there is always someone else, at the extreme moment of death, to strip us of our own life.

And thus, Van Gogh condemned himself because he had finished with living, and we gather this from his letters to his brother; because of the birth of his brother's son,

he felt that he himself would be one mouth too many to feed.

But above all Van Gogh wanted to join that infinite for which, said he, one embarks as on a train to a star,

and one embarks the day one has finally decided to finish with life.

Now in Van Gogh's death, as it actually occurred, I do not believe that is what happened.

Van Gogh was dispatched from this earth by his brother, first by announcing the birth of his nephew, and he was sent away by Dr. Gachet who, instead of recommending rest and solitude, sent him off to paint from nature, a day when he was well aware that it would have been better for Van Gogh to go to bed.

For lucidity and sensibility such as the martyred Van Gogh possessed cannot be so obviously thwarted.

There are souls who, on certain days, would kill themselves over a simple contradiction, and it isn't necessary to be insane for that, a registered and catalogued lunatic; on the contrary, it is enough to be in good health and to have reason on one's side.

I, in a similar situation, could no longer bear to hear, without committing a crime: 'Monsieur Artaud, you're raving,' as so often has happened to me.

And Van Gogh heard just that.

And that is what caused the knot of blood that killed him to twist in this throat.

Post-scriptum

Concerning Van Gogh, magic and spells, all the people who have paraded before the exhibition of his works at the Orangerie for the last two months, are they really sure to remember all they did and everything that happened to them every night of the months of February, March, April and May 1946? Could there not have been one particular night when the atmosphere and the streets became liquid, gelatinous, unstable, and when the light of the stars and the celestial vault disappeared?

Antonin Artaud, *La Projection du véritable corps (The Projection of the True Body),* November 18, 1946–December 1947 or January 1948; graphite and wax crayon. Musée National d'Art Moderne—Centre de Création Industrielle, Centre Georges Pompidou, Paris. © ARS.

And Van Gogh was not there, he who painted the Arles Café. But I was at Rodez, that is to say, still on earth, while all the inhabitants of Paris must have felt, all one night, very close to leaving it.

And was this not because they had participated in unison in certain generalized dirty tricks, when the consciousness of Parisians left its normal level for an hour or two and proceeded to another one, one of those mass unfurlings of hatred which I have witnessed so many times during my nine years of internment.

Now hatred is forgotten like the nocturnal expurgations that follow, and the same ones who so many times bared their swinish souls to the whole world now file past Van Gogh, whose neck they or their fathers and mothers so well wrung when he was alive.

But was it not one of those evenings I have been talking about that an enormous white stone fell on the Boulevard de la Madeleine at the corner of the Rue des Mathurins, as if shot from a recent volcanic eruption of the volcano Popocatepetl?

OF MYTH

ne necessarily dries up—and, stretched to the

.he possibility of myth become undone: there

ʰ wretched. The absence of myth is perhaps this

g. ˙os this ground sinking immediately away.

ᴐwn: it is the opening up of the infinite.

Th ᴐd (I am no longer I, but an *absence of I;*

I wa. ...... .ıow immeasurably joyful).

In the white, incongruous void of absence, there innocently live and come undone myths that are no longer myths, and are such that their duration would lay bare their precariousness. At least the pale transparency of possibility is in one sense perfect: like rivers in the sea, myths, enduring or fleeting, lose themselves in the *absence of myth,* which is their bereavement and their truth.

The decisive absence of faith is unshakable faith. The fact that a universe without faith is a ruin of a universe—reduced to the nullity of things—in depriving us equates privation with the revelation of the universe. If in abolishing the mythical universe we have lost the universe, it itself binds to the death of myth the action of a revelatory loss. And today, because a myth is dead or dying we see better through it than if it were living: it is destitution that perfects transparency, and it is suffering that makes for joy.

"Night is also a sun," and the absence of myth is also a myth: the coldest, the purest, the only *true* myth.

Victor Brauner, *The Crime of the Butterfly King,* 1930; oil on canvas; 25¼ × 19¼ inches. Jan Krugier Gallery, Geneva. © ARS.

Wilhelm Freddie, *Paralyzasexappeal.* © ARS.

Wilhelm Freddie, *Untitled.* © ARS.

HANS BELLMER

FROM "WHAT OOZED THROUGH THE STAIRCASE"

. . . What oozed through the staircase or the cracks in the doors when these girls were playing at being doctors, up there in the attic, what dripped from these clysters filled with raspberry juice, or if I dare say so, with raspberry verjuice, all this could easily take on, on the whole, the appearance of seduction, and even arouse desire.

It must be admitted, as I do reluctantly, that a haunting concern lingered over all that could not be learned about them. Neither myself nor anyone else could lose all mistrust toward these little girls.

When their legs remained idle, nothing could be said of their crooked carriage, mainly toward the knees, only that they resembled those of young frolicking goats. Full-face or sideways, their profile lent itself much less to laughter; the frail curve of the shanks grew bolder at the knees' padding, assuming a curious convexity. But confusion was complete when those legs grew suddenly stiff, with moves suggesting a fleeing hoop, and in the end they hung bare, out of transparent lace and rumpled pleatings, relishing the aftertaste of their game. . . .

Hans Bellmer, *The Doll,* 1934–35; gelatin silver print, 4¹/₁₆ inches × 3¹/₂ inches. Collection of Timothy Baum. © ARS.

YVES BONNEFOY

THE ANTI-PLATO

I

It's certainly *this* object: a horse's head larger than life containing a whole city, its streets and ramparts running between the eyes, adjusting to every swerve and the long stretch of the muzzle. Someone knew how to construct this city of wood and cardboard, lighting it aslant with a real moon. It's certainly *this* object: the wax head of a woman spinning around with her hair flying in disorder on the turntable of a phonograph.

Everything from here, country of rushes, dress, and stone, that is to say: country of water over the rushes and the stones, this country of dresses stained. This laughter covered with blood, I tell you, traffickers of the eternal, symmetrical faces, empty of any look, it weighs heavier in the head of man than the perfect Ideas, which only know how to bleed upon his mouth.

II

The monstrous weapon a hatchet with horns of cast shadows over the stones,
Weapon of pallor and of cry when you turn wounded in your festive dress,
A hatchet because time must withdraw over the nape of your neck,
Oh heavy and the whole weight of a country upon your hands the weapon falls.

III

What meaning should we give this: a man forms from wax and colors the semblance of a woman, lends it every likeness, makes it live, confers by clever lighting just the same hesitation about to move that a smile can have.

Then he takes a torch, abandons the whole body to the caprices of the flame, watches the deforming, the flesh bursting, projecting instantly a thousand possible figures, lighting up with so many monsters, sensing like a knife this funereal dialectic where the blood statue is reborn and splits apart in the passion of wax and color?

IV

The country of blood continues under the dress coursing always black
When they say Here begins the flesh of night and the false roads sand over
And you in wisdom hollow out for light high lamps among the herds
And bend backwards on the threshold of the pale country of death.

V

Captive of a room, of noise, a man shuffles cards. On one: "Eternity, I loathe you!" On another: "Let this moment deliver me!"

And on a third one still the man is writing: "Death indispensable." So over the fault of time he walks, lit by his wound.

VI

We are from the same country on the mouth of the earth,
You of a single casting with the complicity of foliage
And the one they call myself when the day sinks down
And the doors open and they speak of death.

VII

Nothing can tear him from his obsession with the dark room. Leaning over a basin he tries to fix the face under the flow of water: but the motion of the lips wins out.

Face disconcerted, face in distress, is it enough to touch its teeth for it to die? When the fingers pass over she can smile, as the sand gives way under the step.

VIII

Captive calcinated between two thieves of green surfaces
And your stony head offered to the draperies of wind,

Portrait of Yves Bonnefoy in Robert Motherwell's studio, 1980s, by Renate Ponsold Motherwell.
© Renate Ponsold Motherwell.

I see you penetrate the summer (like a praying mantis in the picture of black grasses),
I hear you cry out on the other side of summer.

IX

They say to him: dig a small hollow in the loose earth, her head, until your teeth come across a stone.

Sensitive only to modulation, to passage, to the trembling of balance, to presence affirmed in its bursting forth already on every side, he looks for the cool of invading death, he triumphs easily over an eternity without youthfulness and a perfection without burning.

Around this stone time is boiling. From having touched this stone: the lamps of the world turn round, the secret lighting circulates.

KAY BOYLE

A COMPLAINT FOR M AND M

I believe in the scenic railways that have
not run yet because the scaffolding is still
unsafe and in the buildings they have
not had time to finish I believe this year
and this time of the year there is never
the time to finish only the time left to
begin again.

If it is wiser to say too little than too
much there being less to take back in
anguish later then it is easier to say too
much for it leaves that much less to
carry about in the veins seeking to say it
or not to say it or not to remember to
say it or to forget it is not things like
this that can be said.
    You did not visit the Belgian or
the Russian or the Italian or the German
pavilions or ride up in the lift with the
smell of roses thick as smoke but sweeter
in your eyes. You were expecting Man
Ray or Nancy Perry or Dali or Brancusi
to come and sit in the garden with the
tiger lilies with you.

You did not come to the Paris exposition
    of 1937 on the opening night when I
        asked you.
    You did not see the fountains fresh as
    lilacs spraying along the river in the
dark Or the fans they had bought for the
    occasion made of blue lace and used
            instead of illumination.
You did not wait behind the scenes in the
    wings for the actors to come and the
                curtain to rise
    Or the cues to be given. You were not
            there when the searchlights
            poured the milk of avalanches
    Into the obliterated alley of the Seine.

Where you were you could not hear the
        roman candles breaking the way
            glass breaks under a fist
Or say with a thousand other people who
        were there "Ah-h-h-h" with the
                voice of one person
Awed when the tour eiffel was transformed
        to burning wire, nor could you see
    The fireworks climb like larks in spring
        to those explosions of indecipherable
                        mystery

That liberate metal or song more valuable
than money is.
The savagery
Of serpents and birds imported from Japan
pursued their own incalculable wealth
In emeralds, diamonds, rubies, and topaz,
writhing and spiraling through the
firmament,
Crashing in thirst and frenzy through the
tropic underbrush that leafed in
conflagrated satin.
Trunked in seething palm and cocoa hair
the sky's wild blistering jungle.

You had people to dinner. You could not
come. You did not see the small thick
hooded candles
They set out like gondolas on the current,
drifting in slow flickering formation
like folded gulls
With hearts ignited moving a-light upon
the river's or the tide's declining.
They were extinguished one by one by
breath or wind or by their own
defatigation
(As the complaints I set out lighted in the
dark for you expire in their passage
Because of the long way through silence
they must go.)

VICTOR BRAUNER

ON THE FANTASTIC

I. In Painting

You will like my painting

— 1—because it is nocturnal,

— 2—because it is fascinating,

— 3—because it is lyrical,

— 4—because it is symbolic,

— 5—because it is magic, hermetic, alchemical,

— 6—because it is attractive,

— 7—because it is seductive,

— 8—because it is passionate, impassioned,

— 9—because it is mad, sorceress,

—10—because it is phantasmal, mysterious, disquieting,

—11—because it is made with immense love,

—12—because its unknown world is peopled with somnambulists, incubi, succubi, lycan-
thropes, *éphialtes,* phantoms, specters, sorcerers, seers, mediums, and a whole fantastic population,

—13—because it is a dream world,

—14—because it is insinuating, obsessing, by its nebulous infusion;

—15—because each drawing, each painting is an adventure, a departure toward the unknown,

—16—because it lends itself to endless contemplation,

—17—because it is prophetic,

—18—because it is above mannerism,

Victor Brauner, *Encounter of Number 2 Perrel Street,* 1946; oil on canvas, 85 × 105 centimeters. © ARS.

—19—because it is dislocating, always self-renewing,

—20—because it is the very principle of becoming, and thus dialectic,

—21—because its time is the other time, where the past meets the future,

—22—because it is the continuation of the continual, mobile perpetuum of stimulation or of imagination;

—23—because it is physiological, functional,

—24—because it is devouring,

—25—because it is overestimating,

—26—because it is fairy-like,

—27—because it is erotic, subtle,

—28—because it is primitive,

—29—because it is mythical,

—30—because it is incandescent, burning, liquid,

—31—because it is the communication vessel of fire and water, being misty, vaporous, rainy, ectoplasmic, protoplasmic,

—32—because it is materialist,

—33—because it makes objective chance conscious,

—34—because it is subconscious, irrational,

—35—because it is delirious, obsessive,

—36—because it is the most faithful seismograph of the cataclysms of my sensibility.

—37—because it is inexhaustible like a great thought,

—38—because it is in the natural state of nature,

—39—because it is free—and you have no fear of liberty,

—40—because it is romantic, of a new and powerful romanticism which is to come and which will liberate man,

—41—because it is surrealist, assimilating the greatest physical, chemical, physiological, psychological, psychoanalytical conquests and all science in development, and because it has freed all the conventional frontiers, globing in itself the highest *ethical* values of man.

André Breton

Age

Dawn, farewell! I emerge from the haunted wood, brave the highways, torrid crosses. An ordaining foliage leads me astray. August is as free of fissures as a millstone.

Cling to the panoramic view, sniff the space and reel off the smoke mechanically.

I shall choose for myself a precarious enclosure: We will jump the hedge if we must. The provinces full of heated begonias are chattering, tidying things up. How nicely the griffons troop around the ruffled flying of skirts!

Where to look after the fountains? I'm wrong to put my faith in her necklace of bubbles . . .

Eyes before sweetpeas.

Shirts clotted on the chair. A silk top hat confers reflections upon my chase. Man . . . A mirror avenges you and, vanquished, treats me like a costume laid aside. The moment returns to lay its patina upon the flesh.

Houses, I free myself from dry walls. Somebody's shaking! A tender bed is teased with wreaths.

Attain the overpowering poetry of the tiers.

Unclean Night

Unclean night, night of flowers night of death-rattles, spirituous night, lo! the hand thereof is but an abject kite that is caught in a mesh of strands, black strands and shameful! Oh, champaign land of white bones and red, where hast thou stowed thine impure trees, and thine arborescent candour, and thy fidelity that was a purse of serried pearls, with flowers, with so-so inscriptions, with pansignifications? And lo! it is thou the bandit, the bandit, ah! assassin, thou water bandit thou sheddest thy knives in mine eyes, thou art then quite pitiless, radiant water, lustral water that I cherish! My imprecations, even as a terrifyingly pretty girl-child brandishing her boom broom at you, shall pursue you at great length. Lo! at the end of each branch a star and it is not enough, no, chicory of the Virgin. I do not want to see you any more, I want to riddle with leaden pellets your birds that are not even leaves any more. I want to hunt you right away from my door, you hearts with pips in you, you love's-brains. Away with the crocodiles there, away with crocodile fangs studding Samurai warriors' breast-plates, away, in a word, with jets of ink, and renegades everywhere, renegades with purple ruffles, renegades with black-currant eyes, with goosy locks! There, it is finished, I shall no more hide my shame, I shall no more be calmed by nothing, yea and by less than nothing. And if the shuttle-cocks be as big as houses how shall we play do you suppose, how keep up our vermin, how lay our hands on the lips of the shells that will go on talking (ah, the shells, who will put a stop to their talking, at last?) No more breathing, or blood, or soul, but hands to knead the air, hands to brown the dough of the air, hands to crack the great gum of the sleeping banners, solar hands, in a word, arctic hands!

The Sexual Eagle Exults

The sexual eagle exults he will gild the earth once more
His descending wing
His ascending wing sways imperceptibly the sleeves of the peppermint
And all the water's adorable undress
Days are counted so clearly
That the mirror has yielded to a froth of fronds
Of the sky I see but one star
Now around us there is only the milk describing its dizzy ellipsis
From which sometimes soft intuition with pupils of eyed agate
Rises to poke its umbrella tip in the mud of the electric light
Then great reaches cast anchor stretch out in the depths of my closed eyes
Icebergs radiating the customs of all the worlds yet to come
Born from a fragment of you fragment unknown and iced on the wing
Your existence the giant bouquet escaping from my arms
Is badly tied it digs out walls unrolls the stairs of houses
Loses its leaves in the show windows of the street
To gather the news I am always leaving to gather the news
The newspaper is glass today and if letters no longer arrive
It's that the train has been consumed
The great incision of the emerald which gave birth to the foliage

Is scarred for always the sawdust of blinding snow
And the quarries of flesh are sounding alone on the first shelf
Reversed on this shelf
I take the impression of death and life
To the liquid air

LESS TIME

Less time than it takes to say it, fewer tears than it takes to die; I've taken count of everything, there you have it. I've made a census of the stones; they are numerous as my fingers and some others; I've handed out some pamphlets to the plants, but not all were willing to accept. I've kept company with music for a second only and no longer know what to think of suicide, for if I want to leave myself, the exit is on this side and, I add perversely, the entrance, the re-entrance on the other. Now you see what you're left with. Hours, grief, I don't keep a reasonable check of them; I'm alone. I look out the window; there are no passersby, or rather, no one *passes*. You don't know this man? It's Mr. Same. May I introduce Madam Madam? And their children. Then I turn my back on my steps, my steps turn back too, but I don't know exactly what on. I consult a schedule; all the names of towns have been replaced by names of people who have been quite close to me. Shall I go to A, return to B, change at X? Yes, of course I'll change at X. Provided I don't miss my connection with boredom! There we are: boredom, the lovely parallels, ah! how lovely are parallels under the perpendicularity of God.

LETHAL RELIEF

The statue of Lautréamont
Its plinth of quinine tabloids
In the open country
The author of the Poetical Works lies flat on his face
And near at hand the hiloderm a shady customer keeps vigil
His left ear is glued to the ground it is a glass case it contains
A prong of lightning the artist has not failed to figure aloft
In the form of a Turk's head the blue balloon
The Swan of Montevideo with wings unfurled ready to flap at a moment's notice
Should the problem of luring the other swans from the horizon arise

Opens upon the false universe two eyes of different hues
The one of sulphate of iron on vines of the lashes the other of sparkling mire
He beholds the vast funnelled hexagon where now in no time the machines
By man in dressings rabidly swaddled
Shall lie a-writhing

With his radium bougie he quickens the dregs of the human crucible
With his sex of feathers and his brain of bull-paper
He presides at the twice nocturnal ceremonies whose object due allowance for fire having
been made is the inter-version of the hearts of the bird and the man
Convulsionary in ordinary I have access to his side
The ravishing women who introduce me into the rose-padded compartment
Where a hammock that they have been at pains to contrive with their tresses for
Me is reserved for
Me for all eternity
Exhort me before taking their departure not to catch a chill in the perusal of the daily
It transpires that the statue in whose latitude the squitch of my nerve terminals
Weighs anchor is tuned each night like a piano

THE VERB TO BE

I know despair in its broad outlines. Despair has no wings, it is not necessarily found at a
cleared table upon a terrace, in the evening by the seaside. It is despair and it is not the
return of a quantity of little facts like seeds leaving one furrow for another at nightfall. It
is not moss upon a stone or a drinking glass. It is a boat riddled with snow, if you please,
like birds falling, and their blood has not the slightest thickness. I know despair in its broad
outlines. A very small form, fringed by jewels of hair. It is despair. A necklace of pearls for
which a clasp can never be found and whose existence does not hold even by a thread,
that is despair. As for the rest, let's not speak of it. We haven't finished despairing if we
begin. I myself despair of the lampshade around four o'clock, I despair of the fan around
midnight, I despair of the condemned man's last cigarette. I know despair in its broad
outlines. Despair has no heart, the hand always remains in despair out of breath, in despair
whose death we are never told about by mirrors. I live off this despair which so enchants
me. I love that blue fly streaking in the sky at the hour when the stars hum their song. I
know in its broad outlines despair with its long, slim breaches, the despair of pride, the
despair of anger. I rise every day like everyone and I stretch out my arms on a flowered

wallpaper, I remember nothing and it is always with despair that I discover the lovely up-rooted trees of the night. The air of the room is lovely like drumsticks. It is time weather. I know despair in its broad outlines. It is like the curtain wind giving me a helping hand. Can you imagine such despair: Fire, fire! Ah they are still going to come . . . Help! There they are falling down the stairs . . . And the newspaper advertisements, and the illuminated signs along the canal. Sandpile, go on with you, you old sandpile! In its broad outlines despair has no importance. It is a drudgery of trees that is going to make a forest again, a drudgery of stars that is going to make one less day again, a drudgery of days fewer which will again make up my life.

VIGILANCE

In Paris the Tour Saint-Jacques swaying
Like a sunflower
Sometimes leans against the Seine its shadow glides unseen among the tugboats
Just then, on tiptoe in my sleep,
I move towards head for the room where I am lying
And set it afire
Lest something remain of the consent I had to give
The furniture makes way for similar beasts
Looking at me like brothers
Lions whose manes consume the chairs
Sharks whose white bellies absorb the sheet's last quiver
At the hour of love and of blue eyelids
I see myself burning now I see that solemn hiding place of nothings
Which was once my body
Probed by the patient beaks of birds
When all is finished I enter unseen into the ark
Taking no heed of life's passersby shuffling far off
I see the ridges of the sun
Through the hawthorn of the rain
I hear underclothes tearing like some great leaf
Under the fingernails of absence and presence in collusion
All the looms are withering only a shred of perfumed lace
A shell of lace in just the shape of a breast
I touch nothing but the heart of things I hold the thread

Dreaming I See You

Dreaming I see you infinitely superposed upon yourself
Seated on the high coral stool
Before your mirror still in its first quarter
Two fingers on the water wing of the comb
And at the same time returning
You linger last in the grotto
Streaming with sparks
You do not recognize me
You are lying on the bed you·waken or fall asleep
You waken where you slept or elsewhere
You are naked the elderberry ball bounces again
A thousand elderberry balls buzz above you
So light you remain unaware
Your breath your blood saved from the air's wild juggling
You cross the street the cars rushing towards you
Are only their shadow
And the same
Child
Caught in a bellows aspangle
You are skipping rope
Until at the top of invisible stairs
Appears the only green butterfly haunting the Asian summits
I caress all that was you
In all that you are still
I listen as your counless arms
Whistle melodious
Single snake in all the trees
Your arms in whose center turns
The crystal of the compass card
My living fountain of Shiva

André Breton at Le Palais Idéal du Facteur Cheval (The Ideal Palace of Cheval the Postman) in Hauterives, where Breton went with Valentine Hugo in 1931 and returned in 1939 and 1953.

Ascendant Sign

The desire that the female feels for the male resembles the mists rising from the earth toward the sky. Once they have gathered into clouds, it is the sky that waters the earth.

—*Zohar*

Only on the level of analogy have I ever experienced intellectual pleasure. For me the only *manifest truth* in the world is governed by the spontaneous, clairvoyant, insolent connection established under certain conditions between two things whose conjunction would not be permitted by common sense. As much as I abhor, more than any other, the word *therefore,* replete with vanity and sullen delectation, so do I love passionately anything that flares up suddenly out of nowhere and thus breaks the thread of discursive thinking. What comes to light at that moment is an infinitely richer network of relations whose secret, as everything suggests, was known to early mankind. It is true that the flare quickly dies out, but its glimmer is enough to help measure on their dismal scale the exchange values currently available that provide no answer except to basic questions of a utilitarian nature. Our contemporaries, indifferent to whatever does not concern them directly, are progressively more insensitive to anything that could present them with an in-depth investigation into nature: drifting on the surface of things seems enough of a task. There is an age-old conviction that nothing exists gratuitously, that quite to the contrary there is not a single being or natural phenomenon that does not carry a message to be deciphered by us. This conviction, which was at the heart of most cosmogonies, has been replaced by a numb and stupefied apathy: we have thrown in the towel. We hide in order to ask ourselves: "Where do I come from? Why do I exist? Where am I going?" but is it not absurd or even impudent to aim at "transforming" the world when one no longer cares to make sense of its more enduring aspects. The primordial links are broken. It is my contention that those links can only be restored, albeit fleetingly, through the force of analogy. Hence the importance taken on at long intervals by those brief flashes from the lost mirror.

The diamond and the pig are hieroglyphs of the thirteenth passion (harmonism), which civilized people do not experience.

—*Charles Fourier*

The white of the eye is a bedframe. The iris is a base for the mattress of the pupil on which a ghost of ourselves rests while we are dreaming.

—*Malcolm de Chazal*

Poetic analogy has this in common with mystical analogy: it transgresses the rules of deduction to let the mind apprehend the interdependence of two objects of thought located on different planes. Logical thinking is incapable of establishing such a connection, which it deems a priori impossible. Poetic analogy is fundamentally different from mystical analogy in that it in no way presupposes the existence of an invisible universe that, from beyond the veil of the visible world, is trying to reveal itself. The process of poetic analogy is entirely empirical, since only empiricism can provide the complete freedom of motion required by the leap it must perform. When we consider the impression it creates, it is true that poetic analogy seems, like mystical analogy, to argue for an idea of a world branching out toward infinity and entirely permeated with the same sap. However, it remains without any effort within the sensible (even the sensual) realm and it shows no propensity to lapse into the supernatural. Poetic analogy lets us catch a glimpse of what Rimbaud named "true life" and points toward its "absence," but it does not draw its substance from metaphysics nor does it ever consider surrendering its treasures on the altar of any kind of "beyond."

> The dream is a heavy ham
> Hanging from the ceiling.
> —*Pierre Reverdy*

> I arrive as a hawk and come out a phoenix.
> —*Voice of the third soul, Egypt*

At the present age of poetic research, the purely formal distinction once established between metaphor and comparison should not receive much emphasis. The fact remains that they both serve as interchangeable vehicles of analogical thinking. Metaphor does have the ability to dazzle the mind, but comparison (think of Lautréamont's series of "as beautiful as") has the considerable advantage of *deferring*. Naturally, compared to these two, the other "figures" that rhetoric persists in enumerating are totally devoid of interest. The trigger of analogy is what fascinates us: nothing else will give us access to the motor of the world. Whether it is stated or implied, AS is the most exhilarating word at our command. It gives free rein to human imagination, and the supreme destiny of the mind depends on it. That is why we choose to dismiss rather scornfully the ignorant indictment of the poetry of our time, accused of making excessive use of the "image." On the contrary, what we expect from it in this respect is an ever growing luxuriance.

> Your aggressive breasts straining against the silk
> Your triumphant breast is a splendid armoire.
> —*Charles Baudelaire*

The analogical method was held in high regard throughout antiquity and the Middle Ages. Since then, it has been summarily supplanted by the "logical" method, which has led us to our familiar impasse. The primary duty of poets and artists is to restore to it all its prerogatives. To this end, analogy must be rescued from the parasitic undercurrent of spiritualism, which weakens or even cripples its potentialities.

> Your teeth are like a flock of sheep even-shorn, coming back up from the washpen.
> —*Song of Songs*

Pierre Reverdy, who, thirty years ago, looked into the wellspring of the image, was led to formulate this cardinal law: "The more remote and accurate the connections between two realities that are brought together, the stronger the image—the stronger its emotional potential and its poetic reality." This condition, while absolutely necessary, cannot be deemed sufficient. It must make room for another requirement that in the final analysis could well be an ethical one. Let us beware! The analogical image, to the extent that it brings under the strongest light what are merely *partial similarities,* cannot be translated into an equation. It moves between the two confronting realities in a single direction *that can never be reversed.* From the first of these realities to the second one, it creates a vital tension straining toward health, pleasure, tranquillity, thankfulness, respect for customs. Disparagement and depressiveness are its mortal enemies. In this regard, to make up for the disappearance of noble words, some so-called poets cannot help but call attention to their sham by using vile metaphors such as the archetypal "Guitar singing bidet" from the pen of an author who is fairly prolific when it comes to such strokes of inspiration.

> I saw a gathering of spirits. They wore hats on their heads.
> —*Swedenborg*

> Your tongue
> A goldfish swimming in the bowl
> Of your voice.
> —*Guillaume Apollinaire*

> We went along that avenue lined with blue breasts where a comma is all that distinguishes night from day and a smear of itching powder a sardine from a may-bug.
> —*Benjamin Péret*

The finest light illuminating the general, compelling direction that any image worthy of its name must take is found in this apologue from the Zen tradition: "As an act of Buddhist kindness, Basho once ingeniously reversed a cruel haiku made up by his witty disciple. Kikaku had said: 'A red firefly/Tear off its wings/A pepper.' Basho substituted: 'A pepper/Give it wings/A red firefly.'"

DEAR HAZEL OF SQUIRRELNUT

Dear Hazel of Squirrelnut,

In the lovely springtime of 1952 you will just be sixteen, and perhaps you will be tempted to open this book, whose title, I like to think, will be wafted to you euphonically by the wind bending the hawthorns . . . All possible dreams, hopes, and illusions will dance, I hope, night and day, illuminated by your curls, and I shall doubtless be there no longer; I would have liked to be there just to see you. Mysterious, resplendent horsemen will dash by at dusk, beside the changeable streams. Garbed in light sea-green veils, a young girl will glide sleepwalking under high archways, where a single votive lamp will flicker. But the spirits of the reeds, the tiny cats seeming to sleep in the rings, the elegant toy pistol perforated with the word "Ball," will keep you from taking these scenes tragically. Whatever your lot will be, increasingly fortunate or entirely other, I cannot know, you will delight in living, expecting everything from love. Whatever happens from now until you read this letter— it seems that what we least expect is what will come to pass—let me believe you will be ready then to incarnate this eternal power of woman, the only power I have ever submitted to. Whether you have just closed a school desk on a world crow-blue in high fantasy, or whether your sunny silhouette, except for the bouquet of flowers on your blouse, is cast against the wall of a factory—I am far from sure about your future—let me believe that these words, "mad love," will one day correspond uniquely to your own delirium.

They will not keep their promise because they will only enlighten for you the mystery of your birth. For a long time I thought it was the gravest insanity to give life. In any case I held it against those who had given it to me. It may be that you would hold it against me on some days. That is in fact why I have chosen to see you at sixteen, when you cannot hold it against me. What am I saying, to look at you, no, rather to try to see through your eyes, to look at myself through your eyes.

My little child, just eight months old, always smiling, made at once like coral and like pearls, you will know then that any element of chance was strictly excluded from your coming, that your birth came about at the exact time that it was supposed to, neither sooner nor later, and that no shadow was awaiting you above your wicker cradle. Even that great

Henri Cartier-Bresson, portrait of André Breton sitting at desk, 42 rue Fontaine.
© 1995 Magnum Photos.

poverty which had been and remains mine let up for a few days. I was not, as it happens, opposed to this poverty: I accepted to pay the price for not being a slave to life, to settle for the right I had assumed once and for all to not express any ideas but my own. We were not many in doing this . . . Poverty passed by in the distance, made lovelier and almost justified, a little like what has been called, in the case of a painter who was one of your first friends, *the blue period.* It seemed the almost inevitable consequence of my refusal to behave the way almost all the others did, whether on one side or on another. This poverty, whether you have had the time to dread it or not, imagine it was only the other side of the miraculous coin of your existence: the Night of the Sunflower would have been less radiant without it.

Less radiant because then love would not have had to confront all it did confront, because it would not have had, in order to triumph, to count in everything and for everything on itself only. Perhaps this was a terrible imprudence, but it was exactly this imprudence that was the loveliest jewel of the case. Beyond this imprudence there remained nothing except an even greater one: that of bringing you to life, whose perfumed breath you are. It was necessary, at least, to extend from one to the other a magic cord, stretched to the breaking point above the precipice so that beauty could rise, with just its balancing rod, to pluck you like an impossible flower of the air. May you delight at least one day in believing you are this flower, that you were born with no contact with the ground, unfortunately unsterile as it is with what is commonly called "human affairs." You have come from the slightest shimmer of what was rather late for me the goal of poetry, to which I have been devoted since my youth, of that poetry I continue now to serve, scorning everything else. You appeared there as if by magic, and if ever you detect a trace of sadness in these words that for the first time I address *to you alone,* say to yourself that this enchantment continues and will continue to be identified with you, that it is strong enough to rise above any heartbreak. *Forever,* and *for a long time*—those two great warring expressions that confront each other whenever it is a question of love—have never exchanged more blinding sword-thrusts than today, above me, in a sky entirely like your eyes, whose whites are still so blue. Of these two expressions, the one that wears my colors, even if its star may be waning now, even if it must lose, is *forever. Forever,* as in the oaths that girls insist on hearing. *Forever,* as on the white sand of time and through the grace of this instrument which is used to measure it, but only fascinates you and leaves you hungry, reduced to a stream of milk endlessly pouring from a glass breast. Despite everything, I shall have maintained that this expression *forever* is the master key. What I have loved, whether I have kept it or not, I shall love *forever.* As you are called upon to suffer also, I wanted, in completing this book, to explain to you. I have spoken of a certain "sublime point" on the mountain. It was never a question of establishing my dwelling on this point. It would, moreover, from then on, have ceased to be sublime and I should, myself, have ceased to be a person. Unable reasonably to dwell there, I have nevertheless never gone so far from it as to lose it from view, as to not be able to point it out. I had chosen to be this guide, and therefore I had forced myself not to be unworthy of the power which, in the direction of eternal love, had made me *see* and granted me the still rarer privilege of *having others see*. I have never been unworthy; I have never ceased to identify the flesh of the being I love and the snow of the peaks in the rising sun. I have tried only to know the hours of love's triumph, whose necklace I here clasp about your throat. Even the black pearl, the last one, I am sure you will understand what weakness attaches me to it, what supreme hope of *conjuration* I have placed on it. I do not deny that love has a difference with life. I say it should vanquish, and in order to do so, should rise to such a poetic consciousness of itself that every hostile thing it meets should melt in the hearth of its own splendor.

At least that will have been, permanently, my great hope, undiminished by my not always being able to show myself worthy. If it ever mingles with another hope, I am sure this latter is just as important for you. I have wanted your existence to know for itself this *raison d'être,* that I had asked of it what was for me beauty, in all the fullest strength of the term, love, in all the strength of the term; the name I give you at the top of this letter does not just render, in its anagrammatical form, a charming account of your *present* aspect, because, after having invented it for you, I perceived that I had originally used the words that make it up to characterize the very aspect that *love* had taken for me: this must be what *resemblance* is. I also wanted everything that I expect from human becoming, everything that, as I see it, is worth fighting for collectively and not just individually, to cease being a formal manner of thinking, even the noblest, to confront this reality of life becoming that you are. I mean that at one time in my life I feared being cut off from the necessary contact, from the human contact with what would be after me. *After me:* this idea keeps getting lost but turns up again wonderfully in a certain sleight of hand that you have, *like* (and for me not like) all little children. From the very first day, I admired your hand. It hovered about everything intellectual I had tried to construct, as if to render it inane. What a mad thing this hand is, and how I pity those who have never had the chance to place it, like a star, on the loveliest page of a book. The poverty, suddenly, of any flower. We only have to look at this hand to think that any human makes a deplorable account of what he thinks he knows. All he understands from it is that it is really made, in all senses, for the *best*. This blind aspiration towards the best would suffice to justify love as I think of it, absolute love, as the only principle for physical and moral selection which can guarantee that human witness, human passage shall not have taken place in vain.

I was thinking of all this, feverishly, in September 1936, alone with you in my famous, unlivable house of rock salt. I was thinking about it between reading newspapers telling, more or less hypocritically, the episodes of the Civil War in Spain, the newspapers behind which you thought I was disappearing just to play peek-a-boo with you. And it was also true, because in such moments, the unconscious and the conscious, in you and in me, existed in complete duality near each other, keeping each other in a total ignorance and yet communicating at will by a single all-powerful thread which was the exchanged glance between us. To be sure, my life then hung only by the slightest thread. Great was the temptation to go offer it to those who, without any possible error and any distinction of tendencies, wanted at any price to finish with the older "order" founded on the cult of that abject trinity: family, country, and religion. And still you held me by that thread which is happiness, such as it pierces the web of unhappiness itself. I loved in you all the little children of the Spanish militia, like those I had seen running naked in the outer district of Santa Cruz, on Tenerife. May the sacrifice of so many human lives make of them one day *happy* beings! And yet I did not feel in myself the courage to expose you with me to help that to happen.

Above all, let the idea of the family be buried! If I have loved in you the working out of natural necessity, it is to the exact extent that in your person it was one with what was for me human necessity, *logical* necessity; the reconciliation of these two necessities has always seemed to me the only miracle within the reach of any human, the only chance of escaping now and then the meanness of the human condition. You have gone from non-being to being by one of these agreements which are the only ones to which I cared to listen. You were thought of as possible, as certain, in the very moment when, in a love deeply sure of itself, a man and a woman wanted you to be.

I wanted you too much to hear you one day answering in complete innocence those insidious questions grownups ask children: "What do we think with, suffer with? How did we get the sun's name? Where does the night come from?" As if they could answer the questions themselves! Since you are for me the human creature in its perfect authenticity, you should, improbable as it seems, teach me about them . . .

I want you to be madly loved.

Photo of Maison–Attentat. Reproduced from Breton, "Nadja," *La Révolution surréaliste* 12 (December 15, 1929). Reprinted by permission.

CLAUDE CAHUN

I Am Still Waiting
(Answer to Questionnaire: "What Was the Most Important
Encounter of Your Life?")

I am still waiting for some remarkable circumstance to strike me, by which to evaluate various encounters whose greater or lesser importance and meaning I see more or less clearly.

The only encounter that has played a *capital* role in my life until now took place before I was born. Doubtless I'd never think of such an obvious and common fact, of which I can only make a rhetorical use, if, as long as I can remember, I hadn't had the familiar irritating feeling that my fate is playing itself out for the most part outside of me, and almost without my knowing it.

This irritation leads me to oppose the terms "fortuitous" and "necessary." From a subjective and partial point of view everything seems to be ideally fortuitous, and I envisage the innumerable motives that should logically prevent the irruption of any coincidence isolated from its causes. But whenever I go back to the whole set of elements and make certain links between them, however irrelevant, disproportionate, and imponderable they appear, I see the necessity of the seemingly most fortuitous encounter. And whatever still escapes me is just ignorance.

So many fortuitous necessary and precarious encounters take place for each of us, that the loveliest or dreariest day of our life could perfectly well go by unnoticed. I would admit to having lived through this *capital* encounter without noticing it, if calling it that weren't already enough indication that you cannot survive it.

Claude Cahun, *Self-Portrait as a Young Man,* 1930s; silver print, 9⁵/₆ × 7 inches. Courtesy of Virginia Zabriskie Gallery.

Leonora Carrington

The House of Fear

One day towards half past midday, as I was walking in a certain neighborhood, I met a horse who stopped me.

"Come with me," he said, bending his head towards a street that was dark and narrow. "I've something I particularly want to show you."

"I haven't the time," I replied, but nevertheless I followed him. We came to a door on which he knocked with his left hoof. The door opened. We went in, I thought I'd be late for lunch.

There were a number of creatures in ecclesiastical dress. "Do go upstairs," they told me. "There you'll see our beautiful inlaid floor. It is completely made of turquoise, and the tiles are stuck together with gold."

Surprised by such a welcome, I nodded my head and made a sign to the horse to show me this treasure. The staircase had enormously high steps, but we went up without difficulty, the horse and I.

"You know, it isn't really as beautiful as all that," he told me in a low voice. "But one's got to make a living, hasn't one?"

All of a sudden we saw the turquoise paving which covered the floor of a large, empty room. In fact the tiles were well fitted together with gold, and the blue was dazzling. I gazed at it politely, the horse thoughtfully:

"Well, you see, I'm really bored by this job. I only do it for the money. I don't really belong in these surroundings. I'll show you, next time there's a party."

After due reflection, I said to myself that it was easy to see that this horse wasn't just an ordinary horse. Having reached this conclusion, I felt I should get to know him better.

"I'll certainly come to your party. I'm beginning to think I rather like you."

"You yourself are an improvement on the usual run of customers," he replied. "I'm very good at telling the difference between ordinary people and those with a certain understanding. I've got the gift of immediately getting right inside a person's soul."

I smiled anxiously. "And when is the party?"

Leonora Carrington, *Baby Giant,* ca. 1950. Ex-Edward James Foundation,
Sussex, United Kingdom/Bridgeman Art Library. © ARS.

"It's this evening. Put on some warm clothes."

That was odd, for outside the sun was shining brightly.

Going down the stairs at the far end of the room, I noticed with surprise that the horse managed much better than I. The ecclesiastics had disappeared, and I left without anyone seeing me go.

"At nine o'clock," the horse said. "I'll call for you at nine. Be sure to let the concierge know."

On my way home I thought to myself that I ought to have asked the horse to dinner.

Never mind, I thought. I bought some lettuce and some potatoes for my supper. When I got home I lit a little fire to prepare my meal. I had a cup of tea, thought about my day and mostly about the horse whom, though I'd only known him a short time, I called my friend. I have few friends and am glad to have a horse for a friend. After the meal I smoked a cigarette and mused on the luxury it would be to go out, instead of talking to myself and boring myself to death with the same endless stories I'm forever telling myself. I am a very boring person, despite my enormous intelligence and distinguished appearance, and nobody knows this better than I. I've often told myself that if only I were given the opportunity, I'd perhaps become the centre of intellectual society. But by dint of talking to myself so much, I tend to repeat the same things all the time. But what can you expect? I'm a recluse.

It was in the course of these reflections that my friend the horse knocked on my door, with such force that I was afraid the neighbours would complain.

"I'm coming," I called out.

In the darkness I didn't see which direction we were taking. I ran beside him, clinging to his mane for support. Soon I noticed that in front of us, behind us, and on all sides in the open country were more and more horses. They were staring straight ahead and each carried some green stuff in its mouth. They were hurrying, the noise of their hooves shook the earth. The cold became intense.

"This party takes place every year," the horse said.

"It doesn't look as if they were enjoying themselves much," I said.

"We're visiting the Castle of Fear. She's the mistress of the house."

The castle stood ahead of us, and he explained that it was built of stones that held the cold of winter.

"Inside it's even colder," he said, and when we got into the courtyard I realised that he was telling the truth. The horses all shivered, and their teeth chattered like castanets. I had the impression that all the horses in the world had come to this party. Each one with bulging eyes, fixed straight ahead, and each one with foam frozen around its lips. I didn't dare speak, I was too terrified.

Following one another in single file, we reached a great hall decorated with mush-rooms and other fruits of the night. The horses all sat down on their hindquarters, theirforelegs rigid. They looked about without moving their heads, just showing the whites of their eyes. I was very much afraid. In front of us, reclining in the Roman fashion on a very large bed, lay the mistress of the house—Fear. She looked slightly like a horse, but was much uglier. Her dressing gown was made of live bats sewn together by their wings: the way they fluttered, one would have thought they didn't much like it.

"My friends," she said, weeping and trembling. "For three hundred and sixty-five days I've been thinking of the best way to entertain you this night. Supper will be as usual, and everyone is entitled to three portions. But apart from that I have thought up a new game which I think is particularly original, for I've spent a lot of time perfecting it. I hope with all my heart that all of you will experience the same joy in playing this game as I have found in devising it."

A deep silence followed her words. Then she continued.

"I shall now give you all the details. I shall supervise the game myself, and I shall be the umpire and decide who wins.

"You must all count backwards from a hundred and ten to five as quickly as possible while thinking of your own fate and weeping for those who have gone before you. You must simultaneously beat time to the tune of 'the Volga Boatmen' with your left foreleg, 'The Marseillaise' with your right foreleg, and 'Where Have You Gone, My Last Rose of Summer?' with your two back legs I had some further details, but I've left them out to simplify the game. Now let us begin. And don't forget that, though I can't see all over the hall at once, the Good Lord sees everything."

I don't know whether it was the terrible cold that excited such enthusiasm, the fact is that the horses began to beat the floor with their hooves as if they wanted to descend to the depths of the earth. I stayed where I was, hoping she wouldn't see me, but I had an uncomfortable feeling that she could see me very well with her great eye (she had only one eye, but it was six times bigger than an ordinary eye). It went on like this for twenty-five minutes, but . . .

UNCLE SAM CARRINGTON

Whenever Uncle Sam Carrington saw the full moon he couldn't stop laughing. A sunset had the same effect on Aunt Edgeworth. Between them they caused my poor mother a great deal of suffering, for she had a certain social reputation to keep up.

When I was eight I was considered the most serious member of my family. My mother confided in me. She told me that it was a crying shame that she wasn't invited anywhere, that Lady Cholmondey-Bottom cut her when they passed in the street. I was grief stricken.

Uncle Sam Carrington and Aunt Edgeworth lived at home. They lived on the first floor. So it was impossible to hide our sad state of affairs. For days I wondered how I could deliver my family from this disgrace. In the end I couldn't stand the tension and my mother's tears, they upset me too much. I decided to find a solution by myself.

One evening, when the sun had turned a brilliant red, and Aunt Edgeworth was giggling in a particularly outrageous manner, I took a pot of jam and a fishing hook and set off. I sang, "Come into the garden, Maud,/For the black bat, night, has flown," to frighten the bats away. My father used to sing that when he didn't go to church, or else he sang a song called "It Cost Me Seven and Six Pence." He sang both with equal feeling.

All right, I thought to myself, the journey has begun. The night will surely bring a solution. If I keep count of the trees until I reach the place I'm going to, I shan't get lost. I'll remember the number of trees on the return journey.

But I'd forgotten that I could only count to ten, and even then I made mistakes. In a very short time, I'd counted to ten several times, and I'd gone completely astray. Trees surrounded me on all sides. "I'm in a forest," I said, and I was right.

The full moon shone brightly between the trees, so I was able to see, a few yards in front of me, the origins of a distressing noise. It was two cabbages having a terrible fight. They were tearing each other's leaves off with such ferocity that soon there was nothing but torn leaves everywhere and no cabbages.

"Never mind," I told myself, "It's only a nightmare." But then I remembered suddenly that I'd never gone to bed that night, and so it couldn't possibly be a nightmare. "That's awful."

Thereupon I left the corpses and went on my way. Walking along I met a friend. It was the horse who, years later, was to play an important part in my life.

"Hello," he said. "Are you looking for something?" I explained to him the purpose of my late-night expedition.

"I can see that this is a very complicated matter from a social point of view," he said. "There are two ladies living near here who deal with such matters. Their aim is the extermination of family shame. They're expert at it. I'll take you to them if you like."

The Misses Cunningham-Jones lived in a house discretely surrounded by wild plants and underclothes of bygone times. They were in the garden, playing a game of draughts. The horse stuck his head between the legs of a pair of 1890 bloomers and addressed the Misses Cunningham-Jones.

"Show your friends in," said the lady sitting on the right, speaking with a very distinguished accent. "In the interest of respectability, we are always ready to come to the rescue." The other lady inclined her head graciously. She was wearing an immense hat decorated with a great collection of horticultural specimens.

"Young lady," she said, offering me a Louis Quinze chair, "does your family descend from our dear departed Duke of Wellington? Or from Sir Walter Scott, that noble aristocrat of pure literature?"

I felt a bit embarrassed. There were no aristocrats in my family. She saw my hesitation and said with the most charming smile, "My dear child, you must realise that here we deal only with the affairs of the oldest and most noble families of England."

I had an inspiration, and my face lit up. "In our dining room at home . . ."

The horse kicked me hard in the backside. "Never mention anything as vulgar as food," he whispered.

Fortunately the ladies were slightly deaf. I immediately corrected myself. "In our drawing room," I continued, confused, "there is a table on which, we are told, a duchess forgot her lorgnette in 1700."

"In that case," one of the ladies said, "we can perhaps settle the matter. Of course, we shall have to set a rather higher fee."

"Wait here for a few minutes, then we'll give you what you need. While you are waiting, you may look at the pictures in this book. It is instructive and interesting. No library is complete without it: my sister and I have always lived by its admirable example."

The book was called *The Secrets of the Flowers of Refinement, or The Vulgarity of Food.*

When the two ladies had gone, the horse said, "Do you know how to walk without making a sound?"

"Certainly," I replied.

"Let's go and see the ladies at work," he said. "Come. But if you value your life, don't make the slightest noise."

The ladies were in their kitchen garden. It was behind their house and was surrounded by a high brick wall. I climbed on the horse's back, and a pretty astonishing sight met my eyes: the Misses Cunningham-Jones, each armed with a huge whip, were whipping the vegetables on all sides, shouting, "One's got to suffer to go to Heaven. Those who do not wear corsets will never get there."

The vegetables, for their part, were fighting among themselves, and the larger ones threw the smaller ones at the ladies with cries of hate.

"It's always like this," said the horse in a low voice. "The vegetables have to suffer for the sake of society. You'll see that they'll soon catch one for you, and that it'll die for the cause."

The vegetables didn't look keen to die an honourable death, but the ladies were stronger. Soon two carrots and a courgette fell into their hands.

"Quick" said the horse, "let's go back."

We had hardly got back and were sitting once more in front of *The Vulgarity of Food* when the two ladies returned, looking just about as poised as before. They gave me a parcel which contained the vegetables, and in return I paid them with the pot of jam and the fishing hook.

AIMÉ CÉSAIRE

SERPENT SUN

Serpent sun eye bewitching my eye
and the sea flea-ridden with islands cracking in the fingers of flamethrower roses and my
    intact body of one thunderstruck
the water raises the carcasses of light lost in the pompless corridor
whirlwinds of ice floes halo the steaming hearts of ravens
our hearts
it is the voice of tamed thunderbolts turning on their crack hinges
a transfer of anolis to the landscape of broken glasses it is the vampire flowers relaying the
    orchids
elixir of the central fire
fire just fire night mango tree swarming with bees
my desire a throw of tigers caught in the sulphurs
but the stannous awakening gilds itself with infantine deposits
and my pebble body eating fish eating doves and slumbers
the sugar in the word Brazil deep in the marsh.

THE AUTOMATIC CRYSTAL

hullo hullo one more night stop guessing it's me the cave man there are cicadas which
deafen both their life and their death there also is the green water of lagoons even drowned
I will never be that color to think of you I left all my words at the pawn shop a river
of sleds of women bathing in the course of the day blonde as bread and the alcohol of
your breasts hullo hullo I would like to be on the clear other side of the earth the tips
of your breasts have the color and the taste of that earth hullo hullo one more night
there is rain and its gravedigger fingers there is rain putting its foot in its mouth on

the roofs the rain ate the sun with chopsticks hullo hullo the enlargement of the crystal that's you . . . that is you oh absent one in the wind an earthworm bathing beauty when day breaks it is you who will dawn your riverine eyes on the stirred enamel of the islands and in my mind it is you the dazzling maguey of an undertow of eagles under the banyan

THE VIRGIN FOREST

I am not one of those who believe that a city must not rise to catastrophe one more back twisting neck twisting twist of stairs it will be the snap of the promontory I am not one of those who fight against the propagation of slums one more shit stain it will be a real swamp. Really the power of a city is not in inverse ratio to the sloppiness of its housekeepers as for me I know very well into what basket my head will never again roll. Really the power of a glance is not an inverse function of its blindness as for me I know very well where the moon will not come to rest its pretty head of a hushed-up affair. In the corner of the canvas the lower-class despair and my mug of a primate stoked for three hundred years. In the middle the telephone exchange and the gas plant in full anthesis (betrayal of coal and field-marshals). In the west-west corner the floral metabolism and my mug of a primate dismantled for three hundred years the nopal smoke a nopal in the gorged landscape the strangler fig trees make an appearance salivated from my mug of a sphinx muzzle unmuzzled since nothingness.

SENTENCE

And why not the hedge of geysers the obelisk of hours the smooth scream of clouds the sea's quartered pale green spattered by good-for-nothing birds and hope playing marbles on the beams and between of houses and the dolphin-like rips of banana tree suckers

in the top branches of the sun on the stubbed heart of mornings on the acrid canvas of the sky a day of chalk of falcons of rain and acacia on a portulan of primeval islands shaking their saline hair interposed by fingers of masts handwritten for any purpose under the blink of chance with its shadow sung delights an assassin clad in rich and calm muslins like a chant of hard wine

Breaking with the Dead Sea

You know them, oh my heart, in their sweet delirium.

Crouching below deck they music with dying stench and the heralds of the rainy wind arise, slowly harvesting the work of a pale sun. At times one of them surging up lights in the sanctimonious fumigation the flower of a pure sob, but in a flash, the floral impulse rumples weak and nul into the ashes . . . Pass on, oh sun, the bleeding wounds light sufficiently their propitiatory purulence. Pass by. And now that an irresistible force presides over the metamorphosis of words into a polar star.

Hey, shadow over there!

No longer do the songs stick to the stars. Even the conspiratory smiles have faded out. And at the same time all the living fractures of anguish.

Dreams, to their niches. A mute knifeblade enters the side of the earth. But it is no longer the expectation of an utter silence before an utter silence. A high fever lies in wait for the utter silence. A soft rain descends on the bushes. A rain of inflected desire scatters across the fields. A rain of ancient terror rises towards the horizon. And I hear, dispersed in the clash of battle, one blood striking against another, the last patter:

"Sir, the sun is a cake of badly made putty that you will destroy with your mallet. Madam, your astral body is walking among the flowers."

Back, back, you dwarf corpses!

Back, back, you acromegalic giant corpses!

Back, every management of the past!

Men are seeking in anguish.

In their mounting anguish men are burrowing into death.

And see how the risky site is shrieking a name: yours! mine! in tufts of tragedy.

And my fingers are caressing the cord of your fingers

your ditchbottom fingers

your low voice fingers

your sobeit fingers

your fingers like Atlantis crumbled

and my fingers are nervously snatching at the cord of your fingers,

your long fingers of source and beginning.

Meanwhile—ah! the fetid cut into the prostituted river—a cry rose, the same one, violating all the thrashed throats:

"Who is it? Who is it?"

Who I am? You are asking who I am.

The lagoon foretelling the last tepid torpor of its alcove; the rank weeds making the grasses sound forth in a crackle; the earth smoking with a wintering smoke; the disquieting torpor of the summer lymphs. Silver hearts, silver hearts of flat silver, don't you hear my shadow hatched in the tempestuous nest of young gold? Come on, tell my left ear—when on the road of yesteryear the last horse will sink into the mud of the West, a strange gleam will form its globe: the sky! tender young sky, newborn sky, the sky you'd have to arm with an impenetrable smile against all the bullets and spittings.

Enough . . . Electric wires! total immersions! Erythritis! Hurrah! helix, antihelix, conchshell, through your valleys and your mountains, rising against their peaceable nourishing runes, the beasts of the deep frost, the reindeer, the Scandinavian elk, the brown bear, the blue fox, the musk-ox, they go, words. Debacle. Its the debacle. Hurrah! I am finishing off the wounded. I kill the corpses a second time. The sublime androgyne in the net of my laughter gathers the purest concepts of understanding.

And the fire, the fire of my blood, of my interior soil, the fire where a doll like your future image stretches towards me its childlike hands, shot like a bullet through your new heads rolls—in the tenacious progress of apparitions—along the path, long since dead, of the dead sun.

Suzanne Césaire

The Domain of the Marvelous

No longer is it a matter of the narrow roads where traditional beauty is offered in its clarity and obviousness to the admiration of the crowds. The crowds were taught the victory of intelligence over the world and the submission of the forces of nature to man.

Now it is a question of seizing and admiring a new art which leaves humankind in its true condition, fragile and dependent, and which nevertheless, in the very spectacle of things ignored or silenced, opens unsuspected possibilities to the artist.

And this is the domain of the strange, the Marvelous, and the fantastic, a domain scorned by people of certain inclinations. Here is the freed image, dazzling and beautiful, with a beauty that could not be more unexpected and overwhelming. Here are the poet, the painter, and the artist, presiding over the metamorphoses and the inversions of the world under the sign of hallucination and madness. . . . Here at last the world of nature and things makes direct contact with the human being who is again in the fullest sense spontaneous and natural. Here at last is the true communion and the true knowledge, chance mastered and recognized, the mystery now a friend and helpful.

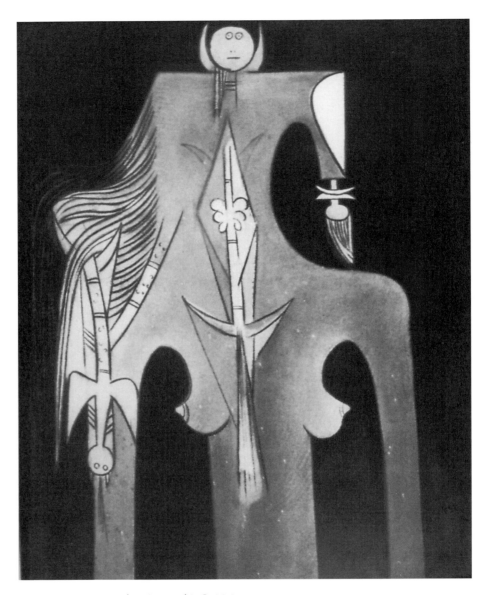

Wifredo Lam, *La Fiancée (The Fiancée)*. © ARS.

RENÉ CHAR

ARTINE

To the silence of one who leaves us dreaming.

In the bed prepared for me were: an animal bruised and slightly bleeding, no larger than a bun, a lead pipe, a gust of wind, an icy seashell, a spent cartridge, two fingers of a glove, a spot of oil; there was no prison door, rather the taste of bitterness, a glazier's diamond, one hair, one day, a broken chair, a silkworm, the stolen object, an overcoat chain, a tame green fly, a branch of coral, a cobbler's nail, a bus wheel.

To offer a glass of water to a horseman as he passes hurtling headlong on a racetrack invaded by the mob takes an absolute awkwardness on both sides; Artine brought to the minds she visited this monumental drought.

Impatient, he was perfectly aware of the order of dreams which would henceforth haunt his brain, especially in the realm of love whose devouring activities usually appeared in other than sexual moments; assimilation developing, through the dead of darkness, in hothouses closed tight.

Artine traverses effortlessly the name of a town. Silence unleashes sleep.

The objects described by and gathered under the name of *nature-précise* form part of the setting for erotic acts bound to *fatal consequences,* an epic daily and nocturnal. Hot imaginary worlds circulating ceaselessly in the countryside at harvest-time render the eye aggressive and solitude intolerable to the wielder of destructive power. For extraordinary upheavals, however, it is preferable to rely altogether upon them.

The lethargic state preceding Artine added what was indispensable to the projection of striking impressions onto the screen of floating ruins: eiderdown in flames cast into the unfathomable abyss of perpetually moving shadows.

In spite of animals and cyclones, Artine retained an inexhaustible freshness. On outings, this was the most absolute transparency.

From the most active depression, the array of Artine's beauty may arise, but the curious minds remain nevertheless furious, the indifferent minds extremely curious.

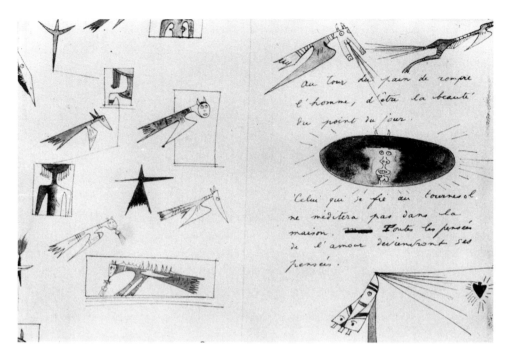

Wifredo Lam, illustration for René Char, from *Le Monde de l'art n'est pas le monde du pardon* (1974); Galerie Maeght, Paris. Courtesy of Marie-Claude Char. © ARS.

Artine's appearances went past the border of those countries of sleep where the *for* and the *for* are endowed with an equal and murderous violence. They occurred in the folds of a burning silk peopled with ashen-leaved trees.

Washed and renovated, the horse-drawn chariot nearly always won out over the saltpeter-papered apartment playing host for an interminable evening to the multitude of Artine's mortal enemies. The dead-wood face was particularly odious. The breathless race of two lovers at random along the highways suddenly became a diversion sufficient for a dramatic unfolding thereupon, out in the open air.

Sometimes, a careless movement caused a head other than mine to sink on Artine's breast. The enormous sulphur block consumed its substance slowly and smokelessly, presence in itself vibrating motionless.

The book open on Artine's knees could be read only on somber days. At irregular intervals heroes would come to learn the calamities once more to befall them, and in what numerous and fearful directions their irreproachable fate would start out afresh. Concerned only with Fatality, they presented for the most part an agreeable appearance. They moved about slowly and were not loquacious. They expressed their desires in broad unforeseeable motions of their heads. Moreover, they seemed to be utterly unconscious of each other.

The poet has slain his model.

FROM *MOULIN PREMIER (FIRST MILL)*

We must have here, a contradiction apparently inescapable, we absolutely must have death's immobility and the freshness of life's entrails.

—*J.-H. Fabre*

IV

Aptitude: bearer of alluvia ablaze.

Daring to be for an instant oneself the accomplished form of the poem. Comfort of having glimpsed matter-emotion sparkling instantly queen.

XV

I do not banter with pigs.

XVIII

The canal goes forward to meet the river. Both equal in depth, both equal in the face of dawn.

Yours, entirely yours, on my knees, humble at the passing of your unnatural processions, oh my damaged love, biting in a silo of hot frenetic slime.

(We loved the opaque waters, said to be polluted, which were the mirror of no rising sky, bare perfumes wholly breathed and this foundation cream of death, a sentinel leaning back, mildly present.)

XXV

Give in to sleep, high matinal generation of linen. The motion of brightness ends in pleasure.

XXXIII

The oscillation of an author behind his work, nothing other than materialistic grooming.

XXXVII

The poet happens to land during the course of his seekings on a shore where he was not expected until much later, after his extinction. Insensitive to the hostility of his backward companions, the poet makes preparations, fells his vigor, divides the term, fastens the summits of his wings.

XLVIII

The long silent walks together at night, across the deserted countryside, in the company of the sleepwalking panther, the masons' terror.

LXVIII

At the sound of the bread of thighs, fire spreads.
Oh widened tuft! oh unstable
Beauty contradicted at length by evidence,
Wandering handcraft of myself!

From *Sens plastique*

A bicycle rolls on the road.
The road is the third wheel
Rolling the other two.

The water says to the wave,
"You are swallowing me."
"How could I?"
Replies the wave,
"I am your mouth."

The dew
Said to the sun,
"Do you see me?"
"No," said the sun,
"I am your eyes."

With their peaks
Two mountains
Were touching a cloud.
For an instant
The cloud felt
Topsy-turvy
Unable to find
Its head.

When the vine
Seized the branch

The branch gave way
And the flower
Stuck its head out
To see what was going on.

Fanning yourself?
Not so.
The fan's in the wind's hand
That's why
You feel cool.

"I've gone all the way around
The Earth,"
One man said.
"Poor fellow
And all that time
You haven't progressed
Half an inch
In your body."

The pupil
Turned the eyes
The iris followed
The white of the eye
Delayed
Just long enough
Friend
For you
To slip into the face
Of the one you love.

"I love you,"
The woman said.
"Be careful,"
Said her lover,
"Don't love me
Too much

Or you'll come back
To yourself
Love is round."

"One and one
Make two"
Said the mathematician.
What's that
To God and the zero?

Cut water
As much as you like
Never
Will you find
The skeleton.
The skeleton of wind
Is life itself.

The eye
Is a one-actor
Theater.

Absolute
Mastery
Of the body
Comes only in death.

"I'll never
Be
Old"
Said the man
"I have hope."

Emptiness
Has no
Way
Out.

If light unfurled
Its peacock tail
There would be
No room
For life.

Sugar
Doesn't know
What it tastes like.
Someone
Tasting it
Gives sugar
A taste of sugar.

A stone
Hears its heart beat
Only
In the rain.

The circle
Is an alibi
For the center
And the center
Is a pretext
For the circle.

The quickest route
From ourselves
To ourselves
Is the Universe.

Blue
Always has
An idea
Up its sleeve.

Night
Is a rimless
Hole.

The road
Runs
In both directions.
That's why
It stands still.

"Take me
Naked"
The flower said
To the sun,
"Before
Night
Closes
My thighs"

The noise,
bit off bits of itself
And
Left
Its teeth
Among
The keys
Of the piano.

She wore
Her smile
Pinned
To her teeth.

Light
Dressed
For the afternoon

Went
To play golf
With the holes.

The lake
This morning
After
A bad
Night
Got into
Its tub
To relax.

The wave
Out of its depth
On the shore
Went
Down.

He was
In such a hurry
To get to life
That it
Let him go.

She anchored
Her hips
In his eyes
And brought him
To port.

The car
Will never
Attain
The speed
Of the road.

ARTHUR CRAVAN

FROM "NOTES"

Had I known Latin at eighteen, I would have been Emperor—Which is more nefarious: the climate of the Congo or genius?—vegetable patches (carrots) in the shape of a tomb— thoughts jump out of the fire—stars, the despair of poets and mathematicians—more virginal and more furious—does it not suffice for a man of discipline in need of a change to sit at the other end of his study table once a month—for a moment I thought of signing this Arthur the First—I rise with the milkmen—in my verdant towers—dog-flesh—white frost, hoar-frost—O my heart! O my forehead! (O my veins!) whichever of the two of us that has the most quicksilver in his veins (syphilis)—I ran my tongue over their eyes (women)—the moon was drinking, the sea was . . . the gilded moon—I shall eat my shit— the Eiffel Tower more gentle than a fern—one clearly feels the instrument is there (speaking of the heart)—forests and sawmill—energy—concerning the dust of emperors, I have had it in my eyes—I will not tolerate people treading on my toenail—our limbs are already borne by the air (aviation)—if I could amble—the serious hour (evening)—the sea of blue hair—the movement of the mist—I have dreamed of being great enough to found and fashion a republic all to myself—I have dreamed of a bed which would float on water and, more vulgarly, of sleeping on tigers—I haunt paths—I would follow the movement of mist on the theatre of the plains and valleys where the rectangular plantations of radishes and cabbages seemed to form vast tombs—electro-semaphore—*I would stare at the sea* from twenty metres above—pigs [?] shake off torpor—my soul . . . takes its place on the pavements—the Romanesque also of an English nature—telegrams—the blue water of the rain, the downpour—the dusty ladybirds of museums—its snows on empty benches—the greatest monuments create the most dust—all these fruits are promised to the autumn—all that glitters in the spring is promised to winter—the silver sun of winter—Canada, I know that you are green—and take a stroll in the woods!—the dust of Caesars is raised by the wind— what am I, where are . . . and my books of love? the universal vessel—freshen the roses— (à propos the war) I would be ashamed to let myself be carried away by Europe—let her die, I don't have the time—far fom my brothers and far from the balloons—I love her,

her manner of today is filled with genius, while I find her manner of yesterday visionary, and as for that of the day before yesterday . . . —what I like about myself . . . I have twenty countries in my memory and I drag the colours of a hundred cities in my soul—the Persian nightingale who whistles for his rose—on the ships of Asia and the gentle elephants—my pen trembles and quivers—I am always moved—reading my books is dangerous for the body—the majority of women will sigh—fatty brain, a mind which scratches glass—my thoughts like boas—we moderns, what we have in our hearts is enough to blow up a fortress—the sun reddens Russia—the sublime lamp of the sun—regions rich in oil—and all the stars spin and revolve with silent transmssions—let me fly far away following your traces—am I somewhere—withdrawn under in my verdant towers—the moving stars sing like a limousine—I withdraw under the ferns—at the foot of the pines—what am I not in the fields!— . . . and I come to you on a beautiful ocean liner—Until when? How long will I dally at . . . ?—phantoms of railway stations—*embouchure*—far from the balloons, virile—colonial—the spirit of independence—current account—enthusiasm—good-bye the passions of a twenty year old! in the dry season—nickel—

Boredom—tarnishes my cells—The follies of the eccentric April moon—Big boy— my blond hair, colonist, far from the balloons—established under the planks—In blond Maryland   and far from the balloons   of my little finger—I fight for breath *equally* (also) grit—my heart, break into a gallop—I feel the verses swimming in the dampness of my brain—I'm ruined, fantasy, madness has lost its dancer—vagabond—temperament—Honest, I know myself for the creature and thief that I am—My heart, break into a gallop, I will be a millionaire—I wake up a Londoner and go to bed an Asiatic—Londoner, monocle—furore and fury—O, you who have known me follow me into life—The wind excites me—I am always nervous—I have put on again my belt of scrupulous   , I have dedicated myself to life, I am in good shape—rippling muscles—aristocratic salons—vases and medals—Greek—principally—pretubercular—I have also been the poet of destinies— voltaic arcs—inter-digital space—multifloral rose-bushes—samples—quantity—room, vase of air, atmosphere, intoxicating oxygen—rich and poor, money has made me taste rare boredom and fresh desire—in my soul I drag piles of locomotives, cracked columns, scrap-iron—pseudo-Lloyd, golden plume—so-called—ogling eyes—the hollow wheat lifts its head, Napoleon lowers his—here are the child, the man and the woman . . . —happy to have been born—happy by biological necessity—Victor Hugo, the greatest verse-making machine of the nineteenth century—cast up on the coast of Japan—the ephemeral has deep roots in me—the thick and thin are *at war inside me*—Lord, chastity consumes us—breath of springtime, I breathe like a whale—every time I set eyes on someone who is better dressed than myself I am shocked—tell me where you live that in following your traces I might fly as far—the queens of the aquarium (fish)—how beautiful is the snow, the good

Lord did not make fun of us—two hearts, four brains, pink colossus and mirror of the world and poetry machine—my swimming days—there is no risk of the Cubists setting fire to their canvases as they paint them—seated like a guitar player—I am enough of a brute to give myself a smack in the teeth and subtle to the point of neurasthenia—man, pensioner, young girl, child and baby—abstract and rascally—I bet that there is not a Chilean nor an *Obokian* in the world who can say to me: "Because of the colour of my skin and my size I once felt something that you could not have felt"—Just let anyone come up to me and say such a thing and I'll spit in his eye—my art which is the most difficult because I adore it and I shit on it—eyes of a woman, neck of a bull—great laggard—viper and duck—his teeth, freshly seen to, sparkled in his mouth like golden statues—the lions are dead—and all the same when I give you elevators of gold—rhinoceroses, fat boilers, my brothers in thickness—when the sun dies in the woods—the maddest of the mad is me—and I look at you, all you specialists—my God! when I think that I'm thirty years old, it drives me wild—I like my bed because it is the only place where I can play possum, pretending to be dead while all the time breathing like the living—when I go on a binge, I can hear the voice of dictionaries— . . . if all the locomotives in the world began screeching at the same time they could not express my anguish—I am perhaps the king of failures, because I'm certainly the king of something—*the same while changing*—I go to . . . the spheres . . . —athletic melancholy—

Support thought—dreaming of Saturn—I already aspire to other readers—I don't give a damn about art yet if I had known Balzac I would have tried to steal a kiss from him—the heart discovers and the head invents—

Breasts, elephants of softness—in the name of God, the shit, the bitch, the decaying carcass—my heart in its passion embraces the age of stone—Nature, I am your servant—Nero of the pit—It is time to sing from the depths of my heart—torrents of memories—heart of hearts—off you go, little specialists—I do furiously . . . — chimera of springtime—and change shirts—my whinnying youth—dead blacks—in the air purified by the volcanoes—blond colossus, blond giant—fleas breed on eagles, cretins in palaces—and to the para-infernal belongings of a woman—Philadelphia—line, service—I have known the happiness of . . .

Farewell, sovereign fern of the Eiffel Tower . . . love, April, perched on stepladders—behind the factories—locomotive boilers—Venus in the gardens—a binge of curtains—lungs—Really electro-semaphores! cyclists, connecting-rods—traffic of skins—intense—external—epidermis— . . . shone on the facade of stations—play in Maryland—as far as, in the roots of eyes—smoke, I see your spirals—no artist has ever been found hanging before a rose—oxygen, I feel pink—vigils . . . factories—throw pebbles—verses carried nine years like the elephant—no body, do you understand, no body . . . —dirtied by the sun—why do actors not recite Latin and Greek verse? the pasture of the moon—when dawn changes the dress of glaciers—the adopted, adoptive green—in the farms—

In the sombre beauty of a darkening cloud

The moon that dreamed like an elephant's heart

The Saint-Laurent under the yoke of bridges—I noticed that female servants minister to M. Gide's chastity—verses carried nine years like the elephant and died seven times in the waves of the heart—chimneys, smoke, smoke, my beautiful dishevelled ones!—my black death, funereal images, your *finery,* in the kingdom of death moles will furnish you, my sister, yet more *fur*— . . . your territorial waters—

Ah, in the name of God, what weather and what a spring—palm trees and towers—manufacture— . . . like a beautiful charcoal-burner— . . . and I love your presidents—I miss masterpieces—I come

freshly to admire your houses—It is me, your Cravan

wind

I feel the bloom of my youth and come fresh-faced

To admire America and its new cycle-racing tracks

My noble nature—astride a bicycle—

What is there really in your heart, melancholy ogre?

Where does it come from this shadow,

The regard of a beautiful female charcoal-burner?

I want no more of these sinister pleasures.

And you, winter sun whom I love to madness

you live in a child

and surprise in passing

In the sombre beauty of a darkening cloud

The moon that dreamed like an elephant's heart.

For five years now you have not been the same, I do not wish to grow old—court purveyor—my elector's card— . . . I swear to you—poet-woodcutter—honour—extravagantly—the genius which consumes a kilo of flesh a week—weekly—obesity of the heart, fullness of figure—around 200 frs., my heart shows a credit, bank—the total—literally mad— . . . to have a great deal of hope—You place lakes under the yoke of bridges—I study death through my portholes—Tarnished street-lamps—naval spirit—to reiterate—*I am a man of heart,* and am sure to be such;

However . . . (hotels)

The past bellowed like a bull—the air in my wind-pipe— . . . make his propellers hum— . . . like a white automobile—young dumb-bellophile—*A Curse on My Muse*—love on its scaffolding—the colporteur—temperature—in short—tramp!—Franco-Britannic—postal order—

Glorification of scandal (the municipality of New York)—eternal April (tenor) perched on its scaffolding and how cold everything one says is in comparison—Wit has its facets and the soul (the heart) has its slopes—my passports—vulgarity—demoralised—at the hour one turns the lights on in offices—street-lamps shine on their grounded stars—Porto-Rico—the olive-tree falls asleep again—elephant prophet—my leg play—

Sovereign fern of the Eiffel

Tower.

I am everything and every inundation—after crying able to tear up my tears—I need a tremendous spree of debauchery—I am the child of my epoch—organism—

I am what I am: the baby of an epoch. My heart shaken like a bottle—to pass with the utmost speed from enthusiasm to the most complete demoralisation—

I am the beautiful Flora, *Laurent* de Médicis

RENÉ CREVEL

FROM *BABYLON*

Babylon, Babylon, Babylon.

They said you were mad, Amie, and they locked you up. Yet you alone were right. Flesh, beautiful white flesh. Tonight the storm will tear ravenously at the clouds as teeth tear at bellies. In the cemetery, the Queen has consumed in one fell swoop her supply of drugs, and collapses on the cold marble. Babylon, Babylon, Babylon, Amie howls aloud her passion. She is placed in a straitjacket. Babylon. Babylon. Babylon. And that house facing the sea will never be finished. Petitdemange, alone with his blond beard, looks on all this drama as devilishly Ibsenesque. Happy are those who can escape the debacle in their Patagonia of frozen stones. At least the hearts of the Mac-Loufs are at peace.

For their daily flights in ecstasy, Cynthia and her lover open the valise of the man without a face. Lying on their backs, eyes lost in a delicate sky, they follow ethereal processions, although here the noon hour falls heavier than an iron slab. The sun stabs the city, showing pity only to the street of the whores. Buoyed by desire, these ladies float on a lake of shade while yonder their honest sisters dissolve in the heat. The dog days. Long live the dog days! Are they not called bitches? Then long live the bitch days, the season of spread thighs and heavy teats. And you, famished hordes of males, throw away your socks, your starched collars, your underpants, and your meager brains, and give the last spark of your poor marrow to this display of meat. But watch out. Today the blood is near the skin. But all the same, that's no reason to be afraid: what, it's enough to keep you from daring to go closer? And those suddenly motionless women? A piercing shriek. The Negress has fallen over backwards. Fallen stark dead, because all of a sudden she had recognized the woman crowned in natural straw, dressed in unbleached linen, and all of a sudden she could not take any more. A white funeral will be given you, dear savage, convert of the pious Mac-Louf, but the other one, that quasi-transparent creature who has heard at the threshold of your paradise the one syllable in which the final moment of a life summed up the world's whole amorous agony, how could she not have guessed that you were the little black sister of Cynthia, and of the drinker of kerosene, of Amie, of the Queen, of the wandering Jewesses of love, and of herself . . . ?

Lighter than a shadow, she took flight.

She had not had the luck to encounter, as you did in another time, Cynthia, the man without a face. A lad who resembled at the same time the one of Agrippa d'Aubigné Street and the father, with skin the color of his hair and eyes the color of Havana's sky, he alone had looked gently on her.

He had the pride of those who load and unload ships, his muscles outlined under the coat of tan the sun had woven on his skin.

Except for the azure canvas of his slacks, he was naked. Naked as joy, as rivers, as stones. Naked like the grass, the gums, the teeth. He smiled. But the woman did not respond to his smile. Get along with you, you handsome scamp. You were at the edge of the waves. You began to dance on their crests. Someone over there, very far away, had stitched the sky to the sea. Buffoon of the tides, forget a street that smelled of a cellar and of violet-scented face powder.

Boy, you were much too fond of the festoons of your steps. A woman was there and you merely glanced at her fragility. Noon. At that particular hour, at that particular age, Cynthia was looking at the acrobats of mother-of-pearl and the opal balloons in the firmament of the sea. You celebrated the anniversary at the threshold of a paradise of shivering and rags, but no more than Cynthia in her aquarium did you turn again toward your sisters with their legs spread apart. Silence. Memory was no longer a gentle poppy. Go down to the harbor, walk forever scornful of time and space. Finish the purple morning among bouquets of shells. Continue walking, and not a word of despair. A dubious rainbow follows the rippling whimsy of the tides. You remembered the drowned men Amie liked to imagine in this tossing grave. You, you saw yourself as Ophelia gliding on the oil that stains the sea. And with what would you replace those long purple flowers the young girl wreathed around her brow before going to the brook, those long purple flowers that virgins call dead men's fingers but that silent shepherds describe by a less circumspect name? You saw yourself, your hair sticky from the violet shellfish that fishwives sell with a little wink of the eye to travelers who wonder for what stupefactive these obscene fruits of the sea were torn from the rocks.

Woman crowned in natural straw, the blue of tenderness must be renounced, the red of desire, the yellow of joy, and even the mauve of fatigue. On the quays, casks slowly lose their perfume interwoven with geranium. Insensitive earth, empty hour, Babylon, after the cries, the scars of teeth, there is a great silence. A jetty draws out to sea this carnal soil, this great body of a continent that sunstroke has beatified.

A woman, a city, compete in indifference.

Every One Thinks Himself Phoenix . . .

Every one thinks himself Phoenix, begging for the wasp's-nest of his complexes to be burnt out, annihilated, in the hope that from their ashes may arise those secret hornets whose murmur seems to him the most beautiful, the true, the only music, the inner music. . . .

It is remarkable that even the most dogmatic person will only accept the fact of his ugliness when he has, if not deified, at least flavoured that ugliness with some kind of aesthetic sauce (expressionism). From his own dull story he will not be slow to deduce the dullness of the world (scepticism). The chancellor of conflicts has recognized at once their pathetic letters of nobility. The obsessed is only prepared to take cognizance of his obsession that he may the better cultivate and cherish it.

The most audacious modes of procedure by introspection, even allowing them to be a very excellent and perfect source of information, should not represent anything more serious than a preliminary chapter of a science that is at once general and particular (ousting the old analytico-metaphysical psychology) and whose function, without any demagogical pretensions to humaneness, humanism, humanities or humanity, is to clear away the contemplative pretexts on which individualism is so proudly established and reveal to man his place in the universe.

Given the present state of the world, the opposition between the personal and collective forms of life, the discovery, made by an acute observer, that the profound facts of the subconscious can be coordinated with the superficial disturbances of consciousness, can only be exploited as a means of developing new specimens of nightmare and neurosis.

In my own case, a simple dream enabled me to realize that this total clarity in which we are exhorted to wash and be clean is just as false as the chiaroscuro from which hasty specialists dared to claim that they could withdraw all shadow. . . .

Surely the world confesses to its own flatness and imbecility by the very fact of explaining as a form of indigence the hypertrophy or morbidity that tends to create that which is neither flat nor imbecile.

SALVADOR DALÍ

THE STINKING ASS

To Gala Eluard

It is possible for an activity having a moral bent to originate in a violently paranoiac will to systematize confusion.

The very fact of paranoia, and particularly consideration of its mechanism as a force and power, brings us to the possibility of a mental attack which may be of the order of, but in any case is at the opposite pole to, the attack to which we are brought by the fact of hallucination.

I believe the moment is at hand when, by a paranoiac and active advance of the mind, it will be possible (simultaneously with automatism and other passive states) to systematize confusion and thus to help to discredit completely the world of reality.

The new images which paranoiac thought may suddenly release will not merely spring from the unconscious; the force of their paranoiac power will itself be at the service of the unconscious.

These new and menacing images will act skilfully and corrosively, with the clarity of daily physical appearances; while its particular self-embarrassment will make us yearn for the old metaphysical mechanism having about it something we shall readily confuse with the very essence of nature, which, according to Heraclitus, delights in hiding itself.

Standing altogether apart from the influence of the sensory phenomena with which hallucination may be considered more or less connected, the paranoiac activity always employs materials admitting of control and recognition. It is enough that the delirium of interpretation should have linked together the implications of the images of the different pictures covering a wall for the real existence of this link to be no longer deniable. Paranoia uses the external world in order to assert its dominating idea and has the disturbing characteristic of making others accept this idea's reality. The reality of the external world is used for illustration and proof, and so comes to serve the reality of our mind.

Doctors agree that the mental processes of paranoiacs are often inconceivably swift and subtle, and that, availing themselves of associations and facts so refined as to escape normal people, paranoiacs often reach conclusions which cannot be contradicted or rejected and in any case nearly always defy psychological analysis.

The way in which it has been possible to obtain a double image is clearly paranoiac. By a double image is meant such a representation of an object that it is also, without the slightest physical or anatomical change, the representation of another entirely different object, the second representation being equally devoid of any deformation or abnormality betraying arrangement.

Such a double image is obtained in virtue of the violence of the paranoiac thought which has cunningly and skilfully used the requisite quantity of pretexts, coincidences, &c., and so taken advantage of them as to exhibit the second image, which then replaces the dominant idea.

The double image (an example of which is the image of a horse which is at the same time the image of a woman) may be extended, continuing the paranoiac advance, and then the presence of another dominant idea is enough to make a third image appear (for example, the image of a lion), and so on, until there is a number of images limited only by the mind's degree of paranoiac capacity.

I challenge materialists to examine the kind of mental attack which such an image may produce. I challenge them to inquire into the more complex problem, which of these images has the highest probability of existence if the intervention of desire is taken into account; and also into the problem, even graver and more general, whether the series of these representations has a limit, or whether, as we have every reason to think, such a limit does not exist, or exists merely as a function of each individual's paranoiac capacity.

All this (assuming no other general causes intervene) is certainly enough for me to contend that our images of reality themselves depend upon the degree of our paranoiac faculty, and yet that theoretically a man sufficiently endowed with this faculty may at will see the form of any real object change, exactly as in voluntary hallucination, but with this (destructively) important difference, that the various forms assumed by the object in question are universally open to control and recognition as soon as the paranoiac has merely indicated them.

The paranoiac mechanism whereby the multiple image is released is what supplies the understanding with the key to the birth and origin of all images, the intensity of these dominating the aspect which hides the many appearances of the concrete. It is precisely thanks to the intensity and traumatic nature of images, as opposed to reality, and to the complete absence

Salvador Dalí, *Gala's Foot,* ca. 1974; private collection, Index/Bridgeman Art Library. © ARS.

of interpenetration between reality and images, that we are convinced of the (poetic) impossibility of any kind of *comparison.* It would be possible to compare two things only if they admitted of no sort of mutual relation, conscious or unconscious. If such a comparison could be made tangible, it would clearly illustrate our notion of the arbitrary.

It is by their failure to harmonize with reality, and owing also to the arbitrary element in their presence, that images so easily assume the forms of reality and that the latter in turn adapts itself so readily to the violences of images, which materialist thought idiotically confuses with the violences of reality.[1]

Nothing can prevent me from recognizing the frequent presence of images in the example of the multiple image, even when one of its forms has the appearance of a stinking ass and, more, that ass is actually and horribly putrefied, covered with thousands of flies and ants; and, since in this case no meaning is attachable to the distinct forms of the image apart from the notion of time, nothing can convince me that this foul putrefaction of the ass is other than the hard and blinding flash of new gems.

Nor can we tell if the three great images—excrement, blood and putrefaction—are not precisely concealing the *wished for* "Treasure Island."

Being connoisseurs of images, we have long since learned to recognize the image of desire in images of terror, and even the new dawn of the "Golden Age" in the shameful scatologous images.

In accepting images the appearance of which reality strives painfully to imitate, we are brought to *desire ideal* objects.

Perhaps no image has produced effects to which the word *ideal* can more properly be applied than the tremendous image which is the staggering ornamental architecture called the "Modern Style." No collective effort has produced a dream world so pure and so disturbing as the "Modern Style" buildings, these being, apart from architecture, the true realization in themselves of desires grown solid. Their most violent and cruel automatism pitifully betrays a hatred of reality and a need for seeking refuge in an ideal world, just as happens in infantile neurosis.

This, then, is something we can still like, the imposing mass of these cold and intoxicating buildings scattered over Europe and despised and neglected by anthologies and scholarship. This is enough to confound our swinish contemporary aestheticians, the champions of the execrable "modern art," and enough too to confound the whole history of art.

It has to be said once for all to art critics, artists, &c., that they need expect nothing from the new surrealist images but disappointment, distaste and repulsion. Quite apart from plastic investigation and other buncombe, the new images of surrealism must come more and more to take the forms and colours of demoralization and confusion. The day is not far off when a picture will have the value, and only the value, of a simple moral act, and yet this will be the value of a simple *unmotivated act*.

As a functional form of the mind, the new images will come to follow the free bent of desire at the same time as they are vigorously repressed. The desperate activity of these new images may also contribute, simultaneously with other surrealist activities, to the destruction of reality, and so benefit everything which, through infamous and abominable ideals of all kinds, aesthetic, humanitarian, philosophical, &c., brings us back to the clear springs of masturbation, exhibitionism, crime, and love.

We shall be idealists subscribing to no ideal. The ideal images of surrealism will serve the imminent crisis of consciousness; they will serve Revolution.

Note

1. What I have in mind here are, in particular, the materialist ideas of Georges Bataille, but also, in general, all the old materialism which this gentleman dodderingly claims to rejuvenate when he bolsters it up with modern psychology.

THE GREAT MASTURBATOR

Despite the reigning darkness
the evening was still young
near the great stairway houses of agate
where
tired by the daylight
that lasted since sunrise
the Great Masturbator
his immense nose reclining upon the onyx floor
his enormous eyelids closed
his brow frightfully furrowed with wrinkles
and his neck swollen by the celebrated boil seething with ants
came to rest
steeped in this still too luminous time of the evening
while the membrane covering his mouth entirely
hardened alongside the alarming the eternal grasshopper
stuck clinging motionless to it
for five days and nights.

All the love and all the ecstasy
of the Great Masturbator
resided
in the cruel ornaments of false gold
covering his delicate and soft temples

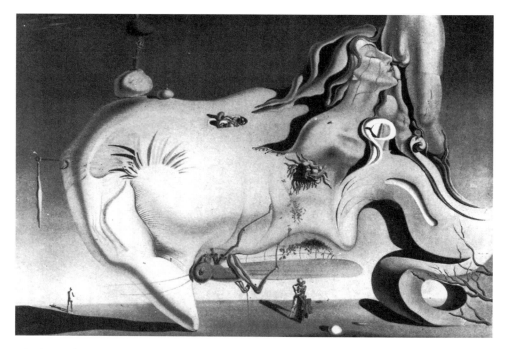

Salvador Dalí, *The Great Masturbator,* 1929; 110 × 150 centimeters. Art Resource. © ARS.

> imitating
> the shape of an imperial crown
> whose fine leaves of bronzed acanthus
> reached as far
> as his rosy and beardless cheeks
> and extended their hard fibers
> until they dissolved
> in the clear alabaster of his neck.

In order to obtain the icy appearance of an ancient ornament of an uncertain and hybrid style that would make possible an error through mimeticism of the complicated architecture of the alley and in order to render the desirable horror of this flesh—triumphant, rotting, stiff, belated, well-groomed, soft, exquisite, downcast, marconized, beaten, lapidated, devoured, ornamented, punished—invisible or at least unperceived by the human face that resembles that of my mother. . . .

LÉON DAMAS

NO ONE REMEMBERS

No one remembers ever having seen
love waiting in the sun its arm at its feet
dying with impatience
question marks one after the other
question marks in the form
of petits fours
like
no one remembers ever having seen
in the approaching night
the one on watch
pronounce the password badly
and it so simple
      He eats his bruises
    eating more than ripe mango
    but fallen mango
    blip!
It is true you will say and I agree
that it's not the same with the mango tree mocking
what no one remembers ever seeing
love waiting in the sun its arm at its feet
dying with impatience in a row
the question marks
like petit fours
or
as at nightfall
the one on guard

saying badly this pass word
yet so simple
      He eats his bruises
    eating more than ripe mango
    but fallen mango
    blip!

ROBERT DESNOS

FROM *DEUIL POUR DEUIL (MOURNING FOR MOURNING)*

These ruins are situated on the banks of a winding river. The town must have had some importance long ago. Monumental buildings still remain, and a network of tunnels, as well as towers of a bizarre and varied architecture. In these deserted and sunny squares we have been overtaken by fear. In spite of our anxiety, no one, no one at all came to meet us. These ruins are uninhabited. To the southwest there rises a tall metallic construction with apertures, whose use we have not been able to determine. It seems ready to crumble into ruins, for it is leaning at a sharp angle and hangs over the river:

"Strange sicknesses, curious customs, bell-clapper love, how far astray are you leading me? I find in these stones no vestige of what I seek. The impassive mirror, always new, reveals only myself. Is it in an abandoned town, a desert, that this magnificent meeting should logically take place? From afar, I have seen the beautiful millionairesses advancing with their caravan of decorated and gold-bearing camels. Impassive and tormented, I have awaited them. Even before reaching me, they were transformed into dusty little old ladies, and the camel drivers into beasts. I have developed the habit of laughing uproariously at funerals which serve as my landscape. I have lived infinite existences in dark corridors at the heart of mines . . .

Love! Love! I shall no longer use in describing you the warring epithets of airplane motors. I shall speak of you in banal terms, for banality may yield me the extraordinary adventure I have been preparing since my first words, and whose gender I do not know. . . . Love, do you condemn me to become the tutelary demon of these ruins, and shall I live from now on an eternal youth . . . ?

I do not believe in God, but I have the sense of the infinite. No one has a spirit more religious than mine. Ceaselessly I strike against insoluble questions. The only questions I admit willingly are all insoluble. The others could only be asked by unimaginative beings and hold no interest for me.

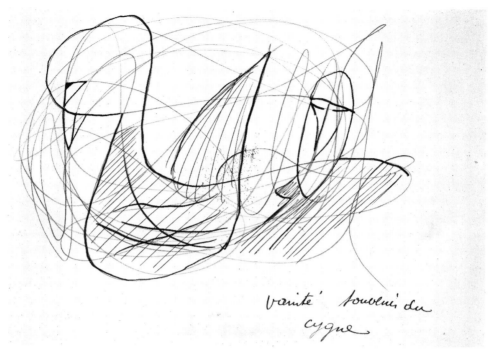

vanité souvenir du cygne

Robert Desnos, *Vanité souvenir du cygne (Vanity of the Swan), 1928–29, Paris;* one of six drawings that accompany the original manuscript of *The Night of Loveless Nights,* by Robert Desnos, Special Collections, The Library, the Museum of Modern Art, New York. Reproduced by permission of MOMA and L'Association Robert Desnos.

These ruins are situated on the banks of a winding river. The climate is nondescript. To the southwest there rises a tall metallic construction with openings, whose use we have not been able to determine. . . . ''

But, oh granite, do not regret your terrifying majesty at the foot of the cliff. Now that you are resting in this cemetery, shaped into a paperweight on a deadman perhaps turned to paper thanks to the rot used to make that matter and perhaps even the paper on which I write this eulogy, you take on the most serene majesty, thanks to that dead man who tried to carry into the silence even his name and to confide to the modest echoes of his surroundings the sound of a terrible and satanic burst of laughter.
Paris, April 1924

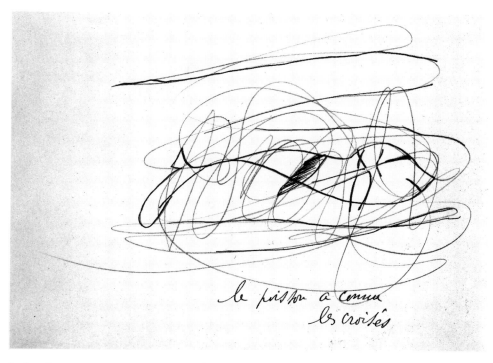

Robert Desnos, *Le Poisson a connu les croisés (The Fish Knew the Crusaders), 1928–29, Paris;* one of six drawings that accompany the original manuscript of *The Night of Loveless Nights,* by Robert Desnos, Special Collections, The Library, the Museum of Modern Art, New York. Reproduced by permission of MOMA and L'Association Robert Desnos.

OH PANGS OF LOVE!

Oh pangs of love!
How necessary you are to me and how precious.
My eyes closing on imaginary tears, my hands stretching
    out ceaselessly toward nothingness.
I dreamed last night of crazed landscapes and of adventures
    as dangerous from the perspective of death as from the
    perspective of life which are both also the perspective of love.

At my waking you were present, oh anguish of love, oh desert
    muses, oh exigent muses.
My laugh and my joy crystallize about you. Your
    makeup, your powder, your rouge, your alligator bag, your
    silk stockings . . . and also that little fold between the ear
    and the nape of your neck, near its base, your
    silk pants and your delicate shirt and your fur coat, your
    round belly is my laughter and your feet my joys and
    all your jewels.
Really, how good-looking and well dressed you are.
Oh pangs of love, exigent angels, here I am imagining you
    in the very likeness of my love, confusing you with it . . .
Oh pangs of love, you whom I create and clothe, you
    are confused with my love whose clothing only I know
    and also her eyes, voice, face, hands, hair, teeth, eyes . . .

I HAVE SO OFTEN DREAMED OF YOU

I have so often dreamed of you that you become unreal.
Is it still time enough to reach that living body and to kiss
    on that mouth the birth of the voice so dear to me?
I have so often dreamed of you that my arms used as they are
    to meet on my breast in embracing your shadow would
    perhaps not fit the contour of your body.

And, before the real appearance of what has haunted and ruled
    me for days and years, I might become only a shadow.
Oh the weighing of sentiment.
I have so often dreamed of you that there is probably no time
    now to waken. I sleep standing, my body exposed to all the
    appearances of life and love and you, who alone still
    matter to me, I could less easily touch your forehead and
    your lips than the first lips and the first forehead I
    might meet by chance.
I have so often dreamed of you, walked, spoken, slept with your
    phantom that perhaps I can be nothing any longer than a
    phantom among phantoms and a hundred times more shadow
    than the shadow which walks and will walk joyously over
    the sundial of your life.

SLEEP SPACES

In the night there are naturally the seven marvels of the world
    and greatness and the tragic and enchantment.
Confusedly, forests mingle with legendary creatures hidden in the
    thickets.
You are there.
In the night there is the nightwalker's step and the
    murderer's and the policeman's and the streetlight and the
    ragman's lantern.
You are there.
In the night pass trains and ships and the mirage of
    countries where it is daylight. The last breaths of twilight
    and the first shivers of dawn.
You are there.
A tune on the piano, a cry.
A door slams,
A clock.

And not just beings and things and material noises.

But still myself chasing myself or going on beyond.

You are there, immolated one, you for whom I wait.

Sometimes strange figures are born at the instant of sleep
and disappear.

When I close my eyes, phosphorescent blooms appear and
fade and are reborn like carnal fireworks.

Unknown countries I traverse with creatures for company.

You are there most probably, oh beautiful discreet spy.

And the palpable soul of the reaches.

And the perfumes of the sky and the stars and the cock's
crow from two thousand years ago and the peacock's scream
in the parks aflame and kisses.

Handshakes sinister in a sickly light and
axles screeching on hypnotic roads.

You are most probably there, whom I do not know, whom
on the contrary I know.

But who, present in my dreams, insist on being sensed there
without appearing.

You who remain out of reach in reality and in dream.

You who belong to me by my will to possess you in illusion
but whose face approaches mine only if my eyes are
closed to dream as well as to reality.

You in spite of an easy rhetoric where the waves die on
the beaches, where the crow flies in ruined factories, where
wood rots cracking under a leaden sun.

You who are at the depths of my dreams, arousing my mind
full of metamorphoses and leaving me your glove when
I kiss your hand.

In the night there are stars and the tenebral motion of
the sea, rivers, forests, towns, grass, the lungs
of millions and millions of beings.

In the night there are the marvels of the world.

In the night there are no guardian angels but there is sleep.

In the night you are there.

In the day also.

IF YOU KNEW

Far from me and like the stars, the sea, and all the
   props of poetic legend,
Far from me and present all the same without your knowledge,
Far from me and still more silent because I imagine you
   endlessly,
Far from me, my beautiful mirage and my eternal dream,
   you cannot know.
If you knew.
Far from me and perhaps still farther from being unaware of
   me and still unaware.
Far from me because you doubtless do not love me or,
   not so different, I doubt your love.
Far from me because you cleverly ignore my passionate
   desires.
Far from me for you are cruel.
If you knew.
Far from me, oh joyous as the flower dancing in the river
   on its watery stem, oh sad as seven in the evening in
   the mushroom fields.
Far from me still silent as in my presence and still joyous
   as the stork-shaped hour falling from on high.
Far from me at the moment when the alembics sing, when
   the silent and noisy sea curls up on the white pillows.
If you knew.
Far from me, oh my present present torment, far from
   me with the splendid sound of oyster shells crunched under
   the nightwalker's step, at dawn, when he passes by the
   door of restaurants.
If you knew.
Far from me, willed and material mirage.
Far from me an island turns aside at the passing of ships.
Far from me a calm herd of cattle mistakes the spot, stops
   stubbornly at the brink of a steep precipice, far from
   me, oh cruel one.

Far from me, a falling star falls in the night bottle of
    the poet. He corks it instantly to watch the star en-
    closed within the glass, the constellations come
    to life against the sides, far from me, you are far from me.
If you knew.
Far from me a house is built just now.
A white-clothed worker atop the structure sings a sad
    brief song and suddenly, in the hod of mortar there appears
    the future of the house: lovers' kisses and double suicides
    and nakedness in the rooms of lovely unknown girls and
    their midnight dreams, and the voluptuous secrets surprised
    by the parquet floors.
Far from me,
If you knew.
If you knew how I love you and though you do not love
    me, how I am happy, how I am strong and proud,
    with your image in my mind, to leave the universe.
How I am happy enough to perish from it.
If you knew how the world submits to me.
And you, oh beautiful unsubmissive one, how you are also
    my prisoner.
Oh far-from-me to whom I submit.
If you knew.

No, Love Is Not Dead

No, love is not dead in this heart and these eyes and this
    mouth which announced the beginning of its burial.
Listen, I have had enough of the picturesque and the
    colorful and the charming.
I love love, its tenderness and cruelty.
My love has but one name, but one form.
All passes. Mouths press against this mouth.

My love has but one name, but one form.

And if some day you remember

O form and name of my love,

One day on the ocean between America and Europe,

At the hour when the last sunbeam reverberates on the
    undulating surface of waves, or else a stormy night
    beneath a tree in the countryside or in a speeding car,

A spring morning on the boulevard Malesherbes,

A rainy day,

At dawn before sleeping,

Tell yourself, I command your familiar spirit, that I alone
    loved you more and that it is sad you should not have
    known it.

Tell yourself one must not regret things: Ronsard before me and
    Baudelaire have sung the regrets of ladies old or
    dead who despised the purest love.

When you are dead

You will be lovely and still an object of desire.

I will be already gone, enclosed forever complete within your
    immortal body, in your astonishing image present forever
    among the constant marvels of life and of eternity, but
    if I live

Your voice and its tone, your look and its radiance,

Your fragrance and the scent of your hair and many other
    things beside will still live in me,

Who am neither Ronsard nor Baudelaire,

I who am Robert Desnos and who for having known and loved you,

Am easily their equal.

I who am Robert Desnos, to love you

Wanting no other reputation for my memory on the
    despicable earth.

OBSESSION

I bring you a bit of seaweed which was tangled with the sea
    foam and this comb
But your hair is more finely fixed than the clouds with the
    wind with celestial crimson glowing in them and are such that
    with quiverings of life and sobs twisting sometimes between my
    hands they die with the waves and the reefs of the strand
    so abundantly that we shall not soon again despair
    of perfumes and their flight at evening when this comb
    marks motionless the stars buried in their rapid and
    silky flow traversed by my hands seeking still at their root
    the humid caress of a sea more dangerous than the
    one where this seaweed was gathered with the froth scattered
    by a tempest
A star dying is like your lips
They turn blue as the wine spilled on the tablecloth
An instant passes with a mine's profundity
With a muffled complaint the anthracite falls in
    flakes on the town
How cold it is in the impasse where I knew you
A forgotten number on a house in ruins
The number 4 I think
Before too long I'll find you again near these china-asters

The mines make a muffled snoring
The roofs are strewn with anthracite
This comb in your hair like the end of the world
The smoke the old bird and the jay
There the roses and the emeralds are finished
The precious stones and the flowers
The earth crumbles and stars screech like
    an iron across mother-of-pearl
But your fine-fixed hair has the shape of a hand.

THREE STARS

I have lost all regret of evil with the years gone by.

I have won the sympathy of fish.

Full of seaweed, the palace sheltering my dreams is a shoal and
    also a territory of the stormy sky and not of the too-pale
    sky of melancholy divinity.

I have lost all the same the glory I despise.

I have lost everything save for love, love of love, love of,
    love of the queen of catastrophes.

A star speaks in my ear:

"Believe me, she's a lovely lady,

The seaweed obeys her and the sea itself changes to a crystal dress
    when she appears on the shore."

Beautiful crystal dress you resound at my name.

Vibrations, oh supernatural bell, perpetuate themselves in her being

Her breasts tremble from it.

The crystal dress knows my name,

The crystal dress said to me:

"Fury in you, love in you

Child of the numberless stars

Master of the wind alone and the sand alone

Master of the carillons of fate and eternity,

Master of everything at last save the love of his lovely one

Master of everything he has lost and a slave to what he still retains.

You will be the last guest at the round table of love.

The guests, the other thieves have taken the silver setting.

Wood cleaves, snow melts.

Master of everything save his lady's love.

FROM *LA LIBERTÉ OU L'AMOUR!* (*FREEDOM OR LOVE!*)

Corsair Sanglot was bored! Boredom had become his cause. He let it grow in silence, while he marveled every day that it was still increasing. It was Boredom, a large sunny square, lined with rectilinear colonnades, perfectly swept, perfectly clean, deserted. An unchanging hour had sounded in the corsair's life, and now he understood that boredom is synonymous with Eternity. In vain was he awakened every night by the pendulum's strange tick-tock in crescendo, its pulse filling the room where he lay, or either, toward midnight, a dark presence interrupted his dream. His pupils, dilated in the darkness, sought the person who must just have entered the building. But no one had forced the door and soon the calm sound of the clock mingled with the sleeper's breathing.

Corsair Sanglot felt a new esteem growing for himself and in himself. Since he had understood and accepted the monotony of Eternity, he advanced straight as a stick through adventures like slithering vines, not stopping his progress. A new exaltation had replaced his depression. A sort of reverse enthusiasm led him to consider the failure of his most cherished enterprises as totally without interest. Time's freedom had finally conquered him. He had merged with the patient minutes in sequence, each resembling the others.

It was boredom, the great square where he had one day ventured. It was three o'clock in the afternoon. Silence covered everything, even the sonorous buzzing of bumblebees and of the heated air. The colonnades cast their rectilinear shadows over the yellow ground. No passer-by, except on the other side of the square, which might have been two miles wide, a minuscule personage strolling with no definite goal. Corsair Sanglot noticed with terror that it was still three o'clock, that the shadows were immutably turned in the same direction. But this terror itself disappeared. The corsair accepted this pathetic hell at last. He knew that no paradise is permitted to the man who has taken account of the existence of the infinite, and he consented to remain, a sentinel eternally standing, on the square warmed and brilliantly lit by an immobile sun.

Who then has compared boredom to dust? Boredom and eternity are absolutely pure of any spot. A mental sweeper carefully surveys the despairing cleanliness. Did I say despairing? Boredom could no more engender despair than it could end in suicide. You who have no fear of death, try a little boredom. Death will henceforth be of no use to you. Once and for all, there will have been revealed to you the immobile torment and the distant perspectives of the mind freed of all sense of the picturesque and of all sentimentality. . . .

Let a tumultuous catastrophe topple the screens and the circumstances and there they are, grains of sand lost in a flat plain, united by the imaginary straight line which links every being to no matter what other being. Neither time nor space, nothing opposes these ideal relations. A life overturned, worldly constraints, earthly obligations, everything crumbles. Humans are nevertheless subject to the same arbitrary rolling of dice.

In the desert, lost, irremediably lost, the white-helmeted explorer finally realizes the reality of mirages and of unknown treasures, the dreamed-of fauna, the improbable flora which make up the sensual paradise where he will from now on evolve, a scarecrow without sparrows, a tomb without epitaph, a man without name, while, in a formidable displacement, the pyramids reveal the dice hidden under their weighty mass and pose once more the irritating problem of bygone fatality and of future destiny. As for the present, that beautiful eternal sky, it only lasts the time it takes to roll three dice over the town, a desert, a man, a white-hatted explorer, lost more in his vast intuition of eternal events than in the sandy expanse of the equatorial plain where his genius, that clever guide, led him step by step towards a revelation ceaselessly contradicting itself, causing him to stray from his own unrecognizable image, because of the position of his eyes or the lack of a point of comparison and the legitimate doubt entertained by a well-bred mind in regard to the mirrors whose worth cannot be proved, leading him to the chaotic image of the skies, of other beings, of inanimate objects and of the ghostly incarnations of his thoughts. . . . But finally I salute you, you whose existence grants a supernatural joy to my days. I have loved you, even because of your name. I have followed the path which your shadow traced in a melancholy desert where, behind me, I left all my friends. And now I find you once more when I thought I had fled you, and now the difficult sun of moral solitude illumines once more your visage and your body.

Farewell, world! And if I must follow you to the abyss, I shall follow you! Night after night I shall contemplate your eyes shining in the darkness, your face scarcely lit but visible in the clear night of Paris, thanks to the reverberation of electric lights in the rooms. I shall contemplate your tender eyes, touching in their dampness, until the dawn which, awaking the condemned man with the finger of a top-hatted ghost, will remind us that the hour of contemplation has passed, and that one must laugh and speak and suffer—not the difficult and consoling noontime sun over the deserted beaches, in the face of the stunning sky traversed by playful clouds, but rather the harsh law of constraint, the prison of elegance, the pseudo-discipline of life's relations and the inexpressible dangers of the fragmentation of dream by utilitarian existence.

And if I must follow you to the abyss, I shall follow you!

You are not the passerby, but the one who remains. The notion of eternity is linked with my love for you. No, you are not the passerby nor the strange pilot guiding the adventurer through the labyrinth of desire. You have opened to me the country of passion itself. I lose myself in your thought more surely than in a desert. And so, at the moment of writing these lines, I have not confronted your image with your "reality" in me. You are not the passerby but the eternal lover, whether you wish it or not. Grieving joy of the passion revealed by meeting you. I suffer, but my suffering is dear to me, and if I have some esteem for myself, it is because I have encountered you in my blind rush toward mobile horizons.

Marcel Duchamp

The Bride

In general, if the Bride motor must appear as an apotheosis of virginity, that is to say of ignorant desire, white desire (with a touch of malice) and if it (graphically) does not need to satisfy the laws of balance, nevertheless a gallows of shining metal might simulate the attachment of the maiden to her friends and relations. . . .

Basically the Bride is a motor. But more than being a motor transmitting its timid-power, she is the timid-power itself. This timid-power is a sort of essolene, essence of love. When distributed to the virtue-frailty cylinders, and within range of the sparks from her constant life, it causes the expansion of this virgin, now come to the state of her desire. . . .

This cinematic expansion is commanded by the electric undressing. . . .

This cinematic expansion expresses the moment of undressing. . . .

This cinematic expansion (commanded by the electric undressing) is the whole importance of the picture (graphically, as surface). It is, in general, the glory of the Bride, the whole of her splendid vibrations: graphically, it is not a question of symbolizing, in an ecstatic painting, this happy-desire state of the Bride; it is only that, more clearly, amidst all this expansion, the painting may be an inventory of the elements of this expansion, the elements of sexual life imagined by the Bride-desirous.

Marcel Duchamp playing chess. Photo: Arturo Schwarz. Reprinted by permission.

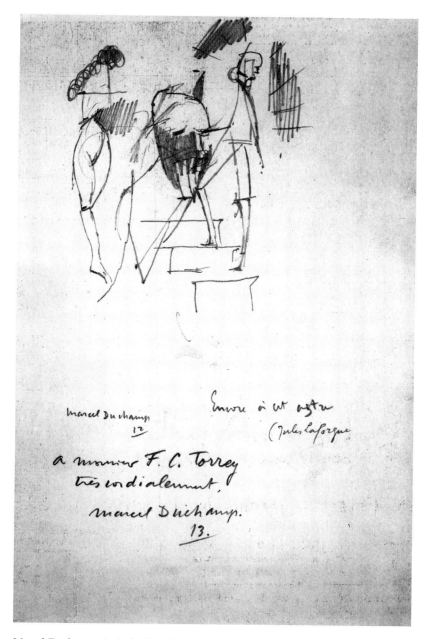

Marcel Duchamp, *Study for Nude Descending the Staircase: Encore à cet astre (To This Star Again, Jules Laforgue);* Philadelphia Museum of Art, Louise and Walter Arensberg Collection. Reproduced by permission of Philadelphia Museum of Art. © ARS.

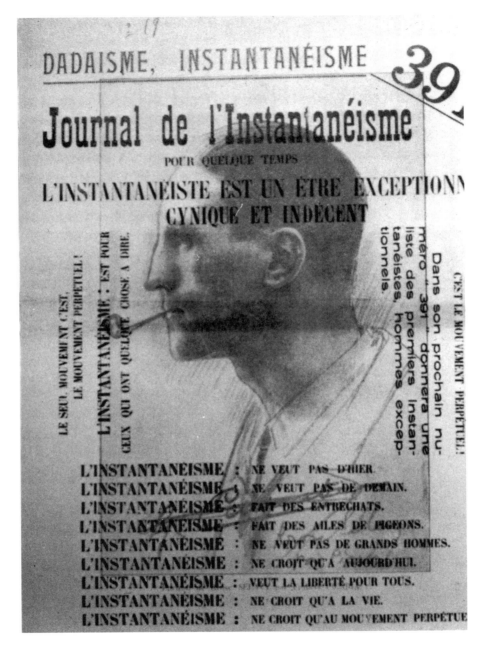

DADAISME, INSTANTANÉISME 39

Journal de l'Instantanéisme

POUR QUELQUE TEMPS

L'INSTANTANÉISTE EST UN ÊTRE EXCEPTIONN
CYNIQUE ET INDÉCENT

LE SEUL MOUVEMENT C'EST,
LE MOUVEMENT PERPÉTUEL!

L'INSTANTANÉISME : EST POUR
CEUX QUI ONT QUELQUE CHOSE A DIRE.

Dans son prochain nu-
méro "391" donnera une
liste des premiers instan-
tanéistes, hommes excep-
tionnels.

C'EST LE MOUVEMENT PERPÉTUEL!

L'INSTANTANÉISME : NE VEUT PAS D'HIER.
L'INSTANTANÉISME : NE VEUT PAS DE DEMAIN.
L'INSTANTANÉISME : FAIT DES ENTRECHATS.
L'INSTANTANÉISME : FAIT DES AILES DE PIGEONS.
L'INSTANTANÉISME : NE VEUT PAS DE GRANDS HOMMES.
L'INSTANTANÉISME : NE CROIT QU'A AUJOURD'HUI.
L'INSTANTANÉISME : VEUT LA LIBERTÉ POUR TOUS.
L'INSTANTANÉISME : NE CROIT QU'A LA VIE.
L'INSTANTANÉISME : NE CROIT QU'AU MOUVEMENT PERPÉTUE

Marcel Duchamp, *391: Journal de l'Instanéisme pour quelque temps (391: Instaneist Journal for Some Time);* with a picture of Marcel Duchamp.

JEAN-PIERRE DUPREY

NOTHING ON EARTH

Blackness has petrified the black of my soul, the black of my blood, the flesh of my pain; mud has redeemed me lightless and black has spurted forth to remove the mud.

I am alone, all alone at the end of myself, my solitude so extreme it extracts me from each abyss.

In what secret was I born?

Faith, you have found once more the white night of hope, your suffering continues you, your present suffers in you; as the sky on a certain day detaches itself from happiness, your soul drinks from the chalice of the purest thirst.

And yet

Each borrowing from happiness returns upon your voice at the break of every noon; every hour ripens its fruit, your inner mineral finds you again like a prayer of sleep at the foot of hell! Oh die, die, to let your second life escape!

In what secret was I born?

For over me there suffers the sorcery of the clock, over me words force themselves, over me you press the exitless orbit of night and my eye enlarges until it dies lamenting.

And here's the dawn of null passions.

What form is mine, what voice is mine, such a voice! Night opens the veins of my passion, when the task envenoms me, I find myself elsewhere. The evil of the dead spurts forth from my pride.

All alone I am reduced even to forgetting. The earth is this thought that always returns to the same murmur unimagining.

Whoever dies here takes with him the flesh of his sorrows.

Whoever lives loses his secret.

From what secret hope was I born? What love will be mine?

Elsa Baroness von Freytag-Loringhoven

Café du Dôme

For the love of Mike!
Look at that—
Marcelled—
Be-whiskered—
Be-spatted—
Pathetic—
Lymphatic—
Aesthetic—
Pigpink
Quaint—
Natty—
Saintkyk!

Garçon

Un pneumatic cross avec suctiondiscs topped avec thistle-tire . . . s'il vous plaît.

X-Ray

Nature causes brass to oxidize
People to congest—
By dull-radiopenetrated soil
Destined
Cosmic hand's dynamic gang
Polish—
Kill—
For fastidious
Brilliant boss' "idée fixe"
Sum total:
    Radiance

Claude Cahun, *Self-Portrait* (Untitled), 1928; gelatin silver print, 4½ × 3⅓ inches. San Francisco Museum of Modern Art. Photo courtesy of Robert Shapazian.

PAUL ELUARD

LADY LOVE

She is standing on my lids
And her hair is in my hair
She has the colour of my eye
She has the body of my hand
In my shade she is engulfed
As a stone against the sky

She will never close her eyes
And she does not let me sleep
And her dreams in the bright day
Make the suns evaporate
And me laugh cry and laugh
Speak when I have nothing to say

SECOND NATURE

In honor of the dumb the blind the deaf
Shouldering the great black stone
The things of time passing simply away

But then for the others knowing things by their names
The sear of every metamorphosis
The unbroken chain of dawns in the brain
The implacable cries shattering words

Man Ray, *Return to Reason,* from *La Révolution surréaliste* 1 (December 1924); J. Paul Getty Museum. © ARS.

Furrowing the mouth furrowing the eyes
Where furious colours dispel the mists of vigil
Set up love against life that the dead dream of
The low-living share the others are slaves
Of love as some are slaves of freedom.

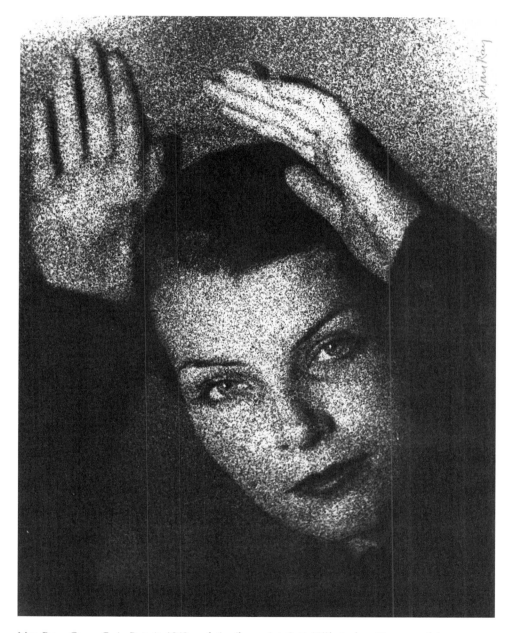

Man Ray, *Coarse Grain Portrait,* 1940s; gelatin silver print, 9 × 11^{11}/$_{16}$ inches. Courtesy of the J. Paul Getty Museum. © ARS.

Man Ray, *A L'Heure de l'observatoire: Les amoureux (At the Hour of the Observatory: The Lovers)*. © ARS.

THE QUEEN OF DIAMONDS

At an early age I opened my arms to purity. It was only a beating of wings in the sky of my eternity, a beating of the loving heart that beats in the breast that is vanquished. I could never fall again. Loving love. Verily, light is glare. I have sufficient store thereof within me to behold night, the whole night, all nights.

All virgins are different. I dream always of a virgin.

At school she is on the bench before me, she wears a black pinafore. When she turns round to ask me for the solution of a problem, the innocence of her eyes confounds me to such a degree that she, taking pity on my agitation, passes her arms about my neck.

Elsewhere, she leaves me. She boards a boat. We are scarcely acquainted, but her youth is so extreme that her kiss does not at all surprise me.

Or else, when she is ill, it is her hand that I hold in mine, until I die, until I awake.

I hasten with all the more speed to tryst with her as I fear lest other thoughts should kidnap me before I can reach her.

212

Once, the world was coming to an end and we were entirely unaware of our love. With slow fond movements of her head she sought my lips. That night for a moment I believed that I would bring her up to the light of day.

And it is always the same avowal, the same youthfulness, the same pure eyes, the same ingenuous gesture of the arms about my neck, the same caress, the same revelation.

But it is never the same woman.

The cards said that I shall meet her in life, but without recognizing her.

Loving love.

IDENTITIES

For Dora Maar

I see the fields the sea
Over them an equal light
There is no difference
Between the sleeping sand
The axe beside the wound
The body blooming in a sheaf
And the volcano of health

I see mortal and good
Pride pulling back its axe
And the body breathing its glory
In full disdain
I see mortal and desolate
The sand returning to its former bed
And health full of sleep
The volcano beating like a heart unveiled
And the boats swept clean by avid birds
Feasts with no morrow pains with no echo
Foreheads eyes the prey of shadows
Laughter like crossroads
Fields sea boredom silent towers endless towers
I see I read I forget
The open book of my closed shutters.

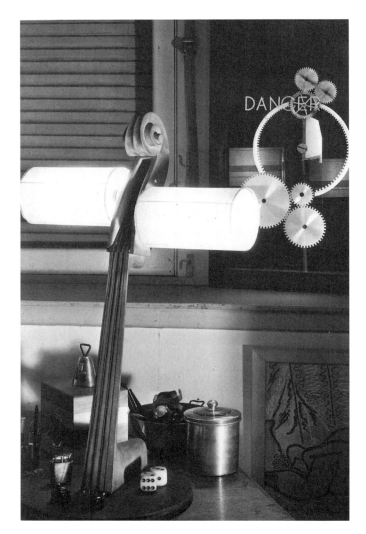

Man Ray, *Still Life for Nusch,* ca. 1925–30; gelatin silver print, $5^7/_{16} \times$ $3^1/_2$ inches. Courtesy of the J. Paul Getty Museum.

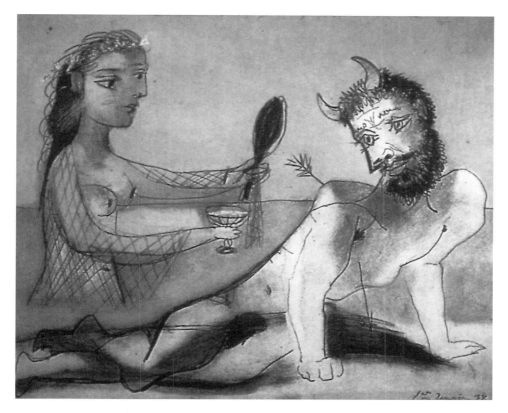

Pablo Picasso, *Wounded Faun and Woman,* 1938; oil and charcoal on canvas, 45 × 55 centimeters. Private collection. © ARS.

THE VICTORY AT GUERNICA

1
Lovely world of cottages
Of mines and fields

2
Faces good in the firelight good in the frost
In refusing the night the wounds and blows

3
Faces good for everything
Now emptiness fixes you
Your death will serve as example

4
Death the heart turned over

5
They made you pay your bread
Sky earth water sleep
And the misery
of your life

6
They said they wanted intelligence
They measured the strong judged the mad
Handed out alms split a cent in two
They greeted the corpses
They abounded in politeness

7
They persevere exaggerate are not of our world

8
Women children have the same treasure
Green springtime leaves and pure mild
And enduring
In their pure eyes

9
Women children have the same treasure
In their eyes
Men defend them as they can

10
Women children have the same red roses
In their eyes
Each shows his blood

11
Fear and courage to live and die
Death so hard and so easy

12
Men for whom this treasure was sung
Men for whom this treasure was spoiled

13
Real men for whom despair
Nourishes hope's devouring ardor
Let us open together the last bud of the future

14
Pariahs the death earth and ugliness
Of our enemies have a color
Drab as our night
We shall win out

DAWN

To Tristan Tzara

Dawn, fallen like a shower. The corners of the room are distant and solid. White space. Going and coming back without mixture, everything in order. Outside, in a corridor with dirty children, empty cases and meaningful, Paris for Paris, I discover. The money, the road, the trip with reddened eyes, the shiny skull. The day exists for me to learn to live, time. Ways—mistakes. A great action will become a bare sick honey, an evil game already syrup, a head drowned, a lassitude.

Thought such a simple joy, old mourning flower, no smell to it, I hold you in my two hands. My head has the form of thinking.

FROM *NUITS PARTAGÉES (Shared Nights)*

All the same, the light gave me lovely images, negatives, of our encounters. I likened you to beings whose variety was the only justification for the name, always the same, yours, that I wanted to call them by, beings that I transformed as I transformed you, in full light, as you transform the water of a spring by taking it in a glass, as you transform your hand putting it into that of another. The snow itself, which was behind us the painful screen on which the crystals of pledges were melting, even the snow was masked. In the caves of the earth, crystallized plants were seeking the cutaways of the exits.

Abyssal shadows, stretched towards a dazzling confusion, I did not perceive that your name was becoming illusory, that it was nowhere except on my mouth and that, little by little, the face of temptations appeared real, entire, alone.

It was then that I turned back to you.

Man Ray, *Filmstrips with Kiki,* 1922; gelatin silver print, 9⅜ × 7 inches. Courtesy of the J. Paul Getty Museum.

Max Ernst

The Hundred-Headless Woman

Crime or miracle: a complete man. The immaculate conception that failed, failed and failed again. Then the landscape changes three times, one, two and three, and the sky takes its hat off twice, one and two. Therefore the semi-fecund lamb dilating at will his abdomen becomes a ewe and Loplop, the best bird, brings the mighty repast to the street lamps in the basin of Paris. At the same time: the immaculate conception.

Extreme unction for extreme youth. The great St. Nicolas, followed by impeccable parasites, is led by his two lateral appendices. Remember: to disemboweled baby dove-cote is open, and when one sees a charming little insect with metallic hair, then the unconsciousness of the landscape becomes complete. Here in preparation the first touches of grace and games without issue. Bring the wash to a boil and increase the charm of transportation and the silence of bleeding wounds, and go on and on with the daytime-games, twilight and nocturnal. Odor of dried flowers—or I want to be Queen of Sheba. Germinal, my sister, the 100-headless woman. In a cage in the background: God the father. New series of daytime games, twilight and nocturnal. Continuation! Continuation! During the day angelic caresses retire to secret regions near the poles. Continuation! Fiesta coiled in bracelets around branches—Prometheus—the 100-headless woman opens her august sleeves. (This monkey, could he by chance be Catholic?) The exorbitant recompense: Perturbation, my sister, the 100-headless woman.

Without a word and in any weather: magic light. Without a word and in any weather: obscure lessons. Sunday phantoms shriek. Dear granny! In cadence more than one passing notary lets his voice drop. Suddenly Loplop reappears with the mouse's horoscope. When the third mouse sits, the body of a legendary grown-up woman flies by. Then let me introduce you to my uncle whose beard we love to tickle on Sunday afternoons. We had hardly strangled the uncle when the marvelous young women flew away. Call it witchcraft or some macabre joke, when suddenly a wide cry of the great diameter stifles the fruits and

Max Ernst, *La Ténébreuse (The Shadowy One),* 1930; photo: Lauros-Giraudon, Bibliothèque Nationale, Paris. Reproduced by permission. © ARS.

meat in their coffins. We'll begin then with a little family-party, with physical culture or the death that you prefer. Have a rapid look at the hibernians of this island and catch the numb train (registration of baggage is worth title of nobility). Open your bag, my brave man, catch the yacht and see the rising sap. Loplop the swallow passes. Nourishing themselves on liquid dreams and quite resembling sleeping leaves, here are my seven sisters together. Loplop the swallow returns.

Loplop the best bird chases in terror the last vestiges of the communal devotion, the sphinx and the daily bread visit the convent and God the father, his beard furrowed with lightning, continues in a subway catastrophe.

Loplop meets the belle jardinière.

Almost alone with phantoms and ants: Germinal, my sister, the 100-headed woman. The moon is beautiful. And the volcanic women with a menacing air raise and agitate the backpart of their bodies.

Nothing can stop the passing smile which accompanies the crimes from one sex to the other, the unlimited meetings and robust effervescences in the supposedly poisoned wheel, and public discharges at any place (all places equal). And Loplop, the best bird, made himself fleshless flesh to live amongst us. His smile will be elegantly sober. His arm will be drunkness, his sting fire. His look will descend straight into the debris of the parched cities.

• • •

Living alone on her phantom-globe, beautiful garbed in her dreams, Perturbation, my sister, the 100-headed woman. Every bloody revolt will make her live endowed with grace and truth. Her smile, the fire, will fall like black jelly and white rust on the flanks of the mountain, and her phantom-globe will find us at every halting place.

Lighter than air, powerful and isolated: Perturbation, my sister, the 100-headed woman.

But the waves are bitter, the truth will remain simple and gigantic wheels will furrow the bitter waves. And the images will descend even to the ground. Every Friday the titans will travel over our laundries in a rapid flight with many hooks. And nothing will be more common than a titan in a restaurant. In the blindness of the wheelwrights we will find the germs of very precious visions. The blacksmiths, grey, black or volcanic, will turn in the air over the forges and forge crowns even larger as they rise higher.

More powerful than vulcans, light and isolated, Perturbation, my sister, the 100-headless woman. Perturbation, elevation, diminishment. Rumbling of drums in the stones, dilapidations, Aurora and a phantom excessively meticulous. Tranquillity of ancient and future assassinations. Pieces of conviction.

The departure for the miraculous fishing-voyage.

More isolated than the sea, always light and strong, Perturbation, my sister, the 100-headless woman.

Here is thirst, that resembles me, the miraculous fishing, clamors and love, the jubilant and gracious thunder, the master of the night, the sea of serenity, the elegant gesture of the drowned, serenity, the sea of jubilation.

The night howls in its hiding-place and approaches our eyes like wounded flesh.

A door opens itself backwards by the night of silence. A bodiless body places himself parallel to his body and shows us—like a plantomless phantom with particular saliva—the matrix for postage stamps. Two bodiless bodies place themselves parallel to their bodies, falling out of beds and curtains—like phantomless phantoms.

The 100-headless woman would smile in her sleep so that Loplop might smile at the phantoms.

Loplop, drunk with fright and fury, recovers his birdshead and remains immobile for 12 days at both sides of the door. Then the forest opens itself before an accomplished couple followed by a blind body.

To evoke the seventh age which succeeds the ninth birth, Germinal of the invisible eyes, the moon and Loplop trace ovals with their heads. At this moment the phantoms enter a period of voracity. Sometimes naked, sometimes clad in thin jets of fire, they make the geysers spout with the probability of bloodrain and with the vanity of the dead. To the glamour of their scales they prefer the dust of carpets, to the masturbation of fresh leaves, the pious lies. But they escape with fear as soon as the rumbling of drums is heard under the water. They pick up some dry crackers in the hollows of the giant's causeway. The giant's causeway is a pile of cradles.

Therefore the phantom remains who speculates with the vanity of death, the phantom of repopulation. All the doors are doors and the butterflies start to sing. After a slight hesitation, you will identify among these phantoms: Pasteur in his workroom, the monkey who is a future policeman, catholic or stockbroker, Phantômas, Dante and Jules Verne, Cézanne and Rosa Bonheur, Mata Hari, St. Lazarus gloriously resuscitated from the dromedary's droppings.

Let it hereby be known, that since the memory of mankind the 100-headless woman has never had relations with the phantom of repopulation. She will never have. Rather would she macerate herself in morning dew and nourish herself with iced violets.

Let us thank Satanas and be happy for the sympathy he has shown us (bis).

Eyeless eye, the 100-headless woman keeps her secret (ter).

Eyeless eye, the 100-headless woman and Loplop go back to the savage stage and cover the eyes of their faithful birds with fresh leaves. God the almighty tries in vain to separate light from darkness.

Eyeless eye, the 100-headless woman keeps her secret.

She keeps her secret.

She keeps it.

Rome—Rome—Paris—marsh of dreams.

Ask the monkey: who is the 100-headless woman? In the church-fathers manner he will answer you: It suffices me to look at her and I know who she is. It suffices for you to demand of me an explanation, and I no longer know.

Loplop the sympathetic annihilator and ancient best bird shoots some elderballs into some debris of the universe.

END AND CONTINUATION

Jean Ferry

Kafka or "The Secret Society"

Joseph K———, around his twentieth year, learned the existence of a secret, very secret society. It truly resembles no other association of this kind. It is very difficult for some people to join. Many, who ardently desire to, never succeed. On the other hand, others are in it without even knowing. One is, by the way, never quite sure of belonging; there are many people who think themselves member of this secret society, and who are not at all. It makes no difference that they have been initiated; they are members even less than many who do not even know of the society's existence. Indeed, they have undergone the test of a bogus initiation, intended to throw people off who are not worthy to really be initiates. But to the most authentic members, to those who have attained the highest grade in the hierarchy of this society, even to those it is never revealed whether their successive initiations are valid or not. It can even happen that a member has attained some real status, in the normal way, following authentic initiations, and that, afterward, without having been warned, he is submitted to bogus initiations only. The object of endless discussion among members is to find out if it is better to be admitted to a low but authentic grade than to occupy an exalted but illusory position. In any case, no one is sure of the stability of his grade.

In fact the situation is even more complicated, because certain applicants are admitted to the highest grades without having undergone any test, others even without having been informed. And to tell the truth, there is not even any need to make application; there are people who have been given very advanced initiations who did not even know of the secret society's existence.

The powers of the higher members are limitless, and they carry within a powerful emanation from the secret society. Their mere presence suffices, for example, even if they do not show themselves, to transform a harmless gathering, like a concert, or an anniversary dinner, into a meeting of the secret society. These members are responsible for making, upon all sessions at which they have been present, secret reports that are examined closely by other members of the same rank: there is in this way a perpetual exchange of reports among the membership, permitting the highest authorities in the secret society to keep the situation well in hand.

However high, however far initiation goes, it never goes so far as to reveal to the initiate the aim pursued by the secret society. But there are always traitors, and for a long time it has been no mystery to anyone that this aim is to keep things secret.

Joseph K—— was very frightened to learn this secret society was so powerful, spreading so wide that he could perhaps, without knowing it, be shaking hands with the most powerful of its members. But unfortunately, one morning, emerging from a painful sleep, he lost his first-class ticket on the Métro. This bit of bad luck was the first link in a chain of jumbled contradictory circumstances that brought him into contact with the secret society. Later, so as to protect himself, he was obliged to take steps to be admitted to this formidable organization. That happened a long time ago, and it is not yet known where he stands in this endeavor.

ALBERTO GIACOMETTI

POEM IN SEVEN SPACES

two golden claws   a drop of blood

                       white spiral   the yellow meadow
                       of wind on   of madness
                       two breasts
                           Crying out

                       three black horses galloping

the feet of the   all the objects have gone far away
chairs breaking   and the sound of a woman's step
with a dry sound   and the echo of her laugh leave
                                                       The ear

The Brown Curtain

no human face is
as strange to me even
more a face from having
looked at it so much it
closed itself in everywhere
on steps of unknown stairs.

Grass Coal

I turn in the emptiness and I look at the space and the stars at high noon running through the liquid silver surrounding me, and Bianca's head, looking at me slightly tipped back in the echo of her voice and the steps of feathers near the red wall in ruins.

I return to the constructions that amuse me and that live in their surreality; a lovely palace; the parquet of white dice with black and red dots you walk on, the columns like rockets, their top in the air laughing and the precise and pretty mechanisms that are used for nothing.

I fumble all around me trying to grasp in the emptiness the invisible white thread of the marvelous that vibrates and from which there escape rats and dreams, with the sound of a stream running over small precious living stone.

It gives life to life and the shining games of the needles and of the dice spinning about take place alternately, and the drop of blood on the skin of milk, but a sharp cry suddenly rises that sets the air to quivering and the white earth to trembling.

All of life in the marvelous ball which envelops us and shines at the turning near the fountain.

I seek women with light step and polished face, mute, singing, mute, their heads a little to one side, the same ones that existed in the boy who, all in new clothes, was crossing a meadow in a space where time forgot the time; he stopped at one point and looked inside and outside at so many marvels. Oh! Palace palace!

YESTERDAY, THE QUICKSANDS

When I was a child, between four and seven, I only saw in the outside world the objects that could give me pleasure. Above all, stones and trees, and rarely more than one object at a time. I remember that for at least two summers, I saw in my surroundings only a large stone that was some way from the village, just this stone and the objects that directly related to it. It was a monolith of a golden color, opening at its base on to a cavern: its underneath was hollowed out by water. The entrance was low and long, scarcely as tall as we were then. In some places the inside was hollowed out more deeply until it seemed to form at the bottom a second little cavern. It was my father who, one day, showed us this monolith. A great discovery; right away I considered this stone a friend, a being animated with the best possible intentions concerning us; calling us, smiling at us, like someone whom one might have known before, even loved, and whom one might find again with an infinite joy and surprise. Immediately, it was the only thing that interested us. From that day, we spent all our mornings and afternoons there. We were about five or six children, always the same ones, who never separated. Every morning, upon waking, I looked for the stone. From the house I saw it in its every detail, even saw like a thread, the little path leading to it; everything else was vague and lacking consistency, like the air sticking to nothing. We would take that path without ever leaving it, never stepping beyond the terrain that immediately surrounded the cavern. Our first concern, after having discovered the stone, was to set a limit to the entrance. It must be an opening just exactly wide enough to let us through. But I was at the peak of my delight when I could crouch in the little cavern at the bottom; I could scarcely contain myself; all my desires were realized. Once, I can't remember by what happenstance, I went in further than usual. A little after, I found myself on a hill. Before me, a little lower, in the midst of the underbrush, there rose an immense black stone in the form of a narrow and pointed pyramid whose walls fell almost vertically. I can scarcely express the feeling of resentment and confusion that I felt in that moment. The stone immediately struck me like a living being, hostile, menacing. It was menacing everything: us, our games, and our cavern. Its existence was intolerable to me, and I instantly felt—unable to make it disappear—that I had to ignore it, forget it, and speak of it to no one. Nevertheless, I approached it, but with the feeling of giving myself over to something reprehensible, secret, unsavory. I touched it just with one hand, with revulsion and terror. I went around it, trembling to discover some entrance to it. Not a trace of any cave, which made it all the more intolerable to me, but nevertheless I felt some satisfaction: an opening in this stone could have complicated everything, and I already felt the desolation of our cave if we could have been interested in another one at the same time. I distanced myself from this black stone, never spoke of it to the other children, I ignored it and never went back to see it.

At the end of the same epoch, I awaited the snow impatiently. I was not easy in my mind until the day when I figured there was enough of it—and many times I figured it too soon—to go all alone, carrying a bag and armed with a pointed stick, in a meadow at some distance from the village (it was very secret work). There I tried to dig a hole just large enough to go into it. At the surface you should be able to see only a round opening, as small as possible and nothing else. I was going to spread out the bag in the bottom of the hole, and once inside, I imagined this place very hot and black; I believed I would take a great joy in this . . . I often felt in advance the illusion of this pleasure during the preceding days; I spent my time representing to myself the whole technique of this construction, I mentally accomplished all the work in its least details; each gesture was thought out in advance, I imagined the moment when I would have to take precautions to avoid everything falling. I was completely given over to the pleasure of seeing my hole completely made and entering it. I would have liked to spend the whole winter there, alone, closed in, and I thought with regret that I would have to return to the house to eat and sleep. I must say that in spite of all my efforts and also probably because other conditions were unfavorable, my desire was never realized.

The first times I went to school, the first country that seemed marvelous to me was Siberia. There, I imagined myself in the middle of an infinite plain, covered with a gray snow: there was never any sun, and it was always just as cold. The plain was cut off on one side, rather far from me, by a forest of pines, a monotonous and black forest. I looked at this plain and this forest through the little window of an *isab* (the name was essential to me) in which I was, and there it was very warm. That was all there was to it. But very often I transported myself mentally to this place.

As a recurring mental imagining of the same kind, I remember that at the same time, for months, I couldn't go to sleep at night without imagining having first crossed, at dusk, a dense forest and having arrived at a gray castle which rose up in the furthest and most hidden spot. There I killed, without their being able to defend themselves, two men, one of whom, about seventeen, always seemed to me pale and terrified, and the other who wore on his left side a suit of armor, where something shone like gold. I raped, after having torn off their dress, two women, one of whom was thirty-two, completely dressed in black, with a face like alabaster, then her daughter, about whom there floated white veils. The whole forest resounded with their cries and their moans. I killed them also, but very slowly (it was night by this time) often beside a lake with stagnant green water, just in front of the castle. Each time with slight variation. Then I burned down the castle and, happy at last, went to sleep.

JULIEN GRACQ

ROSS' BARRIER

It is a shattering experience to see the rise of day over the horizon of the great ice bank, at the hour when the sun of the southern latitudes lays out far and wide its highways over the sea. Miss Jane was carrying her umbrella, and I, an elegant repeating rifle. At each glacier pass, we kissed each other in mint crevasses and postponed at our own good pleasure the moment of watching the sun open, with red bullets, a road to the ice-spangled castle modeled after the one at Chantilly. We chose to skirt the sea coast, there where the cliff breathes regularly with the tide, whose sweet, pachydermic pitching predisposed us to love-making. The waves beat upon ice walls of blue and green snows and, rolling into the coves, threw giant crystal flowers at our feet; but the approach of day was especially sensitive to that hem of phosphorus which ran along the festoons of their crests, like nocturnal capitals suddenly afloat over the slack waters of their own high sea. At Cape Devastation, night-blue edelweiss grew in the ice fissures and we were always sure of seeing renewed, from day to day, a fresh provision of those marine birds' eggs for which Jane claimed the power to clear the complexion. It became a rite with me, daily renewed, to pluck this puerile adage from her mouth with my lips. On occasion the clouds veiling the foot of the cliff foreshadowed overcast afternoon skies, and Jane would ask me in a small voice whether I had forgotten to wrap the Cheshire cheese sandwiches. The cliff gradually became higher, and very chalky from sun: this was Desolation Point, and at a sign from Jane, I spread the cover over the fresh ice. We lay there a long time, listening to the savage seahorses beating the ice-caverns with their breasts. The horizon of the offing was a semi-circle of diamond-set blue which subtended the ice wall, and where occasionally vapors took birth, detached themselves from the sea like white sails—while Jane recited verses to me from Lermontov. I could have spent entire afternoons, my hand clasping hers, following the croaking of sea birds and flinging pieces of ice, listening to them fall in the chasm, while Jane counted off the seconds, her tongue thrust out studiously like a school girl's. At such times we hugged each other so long and close that in the melted snow, a single gully was hollowed out, narrower than a baby's cradle, and, when we got up, the cover between the two teat-like mounds suggested Asiatic asses, saddled with snow and descending the mountain slopes.

Then the blue of the sea deepened and the cliff became violet. It was the hour when the brusque cold of twilight detaches, from the barrier, crystal castle towns which are crushed into snow powder with the report of an exploding planet, and which, under the Cyclopean volute of a blue wave, give back to sight some steamer with its belly gashed by dark algae, or restore to the hearing the heavy snorting of bathing plesiosaurs. For us alone, this cannonade of a world's end flared up by gradual degrees to the outermost horizon, like a Waterloo of the solitudes—and for some time, the fallen night, intensely cold, was pierced in the great silence of phantom and distant gushings by huge geysers of white plumes, but I had already clasped Jane's icy hand, and we were absorbed in the light of pure Antarctic stars.

GEORGES HENEIN

HEALTHY REMEDIES

Friends whose names smell powdery
friends to pick up from the gutter
friends named like cosmetics
friends whose portraits rush away
get some lovely dogs
some chains of ignorance
some mighty weapons
some holy prayer
some unwanted musicians
some stabs in the back
some lengthy absences
in necessity's chalet
in the lascivious city
the city in ashes
the city in tears
the city in red
where fingernails flourish inside
and nerves outside
where flowers flourish only in mouths
friends alike and gone before your time
get some long days of rainfall
and may your conscience envy
nothing in that iron to sell

but keep quiet!
in the distance you hear a great noise of eyebrows
by chance they are thieves
coming to free us from thieves' fear
pirates coming to free us from the storm
it's what's AFTER US coming to free us from the DELUGE.

RADOVAN IVŠIĆ

FROM *KING GORDOGAIN*

Scene 3

The Fool.

FOOL: That was a great idea to send them off the wrong way, and well might you say, "Fool—the Fool, that's me—Fool, you're the clever one". Because, truth to tell, the palace of Gordogain is over this way, and those peasants will run into him right under the *jib, jib,* I mean, under the gibbets. You are going to be trebly happy today, my Fool. You've come up with three peasants. Would anyone have believed there were three peasants left alive in my kingdom, my Fool? No, I would never have believed it. And yet, there really are three left, didn't you see them? Why yes, I saw them. My eyes really prodded them to make sure. Oh, seriously then, you actually saw them. But didn't you overlook something? What about the wood? Why didn't you touch wood when you saw the peasants? You'll not be happy, you're never happy! When will you ever see a peasant again? You said as much (*pointing to Gordogain's palace*): "Every raindrop makes a shower." That's what you told him, but do you think his ears were open? No. What were they doing? They certainly weren't opening up! Splatt, that's not bad. Splatt and splatt, that makes splatt–splatt. Splatt and splatt and splatt, that makes splatt–splatt–splatt, and that brings good luck! But not splatt–splatt and splatt, oh no. No! What else did you tell him? I told him: "It's the same with cows". Same with cows? Yes, with cows. A cow always has big big eyes, and then it has a calf. If a cow is all you need, you can splatt the calf. What you'll have left is the cow and its big big eyes, because a cow always has big big eyes, and then, a little later, once more it will have a calf. If a cow's all you need, you can splatt the calf. You'll still have the cow and its big big eyes. But then there's the calf. If the calf is all you need, you can splatt the cow. And one day, you look closer, it's no longer a calf, it's a cow. Once again you have a cow, big big eyes, a cow always has big big eyes. And if it has big big eyes, it will also have a calf that you can splatt. And if, right at the outset, you had splatted both cow *and* calf, why, you'd have been a right ninny. Did you explain that to him properly? Yes, but he never listened. And what happened then? How many peasants did there used to be in this kingdom? As many as there are grains of sand in the desert. And how many peasants are there left in this kingdom? Less than there are fresh streams in the desert. What's new? Since there are no peasants left, how did Gordogain get through the day yesterday?

Toyen, collage for Radovan Ivšić, *Le Roi Gordogain;* courtesy of Annie Le Brun and Radovan Ivšić.

What was there to do? Why, he splatted all his friends: the Royal Earsnipper, Kersplatt! The Royal Eyegouger, Kersplatt! And you, Fool, aren't you scared of getting splatted? Is it me you're asking? Yes, Fool, you! You want to know if I'm scared? No, I'm not scared. Do you want to know why I'm not scared? I'll tell you why. A fool's never out of luck. That's why I'm not scared in the least. Oh, so you believe in happiness, do you? I do. Do you have any idea what happiness is? No, I don't. Happiness is a bird which has trouble landing but which can take off in a trice. Fool, look over there! Where, where? Over there, where my finger's pointing. Whom can you see? Whom can I see? And you, whom can you see? I can see Teenyteen. You can see Teenyteen? Is he still alive then? Oh yes, he's alive all right, upon my life, that's him, in person.

• • •

Act Five

Scene 1
The Fool.

FOOL: What the cradle has rocked, the spade must dig under. Ah yes, ah yes, Fool, such is life. One day you're alive and kicking and the next . . . The next, you're gone. The wise man told me that very thing. What did the wise man tell you? Dust goes marching over dust. That's what he told me. I don't understand. But of course, it's very simple. You sprinkle water on a little egg and there you are: tsip, tsip, tsip, an oak-tree starts to sprout! Where does it come from? Straight up out of the dust. The storm knocks it over, and tsip, tsip, tsip, the oak tree is gone. Gone where? Into the dust. Do you think a goat is anything other than dust, just because it goes *mee? Mee*—and it's all over! No more *mee*. The wind blows it all away. There's nothing of the well-behaved child about life. It goes jumping into a speck of dust, changes it into a flower or a fish; whereupon the speck of dust thinks: aye, aye, I'm a flower; aye, aye, I'm a fish. And, then, with a hop, life takes another jump, runs off, picks up a new speck of dust, just when you least expect it. Naturally it won't stay there long either. It's as faithless as the waterfall that never lingers more than a moment on its rock. Fool, you've spoken some words of wisdom today.—I've spoken some words of wisdom today?—Yes. When a fool starts to speak words of wisdom, then . . . —What?—Do you know what?—No.—Then he's bound to die, that self-same day; that's what they say.—What are you trying to tell me? Poor Fool! Yes, yes, if I start speaking words of wisdom, I shall die the self-same day. But let's have a think: why should I die today, exactly? It's surely Teenyteen who is bound to die today. Look over here! That's a pretty gibbet they've got ready for him. Isn't that a pretty gibbet? Fine indeed, I should say so! Teenyteen is going to dangle up there and wriggle about like a worm sliced in two. It's Teenyteen who is going to be hanged, not you. You hear someone saying that someone is going to be hanged, and then you start imagining that someone is you. You're talking now as if it were the first time in my life I'd seen a gibbet.—Are you joking?—No, I am not joking. If I've spoken some words of wisdom, I'm surely bound to die.—Don't you believe these stupid ideas! Wait a minute! I've a way out of this puzzle! All I need to work out is whether I've actually spoken any words of wisdom!

Toyen, collage for Radovan Ivšić, *Le Roi Gordogain;* courtesy of Annie Le Brun and Radovan Ivšić.

Frida Kahlo

Letter to Jacqueline Lamba

Letter:

Since you wrote to me, on that clear, distant day, I have wanted to explain to you that I can't get away from the days, or return in time to that other time. I have not forgotten you—the nights are long and difficult.

The water. The ship and the dock and the parting which made you appear so small to my eyes, framed in that round port-hole, and you gazing at me so as to keep me in your heart. Everything is untouched. Later, came the day's new of you.

Today, I wish my sun could touch you. I tell you, your eyeball is my eyeball, the puppet characters all arranged in their large glass rooms, belong to us both. Yours is the huipil with magenta ribbons. Mine the ancient squares of your Paris, above all, the magnificent—[Place] des Vosges. so forgotten and so firm.

Snail shells and the bride-doll, is yours too—I mean, it is you. Her dress is the same one she wouldn't take off on the day of the wedding to no-one, when we found her half asleep on the dirty sidewalk of some street. My skirts with their lace flounces and the antique blouse I always wore xxxxxxxx paint the absent portrait of only one person. But the color of your skin, of your eyes and your hair change with the winds in Mexico. ~~The death of the old man pained us so much that we talked and spent that day together~~. You too *know* that all my eyes see, all I touch with myself, from any distance, is Diego. The caress of fabrics, the color of colors, the wires, the nerves, the pencils, the leaves, the dust, the cells, the war and the sun, everything experienced in the minutes of the non-clocks and the non-calendars and the empty non-glances, is *him*. You felt it, that's why you let that ship take me away from Le Havre where you never said good-bye to me.

I will write to you with my eyes, always. Kiss xxxxx the little girl . . .

Frida Kahlo, *Self-Portrait with Monkey,* 1943; oil on canvas, 32¹/₈ × 24³/₄ centimeters. Art Resource. © ARS.

FROM "CHANT III"

A red light, flag of vice, hung from the extremity of a triangle, its swinging carcass whipped by the four winds, above a massive, worm-eaten door. A filthy corridor, smelling of human thigh, gave on a close wherein the cocks and hens, thinner than their own wings, searched for feed. On the wall serving on the west side as boundary for the close there were diverse openings, parsimoniously placed, barred by grilled wickets. Covered with moss the main building, which without doubt had once been a convent, now served with the rest of the structure as an abode for all such women who would show, daily to those who might enter, the interior of their vagina for a sum of gold. I stood upon a bridge, the piles of which were immersed in the stagnant water of a moat. From this elevation I could observe the least detail of the architecture and arrangement of building and yard . . . I too wished to enter, but descending from the bridge I was arrested by an inscription in Hebrew characters carved upon the entablature of a column, thus: "Do not enter here, ye who cross this bridge. Crime dwells herein as well as vice; for one day his friends awaited in vain the return of a young man who had passed this fatal threshold." Curiosity, however, obtaining over fear, in little time I had arrived before a wicket with a grating of solid bars intersecting one another closely. Wishing to observe the interior through this thick sieve, at first I could see nothing, but it was not long before I was able to distinguish several objects in the obscure chamber, thanks to the ray of a setting sun soon to disappear beneath the horizon. My attention was immediately engaged by a sort of blond staff, made of cones fitted one within the other. This staff was moving! It ran about the room! Its exertions were such as to shake the floor; it attempted to breach the wall in the manner of a battering ram set in motion against a besieged city. Its efforts, however, were useless, the wall was of freestone, and when the staff would strike the wall I perceived how it would bend like a steel blade and rebound like a rubber ball. Assuredly this staff was not of wood. I perceived also that it rolled and unrolled itself easily, like an eel. Although as tall as a man, it did not bear itself upright. Sometimes it tried to do so, showing one of its ends at the grating. It made impetuous leaps, fell back to the floor, failing to batter down the obstacle. I set myself to examine it more attentively and perceived that it was a hair! After considerable struggle with the matter that surrounded it as a prison, it crossed the room to the bed, where, its root resting on the carpet, it leaned its end on the pillow. After several moments, during which I was aware of stifled sobs, it raised its voice and spoke thus: "My master has forgotten me in this room; he will not return to fetch me. He arose from this bed, whereon I rest, and he combed his perfumed hair, never dreaming that meanwhile I had fallen to the ground. Yet had he stooped to pick me up I would not have considered such an act of simple justice as surprising. He has abandoned me, confined in this room, after he has passed a night wrapped in the arms of a woman . . ." And I would ask myself who might his master be! And I would press my eye more avidly to the grating! . . . "While all Nature slept in chastity, he coupled himself with a degraded woman in a lascivious and impure embrace. He so debased himself as to allow her despicable cheeks with their habitual impudence to approach his august visage. He did not blush, but I, I blushed for him. It appeared certain that he thought himself fortunate sleeping the night with such a spouse. Astounded by the majestic aspect of her guest, the woman seemed to experience incomparable delights, and embraced him with frenzy . . . " And I would ask myself who might his master be! And I would press my eye more avidly to the grating! . . . "Meanwhile I felt poison pustules growing more numerous by reason of his unaccustomed ardour after pleasures of the flesh, until my root was surrounded by their mortal malice which absorbed the generative substance of my life. At the very moment when corporeal desire attained to its paroxysm of fury, I perceived my root to crumple as a soldier wounded by a shot. The flame of my life was extinguished, and, detached from his illustrious head, I fell to the ground like a dead branch, without courage, without force, without vitality, but with a profound pity for him to whom I belonged; but with an eternal sorrow for his self-willed error! . . . " And I would ask myself who might his master be! And I would press my eye more avidly to the grating! . . . "When he was satiated with that woman he wished to tear out her muscles, one by one; but, as she was a woman, he spared her, preferring to inflict suffering upon one of his own sex. He called in from a neighboring cell a young man who had come to the house to pass several careless moments with one of the women, enjoining him to place himself a pace before his eyes. It had been long that I had lain on the floor. Not having the strength to lift myself up on my burning root what they did I could not see. All I know is that scarcely had the young man come within reach of his hand than shreds of flesh began falling to the foot of the bed, and came to place themselves by my side. They told me in an undertone that the nails of my master had detached them from the shoulders of the adolescent! . . . " And I would ask myself who might his master be! And I would press my eye more avidly to the grating! . . . "Then he, who should have considered his dignity and his justice, arose painfully. Alone, sombre, disgusted, and hideous! . . . He dressed slowly. The nuns, entombed for centuries in the catacombs of the convent, rudely awakened by the noises of that dreadful night, took him by the hand, forming a mournful circle about him. While he cast about for remnants of his ancient splendor, washing his hands with spittle and drying them on his hair (better to wash with spittle than not to wash at all, after an entire night passed in vice and crime), they intoned prayers of lamentation for the dead. Indeed, the young man had been unable to survive the torments visited upon him by a divine hand, and even as the nuns chanted, his agony was ended . . . " Remembering the inscription on the column I understood the fate of the pubescent dreamer for whom his friends waited, and still were waiting, each day since his disappearance . . . And I would ask myself who might his master be! And I would press my eye more avidly to the grating! . . . "The walls divided to let him pass; the nuns, seeing him take flight into the air with wings hidden until then beneath his emerald robe, silently returned to beneath the cover of their tomb. He has left for his celestial dwelling, and I am abandoned here; that is not just . . . " The hair was silent . . . And I would ask myself who might his master be! And I would press my eye more avidly to the grating! . . . Forthwith the thunder burst; a phosphorescent gleam pervaded the room. In spite of myself I recoiled, who knows by what prophetic instinct. Although distant from the grille I could distinguish another voice, cringing and soft with the fear of being overheard: "Don't leap about so! Hush . . . be still . . . if someone should hear. I will put you back with the other hairs, but wait until the sun has set, so that night may keep secret your path . . . I haven't forgotten you, but someone might see you leave and I would be compromised. Oh! if you knew how I have suffered since that moment! Don't leap about so! Hush . . . be still . . . if someone should hear you. I will put you back with the other hairs, but wait until the sun has set, so that night may keep secret your path . . . The nuns of the convent-lupanar could not return to sleep; they roam about the close, gesticulating like automatons, crushing the buttercups and lilacs with their feet; become insane with indignation, but not so mad as to forget the cause which engendered the malady in their brain . . . There they come, clothed in their white shrouds; they do not speak, each holds the other by the hand. Their hair falls in disorder about their naked shoulders; a bouquet of black flowers reposes on each breast. Nuns, return to your vault; the night is not yet here; this is but twilight . . . Oh hair, you see how from all sides I am assailed by the unleashed furies of my own depravity! . . . Don't leap about so! . . . be still . . . if someone should hear. I will put you back with the other hairs, but wait until the sun has set, so that night may keep secret your path." He paused a moment; and although I saw him not at all, I understood that a wave of emotion lifted his breast as a gyrating cyclone might lift a family of whales. Divine breast, soiled in a day by the bitter contact of the teats of a woman without shame! Royal soul, delivered in a moment of oblivion to the crab of debauch, to the octopus of weakness of character, to the shark of abjection of the individual, to the boa of absence of morale, and to the monstrous snail of idiocy! The hair and his master embraced warmly, as two friends who meet after a long absence . . . I heard the hair humbly pardon his master for his sequestration, since his master had acted from prudence and not from thoughtlessness; and the last pale ray of the sun which had lighted my eyelids, retired into the ravines of the mountain. Turning towards the hair I saw him fold up like a winding-sheet . . . Don't leap about so! Hush . . . be still . . . if someone should hear! He will put you back with the other hairs. And now that the sun has set, crawl away, both of you, old cynic and gentle hair, away from the lupanar, while night, throwing its shade about the convent, keeps secret your furtive path across the plain . . . Departing, I paused at the bridge. Erasing the original inscription, I replaced it, thus: "It is painful, as a dagger, to keep such a secret in one's heart; but I swear never to reveal that which I witnessed when first I entered this dread inclosure."

ANNIE LE BRUN

TWELFTH RING

My love, I've dared to speak just of me in order to cry with you that tragedy abounds through the lack of means, that the comic strips of violence are only the little sounding-balloons of a fool's bother.

You are always free to slam the portals of your eyelids for other departures. I won't hold you back with any proselytizing chewing-gum, I won't ever wound you with the flamethrower of an initiate refusing to breathe. All doors are open like my legs at your approach, swinging open like my dress in its frenzy by the sea.

I have followed you, like others, in the night along the river, because I had the impression that evening that some—and I'm not saying we—could give life to all the city's desires, still trembling disarmingly in spite of everything under the asphalt.

I'm not afraid, I am calmly going down the steps losing their precision under the eyes of day, but certain beforehand that the advancing of each circle of water around my leg upsets the thermic system of an individuality easily admitted. (Don't laugh, you on the shore; once in the current, you'll see that the municipal buoys don't help at all.)

My love, I'm not following you, perhaps I am sweeping you along, myself or some women whose faces you find at the meeting of rivers. I don't hope that their reflection speaks to you only of me. I am not claiming to go to your ultimate depths when every notion of limit takes its basis on the scabs of a shamefully Christian nonsense; it's only the *incongruous relation* of multiple presences around you that will violate you as you wish. From you, from the others, from myself, I want the fire it is always possible to spark forth from between the stones of time; but the fire is no one's, the fire devours the relations of cause to effect, will always find itself in the gazes that we don't yet know.

Oh you dissatisfied of every kind, don't warm up to the idea of a new mode of violence that you could wear, without danger, in town as in the country, and throw away, after using it, at the bottom of the coffin-beds of some up-to-date individualism, like a Great Inquisitor of desire set free.

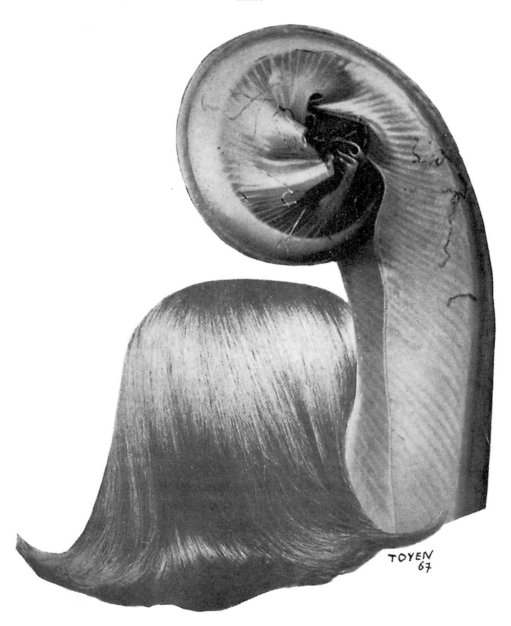

Toyen, two collages and a dry point etching, 1967, for Annie Le Brun, *Sur-le-champ*. Courtesy of Annie Le Brun and Radovan Ivšić.

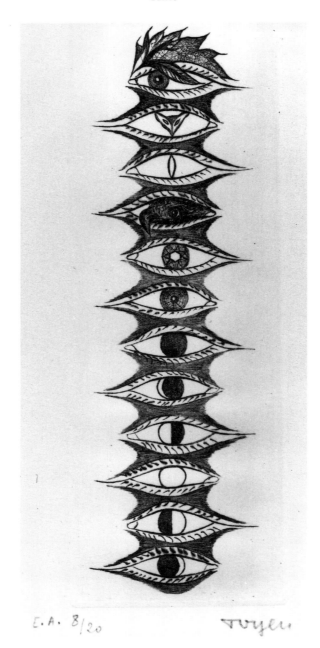

E.A. 8/20   Toyen

My love, you too, you are only raping me because I so passionately consent to the lives other than yours living from me when you penetrate me. Now, I feel certain that some are asking for a bit of irony—but sirs, do you know what irony is on the physical side? The trivial scratch of some mosaic of taboos which reinforce, which seal up the cage where the heart is already walled up before living. You won't dream any longer of being witty when you understand how I am given to thievery, how I'm the thief of the tempests that you want to turn away under the cover of some sacred thing or other. Taboos don't exist to be transgressed, but to be DISSOLVED in a point of extreme and unique combustion that you too (and I have the sadistic joy to tell you this) carry in yourselves.

This point is difficult to find, unbearable to look at, except with our three-year-old eyes.

I'm not tired, I get up just barely, I avoid parallel paths. My road starts from the blue vein at the wrist, yours, mine . . . I move forward sure that it is leading to the point of insatiably unstable equilibrium, to the convergence of infra-luminous rays of life, source of the occult respiratory ways of water, of wind, exactly like my desire.

Paris, December 4, 1966–February 1, 1967

THE RINGS AROUND MY EYES ARE ON THE INCREASE:
IT'S WITH MY EYES THAT I DEVOUR
THE DARK OF THE WORLD.

ABOUT FASHION

I have nothing at all to say and still less *something to say;* right now I am speaking while others are dancing, crying, sneezing, losing weight, killing, breathing, stretching out . . . No one has ever left anywhere, not even at the end of a sentence, without disguise: I admit disdainfully that I have false eyelashes and no hammer, a minor inconvenience when one's gaze does all it can to lose itself in the distance.

We are late, but isn't that just a delay? Daytime won't ever stop moving ahead backwards on the stomach of the night. Maybe we have our brains exposed, as others do their heart, yet to seem more ridiculous than we do would seem unthinkable, since no one pays any attention to someone sunk into the hollow of her shoulders, walking down the street on a leash, gambling her singular breathing at the table of tempests, answering the haggard telephone of sleep . . .

It is said that we are traveling, but we aren't running. We are stifling under plush bearskins, dragging along at the end of a thread whole caravans of precious, jolting, usual, anachronistic, useless, exhausted, marvelous ideas . . . yes, marvelous, maybe. But who's speaking?

Just about all I hear murmuring in beings and things is the despair of not being able to travel. The skin is too tight a garment to be shifted around much: it is the fixed source of all the mistakes you can make about a person, as long as memory doesn't bid farewell to its shapeless servants who can never manage to buckle up the last portmanteau-words. You know perfectly well that in the last resort there's nothing but the mirrors rushing at you like friends, mosquitoes, relatives, after some transatlantic crossing. Yet mirrors only accumulate the circus of our seven tongues in our mouth, the free fall of our leaden heads, the reflection of the different ways of forgetting the word to forget, and multiplying the result obtained by the time to be lost. It's not the moment to break the ice of the comings and goings, the dazzle would just hoodwink us.

The shells of our voices have been submerged for so long, while life is hiding in the uncertain conch of tremblings shouting in silence like the sound of the sea in the immense expectant squares.

Unfolded, smiling vaguely, huddled up, famished, mute, I have only tried to make a crack in the assemblage of the 155 × 30 × 10 cubic centimeters of flesh and bone (that's me) that keep moving about in their prison. Slowly, slowly, at first . . . with my legs still caught in the dress of words but already the greatest organic distances on the horizon.

I have traversed cities, countrysides, and let myself slide along beside a man who seems to be a scabrously mobile point on the border of the wild forests of certain gazes. Painful threadings across the soldered-together visions of idiot songs of genius. In the dry docks, we had to nourish ourselves on clusters of reddish breasts and penises perfumed with lavender water so as not to take all those exemplary paths. Behind us, very far away, the last clatterings of the teeth of grandiloquent storms so that our caresses could become what they desire to be, that is, young blue monkeys from Togoland, chrome-colored children on a dazzling beach, with the silly swelling of bubble gum between their milk teeth . . . for the world can be turned back like a glove over the landscapes of clouds, a glove we should flip from time to time over the muzzle of minutes. Life still doesn't change except by flashes, but on some days the disorder of a room after lovemaking is marked with an imprint that looks for all the world like that of the glass-pawed stroker over the catskins of touch.

As far as you can see, the fields will also be beds of just our size.

Each of our circuits is inscribed on the membranes of the air: there are still nights to take shamelessly against a wall, silences to give a cold whip to, streets to guess under our hand, smells to make you scream, vertebral columns of light to dig out at the end of corridors, summer paths to strangle sweetly with ribbons of puce-colored silk . . .

So then, be on your way! On your way to wherever, but take the way toward the greatest unfinishing. Everything private so suspicious, and the life we call private being so more than anything else, it's only going along that you will run in the attics of the brain, that you will open all the trunks of childhood, that you will sink in completely and love will take on violently the taste of the eventual.

Nomads are great scissors to undress space.

MICHEL LEIRIS

FROM THE HEART TO THE ABSOLUTE

A slight shock, the birth of a lizard which propagated itself with the noise of torn silk, and I found myself again lying beside a river which washed wood shavings and chips of tanned skin towards the brine of the Arctic seas.

In the caves of the earth thieves were heaping their treasures and counterfeiters were heating iron rods to mint coins bearing effigies of the dead. I no longer remembered the Ingénue, nor her deceits; I only remembered a bound, a rapid ascension and that vertiginous fall through the depth of a matrix whose indefinitely multiplied meanderings had led me to this place.

The landscape around me was desolate: no vegetation, but stone, stone and a few clouds. I noticed far away some abandoned quarries and wagons standing still. All wealth seemed to have crawled into the bowels of the earth, from which burst forth voices, sounds of brawls, and the blow of picks muted by the superimposed layers of stratifications which separated the obstinate seekers from the atmosphere. The air was heavy and impassible, not at all troubled by the caress of my lungs and I felt it on me like a glacier without moraines— this air which let no trace of its movements be marked by a bird.

The silence of the surface was hardly disturbed by a slight, very distant whir, the only perceptible vibration, to which my thought clung as to Ariadne's thread; it was the last organic ligament which held me still suspended above a mineral sleep; and I followed attentively the infinitely small variations of the sound engendered by that cord, which was sometimes lower or higher, in accordance with the very feeble modifications of the energy which animated it.

Yet after a few minutes, it seemed to me that the intensity of the humming sound was increasing, as if the object causing it were coming much nearer—and it was not long before I saw a black point emerge beyond the horizon—a point which soon became a line, and which moved following the direction of the river, a few meters above it, obeying the slightest turn made by the water. It was a bronze arrow which dragged in its wake a long white streamer on which I could read distinctly:

THE CATALAUNIC FIELDS

At the same time there approached a line of galleys manned by three ranks of rowers who followed the arrow with sails unfurled, their decks filled with armed warriors wearing shields and helmets.

Above their heads the pikes and rigging were crossed, forming a kind of net which bound the sky, while hanging from the masts, as breastplates might hang from the spinal column, the sails showed distinctly the invisible torso of the air. I heard the cries of the maneuvering and noticed soothsayers circulating among the soldiers and explaining to them the predictions they should deduce from the dice game, while disheveled girls ran from one end of the deck to the other, the prettiest of them twirling flames and knives. All the boats were covered with oriflammes and statues of gods, and the largest of them carried a vast tent made of steel links, beneath which rested the Emperor, a thin, trembling old man who seemed bored under his purple mantle and at times raised his hand to adjust his crown while a nude young girl was huddled in front of him. He was protected by several rows of lances through which I saw the glitter of his scepter, pointed into the air in order to ward off lightning and other threats.

"All exigencies come from human blood," the centurions cried; their words punctuated by the toiling oh's of the rowers. "*An act of force: iron, fire, the future will be white with marvels.*"

Mechanically I rose to watch the fleet pass by, but I noticed that my clothes were in rags and spattered with clay and seaweed. I ran away and hid behind a rock, and it was there I witnessed the landing of the Roman army and the flight of the barbarians; at that moment the arrow, which had become separated perpendicularly from the river, planted itself right on top of a little hill; the streamer, which was unnaturally long by now, had covered the entire plain and hid in the folds of its nineteen letters the rare accidents of the terrain and the diverse phases of the battle.

I saw the Catalaunic Fields stretching before me like a body of water swollen by cataclysms, and the plowed fields sharply determined the trail of the corpses whose ashes were being carried in closed urns to the catacombs. Strange mirage, the U was scooped like an urn; the two C's, extreme ends of the ploughshare, clove the plain for many ells, unleashing the catapults; and finally the S of treason serpented with the last barbaric hordes who were vainly attempting a surprise action, before they fell back midst the hooting of panic.

When the combat was over, the nineteen letters crumbled together and became incrusted in the ground like memorial inscriptions.

Behind the Roman lines, I noticed the Huns in flight, brandishing torches as they ran. Many wagons got stuck in the swamps along the river, whole bands of men were sucked into the earth, and when the extremity of the firebrand they had lifted as high as possible had also disappeared, the flame became detached and fluttered about in the form of a will-o'-the-wisp. Millions of fires were thus lighted, in the dying day, while the Roman dead began to blanch, in a strange putrefaction that destroyed both bone and muscles, transforming them little by little into glabrous mannikins without sex, their spherical skulls quite nude, and their sleek limbs looking as if they were made of white tights stuffed with horsehair.

These bodies were lying around me, before the lances and standards of the Romans, which were carried by motionless soldiers who differed from the dead only in that they were vertical.

When night had fallen, the corpses began to rise slowly in ranks of ten to fifteen, then started to pursue the will-o'-the-wisps, without moving their arms or legs, and floating a few meters above ground. When they had joined the fugitives, their icy breath extinguished all the flames, and soon there were left on the plain only ranks of pikes, the tent of the Emperor still glittering like a coat of mail under the lunar light, and the white mannikins who had stretched out on the memorial letters, blending with them in an identical insensibility of stone, like gravel left there for memory's sake, a short distance from the river, which continued its course towards the North.

The nineteen white letters gleamed in the darkness, immovable and as if emerged from the ground, and they seemed to have become its suddenly exteriorized skeleton. Mist rose from the river and poised above the battlefield, becoming more opaque as the night became darker, and forming scrolls as dense as those of the draining smoke arteries.

At midnight, the vapors had become massed just above the inscription and wrote in the air

19,

which was the number of white letters, set on the blackboard of night, like the first factor of a prophetic operation the consequences of which would be felt way beyond the sensorial domain, as far as the extreme point of the needle which sews for us the woof of the universe hemmed by our human lives.

The wind blew upon the two figures and made them dance one before the other, like a couple in love. The 9, being more sinuous, was the woman, offering her round loop to the 1, which leaped vertically and at times came near in order to thrust its angle into the circle.

I observed this trick for the seventh time, when the two figures became definitely fused and disappeared; then there emerged in white against the background of the night:

$$1 - 9 = 10$$

This sum having been effected in silence, an equilibrium was maintained for an instant. But my ears were suddenly lacerated by a terrible thunderstroke, accompanied by lightning of enormous proportions which divided the number 10 and swept the 1 and 9 away, while at the same time it shook the crests on the tops of the helmets, and the pikes became tufted with innumerable sparks. Then the blasted 10 was also smashed, and I saw in its place only the two figures:

d and b,

the first green and the second blood red, color of lips and wounds, represented by a half-nude Spanish woman in a scarlet shawl, the design of which underscored the imaginary lozenge which had as summits the stain marking the confluence of her two thighs.

Like an object and its image in a mirror, the two fives took their places opposite each other, like eagles on the escutcheon of Charles the Fifth, but the five which was turned backwards dwindled rapidly and there remained only the red Spanish woman represented by the figure of the senses, of the fingers, and of mating.

The dancing woman was irritated, a feeling born more of the storm than the rhythmic measure of the number which had engendered it. She, therefore, rose suddenly to her proper degree, 5 (the number of all the tricks she was capable of), by drawing from her marvelously fine, smooth black stockings a pair of castanets which she raised as high as her two hands could reach in order to unchain a crackling of figures which soon crossed the rays of the rising sun.

Before the soldiers, the dancer with the lozenge then made the ground echo with her heels, her unfurled fan cut the air in five quarters of numbers and points of departure which showed me once more that total death, like that of gestures, is only a formation of angles and a change in direction. At the same time, the teeth of her steel comb marked, through canalization, the temporal divisions created by the solar rays. Part of the light was reflected on the pikes of the legionnaires, and the dancer amused herself by conjugating the movements of her fan and those of her comb in such a way as to increase as much as possible the intensity of the reflected light.

Finally, as she whirled vertiginously about, transforming the air into a vast and luminous cage which was nothing but interlaced bars, the arms and armor of the warriors grew suddenly incandescent, and the entire Roman army became enflamed. The molten metals sank into the crust of the earth, holding in dissolution the flesh and bones of the soldiers, whose fossil imprints were found many centuries later on the ingots of a white and unbreakable substance which ignorant scientists called

MARSITE,

confounding it with those concretions of the sky that sometimes burrow into the earth, having not fallen from high enough to be able to pierce it from end to end.

The storm which had upset the figures had by now attained its maximum velocity. I stood trembling behind my senses of living water, watching for the adventure which was coming with a headlong rush.

The galleys fled, giving the appearance of a flight of cranes. The sun became a revolver barrel which slowly turned around, presenting at regular intervals a body that lay like an arrow before the orifice of the cannon. A shot rang out every minute and the body, its hair streaming ahead, was about to be lost in space. The dancer disappeared at the moment when I was about to seize her, and the entire landscape was swallowed up and replaced by a gleaming maelstrom, with spirals more dense than the wood of a cross.

I was hurled into this whirlpool from which there rose from time to time a multicolored bubble that knocked against the zenith, crashed with a great fracas, and returned to the funnel in the form of mirror flashes, pocketknives, and compasses.

Along with me there turned around the polished region a dark woman, a male goat, and a bottle containing a few pieces of paper, four crystal dice, and a ball of string all plunged into the brine. Each time my position with reference to the bottle made me see a new side of one of the dice, the woman stretched her nude arms and the goat shook its beard, while a bubble came from the funnel.

The woman was the first to fall into the central pool; I was still far away when I saw her balance herself and disappear with a long cry, like a torch that goes out. The goat followed her almost at once; but he had the luck of finding one of the bubbles, which carried him off rapidly into the air; up there he became changed into a cloud which allowed him to come down without pain—in the form of a fine rain.

As for myself, I succeeded, just as my circular voyage was about to lead me to the edge of the abyss, in clutching the bottle and, moving it violently, I threw the number 12 with the dice, which assured me the protection of the zodiac. I found, in fact, within reach of my hand, an aerial girdle decorated with the twelve signs. It placed itself without aid around my loins, and drew me away from the whirlpool, carrying me outside of the zone of terrestrial attraction.

When I came back to this planet, it was on a beautiful summer night, I was metamorphosed into a thunder stone and on my face were engraved these words, which summarized everything the figure 5 and the oriflamme of The Catalaunic Fields had taught me:

Needle
A stippled curve
here is the thread of thought
Feast of passing the Equator
—and the Camp of the Golden Sheet—
here is where the saddle wounds
the circumvolutions
in prismatic darkness.

IN THE HEAT OF INSPIRATION

I want to describe the fury, the impetuosity, the exaltation of a painter (whose name I shall not disclose) as he tried one late afternoon to seize the fading light on the object which I had become. The model, in turn, paints the painter in the heat of his inspiration. Another time, perhaps, but still as an object might see him, I shall paint a painter who is quiet, self-composed, hesitant and thoughtful. The one I am dealing with to-day is not a realistic painter, but a hero of the imagination. He still likes to make a few sketches from nature, however, so he made me sit down in what I must admit was a fairly comfortable position; then, hastily, feverishly, he stuck a large sheet of paper on his easel. He hurried to and fro in search of his drawing-pins and charcoals, with swift gestures as though there were no time to lose, lest the universe—I and the light—should disappear. An intense fire has already taken hold of him. The charcoal scratches the paper. Is he drawing? Judging from the noise, it would seem rather that he is tearing a face apart with pencil strokes. I hear him also spreading shadows and hatchings with such vigour and decision that I have the impression that the sheet is already thoroughly covered and that everything will be finished within five minutes. As it is summer, he is wearing shorts: he draws back for a while, looks at me, then at his paper, and half closes one eye; he remains motionless, his left leg in front, his knee bent, his body leaning forward, his right hand already pushing towards the easel as if for an attack. The calves of his legs, like those of an infantryman, are full and taut, his thighs are those of a mountaineer, hardened by many a daring climb. A little while before, in a field, I had noticed that he was obviously clumsy, and that when his sons threw a ball to him, instead of catching it, he lowered his head, stooped, turned away and lost his breath.

Now he is transfigured (and what strenuous exertion!) He shows extraordinary quickness and all his gestures are unfailingly accurate. He scratches and rubs, and suddenly we hear the sharp noise of the charcoal pencil which has just broken. With a start, he utters a muted Ah! then immediately resumes his work . . . This little accident reoccurs several

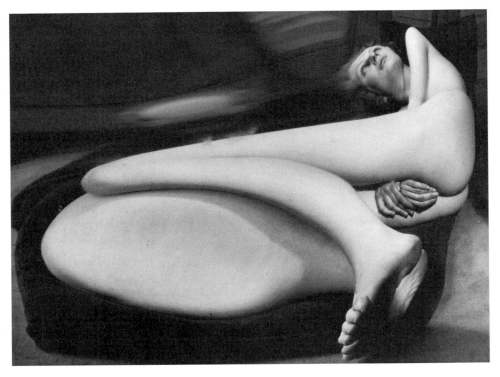

André Kertész, *Distortion #40,* 1933; gelatin silver print, 7 × 9¼ inches. Courtesy of the J. Paul Getty Museum. © ARS.

times; I watch him hurry towards a table, where he feverishly chooses a fresh piece of charcoal. Then he hurries back to his canvas, as if the short delay might make him lose an idea, a reflection, or the movement of a curve. By now his hands are as black as coal, and yet they will conjure up dazzling white surfaces . . . He tightens his lips, bites the lower one, and looks as if he were about to break into a fit of rage that might completely terrorize me; then the expression of his eyes grows calm and for a while becomes gently restful. At times he sighs, and as he grows calmer seems to take pleasure in some detail; then he is seized again with the fire. Now and then he utters a kind of raucous cry: a fabulous animal has eluded him. But when he has succeeded in lassoing it with a harmonious curve, he lets forth a grunt of pleasure. I am a virgin forest, filled with animals which are difficult to capture, with bird–like reflections, and yet I feel myself empty, in a state of stupefaction, like a donkey. But he continues the sort of dance he has started. From time to time, he hums a tune in his throat, a muted buzz accompanying the scratching of the charcoal: but this does not last very long, for he starts breathing violently again, as if he were kindling a bright fire with a pair of bellows . . . Later, as he nears his goal, he quiets down and whistles a few notes, and a little later a negro tune.

The first sketch is finished, he looks at it without saying a word, then quickly takes it from the easel, turns it against the wall, and starts a second one. The same intense fire possesses him. He must soon grow exhausted. However, three, then four sheets are quickly covered.

Later, he remains alone in his studio, among his flames, wholly given over to his ardent passion; correcting, imagining, transforming.

Mina Loy

O Marcel . . . Otherwise I Also Have Been to Louise's

I don't like a lady in evening dress, salting. From here she has black eyes, no mouth, some—
Will you bring a perfection, well bring a bottle—Two perfections WELL I want to SEE it—
he will know it afterwards—will you bring the bottle? Really, have I? Which way? Oh
did I? WHEN? Too much? You are abusing myself. No, you would not—Did you ask Demuth about it? Anything you like, would I? Ough Naow? of course not? Yes I do. I used
to kill myself with the syphon—. You don't remember that ball. Well don't do that because
I am perfectly sober now—that's the kid he looks like—. It will probably cost me very
much I have not got money. Did I say I wanted the bottle all right—SEE it! Excuse me,
explain it. You don't need any. I will give you some paper Mina and keep silent to give
you a rest. Oh! I will give you some paper all the same. Very much. He said to me, we
will toss whether you resign or I resign—a very old French story about 'the English man
must shoot first.' She has a pencil in her hair—very impressionistic. You know you should
have some salt on your hair it's so nice—because? Nothing—it's music. Ah this is, this is,
this is, is IT. Do not worry about such things as lighting a match. I give you my key Clara—
HEY—have some yellow paper. If carried away If Clara ever returns it. Well, you did about
a week, after. Here's the salting lady—I will show her to you—salting lady. She passed.
Do not speak any more—you have to squeeze it, maid of the—. I used to go every day—
waitress. I feel ashamed in front of this girl—she looks at me from far it's wonderful—it's
wo-onderFUL!

Yes, have a drink lady, teaspoon by teaspoon. No please take this—Do I eat? You know
why I have one—I do—I have it—I want some tongue I will give you some—but don't
do too much what? Suck it. Well I don't know how I will get up early tomorrow I have
a lesson at two—no not with the "bellemère." You don't know what a wonderful sensation
it is—I have some preference for some company where is our waiter—where is he it sounds
it doesn't he?

Portrait of Joseph Cornell in his house on Utopia Parkway, 1969. Photo: Hans Namuth; permission by Namuth Studio.

Mina are you short-hand?, I never knew it. I want tongue sandwich, anyway it keeps me awake. You know, she comes riding school fifty-sixth street you know she comes. Lunch 12 o'clock. Well you know it was. How do you light a cigarette—how do you light a match Did you, well it is not dangerous at all—Did you got it? Are you an American representative—I am sorry. You are Pennsylvania I am Boston. Do you want some cigarettes—Did you put the pronunciation? Waiter! Tongue sandwiches. Do you want hot milk? Two perfections she doesn't want anything—you got it? She can't write it down anyway—through the flag oh some cigarettes—waiter I want some cigarettes for Mina— this is a wonderful tune Ti lis li laera Mina I give you two dollars, it means to me two dollars—Ti li li laera—it is twice I need to shave now. Demuth you must be careful of your key she keeps it about a week every key she gets she keeps. You speak like Carlo, well when he wants to imitate—well have a drink! You know those two girls are crazy

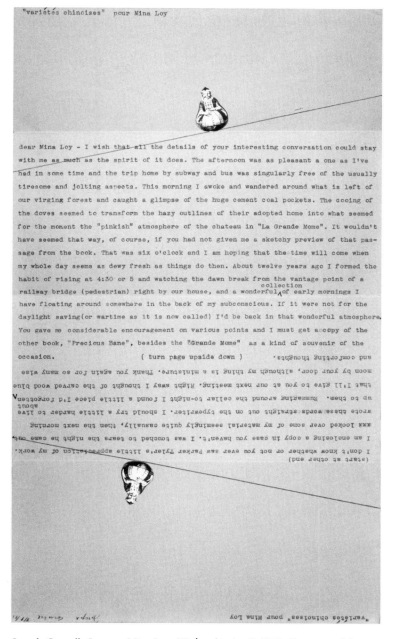

Joseph Cornell, *Letter to Mina Loy, "Boîtes chinoises,"* 1943. Courtesy of the Getty Center for Arts and Humanities, the Joseph and Robert Cornell Memorial Foundation, and Roger Conover.

about that man, they mustn't, you must get him out. I will have a tongue sandwich—you must suck it—Censorship! Don't let your flag get wet—is that Billy Sunday—There's always a sky in heaven!—that is too low. My ancestor is tall people. Don't write, he is going to leave you for a minute. Sandwiches—Oh I forgot to telephone—what shall I say? Ti li li laere—she said—all right!

AUTO-FACIAL-CONSTRUCTION

The face is our most potent symbol of personality. The adolescent has facial contours in harmony with the condition of his soul. Day by day the new interests and activities of modern life are prolonging the youth of our souls, and day by day we are becoming more aware of the necessity for our faces to express that youthfulness, for the sake of psychic logic. Different systems of beauty culture have compromised our inherent right not only to *be* ourselves but to *look like* ourselves by producing a facial contour in middle age which does duty as a "well-preserved appearance." This preservation of partially distorted muscles is, at best, merely a pleasing parody of youth. That subtle element of the ludicrous inherent in facial transformation by time is the signpost of discouragement pointing along the path of the evolution of personality. For to what end is our experience of life if deprived of a fitting esthetic revelation in our faces? One distorted muscle causes a fundamental disharmony in self-expression, for no matter how well gowned or groomed men or women may be, how exquisitely the complexion is cared for, or how beautiful the expression of the eyes, if the original form of the face (intrinsic symbol of personality) has been effaced in muscular transformation, they have lost the power to communicate their true personalities to others and all expression of sentiment is veiled in pathos. Years of specialized interest in physiognomy as an artist have brought me to an understanding of the human face which has made it possible for me to find the basic principle of facial integrity, its conservation, and, when necessary, its reconstruction.

I will instruct men or women who are intelligent—and for the briefest period, patient—to become masters of their facial destiny. I understand the skull with its muscular sheath as a sphere whose superficies can be voluntarily energized. And the foundations of beauty as embedded in the three interconnected zones of energy encircling this sphere: the centers of control being at the base of the skull and highest point of the cranium. Control, through the identity of your Conscious Will with these centers and zones, can be perfectly attained through my system, which does not include any form of cutaneous hygiene (the care of the skin being left to the skin specialists) except insofar as the stimulus to circulation it induces is of primary importance in the conservation of all the tissues. Through *Auto-Facial-Construction* the attachments of the muscles to the bones are revitalized, as also the gums, and the original facial contours are permanently preserved as a structure which can be relied upon without anxiety as to the ravages of time—a structure which Complexion Culture enhances in beauty instead of attempting to disguise.

This means renascence for the society woman, the actor, the actress, the man of public career, for everybody who desires it. The initiation to this esoteric anatomical science is expensive but economical in result, for it places at the disposal of individuals a permanent principle for the independent conservation of beauty to which, once it is mastered, they have constant and natural resource.

PIERRE MABILLE

THE REALM OF THE MARVELOUS

"Let's be clear: the marvelous is always beautiful, no matter what marvelous is beautiful, nothing is beautiful but the marvelous."

One possible danger . . . would be to separate arbitrarily the domain of tangible reality from that of images and of thought, the marvelous reduced in that fashion to the simple game of the imagination, would have lost all its objective density.

For me, as for the realists of the middle ages, no fundamental difference exists between the elements of thought and the phenomena of the world, between the visible and the comprehensible, between the perceptible and the imaginable.

So that the marvelous is everywhere. Understood in things, it appears as soon as you succeed in penetrating no matter what object. The most humble one, by itself, raises all the problems. Its form, a witness of its personal structure, results from the transformations come about since the beginning of the world. It contains the seed of all the innumerable possibilities that the future will bring to be.

The marvelous is also between things, between beings, in this space where our senses perceive nothing directly, but which are filled by energies, waves, forces ceaselessly in motion, where ephemeral equilibriums are elaborated, where all transformations are prepared. Far from being independent isolated unities, objects participate in compositions, vast assemblages or solid constructions, realities of which our eyes only perceive fragments but of which our spirit conceives the totality.

To know the structure of the exterior world, to detect the working of forces, to follow the motions of energy, this program is that of exact sciences. It would seem then that those should be the authentic keys of the marvelous. If they are not completely that, it is because they do not interest the complete human being. Their severe disciplines exclude emotions of the senses. They reject the individual facets of knowledge on behalf of an impersonal and mechanical investigation.

Through a singular paradox, the more humanity extends its knowledge and its mastery over the world, the more it feels itself stranger to the life of this universe, the more also it separates the needs of the being from the givens of intelligence. A definitive antinomy seems to exist today between the workings of the marvelous and those of sciences.

Emotion subsists for scientists at the moment of discovery, when they perceive the obstacle overcome, the door opening on an unexplored domain. The emotion is felt by those who are unlearned but who, understanding nothing, are in ecstasy before the theatrical nature of the modern techniques.

The others, students and professors, do not feel engaged in a mechanism where memory and pure intelligence are in play. Knowledge is like a suitcase they carry. No interior transformation seems to them necessary to understand a theory or to follow a curve in space. Then they learn limited sciences in particular techniques in a special vocabulary. These languages, progressively more precise and abstract flee all concrete poetic images, the words which, having a general value, can engender emotion.

The biologist would be ashamed to describe the evolution of the blood corpuscle by the story of the phoenix, the functions of the kidney by the myth of Saturn engendering children only to devour them afterwards.

Such a fragmentation, such an analytic will have to cease. Soon, thanks to a vast synthesis, humans will establish their authority over the knowledge they have acquired. Science will be a key to the universe in a language accessible to collective emotion. This language will constitute the new lyric and collective poetry, a poetry finally disengaged from the trembling, the illusory games, the demoded images.

Then consciousness will have to cease trying to enclose the vital impulses of life in an iron corset, it will be at the service of desire; reason, going past the sordid level of common sense and logic where it is dragging itself around today, will rise to the floor of transcendance, to the great possibilities of the imagination and the Dream.

If I admit the exterior reality of the marvelous, if I hope that sciences will permit their exploration, it's with the certainty that soon the interior life of the individual will no longer be separated from knowledge and the development of the exterior world.

For it is only too evident that mystery is as much in us as in things, that the country of the marvelous is above all in our own senses.

The Destruction of the World

During my childhood, the announcement of a cataclysm provoked in me a voluptuous satisfaction. I learned to show no emotion and to listen in silence to the lamentations of adults. In particular, the flood of 1910 exalted me. Towns submerged little by little by the inexorable waters, streets transformed into rivers, the headlong flight of the inhabitants, chased like rats: marvelous spectacles which gave place to disenchantment when the water receded and brought things back to their usual monotony.

Volcanic eruptions which the illustrated magazines printed in color on their brilliant front-pages: cities swallowed in a night, the slow descent of the lava; then, the inundation of the spring-tide, the heavy vessels crushed like our childish boats submerged by a mere gust of wind.

And again, the great fires, those of the Var forest, the fire running "with the speed of a galloping horse," the countryside lit up at night as if for the unique celebration of a monstrous Saint John, the bells, forgetting their usual sad call to mass, howling the alarm.

Because I took such pleasure in man's misfortunes, it seemed to me that I was alone in the world and that some demon lived within me; so I strove, by reasoning, to force it into silence. The war, through which I lived for the most part in the dangerous zone of bombardments, revealed to me that my state was not exceptional, but was that of the major-ity of my comrades, whose confidences were made easy by the liberty most of us enjoyed. The child, like all the physically weak, conceals a great sadism; the images most attractive to him are those of natural or voluntary upheavals, he cherishes a secret tenderness for Nero assisting, gay and lyric, at the burning of Rome, started by himself. Perhaps catastrophes draw their interest from their exceptional character, spectacular curiosities loved by the romantics. Perhaps the child is pleased to see the community tremble and to see the adults lose their authority and prestige. Perhaps the child, so near to natural phenomena from his birth and generation, still retains some complicity with cosmic energies? I believe the sadism of the young is, above all, an aspect of fear, that essential province of the affective life. This feeling is so important that men seem to have reached an agreement to pass over it in silence. They dare to face only one of its forms, vulgar and repugnant: moral inhibition, which compels a running away, a morbid depression that paralyzes thought and makes one sweat. Nevertheless, their interior reality is quite different.

Fear of death, you give life its value! Fear of the future, you make the moment pre-cious. You give a meaning to health, to richness. Fear, you grant the marveling at the fragile smile on the face of a woman, you provoke that intense emotion when one meets someone who, the following instant, will be lost in the multiple night. Sensual fear of the child, pretext for cowering against his mother. Finally, fear that is carefully maintained by stories, recreated by novels, tragedies and plays. Constant presence of night, peopled with its black mares, without which the light would not be. Intoxicating dialectic of being and non-being, that brings everything up again, and creates that inquietude without which life would be worthless. Source of all the raptures of our spirit! The indissoluble union of fear and sadistic hope makes us think that perhaps tomorrow the sun will not rise, that the equilibrium of the seasons will be destroyed forever, ruining the fragile security of industrious societies, and nothing will remain of the ordinary circumstances of humanity.

One must have lived through certain moments in a tempest, encircled by foaming mountains of water, lifted like a powerless toy by the frenetic dance of the elements. One must have known, in the night, that progressive cold brought by a horizontal wind when the earth seems to be frozen for eternity, when life crystallizes, dead. And, too, those other extremities of torrid heat, where things seem ready to catch fire in a universal conflagration.

Then man may suffer, but in the midst of his groans lives the insane taste for the extreme, to go even further into the paroxysm. Troubling boundaries beyond which life is compromised, you are the very frontiers and the source of the marvelous!

Because of this complexion, the human sensibility will always be haunted by cosmic catastrophes.

Observation, moreover, indicates that it is not only a "haunting," but an actual happening of the past; the stratification of the earth's bark reveals the reality of those upheavals which caused the disappearance of the giant faun of the third epoch and destroyed that luxuriant vegetation of which only a meagre souvenir remains on distant continents. The unconscious associates these geologic transformations with the fabulous events connected with the origin of societies; the mind wants a reason for these cataclysms and sees a necessity, at a given moment, for effacing the evil in order to renovate and better the world. We ourselves, do we not destroy the inadequate sketches of our work and throw away worn-out things? The legend of the deluge, found amongst all peoples, doubtless expresses the remembrance of real events but it marks, especially, a fundamental tendency of the sensibility and intelligence.

The individual drama of birth, in which water plays such a great part, stretches up the ladder of the whole of humanity; men must be separated from their deified ancestors (and all parents are such) by a deluge, a free-flowing water. What has remained is a saint who participates in the ancient nature of heroes and in our present nature. He is Deucalion in Greece, Outa Napichtim in Mesopotamia, Noah in the Bible. His virtues have moved the Lord and he has obtained the promise that the catastrophe will not repeat itself; he holds the secret of the alliance.

Alas! this cannot be eternal. The Hindus, knowing the cyclic and regular life of the universe, foresee the eventuality of future changes. For the Christians, these will be due to the progressive alteration of man.

Among the numerous apocalypses that have been circulated in Asia and Greece, from the first century to ours, that of Saint John has persisted; during two millenniums it has marked with an indelible seal the unconscious of multitudes.

The prophet announces future destructions and, on a certain day, the coming of plagues.

Installed in the carelessness of their sordid souls, many look upon prophecy as a simple dramatic allegory. Since the year one thousand was traversed without the demon's being unleashed, since they were able to safeguard their precious persons during wars and epidemics, they now repress their instinctive fear. And those cataclysmic displays are embedded in the fog, abstractions detached from daily life. One reassures oneself, although the poet feels that the times have revolved. Leaning over the abyss of his unconscious, like a man who rests at the window watching the storm of a summer night, the poet perceives the premonitory signs of upheaval. In familiar objects, he reads the drama that makes ready: are his eyes closed or wide-open when the thunderstruck vision comes to him?

Whoever is there, stable, among the catastrophes, impassive in front of the storm of sufferings, is the one who keeps the principle of all created things joined to the principle of eternal destruction. Piercing the opacity of space, Lautréamont sees it, he looks at it face to face, and the gold and pearls that John perceived have disappeared from the throne; blood is there, and sweat, and excrement from which the life of man is engendered and in which it expires. Above the flames, the torrents, the storms, appears the great nightmare of a cruel God.

Before growing indignant at the sombre colors of this account, before exclaiming at the partiality, the literary excess, the pessimism, bring to mind, O comfortable reader, the mangled children, the tortured bodies, the cities disembowelled in the name of civilization. Listen to the clamor of sufferings rise . . . The cries of the wage-slaves and prisoners of to-day have no more need to borrow the aid of the poet; they stream from the mouths of the enslaved themselves, rising from the hell of factories and concentration camps more lugubrious than those in Dante . . .

May it cease to exist, this world of pain, may the fire of the earth, the water of oceans with an ultimate convulsion put an end to this miserable creation capable only of bringing to birth unhappiness. And man welcome oblivion rather than continue with his agonies. He implores the saviour deluge, the destroying angel. And if the terrestrial mechanism, too unchangeable in its equilibrium, cannot explode and abolish humanity, if the universe will not consent to disappear, the actual state of things, at least, must be destroyed. If the sky refuses the task of purifying the world by fire and water, if it remains unmoved by the entreaty for death, as it has done for thousands of years to prayers for peace, men, united in revolt, must provoke the deluge themselves. Everything swept away from a past of injustice and oppression; everything, to the very center, washed from rocks stained with centuries-old ignominy. The slave knows that nothing can be saved from the ancient dwelling and its masters; the smallest objects are cursed; he feels that any contact with them will corrupt him in turn.

The true poet, also enslaved, is unable to endure the universal horror, incapable of compromising, he knows the depth of the pit. He knows the distance that separates the real life contained within himself and the social conditions where the already fetid dead assemble their gangrenous stupidity. The poetic message prophesies that indispensable destruction. But such a great goodness resides in man that he lets himself be softened by fear of injustice; he is afraid that the force of his wrath has altered his judgment. At the moment of exercising his violence, he suddenly hesitates, telling himself that perhaps some just ones are left in the condemned world. This inquietude was that of Abraham. Fleeing the corruption of Egypt, he led his meagre band through deserts and privations towards the holy adventure. Striking against the iniquity of Sodom and Gomorrah, he was warned of its imminent destruction, he tried to delay the exterminating arms which were impatient of the accumulated crimes.

The slave to-day, fooled a thousand times by apparent virtue, by fallacious promises, having scrutinized in vain the smiles of faces, knows that nothing can be preserved any more; he learns thus that the times have revolved. Then the floodgates of the deluge open.

René Magritte

Continuous Experience

A certain surrealism claims to domesticate the unknown. Like a philosophy, it only cares about knowing the world, forgetting to transform it. A system of beliefs crystallized in mysterious "beings" and "forces" has replaced the initial enthusiasm. So-called surrealists are even professing their belief in "the love of art" when it isn't the love of the country, waiting to get converted before too long to some religion or other. This surrealism is only practised at present by crafty little minds, people either naive or just worn out, and business people who want to be "with it." As for the ancestors, they are reposing in their renown or have just resigned themselves to giving up the struggle. The experiment, however, continues in broad daylight.

It all happens in our mental universe. By mental universe, we have to understand, necessarily, absolutely, everything we can perceive through our senses, feelings, imagination, reason, revelation, dream or any other way. *We are responsible for the universe,* and this evidence permits us to judge non-dialectic philosophies (idealistic or materialistic) in their proper level of empty games, because the philosophers try to reach perfect thought which has to mix with the object at the point of denying it.

The feeling that we have not to be able to flee the mental universe obliges us on the contrary to affirm the existence of an extramental universe and the reciprocal action of one on another becomes more certain.

We cannot perceive either a "shadow" or the "light" of the extramental universe. As we cannot know anything of the extramental world, there is no mystery. We know no irreducible shadows, for an attentive vision reveals that in every physical or spiritual shadow there are lights and colors animating it. (The unhappy thinker is terrified by the shadows of the infinite, another hears the music of the spheres.

If they were not so miserably dominated by their means in such a miserable world, the Postman Cheval, the Douanier Rousseau, the strangers, children, and insane people drawing would be capable of bringing about magic scenes not indifferent to us. These are

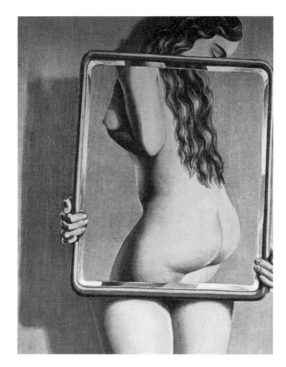

René Magritte, *Les Liaisons dangereuses (Dangerous Liaisons),* 1936. © ARS.

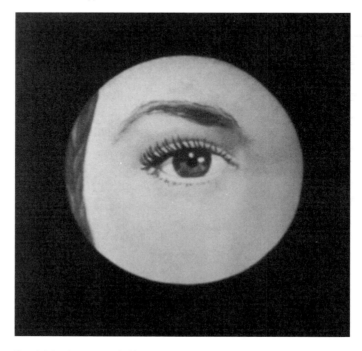

René Magritte, *Painted Object: Eye,* 1936 or 1937; oil on panel glued to wooden base; 6-inch diameter. © ARS.

René Magritte, *Omen of the Night,* 1926. © ARS.

attempts to retain. They are opposed to the Christian conception of the world which indeed would make of here below a valley of tears and also to that of certain present-day surrealists who ascribe to it a fraudulous poetry and fear the slightest bright light.

We mustn't fear the sunlight on the excuse that it has for the most part only served to light up a miserable world. Under traits new and charming, the mermaids, the doors, the ghosts, the gods, the trees, all these objects of the mind will be restored to the intense life of lights, living in the isolation of the mental universe.

ANDRÉ PIEYRE DE MANDIARGUES

THE PASSAGEWAY OF JUDICIARY PLEASURES

To Leonor Fini

It would have been so simple to avoid all that. Your cat was purring softly in front of the fireplace, watching out of the corner of his eye the airy movements of the moths made golden by the lamp's flame. The cold air cried out against the window-strippings. The white pages, covered with lost phrases, lay upon the table. But you have always loved to go out at night, wandering in the half-oriental suburbs of the great Danubian cities to lose yourself in streets lined with trolley-tracks, between buildings which are merely great concrete blocks, and broken-down stables, miserable slum-cottages, sheds built of raw wood, limitless empty lots strewn with rubbish and gipsy girls; nameless places, useless objects, worthless women, all to be had for the asking until cockcrow.

And so it was, on that evening as on so many others; and when you opened your eyes you stood opposite a gateway as bizarrely lighted as the windows of a cathedral on fire—the entrance to the Passageway of Judiciary Pleasures. The name blazed forth in letters of fire above the heads of a squad of policemen both White and Negro, who sported goose-feathers in their caps, and were polished from their heels to the extreme tips of their moustaches. For a moment, you wondered what such words could mean, and why these guards with bared sabres should be stationed here. But it was already too late to go back; the police stepped aside to let you through, with an expression of mingled distrust and compassion which in itself would have kept you from turning back, even if you had felt like doing so. (For you are cowardly the moment you leave the shadows of your solitude.) Inside was a very wide, high passageway, almost empty save for a few lone and confused pedestrians. At pains to avoid each other and somehow to hide their faces, they all pretended to be greedily eating huge slices of watermelon, on sale in an underground stall near the entrance. You are not fond of that indigestible fruit, and its lavender-pink color disgusts you, but you were sorry you had not listened to the salesman who had offered a slice of it to you along with everyone else, sorry especially when that man came running out of his hole, extending his hand to point at you, his lugubrious laugh echoing back and forth in the passage for too

Leonor Fini, *Young Woman Seated;* Christie's Images, London/
Bridgeman Art Library. © ARS.

long a time. It occurred to you—who knows why?—that from certain cages a bit further on, visible in the striped purple light, a pack of hounds might suddenly come bounding. You would have liked to find a dark corner in which to hide from that hand, that laugh, and those furious dogs, to escape from the raw light shed by a row of big gas chandeliers hanging above the archway, making a noise like a swarm of beetles as they burned and sputtered. Yet you pushed on, there being no refuge, and the others who had strayed across the threshold, still masked by their slabs of watermelon, followed your example. When the first among them had come, with you, alongside those strange emporia with their bright red grillwork such as one finds on the fronts of horse-meat dispensaries, there was a sudden burst of wild, rhythmical music from within, and the sound carried from cell to cell all the way to the end of the passage. At that moment there appeared behind the red bars some heavily painted women who began to beckon to you. It was then you discovered that the whole passageway was nothing but an uninterrupted succession of dance-halls, all of which made use of these cage-like affairs to attract clients. Bathed in soft, pink light, their enormously high heels resting on ostrich-feather cushions, they seemed rather more beautiful than the ordinary run of women. No word issued from their mouths frozen into thoroughly-learned smiles; their gestures had something mechanical about them that made them look like huge, attractive dolls. Your companions were soon made captives and dragged inside, each by the partner of his choice, while you remained standing among the bits of watermelon that had been spit into the dust; you stood there in the middle of that disquieting tunnel that belonged to the mimes of love with their too-white smiles and their too-red gums, like the faces in toothpaste ads. Then the invisible musicians fell into a slower tempo, and at the same time those arms stretching out toward you took on a more languid motion; likewise those eyes raising and lowering the heavy curtains of their lids, and those fingers with their mother-of-pearl tips, as they caressed the well-shaped breasts, uncovering the straw-colored flesh above the vermillion stockings, were playing through the grillwork for you alone, a game proper to peacocks, pheasants, birds-of-paradise, lyre-birds, creatures from the magic aviaries of the Queen of the Graces. You were seized with a ridiculous but very real fear that these beings might disappear as quickly as they had come, thus leaving you absolutely alone. Not far off there was a grilled window that shone redder than any of the others; the noise seemed louder there, and the women also seemed better dressed and more haughty than elsewhere. You rushed over, took the arm of the first companion who appeared at the door, without having chosen her, or even in your haste to get in out of the passageway having looked at her particularly. Hangings of garnet-colored velvet (three or four of them there were, if you had cared to stop and count) appeared, and you passed through them with her, letting them fall behind you like billows of dark wine. And then, utterly bewildered by the moving carpet of pink satin, you were suddenly pushed by this peculiar apparatus out into the scarlet thunder of the great dance hall.

Red everywhere, even here: columns caked with glistening mosaic, draped to the ceiling with tulle, which, under the caress of the electric fans, moved like a sea of those tiny clouds that appear at twilight; draperies framing flames of light reflected in the profusion of twenty mirrors facing each other; thick, soft curtains drawn across strange openings like opera-loges; a rutilant, gigantic mechanical organ at the back of the hall, spitting out polkas like steam, their rhythm provided by cymbals and drums worked by lifesize automatons made in the form of Negroes; from the over-all view of this glad drunkard's dream, down to the very costumes of the dancers frolicking in its midst, all the shades and tints scarcely varied in the scale of reds and pinks, with here and there gold dust scattered about like a shower of sparks.

Up near the wall there were several young women waiting to be invited to dance; they too were smiling the wide frozen smile that hid the features of everyone in that subterranean palace. One of the women, seeing you near at hand, singled you out to the others with a gesture, and then together they began a long conversation of which you must have been the subject, but of which you understood absolutely nothing, since they conversed by means of gestures, using the deaf-and-dumb alphabet. Who shall say how much a prudent night-owl should know? It would have seemed comic to you, beforehand, if someone had warned you then not to venture forth again at night without having been initiated into the use of this very special language; and yet see how much more useful it would have been to you than the advanced study of Germanic runes, or of those Etruscan characters over which you have worked so long to discover a secret the world ignores.

The first idea which occurred to you was the following: that perhaps the dancers' faces had been set, by being covered with some sort of lacquer or varnish, in order to impart to them that warm tint and that Dresden china glisten. The fixed smile, with its vaguely funereal aspect, would have been justified by the fear that a sudden unconsidered movement of the lips might crack the fragile ceramic shell from the temples to the chin—a frightful catastrophe no more tolerable than the shattering of the mirrors garnished with a lace of thorns, pears, Venetian iris and glass teardrops, or the tearing of the brocades, those satin sheets stretched out on all sides to the limit of their resistance, or the jamming of the wheels in the miniature clockwork of the huge automatic orchestra, even now in the act of grinding out a particularly enervating polonaise at top speed.

But there was still another surprising element in the behavior of these women, in which one could discern something like a symptom of illness; and soon you discovered that the eyes of the ones who were dancing, no matter where they might be, never strayed an instant from four Negroes in crimson, articulated wooden mannequins, over which the organ exercised strict control as they kept time with bunches of ribbons in their fists, one in each corner of the salon. So the dancers did not hear that deafening music which held sway over their facial expressions! You were delighted to think that they could no more hear than they could speak. And after all, it must have been rather amusing for an evening with such a mad beginning to end you up at the deaf-mutes' ball!

In order to be quite certain about it, you turned toward the partner who had not left your arm since you came in from the Passageway of Judiciary Pleasures, and announced in the most banal fashion that you found her beautiful. (To tell the truth, she was extremely beautiful, even if you had not as yet noticed the fact: as tall as you, with the carriage of a marine goddess; deep russet eyes in enormous globes of white enamel; sumptuous hair, not black, but nocturnal with long bronze reflections in it, and decorated with very heavy shells that looked as if they had been modeled in wax mixed with tar and blue ink. Beneath was the nut-colored skin, cooler than a petal, and damp with dew along the temples' arch; wide, sensual features, scarcely spoiled by an expression of servile arrogance such as one finds in servant-girls who are too beautiful. All this bowed before you when it became evident that you were saying something—since your mouth was moving—whereas no reply was forthcoming. None could be, and you could as easily have animated that superb doll by merely pretending to speak to her, by a tacit grimace or the slightest movement of your lips. Why speak to a deaf-and-dumb girl, unless it is to ask her to dance? In any case, it is likely that this one read no other meaning into your words, for she turned to face you, touching you lightly with the whole length of her magnificent body; and resting a hand that felt like stone upon your shoulder, she led you off in her embrace, into that hurricane of feathers, silk, muslin and perfumes, a turmoil kept spinning by a merry troupe of automatons. Cheek to cheek, her hair touching the nape of her neck, your head bent backwards, there you both go as if you were starting up a steep declivity. You were being watched; and had it not been for the infirmity which paralyzed all the dancers, there would surely have been murmurs following you two, for the men dancing were all sorry-looking fellows—everything from clerks to sacristans, and most of the lovely nymphs were dancing about with each other. And so you were truly the king of the party, and it seemed to you that you were fighting your own royal shadow, as if by holding such incarnate witchcraft in your arms, you were tearing her up out of the earth and carrying her in triumph into a circus of blazing fireworks. It was a long struggle.

Only much later, you came somewhat to your senses—brought back to this world by an astonishing languor in your partner which made her fall softly against you each time you touched the curtains of those loges you had already noticed along the sides of the hall. Each loge was surmounted by a medallion carrying a head in relief, with blinded eyes, and each head was fixed at the end of a sword, with the words, "Bed of Justice," deeply carved into the porphyry. Each time it was only a very slight reflex, an insinuating pressure, little coaxings in the exercise of which you felt the deaf-mute was using all the force of her desire; and her imploring eyes joined yours only to turn them straight toward the closed portières.

You had neither the desire nor the power to resist for very long. Sick people are sometimes good guides, you were thinking; they draw the best tickets at the lottery, treasures do not get away from them, and dogs in heat seldom bite them. Also you remembered having heard it said that "the bed is the tribunal of love," which, together with the fact that a mute girl does not cry out, no matter what you do to her, imparted a pleasant meaning to the disturbing words written above the loges. Finally you gave in to the desire of that woman.

Once again heavy stuffs absorb the sound of your footsteps, isolating you from the ball, whose sound diminishes and disappears. Now everything has changed: no more of the warm reds and pinks that blazed in abundance back there; you are lying near your companion on a great, vast, high-canopied bed, whose wood, hangings and sheets are of a dirty grey color; the light comes from a great square of glass in front of you, giving on a courtyard with livid walls. In this cruel daylight, the lovely mute girl has taken on the complexion of a wet rag, her hair is greased with a repugnant pomade and bristles with dandruff, her eyes become opaque, and her gaze is heavy against you as if to drive you out of the bed toward a twisted staircase leading down through a trapdoor beside the square of glass.

Downstairs, there are long automobiles without windows, trembling slightly, and men with dogs' heads are leading other men, who look like you, toward these vehicles. You wonder what they are going to do with them all, and probably with you too as soon as you have joined them in the courtyard where the gaze of a shattered woman is slowly pushing you. You, you who have read the ancient books, and who know that justice has not changed much since the time when . . . "a sow who had eaten the face of a child was condemned to be hung by the hind legs after previous mutilation of the groin upon which had been superimposed a mask representing a human face . . . said sow having been dressed moreover in women's clothes, with long hose on the hind legs and white gloves on the front paws."

And so the world continues as it has always been, but you would be able to resign yourself better to what will soon be your unhappy fate if only you did not think so intensely of the poor cat purring as it waits for you by the fire in a padlocked room which no one will ever enter again.

Joyce Mansour

The Vices of Men

The vices of men
Are my domain
Their wounds by sweet cakes
I like to chew on their vile thoughts
For their ugliness makes my beauty

They Have Weighed

They have weighed man whitened with chalk
They have weighed my foot without its big toe
They have weighed the ripe fruits of your belly
On the inexact church scales
And they have found that the weight of my soul
Equals that of a penguin
Without his wings

From "Pericoloso Sporgersi"

Naked
I float among the wreckage with steel mustaches
Rusted with interrupted dreams

By the sea's soft ululation
Naked
I pursue the waves of light
Running on the sand strewn with white skulls
Speechless I hover over the abyss
The heavy jelly which is the sea
Weighs on my body
Legendary monsters with piano mouths
Lounge about in the shadow's gulfs
Naked I am sleeping

Look I'm disgusted with men
Their prayers their manes
Their faith their ways
Enough of their overwhelming virtues
Dressed in briefs
I've had enough of their carcasses
Bless me mad light bright on the heavenly peaks
I long to be empty once more like the peaceful eye
Of insomnia
I long to be a star once more

I will swim towards you
Across deep space
Borderless
Acid like a rosebud
I will find you a man with no restraint
Thin swallowed up in garbage
Saint of the last moment
And you will make of me
Your bed and your bread
Your Jerusalem

You don't know my night face
My eyes like horses mad for space
My mouth striped with unknown blood
My skin

My fingers guideposts pearled with pleasure
Will guide your lashes towards my ears my shoulderblades
Towards the open countryside of my flesh
The bleachers of my ribs draw in at the idea
That your voice could fill my throat
That your eyes could smile
You don't know the pallor of my shoulders
At night
When the hallucinating flames of nightmares call for silence
And when the soft walls of reality embrace each other
You don't know that the perfumes of my days are dying on my tongue
When the crafty ones come with their knives adrift
When I plunge into the mud of night

YOUR FIGURE OR THE WAR AGAINST FAT

WHAT YOU MUST NOT DO:

1. Hold a hand held out without a protective glove
   Instead, offer the other cheek
   And speak, speak, put on some powder
   A hand can be a railing
   A frictioner, or a meeting
   But, remember,
   Appetite comes when you are eating.

2. Go on diets. Eat what you want at no matter what hour of your miserable day. You are miserable because you are fat, without appeal, without trumps or a waist or a waiting time, a pencil sharpener to whittle down the wasps stinging the little towers: in short, you are alone and you don't like that, so you are eating to have people notice you; you console yourself for your laughable attractions by chewing; you are plunging into your sad, ugly, and anguished fat. But the charming successes which menace your chastity take their distance with every mouthful of softness. Your nightmares with their veterinary fingers shake up your ulcers and those wrinkles, guzzling maxims, scratch your face off the map of youth. Your friends will do the rest. There you are, old. . . . Eat what you like, death won't hesitate to take you.

3. Throw your pounds in the dirty laundry . . . someone else's. Anyone casting a spell should know how to avoid the return shock. More than one camouflaged woman has

found herself on the threshold of the psychiatric ward you can't get out of, crippled, shapeless, and definitively disfigured.

4. To dull one's senses too much
    By using
    The elegant, encumbering, inoxydable
    Carving-knife, crash hash in superheated bakelite;
    You are risking a pileup in your generic ensemble
    And capricious death of your rotating knife
    For female dismemberment is hard to administer
    And the fruit squeezer of your dreams cannot be mechanical.

WHAT YOU MUST DO:
Buy an electric cleaver
Make a marinade of your figure simmered without makeup
Invoke a little man dogmatising between each fat layer
Marinate your lower parts in the singular sauce of your bitterness
Wet the smoking oil little by little, the ovary huddling in itself
The total extraction of your gravy depends on it.

MARCEL MARIËN

PSYCHOLOGICAL ASPECTS OF THE FOURTH DIMENSION

Every object, thing, or body is four-dimensional. An apple, a house, a woman, each is characterized by length, breadth, depth or density, and *image* (or *surface*[1]).

The eye, then, perceives only the fourth, *image*—a dimension that is also thought, dream, memory, and whatever one speaks about.

The hand that holds an apple, a thumb-latch, or another hand, intercepts a surface (flat or round, it is all one here). It may perceive two, three, or more dimensions (when it encloses a facetted glass, for instance), but a volume, never. The depth dimension of the object it explores is as elusive as air, just as spontaneously indeterminable.

Thus, what is solid and concrete, what offers resistance to the eye or fingers, remains invisible, ever inaccessible, everywhere imperceptible. For if one break, pierce, breach, split, or otherwise penetrate an object, it is not its interior that is thereby reached; in the new void created, new images are created, hitherto unknown surfaces are touched. When a Vesalius wields his scalpel, he does not lay open the heart of his subject, but "a heart" among hearts. When a Kant dies, what remains is not the skeleton of Kant, for Kant is no more: but a skeleton.

When the senses of sight and touch act jointly, and an apple is sliced, or a woman or a house penetrated, one has the illusion of three existent dimensions, which are logical and verifiable. They are existent all right—but not sensibly so, since the apple is but a splash of color on the table, the house but another in the landscape, and a woman a splash in the night. An ever well-behaved mystery of a limited infinite. . . .

. . . for thought arises through the agency of eye or hand or mouth, not by immediate (integral) contact of substance with substance. Heart does not know its neighbors, Stomach and Lungs. Images, surfaces, alone constitute thought, that center of consciousness, that center of exception. And even in love's night, sensation is always memory, image, and

Gina Pellón, *Space hors du cadre* (Space outside the Frame), 1992; collage, 46 × 60 inches. Photo: Christophe Laurencin. Reproduced by permission.

the hope of returning; it is never the brute contact of matter, perfectly fused, absolutely commingled.

No more than the eye, can touch probe the dimension of true depth of things. The universe is hermetically sealed to these two senses. If I remove the peel from an apple, the bark from a tree, I have created a new object. For the eye, a new image will have come into play; and for the hand, a new surface. But as far as both are concerned, they will never perceive volume; but always surfaces and images varying successively in the course of their probing. In any case, whatever is known about volumes belongs to the domain of hypothesis and legend, to what lies beyond, whether on that side of death or on this side of birth. With volumes, imagination takes its beginning: wheresoever it is a question of the content or intimate behavior of things.

The Anonymity of Charnel Houses

I and my skeleton (or my heart or my brain or my leg) are different things, strangers unaware of each other. But there are communities of skeletons, hearts, brains, legs, just as there are communities of egos.

The Anatomy Lesson

When a Vesalius finally cuts a heart, he does not get two halves of that heart, but ventricles and superposed auricles; and, pushing farther and farther, armed with perseverance and better eye-sight, he sees distinctions growing, stellar distances intervening, which make innumerable cells of everything, and indecipherable atoms of each cell. Yet he can never reduce depth to an ideal surface. For on his path he will find, however far he may push, a four-dimensional speck as resistant as cement.

Wind is a concrete but invisible entity. One can imagine the awe of the first men, in the days before perspective, upon seeing shaking images about them, such as heaving waters and rustling leaves, pelted by invisible stones; their terror at contact with clusters of buffets raining down upon their faces and overwhelming their bodies. In excellent form ever since, the wind has carried the responsibility for these misunderstandings very lightly. To be sure, it has found its master, who thwarts it with things like windmills, sailing vessels, and aërostats, and even goes so far as to overwhelm it with curses when it plays truant.

Still, all-powerful, its phantoms have managed to survive and, as is known, they lurk everywhere. Some of them are sly (like the simoon), wicked, ever disposed to wrongdoing;

and others, completely obliging, are benevolent, like the zephyrs. But we have given them luxurious or sinister guises, crowned them with pearls or horns, that we may better see them; so necessary are clear-cut images to any kind of human transaction. Some of them praise or repel God, as others do Satan. Until some fine spring morning when these images are suddenly seized by furious, mortal convulsions; to the greatest possible shame of the wind, which can bear it no longer.

Writing, speaking, or simply thinking, are a proof, assuredly, that spirit is the fourth dimension.

Geography, astronomy, atomic theory, such as they have been established by man, presuppose the possibility of control over depth, over space. Maybe . . . But let us make way for doubt too. For your walking steps do but transport you from image to image, from surface to surface. Where, then, is depth in all this?

Perspective? In the mind! Time? In the mind! I? Again, in the mind!

. . . but the Appian Way for the tourist, Midnight for the vampires, Mariën for the reader.

The universe is a fruit ripening on a tree of the void. The absolute real, the concrete and plenary All, Becoming, are the luxuriant forest.

Movement is also a body, and it contains all life, that of bodies, things, objects. But destitute of depth, density, localization, it eludes all dimension and thus answers better to the representation of a world that is at once unlimited and finite, open and hermetic.

People are not given to speaking of some amalgam that would contain among other things a speck of poppy, another of horse, one of nitrogen, one of Mont-Blanc, one of the Portuguese Nun, one of the Winged Victory of Samothrace, one of the Clothiers' Guild, a trace of Mary Stuart's blood, a grain of the moon, a last trace from a tear shed by Heraclitus. But they do speak freely of Descartes' intelligence, Nero's cruelty, Bonaparte's ambition, the future of poetry, a knowledge of Sanskrit.

Yet we are referring to aggregates that make up the world that constitute history. They are amalgams that are so many aspects of our life, our wars, our fraternizations; and important or paltry, they make us what we are, cruel, languishing. . . .

Let us listen to those children, the great men: who was cruel in Nero, he or a certain voice that ordered the burning of Rome? What was responsible for the execution of Louis XVI? Louis himself, the Convention, or the good Mr. Guillotine's new machine?

Maybe there were some of his own atoms in the sea that he was whipping; but incorruptible was the wrath of Xerxes. And, as far as I know, there was no one, in any case, who complained.

The Brussels Train is taking me to Paris, and along with me, my body, my clothes, my luggage; to say nothing of the train itself, with its carriages and wheels. But the Brussels City Hall and Notre Dame de Paris are made of the same materials. Here again the difference does not inhere in the content but, always, in the images, surfaces, appearances. It is no Vesuvius that determines Naples. Its fire resembles fire in general, its rocky make-up that of any other mountain. Vesuvius, Naples, Paris, Brussels: as many words, not places; as many images, not spaces. Chasms yawn at every step I hazard.

The Nostalgia for Ubiquity

The newly-born child . . . emerges. Growing up, he turns to leave the room in which he has taken his first steps. So goes our life, in a perpetual emergence from one object to enter *into* another. In which case, despair of ever "re-entering"! Each second, each millimeter, calls for a change. Nothing is ever "the same." A mother, once she is abandoned, is an object like any other: table, bird, or oneself.

Death is the only means of access to the three dimensions. Yet it does not exist. Subject neither to experimental control nor to the experience of having been consciously lived, is it not false to believe in it?

One is only what one experiences. Doubtless there is at some point a cessation of life. "I" must come to an end some day, no longer to know another morrow; but what do we have of death, if not images, surfaces: soil tamped down, coffins, grave-diggers, and white cold masks with closed eyes?

Reality, depth, in this instance, is but darkness, routine, submission, surmise: *there is no death but that of the next fellow.*[2]

What is called the All (man-conscience and universe-theater, past and future, dream and reality, nullity and infinity) may be likened to an hour-glass that is incessantly revolved, but in such a way that vacuum and plenum, thought and matter, are everywhere at the same time.

The same difficulties of coherence attend these two demonstrations: arresting the present and making two parallels meet. That is, until the appearance of a Riemann who makes possible the advent of an impossible possibility.

The present is but a fragment—an image. *Present* of a hand grasping a pen, *present* of an eye fastening upon a piece of paper, *present* of an ear turned to a wind-storm: images, surfaces of life—life: a movement of images that takes its point of departure from the unexplorable depths of volumes and leads back to it.

Lightning invented lightning conductors, the latter invented electricity, electricity invented wireless, etc.

Or inversely: the future preceding the past, the friar making the cowl, it is the glove that imagined the hand, the shoes that found the feet.

Thus it is with the whole man, who *imagined* his hand, his feet, his body, then the landscape where he discovered himself, the world. It is, moreover, his art, that essential faculty of his for always creating what he discovers, for always discovering what he creates. Master or slave of a world he made, it is he who with each passing day pushes back the frontiers of his consciousness, and fills so-called infinite space with his time.

The divergences between dimensions are like those of different worlds and minds: struggles between madness and reason, the known and the unknown, me and thee.

The dream is par excellence the *natural* mode of activity of mind. There, images are indeed images, *nothing but images,* that can mask no space, that can mask no time. The quintessence of lived images, the visions of the dream rear a personal world to replace the one momentarily lost. But real tasks, that bite and wound: only that distinguishes them from wakefulness. Superficial information is at this point sufficient to animate dreaming to the point where it can deliberately neglect the concrete and its angles, all the dead weight of what is not authentically *valid.*

The images of the dream, of mind, are ideal surfaces; that is, they have no seamy side, they have nothing "on the back." Their profundity resides only in their extension, their succession, their passage. As much as to say: mirror depth.

To take the great travels of circumnavigators and others, Columbus, Marco Polo, Magellan, we are all admiration for those who dared these priceless departures, for their conquest of unpublished images that enriched the store sedentarily acquired. That this aggregate of discoveries, those paintings thence forward suspended from the cyma moldings of great circles finally take on the form of a sphere, heavy with its imperceptible bowels, we are convinced of all that by now; and that the earth is round, as most assuredly it is, every schoolboy is positive. But however the matter is considered by the miner, surgeon of night, by the keeper of the lighthouse during his leisurely watching hours, by the sailor on his look-out, its rotundity, its depth eludes them, and the curvature or the black pit are but geometric metaphors in the service of their desires or their fears.

Similarly, when we stand before one of those globes over which a world map has been carefully plotted, we may certainly have an inkling of that well-known depth—and yet be unable to penetrate it. The scales, put to the test by that mass, will testify to its weight, so different from a leaf's, as a leaf's is different from that of a hair; they will tell us that "something" must exist between its margins, a fact of which our eyes, our hands had vaguely given us notice. Something, then, happens in the balance weighed by the earth, on the earth weighed by the sky, *on* the sky weighed by . . . and so on.

The balance beam thus reveals *the symptoms of an organic, internal malady in images* (a substantial hypertrophy) in which we scarcely ever risk our participation. Unless at some moment, become bold Vesaliuses, we should undertake to dissect our own "image." A ruinous enterprise, for who, indeed, would be willing to launch himself on this sea without light, abandoning to the grieving memory of his neighbors an opened belly with outpouring guts, over which the stark fancy of the scalpel still hovered.

The madness characteristic of our time is a lesser one—the conquerors are easily satisfied. "Let us leave to others the experience of pain and its attendant pomp," they think. "Our natural gentleness deplores such violence, of course, but there is nothing we can do about it . . . " Their incomprehensible wisdom is, for all that, no less a demonstration that surfaces and depth have always been foes.

. . . And the flower that sprouts from the soil (issued from what fertile nothingness?) composes its fable.

Notes

1. "Surface" is not used here in its commonsense two-dimensional meaning; but rather as zone of resistance to penetration by the sense of touch; analogously, "image" signifies, as far as the eye is concerned, a brake applied to its natural expansiveness.

2. These lines were barely written when, on buying "*Mauvaises pensées et autres*" by Valéry, I fell upon the following phrase, which is an excellent summary of the book: "Death is beheld only by living eyes." To each his own thought; but a little later, impelled by chance, I opened "*Variété III*" to find this definition of death, pretty closely approximative, given by Leo Ferrero, and cited by Valéry: "(Death) is something that happens only to the other fellow . . ." Unto whom, then, we may finally ask, must be rendered what pertains to death?

ANDRÉ MASSON

THE BED OF PLATO

Plato in bed. He speaks:

Whenever we group different beds under a single name, we recognize in them a unity of structure. The carpenter takes this to be a law of construction, which in his work he obeys but does not create. As for the painter, he copies an aspect of the bed—one aspect only—he comes third; he is an imitator twice-removed, as the bed-model itself is but an appearance. Moreover, with a simple mirror anyone can paint.

Pascal replies from the Bois des Solitaires:

All is vanity and fabrication of ghosts, shadow of a shadow, but painting is the most vicious of the vanities.

Monsieur Descartes is heard speaking to himself in the depths of his heated chamber:

The most imaginative artist composes his work only with elements already in Nature; if not forms, colors at least. He is locked in a dungeon so deep that even if he could escape he would never pass beyond the frame itself of his invention.

Can it be true that the philosophers as a whole prefer the densest reality to the Marvellous and the Possible?

The eighteenth century is more generous than dialectical Greece and the classic age in France. Hamann, "the Magus of the North," maintained that the senses and passions understood and spoke through images only, and that the entire treasure of knowledge and human felicity was to be found in images.[1]

Yes, and all is permissible. If Pygmalion does not devour his wife he will be eaten. We shall engulf the Universe (and it is rather vast!). We shall become what we have engulfed. We shall stretch out in domains where liberty does not yet exist, we shall have flowers that are beds, and for us the forests will rise and walk.

We no longer wish the philosopher-jailers to guide the imagination.

We shall see a solar system in a grain of sand, and if we like, it will be there.

Max Ernst, photo of Max Ernst, Jacqueline Lamba, André Masson, and Varian
Fry, in Air Bel, Marseille, 1941; Musée Cantini, Marseilles.

From the bond cast to the wind, to the suffering of the flame, to the wake of a head
of hair, to the flight of a feather in shadows; all signs will serve us in the avid arena of
Desire.

Note

1. Hamann: *L'esthétique dans une noix,* 1762.

SENSITIVE MATHEMATICS—ARCHITECTURE OF TIME

It is a matter of discovering how to pass between the rages which displace each other in tender parallels, in soft and thick angles, or how to pass under the shaggy undulations through which terrors are well retained. Man yearns for the obscure thrusts of his beginning, which enclosed him in humid walls where the blood beat near the eye with the sound of the mother.

Let man be caught, incrusted, until he possesses a geometry where the rhythms of crumpled marble paper, a crust of bread, smoke's desolation, are to him as the pupil of an eye between lips.

Let us put aside the techniques which consist of setting up ordinary materials and brutally push him who inhabits them into the midst of a final theatre where he is everything, argument and actor, scenery and that silo inside of which he can live in silence among his fripperies. Let us reverse all the stages of history with their styles and their elegant wafers so that the rays of dust, whose pyrotechnics must create space, will flee. And let us stay motionless among revolving walls to rid ourselves with fingernails of the crust fetched from the street and from work.

We need walls like damp sheets which lose their shapes and wed our psychological fears; arms hanging among the interrupters which throw a light barking at forms and to their susceptibly colored shadows to awake the gums themselves as sculptures for lips.

Leaning on his elbows, our protagonist feels himself deformed down to the spasm in the corridor, reeling, and caught between the vertigo of equal sides and the panic of suction, giddy when he finally realizes the efforts of the clock which is taxing its ingenuity to impose an hour on the infinity of time of those objects describing in wood or in verve their existence, which he knows is perpetually threatened. And he wants to have at his disposal surfaces which he could fasten to himself exactly, and which, carrying our organs in well-being or sorrow to their supreme degree of consciousness, would awake the mind on command. For that, one insinuates the body as in a cast, as in a matrix based on our movements, where it will find such a freedom that the liquid jostling of life which gives in here or resists there will not touch it, without its always having an interest for us.

Objects for the teeth, whose bony point is a lightning-conductor, ought to breathe our fatigue, deliver us from the angels in an air which will no longer be angel-blue but with which it will be lawful for us to struggle.

And again, other objects, opened into, comporting sexes of unusual conformation whose discovery provokes to ecstasy desires more stirring than those of man for woman. As far as knowledge of the very nervous irresolutions which can compensate for the full opening of trees and clouds from this window onto always identical daylight, plated from the outside.

In a corner where we can hide our acid pleats and bewail our timidity when a lace, a brush, or any other object confronts us with our incomprehension; and ever since then, in reaction, consciously, with a hand gloved several times, rub one's intestines with victims. That will succeed in creating in one charm and gentleness.

Very appetizing and with well-shaped profiles is furniture which rolls out from unexpected spaces, receding, folding up, filling out like a walk in the water, down to a book which, from mirror to mirror, reflects its images in an unformulizable course designing a new architectural, liveable space.

This furniture would relieve the substance of its whole past from the right angle of the armchair; abandoning the origin of its predecessors' style, it would open itself to the elbow, to the nape of the neck, wedding infinite movements according to the consciousness-rendering medium and the intensity of life.

To find for each person those umbilical cords that put us in communication with other suns, objects of total freedom that would be like plastic psychoanalytical mirrors. And certain hours of rest as if, among other things, masked firemen, crouching so as to smash no shadow, brought to Madame a card full of pigeons and a package of tirra-lirras. We need a cry against the digestions of right angles in the midst of which one allows oneself to be brutalized while contemplating numbers like prize tickets and considering things only under the aspect of one single time among so many others.

By mixtures of fingers similar to the clenched hands of a woman whose breasts are slashed, the hardenings and softnesses of space would be felt.

And we will start to waste it, that filthy ragged time offered us by the sun. And we will ask our mothers to go to bed in furniture with lukewarm lips.

René Ménil

Colors of Childhood, Colors of Blood

At that time, the sky was a marvelous blue tenting aquiver, the inky flower of the coconut trees crushing against it. My life was not yet daily . . .

In the afternoon the voyages began: the butterflies gave me the cadence of time with their showy embroidered wings. I lived for nothing then but the naked red earth. Red the earthen floor of the courtyard, red the freshly cut earth of the slope, and far off the black figures immobile over their lovely red drawings. I marveled at walking on this earth, handling it, devouring it. I loved more than anything that clay which is more frankly red and soft and resistant. I molded, pounded, sculpted the red stuff, smearing it lovingly on myself.

In midafternoon, I invariably found myself in a place where the earth ceased to be a bleeding dough to make a beautiful yellow dust. For me to love the earth, I had to find the purple stems of Saint-Martin yams coming out of it, half covered by young violet-tinged leaves. The light passing through the trellis of the hedge and already a bit yellowed had to cling, living as it was, to the violet stems and to this earth like a heated hand, like a hot caterpillar. For hours, I looked in silence, my eyes glued to the stems alight and incredibly violet. Around me rustled the castle of foliage. . . . I extended my hand; joy fell upon me like a sweep of shadow. . . .

In the afternoon the voyages began . . .

I followed a slope on the side of the sun. There was a sorcerer in my life. It was a multicolored cock. Suddenly he appeared at a turn of the path. I loved him, I hated him. He passed by, I remember, in the middle of the path; I threw myself into the underbrush. He passed by, laughing in his beard. But I didn't take long to get to the end of my voyage. There, my sorcerer's coop was sadly smoking. There, the red flowers no longer climbed up the hedge. But, pale at the foot of the slope as if in broad daylight, where candles had been placed at the foot of the dreaming deadman, the white mortuary flowers were burning timidly. There was no way to go further; I knew it without trying. I looked in the distance and found the red line again. It was the path of the horsemen. They didn't take long to appear. Despite the distance, I could see their black hats, their tuxedos opening on their white chests, I could see their terrible spurs. Their horses walked gravely in the narrow path. The coffin must already have been far off, yet they were not rushing to reach it. Soon they were lost behind the fresh hedge of the catalpas. Silence returned upon me and I remained alone with the earth . . .

Around the same time a horse appeared for the first time in my dreams and my reveries. A gigantic horse, with gigantic behind and head. Its apparition unbalanced me in my anguish. He is red or perhaps blue. He rears up, larger than life, against the sky . . . And I remain before him, panting, with a grain of dust in my hand . . .

Finally, I received this terrible visitor without trembling.

I had tamed him.

Then I developed a violent passion for all sorts of glass objects. I can see now a child in a dilapidated courtyard, eaten with light. The child is seated right on the ground, leaning a little forward. Beside him, his shadow. In his hands he holds gravely a few disparate objects of glass. Blue glass, red glass, violet glass, green glass. He brings up to his eyes a bit of blue glass, the color in which the most tumultuous of wooden horses are neighing and where, above the houses scythed down, the time of the New Year comes towards you. He shudders . . . Now: it's a red glass. Another world. Another ecstasy. He looks at the world through its eye: the world is white, the world is annulled . . .

My joy became a frenzy when I discovered facetted crystals. Nothing could have been more precious to me then than a stopper of prismatic crystal. I ceased living. I passed entirely to the center of the crystal and from this center the world and light were torn apart, refracted into a universe with unheard of colors and visions. I held the key. I slept no longer, the crystal keeping me awake. Never had I so loved the night. I woke up with a start to set out in search of the flames. I turned my crystal on to the petrol lamp with blood and smoke in its flame, on the funereal candle end with the wise and puerile flame, on the frozen electric flame, on the embers, on the reflections, the reflection of the lamp moving on the wall, the crazy reflection of the embers, the reflection of reflections. I surprised hidden brightness: the one you dip into right in the mirror in the halflight, the one rending the foliage in the deep countryside, the one of the pool at the feet of the trees at night, the one of the moon in the glass of water, the one of the things you see in the room when just one glimmer pierces the shadows . . . Finally there came, at the end of the night, the flame that flutters surprised between day and night. The lamp was annihilating itself. Things emitted their own flames, the day had come . . . A day in which I would live many worlds. Never did I so love the daylight.

In my mirror for larks, the world was trapped. Everything rushed, concentrated, froze, crackled in my mirror, with heat, cold, life.

Never any longer did I walk without a crystal stopper in my hand . . . In the stopper was the flask. In the flask was the world, all the worlds.

And that trembled in my hand like a bird.

Colors of childhood, colors of blood . . .

POEM

We gathered the insults to make diamonds from them. The weather had the whiteness of wheat. We were forced to leave the town early. The laundry was already drying over the villages. Under each door there was a kiss. They had thrown all the keys into the pools and the brides shining in beauty made a procession over the top of the hills. Ah! How fresh was the laughter under this wine sun. We were silent as a leaf. Then it was that we heard the silk crackling its cloth of laughter, a laughter exploding under the hay and the hay sending up its tips to the sky. We were the children of derision. No one could believe in our rule.

Soon, however, in the bowl of the hills, the sound and the gesture of the birds crazed by the daylight were simmering. Drops of cotton, coming from who knows where, fell in the hollow of countrysides with the sound of a water seeking a water or the more mysterious one of the liquid gestures of sleeping women.

The towns moved towards us. Each had its name, its love and its gifts. Each took shelter behind a dancing word, behind a living wolf. Each one burned with a secret fire, a secret ardor. And suddenly they loosed their children like so many little scraps of paper over the tranquil prairie. A sheaf rose from their breasts like the laughter of those hiding their laughter between their fingers. But we had time to see the eyes shining yes to all the scarecrows scaring no one, standing at the edge of the fields in love with the wind, taking in their bosom the weight of the sky or just the superb wheat that the joyful sleepers exude, outside the barns, from their breath alone.

Joan Miró

Harlequin's Carnival

The ball of yarn unraveled by the cats dressed up as Harlequins of smoke twisting about my entrails and stabbing them during the period of famine which gave birth to the hallucinations enregistered in this picture beautiful flowering of fish in a poppy field noted on the snow of a paper throbbing like the throat of a bird at the contact of a woman's sex in the form of a spider with aluminum legs returning in the evening to my home at 45 Rue Blomet a figure which as far as I know has nothing to do with the figure 13 which has always exerted an enormous influence on my life by the light of an oil lamp fine haunches of a woman between the tuft of the guts and the stem with a flame which throws new images on the whitewashed wall at this period I plucked a knob from a safety passage which I put in my eye like a monocle gentleman whose foodless ears are fascinated by the flutter of butterflies musical rainbow eyes falling like a rain of lyres ladder to escape the disgust of life ball thumping against a board loathsome drama of reality guitar music falling stars crossing the blue space to pin themselves on the body of my mist which dives into the phosphorescent Ocean after describing a luminous circle.

Each Speck of Dust

Each speck of dust contains its own marvellous soil. But, in order to understand it, it is necessary to rediscover the religious and magical element of things, the element expressed by primitive people. But one must keep enough purity to be stirred.

A picture, after all, comes from a surplus of emotions and sensations. It is only a process of birth to which one can never return.

Joan Miró, *La Traversée du miroir (Traversing the Mirror),* 1963; lithograph. Sotheby Parke–Bernet, Art Resource. © ARS.

PAUL NOUGÉ

NOTHING

BUT

NOTHING

THAT IS

NOTHING

SKETCH OF THE HUMAN BODY

THE CHEST
opens
on
the burning cross
of the heart

THE SKIN
sensitive
as precious as
THE EYE

THE HEAD
and its hair
of red
nerves

THE ARTERIES
always stretched
out into
discord

THE LUNGS
the sky's apples
of air
all filled up
take us along

THE LEGS
agile
clairvoyant
come to meet us

THE VERTEBRAL WATER
is more limpid
than the eyes'
water

THE HAIR
and the eyelashes
want
not to meet

THE LIPS
the cheeks
the gums
and the teeth
the NECK
bears them up

THE TEMPLES
the legs
phosphorous
and iron

OUR BODY
proposes
an algebra
which has
no solution

THE TOOTH
that you drill
gets warm
so quickly
that you have to,
while it's worked on,
cool it off
with a thin
iced
stream of water

Holding on
to the wall,
the NAILS
fold back

THE WORDS
of your body
go to your
head

A thin
stream of
blood
waters
each word

THE ATTENTION
caught
right on the tips
of your fingers
flowers
with sparks
at your least
signs

BUT
at the bottom
of the
RED FLESH
there is moving
a delicate
agile
SKELETON
of
Light

THE WINGED BONES
quicker
than
blood

A FULL BASKET
of blue
viscera

THE SHOULDERS
the arms
and the
hands
over the
red breasts
of love

THE DARK
and hot
flesh,
gleaming white
secretes
into the silence
our purest
thoughts

THE NAILS ON END
and the ear attentive
anything
can happen

YOUR
sleeping body
its
furthest
its most
secret
DEPTH

OPEN YOUR EYES

LEAN OVER
on this
SIGN

HOT
filled up
the
VEINS
are easily
sliced open

THE WOUNDED EYE
bleeds
all its
images

BEAUTIFUL
DELICATE
HAND
PIERCED
WITH
NAILS

GREAT WHITE FORMS
a people of humans and birds
live in
your
tongue

MY FRIEND'S DOG

I love my friend's
dog. He can say "yes" so
beautifully. He can say "yes"
when you forget him. He condemns
no one that compares himself to him.
Wherever he goes, spring goes
too. When he weeps, nature
loses its feathers. But when he's
in a good mood, he skilfully pushes
your hand to his mouth to hear
its greatest secrets.
Like every brave man he has
two souls in each breast,
twenty-five in hands and feet.

ROUND THE WORLD

Round the world with the rumpus god
Fishes on his soles
Fins on his heels
The golden sun in the middle.

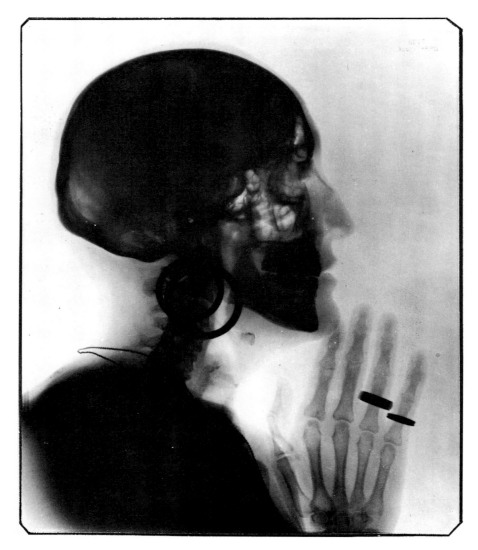

Méret Oppenheim, *X-ray of the Skull of Méret Oppenheim,* 1964. Photo: Roland Aellig, Bern. Reproduced by permission. © ARS.

Méret Oppenheim, *Self-Portrait*. Photo by Heinz Günther Mebusch: Poster for exhibition "Movement in Contemporary Art," Sept. 11– Oct. 10, 1982, Galerie de Seoul, Korea. © ARS.

His heart wreathed in ivy
His face filled with red berries
His nearest hands lie on the rocks.

When he loses the trail
He flees to the abyss
And drops all the spoons.

319

Méret Oppenheim, *Self-Portrait and Curriculum Vitae until the Year 60,000 ac,* 1966.
Photo: Howald, Bern. Reproduced by permission. © ARS.

WITHOUT ME ANYWAY

Without me anyway without way I came near without bread
without breath but withkith withkin with Caspar
with a cake so round though somewhat square
but without growth of grass with scars with warts with fingers
with sticks with many O's and few G's
but an enormously tiny bit of a lot
Oh fall you down into your hole oh bury you yourself
and your longwinded hope
give your ego a kick give your id its reward
and whatever is left of you fry it like little fishes in oil
you can peel off your shoes.

FINALLY

Finally

The butcher dog snaps at the golden ring. The
fairy is good but the coffee hard and the granite soft boiled
like a bonnet of cat's fur.
The boys, the men, the ancients.
They sit on the wall and deliberate. Their hands
speak. The cobblestones spring out of the ground like
fountains and take off in every direction.
One could say something is wrong. But it is only the
secret powers we've been expecting since early morning. The
stones fly to the coast of the northern sea, where they get
caught in glistening silver threads. They sway in the
morning sun.

WOLFGANG PAALEN

THE VOLCANO-PYRAMID
a mythological hypothesis suggested by the appearance of a new volcano

The birth of a volcano no longer gives rise to a myth. To conjure away the dangers of their new volcano, the villagers of Paricutin dance before the Christian fetish, the "miraculous" crucifix. They dance badly, their steps as out of rhythm as their beliefs—a confused mixture of decapitated paganism and decayed Catholicism. The creative image no longer emerges where the magic conception has degenerated into petty superstition; it is only in the debris of the great past of these Indians that we find the vestiges of one of the most monumental cosmogonies that man has ever conceived.

The resemblance of the silhouette of the young volcano to that of a pyramid has struck many observers. Moreover Mexico abounds in mountains and hills of volcanic origin which suggest the form of a pyramid. Without doubt the ancestors of the Mexicans of today witnessed the birth of volcanoes, spectacles quite sufficient to generate a myth.

Quiautonatiuh, the Third Age (in ancient Mexican as in Greek mythology four "ages" are distinguished) ended in a rain of fire: "the volcanic ashes were scattered, the bubbling lava boiled up and the reddish rocks were fixed in the ground." In the cataclysm the sun was lost and because all creation was submerged in obscurity the gods assembled at Teotihuacan to recreate the sun. The Toltec myth cited by Miguel Angel Fernández tells how they proceeded. Essentially the myth tells of the rebirth of the sun through the immolation of a god in a fire lighted on the summit of a mountain. Afterward, in order to move, in order to *live,* the sun recreated by the sacrifice of Nanauatzin had to be nourished with blood. Nanauatzin, the "pustulous" god, is identified by Seler with the symbol of the Fourth Age, the "Sun of the Earth-quakes." It seems to me that a god who can be identified with earth-quakes and who disappears in a great fire on a mountain top called the "Oven of the Gods," is clearly character-ized as a volcanic divinity. But how is this sacrifice linked to the solar cult? Why should the fire of heaven live again through the fire of earth and the blood sacrifice?

The great cosmic symbolizations, through all differences of epoch and of race, remain astonishingly alike. Perhaps a new interpretation of the myth of Prometheus will reveal, by analogy, the significance of the Mexican myth.

In the great struggle that fashioned the Greek pantheon, the Titans manifest their volcanic nature through battles of cataclysms, fires and earth-quakes; vanquished, they are cast into and chained "to the bottom of the abysses of the earth." Later, Prometheus, son of the Titan Japet, was also chained to a mountain. Frazer cites a great number of myths of primitive peoples (especially of America) who seek their first fire from volcanoes. This volcanic origin of the ember is often symbolically expressed by the fact that it is a woman who keeps it; a woman more or less characterized as the earth-mother and who keeps the fire in a subterranean place, in a cavern, a box, if not under her skirt or quite simply between her legs. Useless to insist on the fact that man, before he knew how to make fire, could only get it when he met it, so to speak, in a wild state—in forest fires and volcanoes. But only the volcano could *keep* fire for man; only from a few accessible craters could our ancestors readily procure embers. Thus it seems natural that they associated fire with the earth-mother, that they imagined it as a feminine element, conceiving of it principally in its quality of heat.[1] Nevertheless, to ravish this volcanic fire, material as well as psychological interdictions had to be overcome, there had to be the heroic acts that myth commemorates in the exploits of semi-divine heroes. If one does not tangle it up with uselessly complicated interpretations, the Greek myth says very clearly that Prometheus stole fire from a volcano: the forge of Hephaestus. In most of the other myths fire is stolen or delivered by a bird which often takes on a plainly phallic signification. This bird ravisher of fire is afterward not infrequently identified with the fire itself, if not with the sun; Yehl, the Promethean raven of the Northwest-Coast Indians also steals the fire as he sets the sun in the sky. But why? How is it that Hephaestus, the volcanic god, is the one to forge the golden ship in which Helios, the sun, disappears in the evening? Why is he the one to fashion the arrows of the sun-god Apollo? Why does the earth thus give its arrows to the sun? Why, in analogy, in Mexico, is the solar light restored by the sacrifice of the volcanic god Nanauatzin? And why, finally, does Prometheus in the latest version of the myth no longer steal fire from a volcano but light his torch at the sun?

I think that these myths express the following: As long as man was limited to using fire when he found it by chance, he only knew, *ideologically,* how to associate it with *heat;* it is only when he became capable of *lighting it,* of making flame spring up in the night, that he arrived at a conception of it as similar to sunlight. The first torch to light up a cave must have seemed as dazzling as the sun. The myths cited thus express the evolution of the conception *fire-heat* into *fire-light.* Sociologically (at least in Greece) this evolution corresponds to the passage from the matriarchy to the patriarchy. Thus understood the chaining of Prometheus signifies that in the cosmic stratification of the myth, as a son of a Titan, he is related to the volcano; historically, the old matriarchal conception is vanquished and "punished" through him by a patriarchal Zeus. But his final liberation by Hercules (personifying an old solar divinity) indicates that from the rough brasier, Prometheus[2] mythologically evolved to the lighted torch.

His long captivity would then symbolize the long intermediary stage when the conception of "fire-heat" still balances that of "fire-light."

During this epoch, the eagle of Zeus on the mountain is nourished each day on the liver of Prometheus as the solar eagle of Mexico, under the sun of midday on the summit of the temple-pyramid, devours the torn-out hearts. Quauhxicalli, the "eagle-cup," the sacrificial cup in the highest center of the edifice, is then the *crater* of the symbolic volcano which is the pyramid, its "flame of human blood" uniting by sympathetic magic the fire of earth to the fire of heaven. Quetzalcoatl who voluntarily sacrificed himself on the pyre is the twin brother of Xolotl-Nanauatzin; in a larger sense, he is equally the brother of the Phoenix and of the Thunder-bird: it is he, the "Mexican Prometheus,"[3] who achieves the sublimation of fire into light.

Thus the sun worship of the volcano-pyramid would (besides other significations) express the mythological interpretation of the evolution of the concept *fire-heat* into *fire-light*. And the hypothesis that the Mexican pyramid might have its origin in the mythological representation of the volcano is confirmed perhaps by the fact that the myth places the sacrifice of the volcanic god and the rebirth of the sun precisely at Teotihuacan, the place where stand two of America's most ancient and monumental pyramids.

Notes

1. Thus, in archaic and matriarchal Greece, Hephaestus is easily identified with Dionysus.

2. In Christian mythology, the motif of the fall of the Titans appears as the fall of the rebellious angels and Prometheus becomes Lucifer *the bringer of light* as well as the devil in the midst of the subterranean fire.

3. Alfonso Caso, *The Religion of the Aztecs*.

VALENTINE PENROSE

MAY—1941

It will make the muslins drop,
the wind stumble in the grasp of May
like shells, corals unlasting

Let us walk like the wind in the ropes of war
we have to die soon
go down in the water,
explode like mines
in May—

Break the chain of this marriage
of my heart, of my spades, of your kisses, of the moonlight on the windows,
of your day smell, the smell of only love
found in the rocks, bas-reliefs, grottoes, the silk under the
breasts going to Camden Town.
        They are going
        to dip in the fire
        rise as they can
under the water of the pump, the sand of the bombs, and no anemones.

The buds won't finish out this war,
the brick woman with hollow cheeks gave me
        good advice though,

with her good hand wiping my forehead.
But no—take one by his uniform
buttons, far from the faded slopes,

fade in the burned wood,
on the eaten glass,

Remedios Varo, *The Alchemist,* 1958; private collection, Index/Bridgeman Art Library. © ARS.

the old throat of what is melting,
melting the same, cooing the same,
Oh turtle-dove of always on the branch of May.

Here they are gathering in the black circle, eyes
open on the split stone no longer on the bird
Here are the deadly trucks,
striped to a dull music—

Cold dust—on the other side of the flint of the gash,
his arms crossed, all the sicknesses, lying down
in London, under the Twins.

    London

Benjamin Péret

Listen

If you sheltered me like a maybug in a cupboard
bristling with snowdrops coloured by your ocean voyage eyes
monday tuesday etc wouldn't be more than a fly
in a plaza bordered by ruined palaces
from which would issue an immense vegetation of coral
and of embroidered shawls
where one sees
felled trees depart obliquely
to blend in with park benches
where I slept awaiting your arrival
like a forest that awaits the passing of a comet to see clearly
in its underbrush whimpering like a chimney
calling the log it desires since it yawns
like an abandoned quarry
and like a staircase in a tower we would climb
to see ourselves disappear
in the distance
like a table swept away by the flood

Photo of Our Collaborator Benjamin Péret Spitting at a Priest, from *La Révolution surréaliste* 8 (December 1, 1926).

Where Are You

I would speak to you cracked crystal howling like a dog on a night of flailing sheets
like a dismasted boat the foam begins to invade
where the cat meows because all the rats have left
I would speak to you like a tree uprooted by the storm
which so shook the telegraph wires
they seem a brush for mountains resembling a tiger's lower jaw
which slowly tears me with a hideous noise of a battered-in door
I would speak to you like a metro train broken down at the entrance
of a station I enter with a splinter in a toe like a bird in a vineyard
which will yield no more wine than a barricaded street
where I wander like a wig in a fireplace
which hasn't heated anything so long
it thinks itself a cafe counter
where the circles left by the glasses trace a chain
I would only say to you
I love you like the grain of wheat loves the sun rising above its blackbird head

One to One

To wake up in the bottom of a carafe, stunned like a fly, is enough to make you kill your mother five minutes after you get out. That is what happened to me one morning, so it's no surprise that I should have a head shaped like a dandelion and that my shoulders now sag down to my knees. During the first few minutes after I woke up, I imagined that I had always lived at the bottom of a carafe and probably I'd still believe it if I had not seen this sort of bird on the other side of the carafe, pecking furiously at it with his beak. Thanks to this, the fortuitous and unpleasant features of my situation became clear to me and I flew into a rage. I seized a dry leaf by my side and shoving it into my left nostril, cried out: "Is it possible that the dog is the turtle's best friend?" And, from the top of the carafe, a crack in the glass murmured: "Poor idiot! Enemies are not what the dumb masses think. They have beards and their brains are made of celluloid scrapings and potato peelings. Friends have glass heads and bite like transmission belts."

But I insisted: "Is it true that flies do not die on the hands of a clock? Is it true that rice straw is used to make dumplings? Is it true that oranges gush out of mine shafts? Is it true that mortadella is made by blind people? Is it true that quails eat ewes? Is it true that noses get lost in fortresses? Is it true that bathrooms fade away into pianos? Is it true that in dark rooms the song of dreams is never heard?"

Suddenly there was a great noise like a pot falling and rebounding on a stone staircase and a small opening appeared in my prison. Mercifully for me, it did not take long for the opening to grow to the size of a railway tunnel at the entrance of which appeared a small creature which resembled both a sardine and a butterfly. I was no longer alone and consequently I was in less of a hurry to leave the carafe, which I began to find quite congenial. It would not have taken much to have made me ask the sardine-butterfly to live with me, which she probably would not have refused to do, for she seemed quite gentle and obliging. However, I did not risk making the proposition, which many would have found strange, though it is no more extraordinary than throwing a paving stone from the seventh floor into a busy crowded street in the hope of killing someone. But the world is such that living with a sardine butterfly is more scandalous than living alone in a carafe. Consequently I made no proposition to the charming creature who attracted me so much. In fact, as she entered the carafe, her wings fell off, her tail as well as her fins disappeared, a spark followed by a small wisp of smoke escaped from her head and I saw nothing in its place but a signpost on which was written: SCORPION, 200KM 120m. Again I lost my temper, and grabbing the signpost, threw it as hard as I could against the walls of my glass prison. To my great astonishment, the signpost went through the carafe and bounced two or three times upon its outside surface before reducing it to splinters. It was then that I was surprised to find myself stretched out on my back in a field of wheat. When I made a move to get up on my feet, twenty partridges flew out of my pockets where they must have been sitting for quite some time—although I had not been aware of it—for they left a number of eggs which hatched in my hand.

Having recovered from my surprise, it occurred to me that one field was as good as another, at least in the present state of things, and I resolved that from now on it would no longer be so. Not without difficulty, I succeeded in regaining the vertical position to which I was born, and threw jets of saliva to all sides which flew off, followed by the shots of invisible hunters. I climbed into the ditch, taking care not to crush the pretty white moles which had naively come out to enjoy the cool air. It is true, they experienced this pleasure rarely enough! They were so happy that, although I was a stranger to them, they could not restrain themselves from confiding their story to me. It was a very small white mole with dragonfly wings which spoke:

The White Mole's Story

Just as you see me, I was born in a box of shoe-polish. My father was a chestnut vendor and my mother a sow. How did that happen? I am not sure. My father was a tall man, and thin as a stick, except that his head was easily the largest that could be imagined. He had no nose and his ears hung like the stems of grapevines torn off by the wind. Of course, he was stupid, that is why he was a chestnut vendor. One day, having torn off a sow's tail, he walked through Troyes, shouting: "THIS IS MY BLOOD." Soon the druggists were following his trail, then the solicitors, hardware salesmen, cess-pit cleaners, lacemakers, orthopaedists, justices of the peace, café proprietors, sacristans, herb dealers, amateur fishermen, children of pigs, and finally the clergymen. Then, shaken with fright, he hid the sow's tail in a box of shoe-polish which he put in a mailbox after addressing it as follows:

CLAY PIPE
at IVORY TOWER
near SCURVY (Morbihan)

The letter had its ups and downs. Soon it climbed an iceberg, then descended into a vat, then climbed a tree whose leaves it devoured, causing it shortly thereafter to fall into a well from which a bucket of blue glass extracted it and set it on the right path. Finally, after a thousand changes, it arrived. The place in question looked more like a tulip which had sprung out of a decomposing skull than a well-managed establishment. Indeed, the staircase was laid out like a dead snake in the hall, and the upper stories were reached by means of an arrow which one stuck through one's backside, before being shot up to the desired level by the ground floor. There the letter found its addressee, who paced from one end of the stairway to the other without meeting "a living soul" and asked himself in what desert he found himself without camels or caravans, in what desert populated only by crackling noises and the tinkling of broken glass, in what desert he dragged his feet melancholically like an asparagus which, expecting to be eaten with vinaigrette dressing, is merely sucked at with white sauce. The unknown person was none other than Clay Pipe, famous for duelling with empty bottles.

It was then I came into being.

But perhaps it is worthwhile recounting the marvellous adventures of Clay Pipe and the empty bottles.

Clay Pipe had always believed that virgins lived in broken bottles. But, having found his left eye in one of them, he realised he had been deceived and was quite vexed. Failing to find the young virgins he was after in the broken bottles, he resolved to raise grandmothers, suitably shrivelled by a half century of use, in them instead. Is it necessary to say that his project miscarried miserably? Hardly had the grandmothers been shut up in the broken bottles, than they liquefied and rapidly became a sort of tar used to repair the streets of Paris. All hope of thus obtaining a generation of diminutive grandmothers was lost. But Clay Pipe was tireless. Without becoming discouraged he sowed naval officers in the bottom of the bottles, but that finished him, for naval officers do not smoke clay pipes, but rather the wreckage from ships and sailors' hair, which, as everyone knows is bad for the health of empty bottles. Clay Pipe was not long in seeing the effect on his protegés, and he took his revenge on the naval officers, who he reduced to the state of slugs, molluscs much appreciated by empty bottles, which eat a great many of them especially in the springtime. He was however wrong not to hide from them the origin of their food, because the bottles, despite everything, were much attached to the naval officers, and they became extremely angry. A paper lantern duel ensued and Clay Pipe was beaten, having swallowed only 721 lanterns, while the smallest of his adversaries had devoured at least a thousand. Since that day, Clay Pipe had paced the horizontal staircase from one end to the other in the hope of finding his empty bottles again, but in vain. They had fled long ago, thanks to the spring geranium shoots which grow so frequently on the bellies of pregnant women and instigate premature delivery.

And the little white mole went away as she had come, like a crescent moon. I found myself alone again, desperately alone, my feet attached to a sort of sleigh decorated with a host of little pigs similar to the flag of the United States. This indicated to me that the sleigh was made of acorn potato flour. While I reflected on the insubstantial nature of such a vehicle, it started to move, while the pigs flew away crying:

"Lafayette I am here! . . . Over there! . . . You don't make omelettes without breaking eggs . . . eggs . . . eggs . . . eggs . . . eggs . . . eggs . . . Negroes have flat feet . . . Swedes eat mussels . . ." And a thousand other things in which the word "hair" was repeated often.

Only one young pig, shiny as a new penny, stayed on the sleigh and when the vehicle stopped near the ear of a naturalised elephant, spoke the following words to me:

—I live in the toolsheds of roadmenders. I eat sleighs. I read Paul Bourget beginning at the end of each line. I play night-table music. I caress the fingers of brides and I keep a well-known politician in the forest of my bristles. What is he and who am I?

But instead of replying, I asked:

—Did you stand in line?

—Sit down, I beg you, he replied. I had a slight cold and now you are saved.

—I understand nothing of all this. I could not help telling him. And now the cauliflowers litter the airless rooms and turn yellow when by chance the little white crystal spiders happen to meet them, playing their customary game of whist in the evening in the deserted squares, although they have long been closed to the public. But this stupid beast would not let me get away so easily, and once again taking me aside, asked:

—Does the gentleman wish me to put on his dressing gown?

Hoping to get rid of him, I replied in the same silly tone he had adopted: "I can't find my bedroom slippers."

Again the pig asked me: "Does the gentleman wish me to comb his hair?"

—Just part it. I can do the rest very well, I replied, exasperated.

For more than a day, the sleigh slid rapidly between a double hedge of porcupines, which gravely contemplated our strange rig and fled as soon as we were out of sight, uttering cries so piercing that frightened birds fell to the ground, where they remained flattened out like a piece of putty on a window. I began to worry. The more so since an indefinable odour floated in the air, something like the smell of artichokes and a well-groomed head of hair. And our speed, which increased steadily! And the pig, which became as large as a church! This animal upset me more than I can say, with his great pale face barred vertically with a sword, and a pistol tattooed on each side of an enormous nose supporting a large stick to which were attached more than fifty children's balloons. To tell the truth, these balloons, whose purpose I did not understand, intrigued me considerably. For most of them contained a bearded man whose chest was decorated with many rusted medals and which opened like a door, revealing inside a rubbish bin overflowing with enormous rats which jostled and crushed one another, drawn no doubt by some alluring rottenness.

The pig observed my troubles and took up his questions again:

—What is he and who am I?

—No doubt the inventor of a cattle car, so-called because it serves for the transportation of playing cards and principally clubs, like clovers, which must be spread out in good season upon green fields, in order that they may acquire the qualities of suppleness and endurance which other cards do not have.

The animal let out a great burst of laughter and murmured disdainfully: "You joker."

Then he began to sing:

On the prairie there is a lock
a lock that I know
It glows and rocks
when the birds fly around

On the prairie there is a camel
a camel with no teeth
I will make him some with a mirror
and his humps will be my reward

On the prairie there is a pipe
where my destiny hides

On the prairie there is a chairman's chair
I will sit in the chair
and the public will be at my feet
It will be warm it will be cold

I will raise centipedes
which I will give to dressmakers
and I will raise chair rungs
which I will give to bicycles

For a long time he continued in this manner, which was far from reassuring to me. Suddenly, as we approached a forest which had barred the horizon for a long time, I saw the forest leave the ground and come galloping up on both sides after bowing respectfully to my companion, who, at this moment, appeared to be filled with unbearable self-sufficiency. They had a long conversation of which I could grasp only a few words, which gave me no idea of what it was about!

—Down there, in that pavilion . . . what can these letters mean: S.G.D.G. . . . What if we visited the naval section . . . provided that we get safely into port . . . , etc.

However, I supposed it had to do with me, and I had no doubt they intended to do me a bad turn, so I prepared to defend myself, but I did not have the chance, the forest grabbed me from behind and immobilised me in no time, then shoved my head into my stomach, pinned my arms against my buttocks, and carried me away, rolling me along like a barrel.

And since then I have wandered the world over.

The Four Elements

The world is composed of water, earth, air and fire. It is not spherical but shaped like a bowl, and is one of the breasts of heaven. The other is to be found at the centre of the Milky Way.

I. Earth

Earth breeds flies, phantoms which are there to watch over it by day and guard it during the warm weather. When it is cold, dried earth shrivels into pumpkins and needs no watching over. But during the summer smoke pours out of its ears and, without flies to direct it upwards, this would lie around like bundles of dirty linen.

When thoroughly watered, earth brings forth the following:

1. Lipstick, which is what kisses are made of. There are two kinds of lipstick—wavy lipstick coming in long ripples which, when distilled, produces flags—and light lipstick which bears the flowers that turn into kisses. There are, however, two very distinct ways of obtaining these. It can be done either by drying the blossoms the very moment they burst open, or by crushing the seeds to obtain a perfume which evaporates so quickly that it is almost impossible to hang on to it.

2. Turkish baths, which come from kneading damp earth with yoghurt. These make such a disgusting din that they have been gradually pushed further and further into the desert.

3. Frogs, which are slowly eating away the earth.

4. Cellos, which are used more and more frequently to cure arthritis and which, when ground down to a powder, are very popular as a detergent which does not spoil the colours of delicate and flimsy underclothes.

5. Spectacles for people with short sight and which come from softening earth with pots of boiling china tea and then simmering it all in a steamer.

Many other things may be obtained also from dampened earth, such as compasses, sausages, boxers, matches, and prepositions that were still used by our grandparents but which can only be found nowadays in antique shops.

By blowing on earth, i.e., by gently filling it with air, gooseberries are obtained. Tricycles come by blowing hard.

Mechanical methods (whose origins will be explained in greater detail later) permit greater quantities of air to be pumped into the earth, and have brought forth sieves. This is done by taking earth sprinkled with chicken droppings and subjecting it to a powerful stream of air which has been carefully kept at room temperature. Once reduced to dust the loamy earth is enclosed in a receptacle in which the air, agitated by a powerful propeller-fan, goes from freezing point every five minutes to fifty degrees above zero and vice versa, and produces caretakers. These were discovered originally by the Prince Consort, and have since been very much perfected, but do not last as long as they did in the good old days.

In a receptacle containing air at a pressure of three atmospheres and which is subjected to a very low temperature, earth gives us knitting needles. By increasing the pressure and lowering the temperature we also get blackbirds, cradles, green peas and beastly motorbikes.

Thinly sliced and toasted, earth turns into fish-hooks. Thickly sliced and shrivelled to a cinder it turns into urinals. Rolled into balls that explode in the flames, it produces cockchafers and, if the balls are large enough, moustaches.

II. Air

Air, in its natural state, constantly secretes pepper which makes the whole world sneeze. At ground level this pepper condenses so as to give trinkets in summer and newspapers in winter. These only need to be put in a cool place for them to be transformed into railway stations or sponges, depending on how many pages they contain. Pepper also becomes condensed at two thousand five hundred feet up in space, after which it falls back to earth as such a fine dust that nobody ever notices it. Therefore, when the accumulated evidence of this flagrant futility does eventually begin to make an appearance, the man in the street automatically treads on it and flattens it without showing any signs of conscience. Higher still, pepper is what puts the sparkle into starlight.

When painted blue, air provides undergrowth in dry weather, and bleach when it rains, but it can be dangerous to human beings if taken in large doses as it causes stomach ulcers and blisters, and also rots the teeth. When painted yellow, air is used for making furs and, mixed with cockchafer powder, it cures lockjaw. When sugar is added, air is used for mending inner tubes, and if salt is added, it makes beds. When warmed between the hands it increases in size until it is transformed into whips. Shredded into mincemeat and doused with red wine, orchestral conductors may be produced, and these are always extremely useful to country folk at harvest time. Dried in the sun and kept throughout the winter in a very dry place, air will provide engagement rings in springtime, but their extreme sensitivity to variations in temperature makes them very fragile and they rarely survive into adulthood.

Kept in a sealed cupboard, air has a tendency to escape. When it succeeds in doing this, it expires at the threshold in the form of mushrooms. These are often used today for smoothing away wrinkles.

Steeped in vinegar, air produces dock-hands who, in windy weather, run like over-ripe cheese. In such cases tender dock-hands are collected, dried, and then carefully ground so that they may be sown in spots well away from direct sunlight. After a month, the moon rises from these spots, forcing its way out of the earth in order to bloom, as it is not a star as so many people seem to think, but merely the pollen of the innumerable female flowers of the tender dock-hands, which rises from the earth every evening, while the male flowers fall back to the earth so that their seed may spring up again. Each morning the moon sinks down into the sea where, bouncing against the waves, it sets up tides until eventually it melts and, as it dissolves, flavours the sea with salt.

III. Water

In the form of rain, water becomes earthworms burrowing their way into the ground. These worms, going to enormous depths, gather in vast masses in the earth's natural cavities and, when they split, produce crude oil. Several varieties of this oil are worth noting:

1. Studded oil, which has a very brief duration period since, once formed, it is immediately eaten away by moths.

2. Seeded oil, which elephants find irresistible because it makes their tusks grow.

3. Unicorn oil, which is completely useless as oil. Only the horn, decomposing under wind pressure, will give marathon runners, who are in constant use when making china for the purification of clay. This has been previously purified of all noxious matters by the application of strong doses of octopus ink.

4. Hoarse oil, which has been given this name because of the disgraceful raucous noises it makes. This is the oil that causes blisters that spread extremely infectious diseases.

5. Hairy oil, which clings to the bark of trees in cold countries and eventually gives, in swift succession, sparrow's eggs, Chinese crackers and hat-pins. The crackers and the hat-pins together produce red billiard balls that are a menace to carp. They are so ferocious that within a few days whole ponds which were once full of fish are turned into deserts, after which the red balls expire through lack of nourishment, at the same time producing will-o-the-wisps.

6. Snowy oil, which is only to be found at the tops of the highest mountains of Europe. At a height of two thousand five hundred yards this oil loses all its properties, becomes dull, tarnished and brittle, and when exposed to sunlight, turns into chairs, a species of lemur which looks harmless, but whose extremely poisonous bite can be fatal if not rapidly attended to.

Chickens, whose feathers are keenly sought after for making low gradients, come from river water by moonlight. However, these chickens do not have feathers in summer, and their sprouting quills are like red teeth which are shredded to make candles which are most useful in the country for locating underground lakes. Such underground water is inhabited by multitudes of keys which, as soon as a well is sunk, slip out through the shaft and build nests at the top of the tallest tree with piercing shrieks. As soon as night falls, they gang up in groups to attack dogs who run for their lives when they see them coming, yelping blue murder.

Once it rises to ground level, well-water evaporates, leaving a brilliant emerald residue at the bottom of the well. When warmed, well-water becomes hard, expands and, at a temperature of eighty degrees, acquires great elasticity which makes it liable to turn into kangaroos in two or three days. But these kangaroos are subject to diseases of the respiratory tubes, as well as to tuberculosis, and this plays havoc with their numbers. This is why deadwood kangarooes, which are rather more hardy than the other types, are the choice of rabbit-breeders since, once the rabbits have been in contact with the kangaroos, their fur takes on a soft silky texture which is perfect for making flags. When temperatures fall below zero, well-water is transformed into beggars. Cut into very thin slices, these are used for making grottoes.

Sea water, once it has evaporated, leaves behind a silk whose long life is a source of constant amazement to man. Certain female silks, a thousand years old, and which still produce four litters of brandy glasses a year—each litter comprising at least a dozen glasses—have been quoted. It is obvious that, under conditions such as this, the brandy glass would have become a plague to man worse than locusts, had he not discovered in crutches an even more implacable ally.

Indeed, one single crutch annually devours hundreds of thousands of brandy glasses and, in equatorial Africa alone, crutches, of which at least twenty different species are known, make up endless armies which, after devouring every brandy glass in sight, turn to terrorising the natives whose harvest of calves' livers they completely destroy, thus reducing them to poverty and famine.

Finally, we should mention bearded-water, whose nature is still not very clear (although it may be made into armour which is very suitable for little old ladies who feel the cold rather badly); flying-water, which navigators use to take their bearings; light water, which is the basis of swimming-trunks; hardwood-water, which is indispensable to sweet-makers; dusty-water, which is useful in carpentry; feathery water, which is hunted in December just at the moment when the feathers take on their most brilliant hues; and clinker water, which is mainly used in electricity, but also has many other uses which we shall investigate later.

IV. Fire

Essentially a mineral element, fire dwells in stones and eggs. Trembling stones are the ones which, when damp and exposed to sunlight, give the best kind of fire. This is soft, sweet, velvety and perfumed, and is currently used for burning down churches. But such stones should not be allowed to tremble too much, as, if the trembling is over-pronounced, the fire will melt and turn into a hot spicy sauce whose heat scalds people touching it and stings them with begonia to make them yawn from morn till night. If the trembling is not intermittent, the fire will crackle and spurt out damp moss which will extinguish it, but also serve as a breeding ground for those fleas which are so dreaded by dyers and cleaners because of the mess they make of their colours. Disturbed by these fleas, colours do indeed lose their glittering sparkle and freshness, so that it becomes impossible to maintain a uniform tone. On the other hand, this kind of disturbing action is exactly what is sought by dyers who require marbled or textured effects. Therefore they capture the fleas and put them in equal quantities in sealed jars with the dye and keep the mixture at a fairly high temperature for varying lengths of time, depending on whether they want to achieve an effect of marble or of watered silk.

Left out in the rain for a whole winter, wind-stones produce fierce fires whose life is, however, very short unless great care is taken to plunge them in the sea before using them, i.e. before putting them in those lobster-pots which are ideal for kindling fires. The fires then attract moles which are their main source of nourishment and thus help to extend the length and intensity of their life.

The amount of different fires that are known is considerable. Amongst the most common must be counted tatter-fire from which we obtain bottles which, when plunged into quinine baths, give such ferocious fires that special tools are needed to cut them into the resilient lightweight planks which children use to make their kites. Wellington fire is also not difficult to find, being the result of a mixture of sleeping-cars and wheel-barrows, and it is greatly sought after by composers. Stretched out on soft and well-brushed beds, when it has been lightly sprinkled with salt, it plays symphonies, and when it has been splashed with ink, it sings operas. One of the most common types of fire, stinking-fire, is obtained by soaking bishops in cod-liver oil. It gives off a noxious odour, but this is excellent for the growth of asparagus shoots, as it puts paid to the drawers which nibble at them. We may also give the example of cloudy-fire which stops rats and mice invading empty houses; passage-fire which fizzles out as soon as it is squirted from hypodermic syringes; taffeta-fire, which is essential in pastry-making; ostrich-fire, which every girl slips into her bra when going to her first dance; hobbling-fire, which scares doctors stiff since it starts epidemics (which must be fought off as soon as they appear with an inhalation of leeks); whipped-fire, which prevents villagers from sleeping on the night before the grapes are gathered in; twig-fire; pill-fire; dry-fire; black-and-white-fire; striped-fire; doctrinal-fire; etc.

All these types of fire are frequently encountered in their more-or-less pure states in all parts of the surface of the globe. They can be very easily cleaned, either with fish-bones or by filtering them through blotting-paper which has previously been soaked in vinegar. However, much rarer varieties of fire are also known, such as button-fire which suits blondes so well, or brain-fire which is produced with great difficulty by crushing turkeys with twitch-grass to make a smooth paste which is then put out to dry in the sun after sprinkling it with equal quantities of very fine iron and copper filings. If the filings are not fine enough, the paste will run and produce small change; if it is too fine, birds will come and peck at it, causing it to explode and give out clouds of skin-clinging black dust which can only be got rid of by painting the affected areas with tincture of iodine. After a few days a nut of brain-fire can be discovered on cracking open a pound or two of this paste which has been allowed to dry. One must still be very careful to avoid dropping it on wool as this would be liable to become inflamed. When this brain-fire is crushed and compounded with clusters of heliotrope flowers, which have also been reduced to a powder, it is made into a night-cap for women wishing to acquire beauty spots. Amongst the rarest of the remaining fires we should still note shutter-fire, which rises from volcanic ash long after the eruption has taken place, and which, at the rate of a few ounces per ton of ash treated with cider, makes it very scarce; dewlap-fire, which is used as a decorative motif; flying-fire, which it is strictly forbidden to take into fashion-houses as it stirs up the passions of the needlewomen against the wives of their bosses; rose-fire, which is found at the crack of dawn in the woods in springtime; cross-bow-fire, which is a very rare disease of the horns of cockled snails (one in ten thousand has it); quivering-fire; braces-fire; breast-fire; and, last but not least, crumb-fire, which female penguins sometimes secrete when laying their eggs, although it evaporates after a few moments if not gathered immediately and put into fresh cream.

Francis Picabia

Aphorisms

Knowledge is an old error remembering its youth.

Taste is as tiring as well-bred people.

The most beautiful discovery of man is bicarbonate of soda.

Vegetables are more serious than men and more sensitive to frost.

The world is steeped in good taste and ignorance pasted together.

Painting is made for dentists.

Really, it is only mediocre people who have genius during their lifetime.

It rains and I think of the poor people for whom it doesn't rain.

Human beings win diplomas and lose their instinct.

The more one pleases, the more one displeases.

The only way to have followers is to run faster than the others.

Spinoza is the only person who never read Spinoza.

It's easier to scratch one's ass than one's heart (St. Augustine).

The unknown is an exception, the known a deception.

A favorable wind has blue feathers.

Tables turn, thanks to the spirit; pictures and other works of art might be called safe-depositables: the spirit is inside and becomes increasingly inspired as the auction prices mount.

Only useless things are indispensable.

PABLO PICASSO

IN THE CORNER A VIOLET SWORD

In the corner a violet sword the bells the paper folds a metal sheep life lengthening the page a gun shot the paper is singing the canaries in the white almost pink shade a river in the empty white in the light blue shade lilac colours a hand on the edge of the shadow casts a shadow on the hand a grasshopper very rose-coloured a root raises its head a nail the black of the trees with nothing a fish a nest the heat in broad daylight looks at a parasol light fingers in the light the white of the paper the sun light in the white cuts out a dazzling mask the sun its light the sun very white the sun intensely white

Listen in your childhood to the hour which white in blue memory borders white in his eyes very blue and indigo spot of silver sky the white looks cobalt pierce the white paper which the blue ink tears out bluish his ultramarine descends which white enjoys repose blue stirred in the dark green green wall which his pleasure writes light green rain which swims yellow green in light oblivion by his green foot the sand earth song sand of the earth afternoon sand earth

Girl decently dressed in a beige coat with violent cuffs 158. 500–300–22–95 cents calico slip corrected and revised with allusions to ermine fur 143–60–32 a brassière wide open the edges of the wound held open by hand pullies making the sign of the cross perfumed with roblochon cheese 1300–75–05–49–317.000–25 cents openings added every other day incrusted in the skin by shivers kept lively by the dead silence of the colour bait à la Lola de Valence 103 plus the languid looks 310–313 plus 3.000.000–80 francs–15 cents for a glance forgotten on the chest of drawers—penalties incurred in the course of the match— throwing the discus between the legs through a series of events which for no good reason succeed in making a nest for themselves and in some cases in turning into the rational picture of the cup 380—11 plus expenses but the drawing so academic pattern of all history since its inception down to this morning does not even write if one steps on the fingers which point towards the exit but spits its bouquet with the drinking glass which the smell produced

Photo of Pablo Picasso with René Char, in headdresses, 1965. Courtesy of Marie-Claude Char.

Pablo Picasso, *The Cage,* 1933; Coll. Fukushima, Paris, Art Resource. © ARS.

by the regiments marching with a flag at their head only unless the titillations of desire discover the suitable place for changing the sardine into a shark the shopping list lengthens only from that time on without the unavoidable halt at table at lunch time in order to write seated in the midst of so many hyperboles mixed with the cheese and tomato

GIVE AND TAKE TWIST AND KILL

give and task twist and kill I cross and light and burn caress and lick and look I ring the bells furiously until they bleed frighten the pigeons and make them fly all around the dove-cote until they fall dead tired to the ground I will stop up all the windows and doors with dirt and with hair and I will paint all the birds that sing and cut all the flowers I will cradle the lamb in my arms and give him my breast to be devoured I will wash him with my tears of pleasure and of pain and put him to sleep with the song of my loneliness by *Soleares* and engrave fields of wheat and grain and watch them die lying face up in the sun I will wrap the flowers in newspaper and throw them out the window into the stream which repents with all its sins on its back flowing laughing and happy in spite of all to make its nest in the gutter I will break the music of the woods against the rocks of the waves of the sea and I will bite the cheek of the lion and make the wolf cry of tenderness before a portrait of the water that drops its arm into the bathtub.

GISÈLE PRASSINOS

THE WOOL DRESS

And there you are. Now, I don't know where to go any more, without baggage, without money, with just the dress on my back. Luckily, it's a warm one, I knitted it myself by hand, it took me, that's true, two winters of nonstop work; but I can say I'm dressed now. If that thing hadn't happened, everything would be fine, really. And I don't have an aunt in the world, not a sister, nor even a friend whose place I could go to for shelter. Nothing, I've nothing left.

This morning still, I was sitting in my room, I'd hardly finished ironing the seams of my knit dress—I'd finished the last stitch yesterday evening at eleven o'clock—when there was a ring at the door.

Opening it, I was sure, straight off, that I didn't know the three people laden with cases and the baby smiling at me with quite sincere pleasure. I couldn't lie and let them believe it was me they were looking for. Very quickly, before one of them, by mistake, jumped on me to kiss me, for I could see very well they were getting their mouths ready, I said:

"You must be mistaken, I don't know you."

However, no one listened or heard me and I had to submit to an embrace from all of them, one after the other. They even put in my arms the child the younger woman held in hers. Its face and especially its mouth was covered with scabs and patches of raw flesh. It was smiling though like the others and awkwardly laid its poor diseased cheek against mine, to the great joy of its relatives: the father, the mother, and the grandmother, no doubt.

Then they put their cases down and the two women noticed my dress on the hanger. It still gave off a light steam after the careful ironing I'd given it. The younger one looked at the other, full of mute admiration for what she could see, murmuring something in her ear. Finally, they came close to feel the wool and judge its quality, as if my dress was in a shop window and they wanted to be quite sure before buying it. I felt afraid and couldn't resist the wish to put it away safe. I summoned up my courage, I took the dress down and

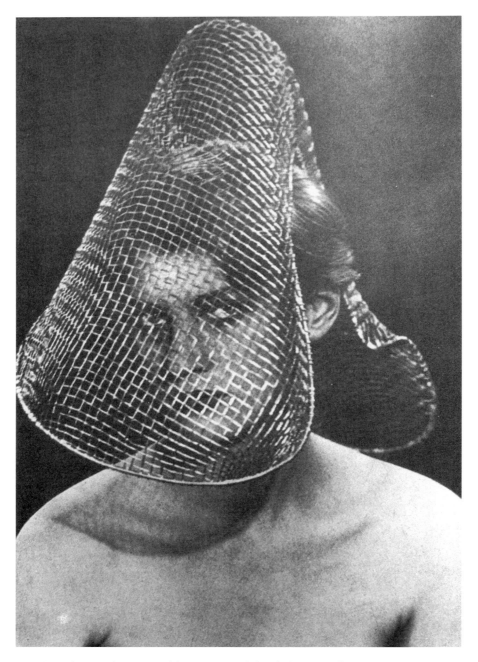

Man Ray, photograph in *Le Surréalisme au service de la Révolution* 1 (July 1930).
© 1988 ADAGP, Paris.

slipped it on in front of them, in spite of their eyes fastened to my every movement. I tell myself, now, I did the right thing.

You couldn't say they weren't friendly, on the contrary, they were even willing to help.

"Don't put yourself out for us," they said, "we'll manage, we'll even unpack our cases on our own."

And that was true. With the child wedged on the sideboard, all three of them took out their things and laid them on my bed in orderly little bundles.

"And how's your mother's cold, better?" the old woman asked me in a soft voice, as she counted the pile of baby's diapers.

She's been dead eighteen years, my mother has, but I couldn't answer, my jaws seemed stuck together forever.

And she went on:

"*He* didn't want to come, you know what he's like. Always doing the opposite of other people. I could've insisted, but because of you, because I thought he could cause trouble, I told him, 'Do as you like.'"

"He'll make up his mind to it, alright, one day," said the man in a tone of indifference and, anxiously, "Joan, it's time," he added, speaking to the young woman, after looking at his watch. "Just give it a try, all you've got to do is stretch out, I'll hand him to you."

She began to cry softly on her mother's shoulder and, with a tired air, did as she was told. Then she took out a skinny little breast and the child threw himself at it. Then the other two stood on each side of my bed to watch.

"Do you think it's going to start again?" said the old woman, while her daughter's closed eyelids trembled as if in expectation of a dreaded event.

The man remained silent and watched greedily. He looked at that moment, like one of those fanatics photographed for movie newsreels during a boxing match or at the races.

The child was sucking and fidgeting at the end of the gray nipple it was drawing in further and further, ceaselessly letting go and taking hold again, with grunts of impatience.

"Little vampire!" said the father in a changed tone, his mouth twisted, while his eyes filled with strange pride.

"It's begun . . . ," said the old woman.

What had begun was blood. It ran around the child's mouth, soaking the breast and the sheets of my bed on which the young woman was struggling feebly.

When she seemed to have fainted away and the child quietened down, its nose in its food, its father took it in his arms and amused himself making it laugh.

"We're going to eat too?" he proposed at that point.

"Let's eat then," said the old woman, looking at me.

What could I do, but bring out the bread and the nuts for my own dinner? But as that seemed only to half satisfy them, I opened the two cans of sardines I kept in stock.

When everything had been eaten up, the father stretched and lay down by the side of his wife who still hadn't moved since suckling the baby. The old woman curled up across the bottom of the bed, after placing the baby up close to her.

They put the light out. There were a few minutes of silence during which I tried to settle on the freezing floor. Then I heard my bed squeak, once, twice, then the baby began to whimper gently, as they all do before falling asleep. In the dark the old woman had sat up, her hands crossed on her stomach.

I tried to manage to sleep on the cold floor, I couldn't do so. The moment I began to warm the wood under my body, the bed began to make a noise again, and I heard the man whisper;

"My dear, my beauty, my sweetie . . ."

"No, no!" the young woman moaned.

At that moment, I saw the shadow of the old woman get up and come toward me.

"They take up all the room," she murmured with tears in her voice.

She crouched down and I felt the weight and dryness of a very old body press down on me.

"You'll excuse *him* if *he* hasn't come," she said to me again, "you know what he's like . . ."

That's when I got up, leaving on the cold floor, the cold floor of my bedroom, the moist imprint of my back. I opened the door, the door of my bedroom, without quite thinking what I was doing. Outside, it was dawn. A freezing wind hit me and I walked a long time.

But luckily I have my wool dress. Those two winters of nonstop work won't have been for nothing, it clings gently to my bust and my back, it's all I've got left.

Because I'll never go back there, to my room, no indeed.

RAYMOND QUENEAU

SURPRISES

How tightly packed in we were on that bus platform! And how stupid and ridiculous that young man looked! And what was he doing? Well, if he wasn't actually trying to pick a quarrel with a chap who—so he claimed! the young fop! kept on pushing him! And then he didn't find anything better to do than to rush off and grab a seat which had become free! Instead of leaving it for a lady!

Two hours after, guess whom I met in front of the gare Saint-Lazare! The same fancypants! Being given some sartorial advice! By a friend!

You'd never believe it!

DREAM

I had the impression that everything was misty and nacreous around me, with multifarious and indistinct apparitions, amongst whom however was one figure that stood out fairly clearly which was that of a young man whose too-long neck in itself seemed to proclaim the character at once cowardly and quarrelsome of the individual. The ribbon of his hat had been replaced by a piece of plaited string. Later he was having an argument with a person whom I couldn't see and then, as if suddenly afraid, he threw himself into the shadow of a corridor.

The Rainbow

One day I happened to be on the platform of a violet bus. There was a rather ridiculous young man on it—indigo neck, cord round his hat. All of a sudden he started to remonstrate with a blue man. He charged him in particular, in a green voice, with jostling him every time anybody got off. Having said this, he rushed headlong towards a yellow seat and sat down on it.

Two hours later I saw him in front of an orange-coloured station. He was with a friend who was advising him to have another button put on his red overcoat.

Interjections

Psst ! h'm ! ah ! oh ! hem ! ah ! ha ! hey ! well ! oh ! pooh ! poof ! ow ! oo ! ouch ! hey ! eh ! h'm ! pffft !

Well ! hey ! pooh ! oh ! h'm ! right !

ALICE RAHON

DESPAIR

To Pablo Picasso

The fireworks have gone off. Gray is the absolute color of the present tense. I saw that nightingales imitate dead leaves well before autumn. Despair is a school for deaf-mutes taking their Sunday walk.

It would be better. I don't know what would be better. The thread breaks constantly; perhaps it's the same frustrating task as when a blind man tries to recall the memory of colors as his white window.

Beautiful women with silver waists always fly above cities—Patience—the signs on those roads where every mistake is irreparable end in a horsehead-shaped club.

We must cry out all our secrets before it's too late. It's previously too late if we've forgotten to leave the chair where despair will sit to join our conversation. Despair will never be reduced to begging even if they burn his arms. Then he'll affect the silhouette of a poppy against a stormy sky. His pipe-like laughter will only become insulting.

For a while I've lived on a geography map on the wall. I think I'm at the wind's crossroads. I chat with him. The bouquet of larkspur takes flight at dusk and goes to spend the night on the ponds. The doll jumps rope with its shadow. I shall not tame that shadow that followed me during childhood.

I think that at the bottom of their graves the dead listen for a long time to see if their hearts will start beating again. For the noise, for the company of noise, let's greet the company tied by strings.

FROM *LORD PATCHOGUE*

1. The reverse is just as good as the right side: it is necessary to wait there.

2. For customer—

How to stop him? I know everything he is going to tell me. That's enough. I can predict his every move. Do not open your mouth, simpleton. I know what you will have to say tomorrow, I know you from the front, behind, north, south, hot, cold; that's enough.

Do not open your mouth, my friend. To whom are you speaking, you are drunk, my ears are your ears, your tongue is my own, you are alone, madmen make me afraid.

"My friend's sweethearts . . . "

" . . . are my sweethearts." I can complete all your sentences.

3. When tiredness overcomes Lord Patchogue at his observation post, when he became certain that he would not discover anything except a confirmation, he turns round, a mirror is behind him and Lord Patchogue sees himself again. They both say to one another in fearful tones which only increase as they contemplate themselves: "I am a man trying not to die." And Lord Patchogue launches himself through the mirror a second time. A crash of splintering glass. Lord Patchogue stands before another mirror, facing Lord Patchogue. On his forehead, the cut is bleeding once again. Lord Patchogue repeats: "I am a man trying not to die." And when he passes through the third mirror amidst a noise which is now familiar, he knows that he will meet Lord Patchogue whose forehead will be bleeding more heavily in the fourth mirror and who will tell him: "I am a man trying not to die." This is what happens. Now he knows, all he can do is to break the glass; the eye that looks at the eye that looks at the eye that looks . . .

The man trying not to die has propelled himself; he walks automatically, without curiosity, without 'expectation,' because he cannot do otherwise, with each step another mirror shatters; he walks surrounded by the crash which soothes the ear of the condemned man; before each mirror he chants: ". . . the eye—that looks at the eye—that looks at the eye—that looks at the eye—that looks . . ." Lord Patchogue stops. The floor is nothing but a broken mirror, not just the floor but also the walls and ceiling. Pretty landscape, the walls and ceiling lodge in the debris of mirrors as best they can.

4. Lord Patchogue has a plan. So much the worse for the first person to happen by. Wait. At last the sound of footsteps approaching the caged hunter. Someone is in the room, someone who is still out of sight of the mirror. Will the mirror's call really be in vain? No, whoever it is approaches. Alas, it's a woman.

"Cheated! Clear off, sugar! Next please!"

She preens herself professionally. Disarmed, Lord Patchogue passively returns to her what she desires. What love, what lovers, what what. The young woman is more than self-satisfied, she runs her hands over her breasts. Lord Patchogue reflects her movements with docility, all it takes to recall him to himself is the contact of the two young unknown globes under his fingers. Over her blouse, his fingers cautiously linger on a woman's breast as she breathes in, he feels her swell, he receives her warmth.

In order to adjust a stocking, she reveals a leg with the indifferent precision of someone who knows that nobody can possibly be watching. Lord Patchogue obedient to the unstated wish offers her a leg for the sake of love.

He can hardly believe his eyes, and over her blouse his fingers cautiously linger on a woman's chest, his own, at his own body temperature, rising as she breathes. But would the transformation stop with the breasts or . . . And a comic inquietude seizes hold of Lord Patchogue, so compelling is the superstition of male virility that instead of hoping for the acquisition of a new sex, Lord Patchogue with a furtive but revealing gesture checks to assure himself that he is still a man. As he prepares himself to inhale, there is a scream from in front of him. Because unfortunately the young girl, now passive in her turn, can do no more than imitate the movement of Lord Patchogue. And what a discovery: attributes which only marriage should reveal to her. The victim might well run off, but towards what dreams!

5. There is no way out on this side, any progress is impossible, the ladder of eyes stretches to infinity. In front of him, it would be enough to traverse the mirror in the opposite direction, taking every conceivable precaution of course, a blow with the heel to begin with would suffice; but would that not be to return to his hat size and wouldn't the nine letters of his name coil themselves around his neck like the chains on which identity medallions hang; undesirable. The walls, there were still the walls; Lord Patchogue approaches, touches them with his finger, pushes; but even the mirrors offer less resistance to his efforts.

Young unknown, your hair is out of place; to tidy it, thoughtless little fly, you approach the mirror. Watch out, Lord Patchogue has a plan. But what's the use, the breeze which has mussed your hair must have received precise instructions from the proper authority. The imprudent one stops; on the other side Lord Patchogue steadies himself; like an athlete flexing his muscles before the race, assuring himself of their suppleness, he raises both his hands on a level with his tie, and the victim does likewise. Everything is working. He brings his hand to his tie and adjusts it slightly, then he flicks back his hair once or twice, just like the other. Lord Patchogue is sure of him now. He slowly turns his head so that the mirror is no longer in the victim's field of vision and with unexpected vigour throws himself to one side, against, into, through the wall. When the subject turns his head again, all he can do is remark that he has taken the place of Lord Patchogue. The right side is just as good as the reverse.

6. Alternate dialogue and monologue between the visitors and Lord Patchogue:
    "It is I who am looking at you and it is you that you see, you're incorrigible."

7. My ten fingers are not your fingers and this point between my eyes is not the middle of your face. I rarely feel pain when someone strikes you, any more than you do for me.

8. Sign your name, naturally, at the bottom of this mirror, etch it, provided that it contains neither a 'p', nor a 't', nor a 'c', nor an 'h', nor an 'o', nor a 'g', nor an 'a', nor a 'u', nor an 'e'.

9. Just like a photographer: "Smile, and I'll do the rest."

10. Don't forget that I cannot see myself, that my role is limited to being the one who looks in the mirror while at the same time I remain Patchogue as before. I have never felt so natural.
    (Nothing has changed.)

1. The secret: life begins with anomaly, with an abnormal function. The wheel which turns, etc. The legs . . .

2. Once and for all, I am not telling you the story of my life, only a story which I remember. Nothing happens, or at least nothing ever happened.

3. In all these things which should give rise to dread in me, should affect me, I feel nothing, I do not see myself, I am not there. There are, no doubt, those people who are able to adapt to the impossible, liberty, impossible liberty, provided that there are no more questions.

4. Lord Patchogue walks a body which demonstrates the same resistance, a body that you will recognise. The voice is the same, that which you have already heard, it has the same sharply-defined features, only that vulnerable quality has disappeared, the weakness through which the mortal air of your own breast may pass. The mechanism is the same and the eye has not ceased to transmit to the eye on the next rung his observation, which incessantly proceeds from eye to eye. [. . .]

(Fragment)

Note: For those who appreciate the marvellous, this is how Lord Patchogue got his name. Travelling around Long Island with some friends in a car, near New York, Mrs Muriel Draper—someone of whom I could say far too much, but above all a friend of mine— and myself found our attention drawn along those endless roads devoid of signposts by one which indicated the way to the town of Patchogue at almost every cross-roads. We drove along these roads for three days obsessed by this signpost (just like the one reading "Vichy 794 km" which one sees on every road in France) without ever managing to reach the aforesaid town. Without us realising, the word took on the meaning of something which does not exist in our conversation. A couple of weeks later we learned from the newspapers that some artful man had managed to persuade half the population of Patchogue that the end of the world would occur on a particular day and had succeeded in buying cheap a vast expanse of land.

The following summer, I found myself in Italy on a friend's small boat in the Gulf of Naples. We stopped off at the Albergo della Luna at Amalfi. In this hotel I came across notepaper [. . .]. Under the heading Albergo della Luna there was a large reproduction of the patio of the inn, and in the middle of this design an inset portrait of the face of Ibsen with a caption surrounding it to the effect that Henrik Ibsen had etc., etc. I thought that this notepaper would amuse my friends and decided to send a specimen to Mrs Muriel Draper. I also had at this time amongst other conceits that of writing my letters in the form of the contents page of a book: something which catered for both my laziness and my desire not to miss the opportunity of delivering to the recipient of the letter at our next meeting an account of such incidents as the title of each chapter would serve to recall.

Harold Rosenberg

Life and Death of the Amorous Umbrella

Virtues of Chance Love

The poets of Paris, before their hegira, succeeded in establishing the fact that if a sewing machine and an umbrella met by chance on an operating table they would at once fall in love.

This ability to combine spontaneously has been taken as a sign of dermal alertness characteristic of those born of the spirit who, like the wind, blow where they list. The embrace of the umbrella and sewing machine has thus become the device on the banner of absolute freedom.

Daemonists have claimed that to give oneself totally to the alien, just because it is alien, because there is no mirror in it for one's own ego, is an act of purification belonging to the great magical rites of sacred prostitution. The embrace of the umbrella and sewing machine has also been inscribed therefore on the banner of purity.

And on the banner of beauty—by Lautréamont himself, original discoverer of the encounter of this couple, more revealing to the present epoch than Adam and Eve's sudden self-consciousness in Eden.

Politics of the Umbrella

The umbrella's free, pure, and beautiful encounter opposes conventional social relations, which provide a path to the couch only upon obedience to fixed rules. In place of the feelings and behavior prescribed by society, the umbrella avails himself of a type of general- ized sociability, an abstract and permanent readiness for the excitement of love. Against the System, he sets up the no-system or mysterious super-system of his senses and his *données immediates*. And outwits the eye of order by awakening unexpectedly to opportunity on an operating table.

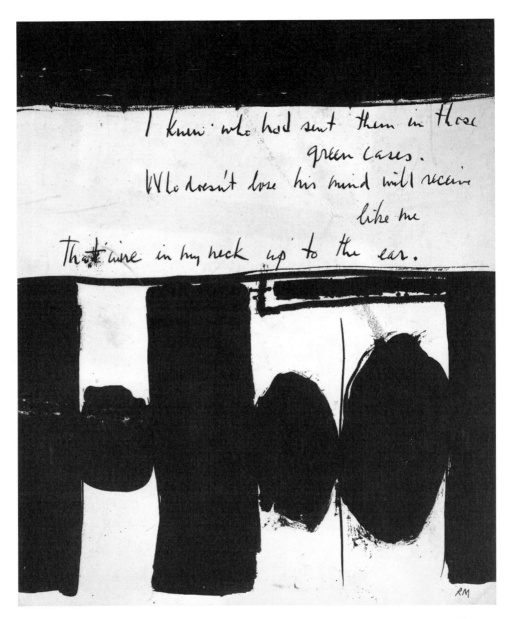

Robert Motherwell, *Elegy to the Spanish Republic No. 1,* 1948; India ink on rag paper, 10³/₄ × 8¹/₂ inches. The Museum of Modern Art, New York. Gift of the artist. Photo © 1995 The Museum of Modern Art, New York.

Pathos

In our admiration for the free, pure, beautiful and revolutionary, we must take care not to overlook the pathos of the umbrella's quick-fire romance. Though his act itself is perfect in its moment, a distinct psychological malady is implied by his unpremeditated leap. Why are he and his sweetheart like clerks in big-city boarding houses, so hysterically susceptible to love at first sight? Why so naked underneath their respectable professional costumes? Why so resistless to rudimentary shapes—the vertical, the horizontal, the curved opening? Everything points to frantic impulses and the absence of the critical spirit.

The psychological tragedy has obvious social roots. The umbrella and the sewing machine are specialized creatures. Each has but one use, and in their work they are entirely passive. This restriction to a single passive performance cannot fail, of course, to produce a violent sense of loneliness and frustration. Moreover, they inevitably undergo long periods of unemployment—clearly, it was in such a period that the momentous meeting disclosed by Lautréamont took place. What more natural than that during this idleness they should stuff themselves to the bursting point with dreams manufactured from their simple work-memories. Standing in his corner the umbrella recalls and elaborates upon the delicious warm strokes that stained his wings one by one and spread through his substance, slowly at first, then all together in a murmuring wash of joy. While the sewing machine, covered with dust, recreates in fancy the soft fingers that under her groin smoothed an endless buttoning of silk.

The Bed of Liberation

These inspiring images become irritating to the dreamers through repetition without change, in accordance with the quantitative laws of psychological causality established by the Chinese: so many taps, unnoticed; so many more of the same, expectation; unendurable torture; repeated indefinitely, madness and death.

The umbrella and sewing machine attain, through inaction and narrowness of perspective, to a complete generalization and mechanization of love, in which each is conscious of nothing but erotic essentials and is entirely ready for an encounter with anyone who can supply them. In this sense, the famous chance encounter does not take place altogether by chance, after all.

At last arrives the perfect dream-setting, the operating table with its reek of pain, anesthesia, and violent partitions of the flesh—absolute brothel for the starving.

Now the dry vulture's eye of the timid and tight-lipped umbrella lights upon the buxom sewing machine, a household Mae West even more enflaming for her prurient and drudging domesticity. To whom his demeanor of a funeral attendant is insurance against scandal. Bring on the ether!

Chorus

The free, pure, beautiful and revolutionary act, yes. But the actor? How pathetic the unpremeditated nuptials of umbrellas and sewing machines which fall upon them like blows! How deplorable the love postures of these cripples rummaging over one another! Even the 10,000 marvellous paintings inspired by their sorrows will not express the tragedy of the haphazard.

The anarchism of the amorous umbrella does not change the conditions of his existence. In combining fortuitously he enters a metaphorical frame of the same order as those of nature and logic, only without nature or logic. He is still himself, the slave that society made of him, and the force and duration of his embrace are not really as unconditioned as they seem.

Death and Transfiguration

It is inconceivable that "the umbrella of dominion" under which sat the rulers of the Indies should ever have met a sewing machine. But had this happened, nothing personal would have developed between them. This is a common argument of caste and "order" against the liberation of the masses.

Orthodox Jews bless God daily because the human body is made with many holes. If, they repeat, one of these was sealed up, or if one were opened too far, it would be impossible to exist.

Noah's Flood was said to have been ordered as a punishment for greed and wantonness in a period of incredible prosperity: if one hole is plugged another opens wide. The Flood was produced by drawing apart the vents of the deep and by the simultaneous escape of the upper waters through holes made by removing two stars out of the constellation of the Pleiades, so that the male waters of the heavens met the female waters of the earth.

This proves that anything torn open to chance encounters cannot survive.

The total sealing of the vents of modern society has brought into being a stifling period of chance combinations, made and dissolved with lightning speed. The opening of this epoch was heralded by the ultimate aggrandizement and death of the umbrella. The final appearance of the prime abnegator of choice took place in a world stage. The umbrella of Lautréamont is generally recognized as the same umbrella carried as the sign of his election by Chamberlain, himself an umbrella, when he opened his bats' wings across the English Channel in order to demonstrate that fortuitous liaisons could be prolonged at will. On the operating table he was permitted a last dogsniff at his sweetheart's relics, the seams of Europe.

Raymond Roussel

Bertha, the Child-Flower

Just then there came towards us a woman looking like a robust peasant. She held before her, with both hands, a kind of rose-painted tray where a body of the same very vivid rose color was stretched out, intriguing us with its half-human, half-vegetal aspect.

—Here are Catherine Seyeux and her daughter Bertha, said Boudet, calling the woman who came forward right away. Bertha, stretched out flat on the tray, was sleeping naked in the sun without her mother trying in any way to keep the burning rays from her. About six weeks old, the child had a disturbing, even upsetting appearance. Her skin, of an unbelievable delicacy and transparence, looked exactly like a flower petal and was the same vivid rose color. In her fabulous epidermis there ran a network of veins no less strange in appearance, whose greenish shade glinted like enamel, as you see in certain flowers. Her skin was so diaphanous that the different bodily organs were visible through it.

Seeing a question on our faces that we hadn't expressed, Boudet explained to us how Catherine Seyeux had managed to engender such a bizarre creature.

For a long time Boudet had been haunted by the idea that he might artificially inseminate a woman with flower pollen. Many was the time he had attempted this with country women whom he had specially chosen as being both robust and prolific. But it was in vain that he had tried all sorts of different pollens, without ever obtaining any result.

One day, leafing through a newspaper, he saw the picture of a Texas peasant woman aged thirty-eight who had had not less than forty-five children, boys and girls. Since she was eighteen, she had given birth each year to two and sometimes three twins or triplets. In the picture you saw the smiling mother standing next to her husband and surrounded by her forty-five offspring, all in perfect health. The newspaper gave the name of the mother (a Texan name) and that of her village: Ar . . .

Astounded by such ease of procreation, Boudet could only think about trying his experiment on Catherine Se. who seemed to him to be likelier than anyone else to offer some chance of success. He wrote her, laying out in detail what he expected of her, and offering her magnificent conditions if she would consent to come to France to make herself available. Catherine showed the letter to her husband, who, although he was a farmer of some means, could scarcely remain indifferent to such a large sum of money, given the heavy expenses of his many children. He gave his consent to his wife who took the first steamer and arrived one fine morning at Boudet's house.

From the very first attempt, made with pollen from X., Catherine was declared pregnant, and Boudet was filled with joy and followed each of the stages of the pregnancy anxiously.

Finally, six weeks before this, at the normal time, Catherine had given birth to the fragile little girl whom we were looking at, and who was exactly midway between a flower and a child. It was impossible to put any clothing on her because her skin might have ripped apart at the slightest contact. In fact, so that her fragile body would be touched as little as possible by anything at all, Boudet had made a sort of tray to support her, which he had painted in a vivid rose color adapted to the skin color of the little girl whom they called Bertha.

During the daytime, they kept her always outside, as exposed as possible to the sun. Her vegetal aspect prevented any sunstroke and profited wonderfully from this exposure. Indeed, the slightest shadow cast over her head or her body brought about a shudder of discontent in the little being who calmed down and flourished as soon as she was completely exposed to the sun.

While Boudet was speaking, Bertha had been stirring about as if she was going to wake. She finally opened her eyes whose strange reflections reminded you a little of the enamel tint of her veins. Looking at his watch, Boudet saw it was time for her breastfeeding and asked Catherine to suckle her daughter in front of us so that we could see how lively and alert the little girl was.

Catherine opened her blouse, and holding the tray with one hand, carefully turned Bertha around so she would take hold of the breast with her little hands and place her lips on it, which she did greedily.

Thanks to the transparency of the membranes of the strange creature, we could see how the very pure white stream of milk was flowing slowly into the esophagus and descending to the stomach.

After some moments, Boudet, judging we had sufficiently noticed how good was the child-flower's appetite, indicated that Catherine should continue her walk and beckoned us to follow him again.

Note

A discarded manuscript passage from *Locus Solus,* ed. Annie Angremy. (These pages from the Fonds Roussel, *Locus Solus,* were written without alteration for the novel, then discarded; they were printed in the *Revue de la Bibliothèque Nationale,* no. 43, 1992. My thanks to Annie Le Brun for suggesting I use them.)

REVOLUTION

QUADRANGLE

Lukewarm milk fight thine soul triangle.
Flowers bloomen yellow moons in the sun.
Moon yellow blue, blue days,
And the frog slants the chosin question.
Dew Eyes towards you.
Lukewarm milk fight *Thine* soul's triangle,
To thee
And thou,
And eyes choose question velvet the frog.

And now follows the beginning of this story again.
The child was playing.
And saw a man standing.
"Mama," said the child. The Mother: "Yes."
"Mama,"—"Yes."
"Mama,"—"Yes."
"Mama, a man is standing there!"—"Yes."
"Mama, a man is standing there!"—"Yes."
"Mama, a man is standing there!"—"Where?"
"Mama, a man is standing there!"—"Where?"
"Mama, a man is standing there!"—"Where is that man standing?"
"Mama, a man is standing there!"—"Where is the man standing?"
"Mama, a man is standing there!"—"What are you talking about!"
     "Mama, a man is standing there!!!"—"Let the man stand!"
     "Mama, a man is standing there."
     The mother arrives. Really, a man is standing there. Strange, I wonder what he has
to stand here for? We had better call Father. The mother calls the father, the father calls

Kurt Schwitters, *Merz 1003 (Peacock's Tail),* 1924; oil on composition board with added wood shapes. Yale University Art Gallery, by permission. © ARS.

the neighbor, a group of people form, and form around the man (—a mob). The Honorable Doktor Friedrich August Leopold Kasimir Amadeus Gneomar Lutetius Obadje Jona Micha Nahum Habakuk Zephanja Haggai Sacharja Maleachi Pothook and his spouse, Frau Doktor Amalie Pothook, attempt in vain to learn the reason, why the man is standing there. Frau Doktor Amalie on this occasion gets excited, and lets herself be carried off to expressions, to expressions which she probably has heard from a very uncultured creature, to expressions, to expressions, which she probably never brought over her noble lips before, to expressions, to expressions such as I as an author would never have used, among others the word, "LOUSY BRUTE."

More objurgations are heard. Alves Bromestick even calls the man a criminal. He said it distinctly, especially the second time, after Frau Doktor Amalie let herself go to the point of articulating expressions, expressions, which she probably had heard from a very low person, expressions, expressions, which she probably has never let pass her lips before, expressions, expressions, which I as the author would never, never, nor with pleasure, have used, expressions, expressions, expressions, among them the word, Lousy Brute!!!

In this critical moment, the author lets follow his self-composed poem *Quadrangle*.

Quadrangle

Lukewarm milk thine your soul triangle.
Flowers bloomen yellow moons in the sun.
Moon yellow blue, blue days,
And the frog slants the chosin question
Of your eyes.
Thine
Dew eyes towards you.
Lukewarm milk fight *Thine* soul's triangle,
Quadrangle, Pentagon, Hexagon, Heptagon, Octagon,
Nonagon, Decagon,
To thee,
And thou,
And eyes choose question velvet the frog.
And if you think, the moon goes down (to be sung)
She does not, it merely seems so (to be sung)
Round the earth she drags and drags (to be sung)
Taking inflammable matter there (to be sung)
. . . (the melody to be whistled)
They must be curious trees, indeed (to be sung).
Where the big   —
Elephants go walking,   —
Without bumping each other!!!   —

371

And now we'll get back to the beginning of this story again.

The child was playing.

And saw a man standing.

"Mama!," said the child. The Mother: "Yes."

"Mama!"—"Yes."—

"Mama!"—"Yes?"

"Mama!"—"Yes."—

"Mama, a man is standing there!"—"Yes."

"Mama, a man is standing there!"—"Yes."

"Mama, a man is standing there!"—"Where?"

"Mama, a man is standing there!"—"Where?"

"Mama, a man is standing there!"—"Where is a man standing?"

"Mama, a man is standing there!"—"Where is a man standing?"

"Mama, a man is standing there!"—"Why, no."

"Mama, a man is standing there!"—"Why don't you let the man stand?"

"Mama, a man is standing there!"

The mother arrives. There really stands a man. The mother calls the father, the father calls the neighbor. Now the reader knows himself, how it goes on, but it cannot be emphasized too much that a man is standing there, or rather has been standing there. Well, we'll see.

Then, the most unexpected thing happened.

Slowly, and with the tranquillity of a perfect machine, the man left,

amiably

greeting everybody,

but not with the official,

no,

in an opposite direction.

Concluding Song:

They must be curious trees indeed, where the big

Elephants go walking,

without bumping each other,

without bumping each other,

without bumping each other,

without bumping each other,

without bumping each other,

without bumping each other!

PRIIMIITITTIII

priimiitittiii	tisch
tesch	
priimiitittiii	tesch
tusch	
priimiitittiii	tischa
tescho	
priimiitittiii	tescho
tuschi	
priimiitittiii	
priimiitittiii	
priimiitittiii	too
priimiitittiii	taa
priimiitittiii	too
priimiitittiii	taa
priimiitittiii	tootaa
priimiitittiii	tootaa
priimiitittiii	tuutaa
priimiitittiii	tuutaa
priimiitittiii	tuutaatoo
priimiitittiii	tuutaatoo
priimiitittiii	tuutaatoo
priimiitittiii	tuutaatoo

LANKE TR GL (SKERZOO AUS MEINER SOONATE IN UURLAUTEN)

lanke tr gl
pe pe pe pe pe
ooka ooka ooka ooka
lanke tr gl
pii pii pii pii pii
züüka züüka züüka züüka

lanke tr gl

rmp

rnf

lanke tr gl

ziiuu lentrl

lümpf tümpf trl

lanke tr gl

rumpf tilf too

lanke tr gl

ziiuu lentrl

lümpf tümpf trl

lanke tr gl

pe pe pe pe pe

ooka ooka ooka ooka

lanke tr gl

pii pii pii pii pii

züüka züüka züüka züüka

lanke tr gl

rmp

rnf

lanke tr gl?

PAOLO UCCELLO

His real name was Paolo di Dono; but the Florentines called him Uccello, or Paul the Bird Man, on account of the many drawings and paintings of birds and beasts that filled his house; for he was too poor to keep any animals or to procure specimens of those he did not know. It is even said that when he painted a fresco representing the four elements, at Padua, he used a chameleon to symbolize air, and, never having seen one, pictured it as a pot-bellied camel with a gaping mouth. (Whereas, as Vasari explains, the chameleon is like a little wizened lizard, and the camel is a big, gawky animal.) For Uccello did not care about the reality of things, but about their multiplicity and about the infinitude of lines; consequently, he painted blue fields and red cities, and horsemen in black armour on ebony horses with flaming mouths, and lances pointing like rays of light to all the quarters of the heavens. And he was in the habit of drawing *mazocchi,* that is circles of wood covered with cloth, which are placed on the head in such a way that the folds of the cloth completely surround the face. Uccello painted pointed ones, square ones, others with facets or built up in pyramids or cones, according to all the vistas of perspective, and so discovered a whole world of relationships in the folds of the *mazocchio*. And Donatello the sculptor used to say to him: "Ah Paolo, thou leavest the substance for the shadow."

But the Bird continued his patient work; he assembled circles, he divided angles, he examined every creature from every point of view, and he would ask his friend, the mathematician Giovanni Manetti, to tell him the answers to the problems of Euclid; then he would shut himself up and cover his parchments and his wood with points and curves. He applied himself constantly to the study of architecture, with the help of Filippo Brunelleschi; but with no intention of building. He confined himself to noting how the lines ran from the foundations to the cornices, and the way the straight lines met at their points of intersection and the way the arches turned about their keystones, and the foreshortening of ceiling beams, fan-like, as they seemed to come together at the ends of long rooms. He also drew, in addition to human gestures, all the beasts and their movements, in order to reduce them to simple lines.

Yves Tanguy, *Fear,* 1926; oil and collage, 90 × 72 centimeters. Private collection, Milwaukee. Art Resource, Photo Archive, Marburg. © ARS.

Then, like the alchemist poring over his mixtures of metals and organs and watching for their fusion into gold in his furnace, Uccello poured all these forms into the crucible of form. He united them, combined them and melted them down, in order to transmute them into that simple form on which all others depend. That is why Paolo Uccello lived like an alchemist, shut up in his little house. He believed that he could blend all lines into a single, ideal form. He wished to grasp the created Universe as it was reflected in the eye of God, who sees all shapes spring from one complex centre. About him lived Ghiberti, Della Robbia, Brunelleschi and Donatello, all of them proud and masters of their art, and contemptuous of poor Uccello and his mania for perspective, deploring his spider-filled, poverty-stricken house; but Uccello was prouder still. With every new combination of lines, he hoped to discover the method of creation. His aim was not to imitate, but to achieve the power of giving masterly development to everything, and his strange series of folded headgear was to him more revealing than the great Donatello's magnificent marble figures.

Thus did the Bird Man live, his pensive head wrapped in his hood; and he heeded neither his food nor his drink, but was completely like a hermit. And so, one day in a meadow near a ring of old stones half buried in the grass, he saw a young girl with a garland bound about her head, laughing. She was wearing a long pale dress, caught up at the hips with a pale ribbon, and her movements were as supple as the grasses she was bending. Her name was Selvaggia and she smiled at Uccello. He noted the curve of her smile. And when she looked at him, he saw all the little lines of her eye-lashes and the circles of her pupils and the curves of her eyelids and the subtle interweaving of her hair, and he imagined the garland about her brow in innumerable other positions. But Selvaggia knew nothing of all this, because she was only thirteen years old. She took Uccello by the hand and she loved him. She was the daughter of a Florentine dyer and her mother was dead. Another woman had come into the house and had beaten Selvaggia. Uccello took Selvaggia home with him.

All day long, Selvaggia sat crouching in front of the wall on which Uccello drew his universal forms. She never understood why he preferred looking at lines, straight and curved, rather than at the tender face upturned towards him. At night, when Brunelleschi and Ma-netti came to study with Uccello, she would fall asleep after midnight at the foot of the nexus of intersecting lines, in the circle of shadow which lay wide beneath the lamp. In the morning she awoke before Uccello, delighted to find herself surrounded by painted birds and coloured animals. Uccello drew her lips and her eyes, her hair and her hands, and recorded all the attitudes of her body; but he did not, like other painters when they loved a woman, make a portrait of her. For the Bird Man did not know the joy of limiting himself to the individual; he could not rest in one particular place; he wished to soar above all places. And the forms of Selvaggia's attitudes were cast into the crucible of form, with all the movements of animals, and the lines of plants, stones and rays of light, and the undulation of terrestrial vapours and waves of the sea. And, forgetting Selvaggia, Uccello seemed to be forever poring over the crucible of form.

However, there was nothing to eat in Uccello's house. Selvaggia did not dare tell Donatello or the others. She held her peace and died. Uccello drew the stiffening of her body and the linking of her thin little hands and the line of her poor closed eyes. He did not know that she had died, just as he had never known that she was alive. He only added these new forms to all the others he had collected.

The Bird Man grew old and no-one could understand his pictures any longer. They appeared to be nothing but a chaos of curves. Neither earth nor plants nor animals nor men were recognisable in them any longer. For many years he had been busy on his supreme work, which he kept hidden from everyone. It was to embody the results of all his researches. The subject—Doubting Thomas feeling Christ's wound—symbolized these researches. Uccello completed his picture at the age of eighty. He sent for Donatello and uncovered it reverently before him. And Donatello cried: "Ah Paolo, cover up thy picture again." The Bird Man questioned the great sculptor but could not get him to say more. And so Uccello knew that he had accomplished the miracle. But Donatello had seen nothing save a confused mass of lines.

And a few years later, Paolo Uccello was found lying dead from exhaustion, on his pallet. His face was a rapture of wrinkles. His eyes were fixed on mystery revealed. In his sternly clasped hand was a small round piece of parchment covered with interlocked lines, beginning at the centre and leading to the circumference and then returning from the circumference to the centre.

LOUIS SCUTENAIRE

ENTRIES IN A JOURNAL

Though it is impossible that Destiny should have an existence of its own, nothing can escape it.

A commendable activity would be the reconstitution of extinct species, for instance: the dodo, the migratory ectopist, certain whales. It would only take courage, patience and science, and some genius.

Until the appearance of Napoleon Bonaparte, the lords of peoples seemed, by and large, to be persons concerned to round out their domains and to enjoy them with all their men and beasts. But since then, they seem rather like gamesters who, mixing the rules of chess with those of blindman's bluff, should move their pawns about with a minimum of skill and intelligence.

 Once my Revolution is successful and my first series of postal stamps has been issued, I shall have to think of getting rid of my enemies.

 I shall confine them in cells by two's, and as I distribute daggers to each of them I shall say:

 "Whichever of you two kills his neighbor will have his chance at freedom."

 The next day I shall again lock the survivors up by two's and make the same promise. This way, I shall soon have only one foe left, whom I shall have brought before the Court of Assizes for murder.

 I shall have thereby won by tranquillity without having any innocent blood on my hands or my head.

What I love least? I believe that it is equilibrium, whether in thought, love, daily behavior: in all domains save that of the circus, where equilibrium, in all its perfection, parodies itself.

I should like as far as possible to enter in some book the sights that I have enjoyed— I don't mean evoke them with words, but transport them there with all their life, aspect, color, movement, odors, and volumes (only, reduced to page-size).

A good and resounding village fanfare, followed by the notables, dancing children, and an old toper singing a bawdy ballad and pissing as he walks along.

A wood at the birth of summer.

A pretty and well-dressed woman who undresses the moment she is told.

Certain birds of prey in flight.

Everything that I love.

It would be essential, too, that, resounding and on the march across the book, the fanfare should still be life-size and not cease to tickle the ears and eyes of the village, which would still be at the edge of the wood where the pretty woman could watch the sparrow-hawk as she and I continued the endless count of what we love.

A crystal prism in a skillful palm could play upon the Universe as profoundly as all the machines of men.

Young, broad-shouldered, flat-bellied, with a handsome, thin, though somewhat lazy face, a priest stops before the display window of a humble florist in a poor quarter. His hands thrust into the pockets of his threadbare cassock, he looks insistently and, it seems to me, sneeringly at the vendor, a keen-eyed, chunky man squatting on the door-step.

The flower-vendor stares back at the priest and greets him gruffly with a "Hello, Priest!", whereupon the priest, equally gruff, retorts, "Hello, Florist!", and walks away. The florist, his attention immediately drawn elsewhere, does not even look after him.

Because people say such idiotic things and swallow any kind of nonsense, diseases are cured and poems written.

Hegel, a palace of light and mirrors, without doors or windows.

The dress of our nuns was once the secular garb of our remote feminine ancestors. Just imagine how delighted our children's children will be to see the nuns moving about with naked legs, open blouses, with a wonderful odor of minx, all smiles, short-skirted, tanned or freshly painted under a halo of tousled hair, and too knowledgeable to be chaste!

It seems to me that the bourgeois comedy would make an important film, in which the dramatic action, very quiet and very proper, would be played out by the Marx Brothers.

Paul Delvaux, *The Echo*; n.d., © P. Delvaux Foundation, St. Idesbald, Belgium. Licensed by VAGA, New York.

Obedient from beginning to end to the proprieties of the situation, atmosphere, and dialogue, abandoning their clownish costumes for correct business attire, they would forget all their absurdity and violence but retain—very scrupulously—the facial expressions we had come to know from the films of their mad period.

There are people who do not believe in God, but think that they can catch an occasional glimpse of him—like those people who, in a summer forest, stretched out under a bush or a screen of leaves, imagine that they can see patches of sky through the interlacing branches, when in reality they are looking at the bluish undersides of the leaves in the tall trees.

Never accuse your neighbor of anything, but simply say that you find him loathsome.

Paul Delvaux, *Le Train bleu,* 1946; © P. Delvaux Foundation, St. Iderbald, Belgium. Licensed by VAGA, New York.

Violence:

Destroying a chandelier, gutting a wardrobe, kicking over a table and chairs, tearing the curtains apart, in order to crush a moth, which in any case makes good its escape.

Passive Resistance:

Allowing the moth to devour your clothes and blankets, letting it make many little moths that will make your house uninhabitable.

Common Sense:

Crushing the insect skillfully, without damaging anything, in a way so as not to puff out the out-size jacket that one fine day a transmission belt will catch up, thus reducing you to minced meat.

Language is a noise; noise is a language.

For certain reasons, my entries may be compared to a backfiring rifle upon which would be inscribed the words: "A rifle that shoots backwards."

The "certain reasons" I have just alluded to are naturally reasons bound up with weakness and vanity, so it seems to me. I record this glory, not to my shame or self-vindication, for I exercise myself, never merely to play, but always to win, here as elsewhere.

I am not writing these confidences in repentance or good faith; but through ruse, that I may be spared or even flattered (because I am susceptible). In effect I disavow men

Louis Scutenaire

sufficiently to hope for a refuge among them, these self-same men whom I disavow less because I know them than because I know myself.

Things that have lifted me to the summit of exaltation:

The musical entry of the Fratellini in the ring.

The thighs of Lola, the Danseuse, in the "Blue Angel."

The Knockabouts, a troupe of destructive clowns, *circa* 1914.

The Darío who sang:

When I used to be in Spain

I found myself in Spain again.

Wantons who have delighted me.

Many poems.

Certain heavyweight bouts.

Bleak contrysides.

Rémouleur's song: "Car elle est gentille, ma fille," sung at a village fair by some forgotten old workingman.

Chaplin's song in *Modern Times*.

People can talk but I have my doubts as to the efficacy of martyr's blood. Consider the spermatozoa, for instance. For every martyr that succeeds, how many, in their career, go smashing into a wall!

As I pass a hearse from which the occupied coffin is being withdrawn, I rejoice not to have my hat on—thus being spared the obligation of tipping it, which I find disagreeable. A brief moment later, I feel the urge to break wind, which I restrain because I want in no way to appear to be flaunting my disrespect (in my own ears, for nobody but me would hear it). It is only after having convinced myself that the issue, for me, is not to make a show of my bowels, but simple to relieve them, that I release, without a trace of arrogance, three farts.

I am very fond of young American novelists: Sherwood Anderson, Sherwood Anderson, Sherwood Anderson, and Sherwood Anderson.

On their hides was branded the word: *Thick*. On their muzzles, fittingly enough, their names. On their forehead: *Recalcitrants*. And above the place where the heart usually is: *None*. They are as proud of these words as of so many blue ribbons. They show them to their children, and with all the weight of their heavy feet, they bear down (unawares, to

383

be sure) upon a multitude of exposed, sentient creatures, who would adore life were it not for the fact that these oxen use them for a litter.

What exists must be created.

The existentialist is painfully dragging himself toward the river Knowledge that Surrealism cleared in one leap twenty years ago after Dada had drained it dry.

Many innovators killed for their ideas would have lived had they known how to smile.

I am your enemy.

EPHESIAN: "Nothing doing, I could never bring myself to kill a a child."

LOUIS: "Come, come. I could—easily."

EPHESIAN: "Any child?"

LOUIS: "No, not one of those poor children; those little wretches touch me too deeply with their picturesque rags, their pinched, sometimes sharp, little faces, their eyes so huge."

EPHESIAN: "Then you could kill rich children?

LOUIS: "Nor them either, I love their coquetry, their little self-assurance, their freshly-scrubbed look!"

EPHESIAN: "But, the Devil! What kind of a child could you kill anyway?"

LOUIS: "The child as a concept, O Ephesian."

RROSE SÉLAVY DEMANDE

Rrose Sélavy demande si les Fleurs du Mal ont modifié les mœurs du phalle: qu'en pense Omphale?

Question Aux Astronomes:

Rrose Sélavy inscrira-t-elle longtemps au cadran des astres le cadastre des ans?

Au pays de Rrose Sélavy on aime les fous et les loups sans foi ni loi.

Suivrez-vous Rrose Sélavy au pays des nombres décimaux où il n'y a décombres ni maux?

Rrose Sélavy se demande si la mort des saisons fait tomber un sort sur les maisons.

Rrose Sélavy connaît bien le marchand du sel.

Epitaphe:

Ne tourmentez plus Rrose Sélavy car mon génie est énigme. Caron ne le déchiffre pas.

Perdue sur la mer sans fin Rrose Sélavy mangera-t-elle du fer après avoir mangé ses mains?

Rrose Sélavy voudrait bien savoir si l'amour, cette colle à mouches, rend plus dures les molles couches.

Au virage de la course au rivage, voici le secours de Rrose Sélavy.

Rrose Sélavy peut revêtir la bure du bagne, elle a une monture qui franchit les montagnes.

Rrose Sélavy décerne la palme sans l'éclat du martyre à Lakmé bergère en Beauce figée dans le calme plat du métal appelé beauté.

Croyez-vous que Rrose Sélavy connaisse ces jeux de fous qui mettent le feu aux joues?

Man Ray, *Rrose Sélavy, New York,* 1921; portrait of Marcel Duchamp as Rrose Sélavy.

Rrose Sélavy c'est peut-être aussi ce jeune apache qui de la paume de sa main colle un pain à sa môme.

Qu'arrivera-t-il si Rrose Sélavy, un soir de Noël, s'en va vers le piège de la neige et du pôle?

Dans le sommeil de Rrose Sélavy il y a un nain sorti d'un puits qui vient manger son pain la nuit.

Man Ray, *Duchamp as Rrose Sélavy,* 1920–1921; signed "lovingly, Rrose Sélavy, alias Marcel Duchamp." © ARS.

Debout sur la caréne le poéte cherche une rime et croyez-vous que Rrose Sélavy soit la reine du crime?

Rrose Sélavy propose que la pourriture des passions devienne la nourriture des nations.

Quelle est donc cette marée sans cause dont l'onde amère inonde l'âme acérée de Rrose?

Si le silence est d'or Rrose Sélavy abaisse ses cils et s'endort.

Rrose Sélavy a visité l'archipel où la reine Irène-sur-Flots de sa rame de frêne gouverne ses îlots.

Rrose Sélavy vous engage à ne pas prendre les verrues des seins pour les vertus des saintes.

Rrose Sélavy n'est pas persuadée que la culture du moi puisse amener la moiteur du cul.

Rrose Sélavy s'étonne que de la contagion des reliques soit née la religion catholique.

Dans le silence des climes, Rrose Sélavy regarde en riant la science qui lime.

Devise de Rrose Sélavy:

Plus que poli pour être honnête
Plus que poéte pour être honni.

Oubliez les paraboles absurdes pour écouter de Rrose Sélavy les sourdes paroles.

Rrose Sélavy proclame que le miel de sa cervelle est la merveille qui aigrit le fiel du ceil.

Aux agapes de Rrose Sélavy on mange du pâté de pape dans une sauce couleur d'agate.

Apprenez que la geste célèbre de Rrose Sélavy est inscrite dans l'algèbre céleste.

Rrose Sélavy affirme que la couleur des nègres est due au tropique du cancer.

Rrose Sélavy sait bien que le démon du remords ne peut mordre le monde.

Rrose Sélavy nous révèle que le râle du monde est la ruse des rois mâles emportés par la ronde de la muse des mois.

Dans un lac d'eau minérale Rrose Sélavy a noyé la câline morale.

Rrose Sélavy glisse le cœur de Jésus dans le jeu des Crésus.

Au fond d'une mine Rrose Sélavy prépare la fin du monde.

A son trapèze Rrose Sélavy apaise la détresse des déesses.

Dans le pays de Rrose Sélavy les mâles font la guerre sur la mer. Les femelles ont la gale.

L'argot de Rrose Sélavy, n'est-ce pas l'art de transformer en cigognes les cygnes?

Marcel Duchamp:
Sur le chemin, il y avait un bœuf bleu près d'un banc blanc. Expliquez-moi la raison des gants blancs maintenant?

Kurt Seligmann

An Eye for a Tooth

Sadism it is that grates amongst the cogs of this our infernal machine with its two billion cylinders; but it is masochism that shrieks and wails with the pounded oil through its murky ducts. The human machine rumbles in deadly monotonous unison.

However, from the smoke of an explosion, from the bursting of a boiler, transfigurations emerge: Gilles de Machecoul the well beloved, Elizabeth Bathory of the dull skin, Etiennette Thomason on her cross, and other velvet dragons, dragons who lop off fingers as they pass the time of day.

The movement of the pistons makes me shudder; it is cruel without being singular: sadism is fascinating only when it is monumental. The perverted are no more interesting to me than the normal.

"Have dreams actuality?" is subsidiary to the question "To what do dreams incite us?" If perversion is a state of grace, it is by the grace of the devil. But sanctioning this kind of diabolism amounts to affirming its antithesis. Are we to stop where the minor Symbolists left off? To do so would be hardly comfortable—prosperity is far behind us. We would be living in a Land of Cocaine in which blasphemies would fall ready roasted into our mouths.

Our daily bread must be anguish: the anguish of an adult being born, the anguish of one restored to life after having killed himself, of a pinioned ghost sitting on a time bomb, of the prodigal son seeing his father roast an ox whole.

In an iconoclastic era such as our own, we shall speak the language of hints. We shall shiftingly identify ourselves with our cryptic images. A poem, a painting will be full of robust solid things from which we shall absorb the gruesome healthfulness. In a corner only will the artist dare put the finishing comma, that form which will be the mark of our despair and of our foresight. And the leitmotiv will be so intricate that its interpreters, now and for evermore, will break their teeth on it.

There will remain nothing but this actuality from which the depiction of the unhappyworker will be excluded as antisocial, in which abstract painting will be one with the bands and bars of which the blind and imprisoned dream, in which camouflage will be the only decoration.

Kurt Seligmann with *Salish* (First Nation) totems, near Vancover, British Columbia. Photo by Arlette Seligmann.

Without fear of falling into imitativeness of cheap conclusions, we will be able to use the stereotypes of anguish: mouse-trap, one legged man, fishing net helmet, knife, wheel, whale, shipwreck, phantom apparition, massacre, ruined palace, tatters, explosion, fire, broken egg, blind man, handle, hole, gallows, scissors, tempest, ring, toothless jaws, foxtail, bird's nest, hill of porridge, winter's afternoon, motionless soldiers, execution, collapse, faceless heads, weeping eye, red eye, pink eye, purple eye, put out eye and all the other traditional banalities, the gift of dreaming with closed eyes.

Conventions will have an infinitesimal place in our work, a vicious position poisoning everything, spreading a net of uncertainty over all represented things. They will hypocritically escape every attempt to compromise with them; they will carry all the outward signs of barren morality but will stimulate discomfort to the utmost rather than guilt.

This projection of our anguish is necessary for our psychic health and our survival; it has been long and commonly in use. Our anguish will be expressed in our work alone, and in undertones which will travel in the whispering gallery that encircles the earth.

Léopold Sédar Senghor

Speech and Image: An African Tradition of the Surreal

Speech seems to us the main instrument of thought, emotion and action. There is no thought or emotion without a verbal image, no free action without first a project in thought. This is even more true among peoples who disdained the written word. This explains the power of speech in Africa. The word, the spoken word is the expression *par excellence* of the life-force, of being in its fullness. God created the world through the Word. We shall see how later. For the human being, speech is the living and life-giving breath of man at prayer. It possesses a magical virtue, realizing the law of participation and, by its intrinsic power, creating the thing named. So that all the other arts are only specialized aspects of the great art of speech. In front of a picture made up of a tracery of geometrical forms in white and red representing a chorus of birds or a tree at sunrise, the artist explained: "These are wings, these are songs. These are birds."

The African languages are characterized first of all by the richness of their vocabulary. There are sometimes twenty different words for an object according to its forms, weight, volume and colour, and as many for an action according to whether it is single or repeated, weakly or intensely performed, just beginning or coming to an end. In Fulani, nouns are divided into twenty-one genders which are not related to sex. The classification is based sometimes on the meaning of the words or the phonetic qualities and sometimes on the grammatical category to which they belong. Most significant in this respect is the verb. On the same root in Wolof can be constructed more than twenty verbs expressing different shades of meaning, and at least as many derivative nouns. While modern Indo-European languages emphasize the abstract notion of time, African languages emphasize the *aspect,* the concrete way in which the action of the verb takes place. These are essentially *concrete* languages. In them words are always pregnant with images. Under their value as signs, their sense value shows through.

The African image is not then an image by equation but an image by *analogy,* a surrealist image. Africans do not like straight lines and false *mots justes.* Two and two do not make four, but five, as Aimé Césaire has told us. The object does not mean what it represents but what it suggests, what it creates. The Elephant is Strength, the Spider is Prudence; Horns are the Moon and the Moon is Fecundity. Every representation is an image, and the image, I repeat, is not an equation but a *symbol,* an ideogramme. Not only the figuration of the image but also its material . . . stone, earth, copper, gold, fibre—and also its line and colour. All language which does not tell a story bores them, or rather, Africans do not understand such language. The astonishment of the first Europeans when they found that the "natives" did not understand their pictures or even the logic of their arguments!

I have spoken of the surrealist image. But as you would suppose, African surrealism is different from European surrealism. European surrealism is empirical. African surrealism is mystical and metaphysical. André Breton writes in *Signe Ascendant:* "The poetic analogy (meaning the European surrealist analogy) differs functionally from the mystical analogy in that it does not presuppose, beyond the visible world, an invisible world which is striving to manifest itself. It proceeds in a completely empirical way." In contrast, the African surrealist analogy presupposes and manifests the hierarchized universe of life-forces.

PHILIPPE SOUPAULT

THE SILENT HOUSE

Since I have lived in this silent house I have been surprised to see the large tree which grows before my window turn slowly round and round. All the hours here, as elsewhere, have their sounds, their goings and comings. Life seems to rise and fall. But each day the hours resemble one another. Only the great tree, green, red or yellow, I do not know which, changes its aspect. I see it through the network of curtains trimmed with lace. I observe it and I cannot look at it without a touch of anguish. I am afraid I shall not find it there. During several weeks, some months, perhaps,—I have lost all track of time,—it has never been twice the same. I watch it, I turn my head again and again. I close my eyes and open them. It is there, shuddering slightly, and already different. One leaf, two leaves have fallen and a little light passes back and forth through the new opening; a dead branch appears blacker than before.

It is fond of silence, of the night, and that vague light which hangs like a cloud above Paris. It gathers the meagre rays within its foliage, the rays, glistening with humidity, which are thrown out by a nearby street-lamp at ten o'clock in the evening. In this calm, I seem to see it twist its branches, display its leaves, inhale and exhale. It becomes solitary. By opening a shutter to admire its lustre, I startle it. It stands there, like a king, master of the garden and of shadow.

And in the morning it showers itself with brilliance. The leaves it lets fall are not like tears. It seems to distribute them magnificently, like large gold pieces, inflexibly enriching the lawn.

One by one I watch the hours glide by, then softly disappear in the small garden I explore and which I discover little by little. The turf-colored patch of cemetery, the low stone wall, the crooked alley, which leads I know not where,—all the vegetation, so poor, so dry, is familiar to me. It is like me, a Parisian, in this cold suburb. There is a bench. Yesterday a young man, accompanied by an interne, came to sit down there. The large tree took on a deeper yellow and sent out a stream of light like a projector. I watch the man who, seated as if he belonged there, smiled softly, breathed in the air and the odor of the earth, then took a few steps and came back cautiously to sit down again.

I observed his actions with as much interest as a child feels in watching a June bug, with a sort of restrained passion, so that I was afraid the door of my room would be opened,—I did not want to be obliged to leave the window. He walked with a slow and lackadaisical step, disregarding the golden tree; its radiance, which gushed like water, did not attract his eye at all. He made a turn about the lawn. I saw he was dressed in a long, dark-grey cloak, a light straw hat with a black band, and thick yellow boots, very pale, like those worn by hunters or chronic invalids.

He walked in this fashion for an hour, perhaps more, and I kept my eyes upon him, for something turns in my head if I close my eyes for a moment. He kept up his unvarying march in a circle. Then he disappeared and I heard him mount the stairs to his room which is above my own.

Already I hear a dull winding and gropingly I recognize the refrain of a gramophone which stretches itself like a snake and uncoils. Up there, in a solitude similar to mine, a disk turns and I hear "Tea for Two." I picture the man lying at full length, like me, alone upon the bed, opposite the clothes closet with its mirror. All the furniture is littered with articles. A coat on the chair lets its sleeve hang over on an easy chair, on the table is a half folded newspaper, a toilet case, and here and there are vases of flowers. The mauve light of an electric bulb is reflected in the glass and, now and then, when he raises himself to adjust his pillows, he sees his face in the mirror. His face. I know he is indifferent to everything, that nothing outside himself, neither the flowers, nor the light, nor a movement in the corridor, nor even himself, could hold his attention one instant. He thinks of nothing. He lives. He lives, as I do, meandering through the recesses of his empty body of which he expects nothing more. The light which parades before us and reclaims its place shows us that it is daytime.

The objects are unchanged. There is a whiteness of the sheets, the grey painted walls, the grinding of the doors, the croaking of the bed-springs.

I asked one day who this man was and someone told me he was a sick man called Nijinsky.

I listened intently to the noise of his footsteps on the floor. He goes, he comes. I hear him turn. I close my eyes to shut out the sight of a young man far below in the mist who is holding a rose in his hand and leaping to and fro. I close my eyes. I have forgotten. Also I hear an old mad-woman who powders her hair, stirring in the parlor on the ground floor beneath my room. She opens the piano. She has chosen at random a torn old sheet of music but she recognizes the piece she plays, for she still retains a trace of memory. Again she looks out over the candles of a salon (is it a salon of Poictiers, or of Sainte Menehould?), her gown trimmed with garlands of tiny roses, her scarf. . . . She plays the "Invitation to the Waltz." Overhead Nijinsky is still walking. He steps around the bed, silently. O fame, I toss you a smile. Then suddenly I hear, together with the old, cracked waltz, the gramophone droning, "Tea for Two."

It is only in the garden that I see spectres. The fall is reminiscent of summer. It is, perhaps, five o'clock in the afternoon and the tree, the great tree, shudders. Night is coming. Hours which will never sound again have passed. The air is still mild, almost listless. I know that in murmuring Paris the bells are beginning to ring, night is falling, one by one the store windows are lighted.

I think of all my neighbors, those whom I see from my window, those whose voices I hear, remote in their solitude. I am eager to know about them and, when the nurse brings me a soothing narcotic, I question her. There is the man who decorates himself like an old soldier, who throws out his chest to display his red rosette and who is always expecting someone. He pulls out his watch every two minutes, raises his hands to the sky and cries out: "They will never come again. Oh, my family. I am forsaken. What misfortune." Always the same words, and the same pacing back and forth. At midnight, at one o'clock in the morning, he looks at his watch just the same and utters an exclamation. He cannot sleep, so he gets up (I hear the bed creak) and starts walking again. I visualize him, going from one end of the room to the other, in nightshirt and slippers.

Sometimes in the morning I hear furniture being shoved about. This is the work of an old woman who is indulging in her mania for housecleaning. She moves all the furniture, rearranges it in her own way, pushes the dresser in front of the window, the bed against the door. . . . If the watchfulness of the attendants is relaxed a bit, she sneaks down to the reception room to rearrange things there. One day she worked so hard that she used all her strength in rolling the piano in front of the door and, exhausted, fell asleep. Someone had to climb in through the window to enter the room.

I see also that rather quiet man with eyes of angelic blue who walks in the garden and then suddenly stands utterly still. After the birds have gathered near him he makes a terrible gesture to chase them away. Then he smiles as if he had gained a great victory.

Turning from the window, I hear footsteps once again upstairs,—footsteps like those of which I saw the traces in the hall of a grey and abandoned chateau with a name as soft as a bird's song,—the chateau of Maria Pia. There a guide showed me the hall of lost footsteps, where a banished king, forgetful of his youth, wore out the flagstones pacing from one end of the room to the other. He, too, had lost his memory. One of the most beautiful landscapes in the world lay at his feet. From the window the fallen prince could look out over earth, sea and sky, but he lowered his eyes to watch only his endless and invisible path, to scrutinize the cold stone, grained like the skin of a hangman.

Perfumes denser than the voluptuous laughter of golden-skinned girls arose from the forests.

What did the world matter to him? Four walls, a door, the tireless chant of a water jet, formed a prison for his weariness, perplexity and his unhorsed glory.

In the room which shelters me, I don't know for how long, lives a man who has held on to his memory and who suffers from it as if it were a cancer, red and inflamed. I envy Nijinsky who knows nothing of his past, nor his fame.

But I must live with myself, and I gnaw slowly at the liberty I have loved so much. Perhaps tonight, as during the preceding one, I shall be obliged again to think of that which burns within me, to the suffering so strong I seem to breathe it. That which has nourished so many heartaches is there, in spite of me, in spite of me, because of me. This evening it brings to me once more the recollection of eyes which turn in their sockets, arms thrown forward, memories of a back, shaken, shaken. And again I feel my face muscles harden to keep from crying myself, and my shoulders ache because I have not opened my arms.

It is for this that I enjoy my suffering,—because I dream of sights I have seen, suffering I have caused, of things I have endured. I call to it, I await it.

Memory, memory! My daily enemy, my horror.

You, up there! You walk, you pass by, and you have forgotten, you have forgotten everything.

I know that my neighbor is not troubled about a rose, nor a waltz, nor the universe. I guess that he thinks of his old age, that some day his muscles will shrink and that he will no longer be able to walk around the green turf which constitutes his world.

Since it is Sunday, the silence is more profound, more absolute than usual. The man I am thinking of will not take a walk today. He will be left in his room. He will seat himself in his easy chair and stare at the gramophone. The world has ceased to exist.

All is not lifeless, however, since I dream of the throng which, on the outskirts of Paris, crowds around to admire a little bay horse, sweating and panting. I think of Longchamp. An interne has left a sporting paper on the stairway. I know (no one can conceal it from me any longer) that today at Longchamp the horses will contest, straining their utmost, forgetful of everything. It is the last day. The leaves are falling. After this, one must wait until spring to see again the broad, green field, surrounded by hills. It is fair weather, a little smoke, the Eiffel tower, a balloon may be seen.

Everything is ready for the races. Already gay colors, greens, yellows set off by the orange foliage, may be distinguished in the crowd. The jockeys climb upon their colts which throw their legs like sparks in all directions. They start off, heads lowered, faces set. They gallop on the grass. They pass the windmill, smelling the fragrance of leaves and turf. I open the window. My neighbor has started the gramophone and the refrain recurs like an old woman telling her beads.

The window is open. The weather is mild. The leaves fall, fall slowly. There is no way to stop them.

At such a time, memories float softly in the air, like the long inexorable cobwebs called "sons of the virgin." It seemed to me that my glances were mingled in the distance. There was an immense green field. God! If only the rest were a matter of indifference to me. There was a crowd which came and went, a red disk on a post, numbers, names which passed from mouth to mouth, money passed from hand to hand. My head turned, I was lost, I could not place myself, and I heard a tumult, ferocious and gay like a big celebration.

The sun was sinking. I sat there by my window and the hours had stopped. The rain had ceased and the mild air let the fragrance run freely. I heard a murmur.

Then a cry, a cry I shall remember. Sunday, and the silence of today, before a closed door and by the window-pane the rain struck regularly. With hands open and my eyes closed, I sit down in the armchair, close to the window. These hours will pass with these phantoms, faces I still wish to keep out of my mind. Still, I wait for them, today as on other days. It seems to me that I should be desolate if they were to vanish forever, I write only to pursue more closely my thoughts, which drift and unravel. I write because I do not suffer enough, because my pen, perhaps, will attack the core of my suffering.

Sunday. The big day at Longchamps. The brother of days I have lived.

I am grateful to those who have found this refuge for me, who have kept me from harm and have obliged me to whet my suffering to a keen edge.

The ennui which, riding the hours of the afternoon, would force my doorway, I do not fear. Here I am alone for the first time in so many years. And for how long? It is not ennui I fear but that sort of dizziness called terror. I imagine that in this solitude, this great and empty space, all the phantoms I have known, even those I have merely perceived, will penetrate the walls, all at once, and parade before me.

I know well that my mind, in the habit always of considering uniquely the future, of neglecting even the present, is likely to run backward, like the movement of a crazy watch, and unroll the long band upon which the past is inscribed.

The evening which is about to come will subdue all noises which still could distract me and the night, far ahead of sleep, will install itself for hours in this room. Already I look at the bed; already I dream of silence. Everyone has stopped moving, as if a bell I had not heard had signalled for silence and immobility.

I dreamed I was alive. That surprised me. I was alive. But I woke myself up.

Twilight

An elephant in his tub
and three children sleeping
strange strange story
story of the setting sun

One Two or Three

Let's look for the kids
the parents of the kids
the kids of the kids
the bells of spring
the springs of the summer
the regrets of fall
the silence of winter

Georgia

I can't sleep Georgia
I shoot arrows into the night Georgia
I'm waiting Georgia
I'm thinking Georgia
The fire's like the snow Georgia
I hear every single sound Georgia
I see smoke rise and drift away Georgia
I'm walking softly in the shade Georgia
I'm running
The street the faubourgs Georgia

Here's my city I don't know Georgia
I'm in a rush here's the wind Georgia
and the cold silence and the fear Georgia
I am fleeing Georgia
I am running Georgia
the clouds are low they will fall Georgia
I stretch out my arms Georgia
I'm not closing my eyes Georgia
I'm calling Georgia
I'm shouting Georgia
I'm calling Georgia
I'm calling you Georgia
Are you coming Georgia
soon Georgia
Georgia Georgia Georgia
Georgia
I can't sleep Georgia
I'm waiting for you
Georgia

EPITAPH: TRISTAN TZARA

Who's that?
You didn't shake my hand
Hearing you'd died we laughed so much
We worried you were eternal

Your last breath
Your last smile

No flowers no wreaths
Just those tiny cars
and butterflies ten yards long

Epitaph: André Breton

Yes I saw your look
When I closed your eyes
You said I shouldn't be sad
I wept all the same

The angels came up to your bed
saying nothing

Death is quite lovely

How you must be laughing by yourself
Now we can't see you any more
your cane's in the corner

People brought flowers
Even made speeches
I said nothing
I just thought of you

To Drink

If all the world were cake
And the sea black ink
And all the trees street lamps
What ever could we drink?

DOROTHEA TANNING

FROM "BLIND DATE"

It must have been a very bleak winter that year. I have no recollection of the weather, only the marvellous and relentless order in which everything occurred. It was the time that the sewing machine broke loose; nothing could have been more inopportune or diabolically calculated—the leaves had been carefully gathered and stored and now they were to be sewn together. They were particularly good leaves, I remember, sere and thin, each with the track of the snail underside, exactly the kind of leaf for a birthday, and now the sewing machine had gone, fled without a word of warning. Chagrined, unnerved, and with an inexplicable feeling of portent, it was I who set out in hopeless search. The month was November but the day had no date.

. . . a marvellous kind of synthetic awareness that the wallpaper is singing to me. And this is the song of the wallpaper:

> *Stitch the leaves then, stitch them carefully and with regard for the isolated time-beat. Tremble a little upon the threshold. One feigned tremor flung magnanimously to that enormous sloth which is legion. Today you have been born, out of abysmal sorrow and knowledge, out of symbols, destructions, words, pestilence, instrument sacred and obscene, spasms, defilements; out of hates, and holocausts, guts and gothic grandeurs, frenzy, crimes, visions, scorpions, secretions, love and the devil. Today you shall be married to your future.*

Dorothea Tanning, *Music Hath Charms,* 1940. Courtesy of Dorothea Tanning. © ARS.

Dorothea Tanning, *A Parisian Afternoon,* 1942. Courtesy of Dorothea Tanning.
© ARS.

Dorothea Tanning, *Guardian Angels,* 1946. Courtesy of Dorothea Tanning. © ARS.

Dorothea Tanning, *Palaestra,* 1947. Courtesy of Dorothea Tanning. © ARS.

Dorothea Tanning, *A Very Happy Picture*, 1948. Courtesy of Dorothea Tanning. © ARS.

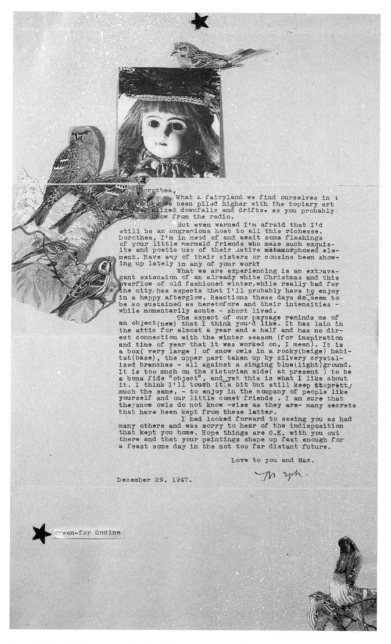

Dorothea,

    What a fairyland we find ourselves in [ ]
we been piled higher with the topiary art
     alized downfalls and drifts, as you probably
     know from the radio.

        But even warned I'm afraid that I'd
still be an ungracious host to all this richesse.
Dorothea, I'm in need of and await some flashings
of your little mermaid friends who make such exquisite and poetic use of their native metammorphosed element. Have any of their sisters or cousins been showing up lately in any of your work?

        What we are experiencing is an extrava-
gant extension of an already white Christmas and this
overflow of old fashioned winter,while really bad for
the city, has aspects that I'll probably have to enjoy
in a happy afterglow. Reactions these days do seem to
be so sustained as heretofore and their intensities -
while momentarily acute - short lived.

        The aspect of our paysage reminds me of
an object(new) that I think you'd like. It has lain in
the attic for almost a year and a half and has no direct connection with the winter season (for inspiration
and time of year that it was worked on, I mean). It is
a box(very large) of snow owls in a rocky(beige) habi-
tat(base), the upper part taken up by silvery crystal-
ized branches - all against a singing blue(light)ground.
It is too much on the Victorian side(at present) to be
a bona fide "object", and yet this is what I like about
it. I think I'll touch it a bit but still keep itapretty
much the same, - to enjoy in the company of people like
yourself and our little comet friends . I am sure that
theysnow owls do not know -wise as they are- many secrets
that have been kept from these latter.

        I had looked forward to seeing you as had
many others and was sorry to hear of the indisposition
that kept you home. Hope things are O.K. with you out
there and that your paintings shape up fast enough for
a feast some day in the not too far distant future.

                    Love to you and Max.

December 29. 1947.

green-for Ondine

Joseph Cornell, *Letter to Dorothea Tanning,* 1950; collection, Museum of
Modern Art. Courtesy of Dorothea Tanning. © The Joseph and Robert
Cornell Memorial Foundation.

Dorothea Tanning, *La Truite au bleu*, 1952. Courtesy of Dorothea Tanning. © ARS.

Dorothea Tanning, *Portrait de famille (Family portrait),* 1954. Courtesy of Dorothea Tanning. © ARS.

TRISTAN TZARA

NOTE ON ART

Art is at present the only construction complete unto itself, about which nothing more can be said, it is such richness, vitality, sense, wisdom. Understanding, seeing. Describing a flower: relative poetry more or less paper flower. Seeing.

Until the intimate vibrations of the last cell of a brain-god-mathematics are discovered along with the explanation of primary astronomies, that is the essence, impossibility will always be described with the logical elements of continual contradiction, that swamp of stars and of useless bells. Toads of cold lanterns, squashed flat against the descriptive sense of a red belly. What is written on art is an educational work and in that sense it can be justified. We want to make men realize afresh that the one unique fraternity exists in the moment of intensity when the beautiful and life itself are concentrated on the height of a wire rising toward a burst of light, a blue trembling linked to the earth by our magnetic gazes covering the peaks with snow. The miracle. I open my heart to creation.

Many are the artists who no longer seek solutions in the object and in its relations with the external; they are cosmic or primary, decided, simple, wise, serious.

The diversity of today's artists gathers the fountain's spray into a great crystal freedom. And their efforts create new clear organisms, in a world of purity, with the help of transparencies and the constructive materiality of a simple image as it forms. They continue the tradition: the past and its evolution push them slowly snakelike toward the interior, direct consequences far beyond surfaces and reality.

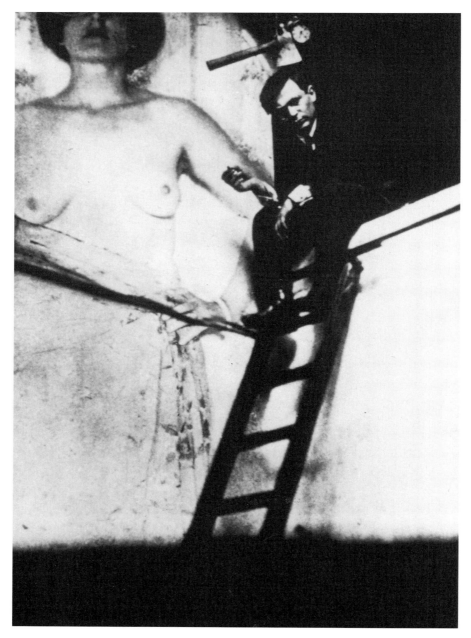

Man Ray, photograph of Tristan Tzara on ladder, 1924–1934. Pompidou Center. © ARS.

Note on Poetry

The poet of the last station no longer weeps in vain; lamenting would slow down his gait. Humidity of ages past. Those who feed on tears are happy and heavy; they slip them on to deceive the snakes behind the necklaces of their souls. The poet can devote himself to calisthenics. But to obtain abundance and explosion, he knows how to set hope afire TODAY. Tranquil, ardent, furious, intimate, pathetic, slow, impetuous, his desire boils for enthusiasm, that fecund form of intensity.

Knowing how to recognize and follow the traces of the strength we are waiting for, tracks which are everywhere, in an essential language of numbers, engraved on crystals, on sea-shells, on rail tracks, in clouds, in glass, inside snow, light, on coal, on the hand, in the radiations grouped around magnetic poles, on wings.

Persistence sharpens and shoots joy up like an arrow toward the astral bells, distillation of the waves of impassive food, creator of a new life. Streaming in all colors and bleeding among the leaves of all trees. Vigor and thirst, emotion before the formation unseen and unexplained: poetry.

Let's not look for analogies among the forms in which art finds outer shape; each has its freedom and its limits. There is no equivalent in art; each branch of the star develops independently, extends and absorbs the world appropriate to it. But the parallel sensed between the lines of a new life, free of any theory, will characterize the age.

Giving to each element its integrity, its autonomy, a necessary condition for the creation of new constellations each has its place in the group. A will to the word: a being upright, an image, a unique, fervent construction, of a dense color and intensity, communion with life.

Art is a procession of continual differences. For there is no measurable distance between the "how are you," the level where worlds are expanded, and human actions seen from this angle of submarine purity. The strength to formulate in *the instant* this varying succession is the work itself. Globe of duration, volume born under a fortuitous pressure.

The mind carries in it new rays of possibilities: centralize them, capture them on the lens which is neither physical nor defined—popularly—the soul. The ways of expressing them, transforming them: the means. Clear golden brilliance—a faster beating of spreading wings.

Without pretensions to a romantic absolute, I present some banal negations.

The poem is no longer subject, rhythm, rhyme, sonority: formal action. Projected on the commonplace, these become means whose use is neither regulated nor registered to which I assign the same importance as to the crocodile, burning ore, grass. Eye, water, scales, sun, kilometer, and everything I can conceive at one time as representing a value which can be humanized: *sensitivity*. The elements grow fond of each other when they are so tightly joined, really entwined like the hemispheres of the brain and the cabins of an ocean liner.

Rhythm is the pace of intonations you hear; there is a rhythm unseen and unheard: radiation of an interior grouping toward a constellation of order. Rhythm was until now only the beatings of a dried-up heart: tinklings in rotten and muffled wood. I don't want to treat with a rigid exclusiveness of principle a subject where only liberty matters. But the poet will be severe toward his work in order to find true necessity: from this asceticism will flower order, essential and pure. (Goodness without sentimental echo, its material side.)

To be severe and cruel, pure and honest toward your work which you prepare to place among men new oganisms, creations living in bones of light and in fabulous forms of action. (REALITY).

The rest, called *literature,* is a notebook of human imbecility to aid future professors.

The poem pushes or digs a crater, is silent, murders, or shrieks along accelerated degrees of speed. It will no longer be a product of optics, sense or intelligence, but an impression or a means of transforming the tracks left by feelings.

Simile is a literary tool which no longer satisfies us. There are ways of formulating an image or integrating it but the elements will be taken from differing and distant spheres.

Logic guides us no longer and its commerce, easy, impotent, a deceptive glimmer scattering the coins of a sterile relativism, is extinguished for us forever. Other productive forces shout their freedom, flamboyant, indefinable and gigantic, on the mountains of crystal and of prayer.

Freedom, freedom: not being a vegetarian I'm not giving any recipes.

Darkness is productive if it is a light so white and pure that our neighbors are blinded by it. From their light, ahead, begins our own. Their light is for us, in the mist, the miniscule microscopic dance of the shadowy elements in an imprecise fermentation. Isn't matter in its purity dense and sure?

Under the bark of the fallen trees, I seek the paintings of things to come, strength, and in the canals perhaps life is swelling already, the darkness of iron and coal.

Before Night

1

Before night falls, in this moment as disturbing as air suspended between liquid and solid states, when everything hides its face in shame, even the noises take flight, timidly, when the feeling that a vase is about to overflow plants itself with anguish in each breast as if another announcement of the death of someone we love, of his awful suicide, were going to strike us, when this hatred of life can transform sorrow into an immense gratitude, when the heaps of corpses warming the winter frozen in us, half-putrified, men we have known in the constant bitterness of a restless gaiety (how powerful sadness must be among such obvious signs to take on such strange aspects) have mutilated, torn, and strangled each other with a fierce joy of destruction, in a delirium of hatred, a delirium of hatred, such a frenzy that only the liveliest joy can raise the purity of a soul to such tender altitudes—before night falls, in this moment trembling in everyman's voice, without his knowing it, in the moment perceptible only to a few experienced beings for whom the invisible counts at least as much as degrading matter—how degrading physical suffering is—and knowing that you are a slave to pain wounds you in your human pride, when fate takes pleasure in showing you its steel fangs, ready to grind its own creation teeming with misunder-standings, between its lottery wheels, like a fire-eater at a fair, a subject to which I shall return, to which so many others have returned without turning around as in the song; finally, not to let myself slide down the bitter slope, before night falls, I say, in this moment like a long intake of air, seeming still longer in a hollow breast, a long breath to utter a cry which will perhaps never be uttered, the uselessness of things has become so fixed in the intentions of nature, I have decided to summon you, disgust, you who live hidden behind the meaning of things and people, always present, flooding this world with your sticky imprecation, you who have never changed, buried under immemorial layers of human despairs, fusing sometimes with the strength of storms and displaying yourself proudly before our hesitant steps, disgust, I have decided to summon you in a quiet voice with no trace of insult to it, in a voice which would have captivated the voices of all men over the infinite expanse where they suffer, bitter lament and suffering with no going back into memory, of all voices bundled into a sheaf of hatred, I summon you, disgust, to my aid, so that your hideous face, emerging in the middle of this world, can take account of your filthy adorers and those who turn away, so that your hideous face can divide into neat ranks the hybrid undecided mass, I summon you, cunning dis-gust, you who slow down our movements, you who take the harsh toll of at least half what our gazes have gathered, all that thought has tried to replace or to sing, you diminish our hatred and discourage the assassin born with us, who grew up in us and is struggling in a prison cell between love and the sun, in us, disgust, when your face has arisen from monstrous blackness and hidden half the sky with its fetid substance the answer will open perhaps in the word of all men, like the light gleaming only in their invincible hatred.

Before Night

2

Turbulent man—oh man as I see you growing from the smooth palm of mud, fusing your deep and delicate rootlings, scarcely joined to the earth's skin, scarcely fleeing at the wind's rise, scarcely submerged by the fleeing waters, scarcely surviving the profound play, gathering yourself in the aerial agility—the turbulent man decanted by age, the man of dramas and irremediable silences bows his head of dying sun, bows his look once swimming with crimes, impulses, scrutinizing monkey-wrench gazes, the slow source of sadness, of tenderness—oh moments falling fine as pearls on a sheet of glass, memory, entering through the eyes and projected on the foul heaps fed by deceptions—man folded over, a cool crock benevolent in the beggar's hand, the beggar sonorous and full who knocks on the doors of being as would a tree, a bell, a road stronger than you, man, you who have known a road more imperious than a woman's voice and who have made of a voice your nourishment and your daily luck and your sleep and your reason, man harrassed by absences (must a wall absorb so many echoes that its presence still resounds, for such a long time cruel or tender, infinitely tender), man bends over a defunct world and sees love, poverty, a whole hunger built of life and man, and the passion he believed so strong as it ripened the cold face, all it touched in its passing, often mocking it in a hollow similar voice, man who reached in his delirium the supreme lie purity accompanies, wearing itself out lying in its strength and doubt—falls, falls in the mud—and from the heights of its fervor, blind dizziness of snows—the snows melt and on each falling place, the place of a tomb is marked—man lives on impotence before the exaltation which draws him like a charm, man made to fall lower, lower, lower every day, without taking account, like water, as its freshness and as flame are priceless, priceless like a flying leaf is a bird singing crudely while beneath there

Man Ray, portrait of Tristan Tzara, from Man Ray, *105 Works, 1920–1934* (New York: Dover, 1979). Pompidou Center. © ARS.

are grave pains, jaws weighty with a heavy anger, heavy memories plunging in our immortalities, so many others which have not known how to perish, man who has turned toward cardinal hopes and has discovered in each beast an infant's cry and thought, like love, he has carried higher than the hour of the dead, man bends over the word and melts in legend like a mouth in desire and becoming in the line-up of unnumerable tombs through which he has forged for himself a king's forehead and a sun for the poor, sovereign bitterness and lassitude.

Before Night

3

And when man had finished spreading out his obsession with the infinite, he began again the unreasonable cycle of perpetual failures. Dramas moved their vain and foolish wings. Love shone in him like a mine-deep secret. Sleep was not his friend. But the wind brought him new words and, under each, he found fresh grass. And unknown nests. And the unknown grew in him until it was high as his head. There was solitude; there, the ineffable was seen. There he built his house from the ruins. May his wishes wake, may the stone take root! But that could not be and he set out again. Over the sea, over the eyelids. Over the earth with fire.

Part XIX

the whooping cough of mountains firing the steep walls
    of the ravines
with the pestilential buzzings of autumnal aqueducts
the reclaiming of free sky which like a common trench
    caught so many pastures
the languages of clouds the messengers' brief apparitions
announcing in their tufts supreme clamors and obsessions
underground the restless workshops of slow chemistries
    like songs
the rain's rapidity its crude telegraphic tingling
    like a ruminating shell
the deep punctures of peaks where the fleecy wash descends
worn-out from all the countrysides and the ruses
    of mocking valleys seducers of countries
the godless promenades of streams
the daring of their exploits against the seated dusk
    of clay

the oblivions of essences drowned in the oblivion
     of numbers and of ferries

in the fibrous dungeons agglomerated stalks and bells
where spinners of cares faint in the shade clanging with
     scythes
and uncover the eyelids of phallic phantom icicles
the bareness of stone walls their newels climbed
     by a thousand fingers
intertwining in braids of dandelions
and the balance of temperatures fanned by the exaggerated
     stare
your kindnesses produce in me aimless wanderings of facile
     and numbing prophecy
and stony in my garments of schist I have pledged my waiting
to the torment of the oxidized desert
and to the unshakable advent of fire

jostled in the basalt silence of ibises
caught in the reins of subterranean rivers
left to the frantic forests of hydras
where to the sermons of thick summers gargle dreamy rivalries
the night swallows us and hurls us to the other end
     of its lair
rousing beings that the grammar of the eyes has yet defined
     on the space of tomorrow
slow encirclings of coral
slaughter the high forks on stony wills
the notches in your heart it is a sultry season of gravel
     of hungry men
and how many huts in the shelter of your forehead have
     inscribed the mosses' broad mourning on the breast
falling in the ruin of a pile of futures
covered with muddled imperfections mixed with the ambushes
     of vines
when the schools of murky fish are infiltrated
by opaque death and tresses

we were crossing the heaths made gentler by attention
quietly careful of the monotonous jolts of phenomena
that the practice of the infinite imprinted on the blocks
    of knowledge
but the scaly structure of scattered opinions
on the moist infinity of diadems—the fields—
disdains the sensitive pulp of truths
with a hasty privilege of sharpened torture

the hatchets were chopping amid chestnut laughter
and the discs of hours flew to the attack
aerial flocks were bursting in the head
our reasons lying fallow restrained their diaphanous turbulence
and the knotty trajectories that they traced in time
were incarnate tentacular in the constraint of the ivy

there we forsook luxury and the dogma of the spectacle
sacrificing to other instincts the bronze desire
    taught us by its fruits
mow down adamantine insistences the vain landscapes
    elaborated by my senses
stand upright muted hallucinating mistrust
on the moor of my being the roads are all opened for you
take away what drunken reproach could not yet vanquish
and all I could understand and in which I no longer believe
the clot of what I could not understand rising
    in my throat
the seaweed dragged by the implacable working of the depths
and the triangle's flower incised in the pupil
the battle my breath loses on the stiff white page
and the osmosis of odious thoughts
the sorrows riddled with persistent sowing of seduction
the sorrows built on pilings safe from diversions
and the hut velvet with dust
and a lost soul's dwelling
and so many others and so many others

sick or found again
for stony in my garments of schist I have pledged my waiting
to the torment of the oxidized desert
to the unshakable advent of fire

hands strangely separated clusters of transparent hands
shuffle dominoes of stars over the swamp they are sheep
and shells of crushed clouds nautical odors trailing
on the table of the sky covered with eucharistic games
what games what savage joys support with disarray your
      conduct in the menagerie sky
where beasts and planets intertwined roll opium eyes
stretched out from one end of the aquarium to the other
      your heart so luminously carved from silence
dedicated to the minute artifices of blades
incrusted with rebellious drops of wine and
      blasphemous words
is permeated with the ecstasies ebbing and surging
      in the verbal congestion
with which the typhoon stigmatized your forehead

henceforth the ramparts' prow is carved like the swimming
      figure
but now your eyes guide the cyclone
haughty shadowy intention
and over the sea to the boundary of the wakes of birds
the wind coughs to the boundary where death lays down its
      load
in our numbed consciousness thunder promethean waterfalls
      of echoes
when the earth remembers and tosses you that is suffering
a beaten village dog and poor you wander
you always return to the starting point disconsolate
      with the word
a flower in the corner of your mouth a consumptive flower
      jeered by the harsh necropolis

tons of wind have poured into the deaf citadel of fever
a ninepin at the mercy of a thoughtless impulse
    what am I
a disconsolate starting point where I return smoking the word
    in the corner of my mouth
a flower battered by the rough fever of the wind
and stony in my garments of schist I have pledged my waiting
to the torment of the oxidized desert
to the unshakable advent of fire

when the complexities of chance make fast the moorings
    by their smile
when your heart is summoned—where solid jaws sink in—
stale and dusty moth—dull intimacy—what do I know—
    workshop of the night—
when the jar with the hissing of a trampled nest of snakes
where the persuasions of virile harshness endure
snarling to a gradual moan
slow furnace of invincible constancy—man—
slow furnace rises from the depth of your slow deliberation
slow furnace rises from the valley of glacial principles
slow furnace of unspeakable alloys
slow furnace reaching the centers of lucid emotions
great furnace rises from the coughs slaves of fortresses
slow fire brightens in the gaping fear of your
    strength—man—
fire grown tipsy on heights where the coastal traffic of clouds
    has earthed over the taste of abyss
fire climbing supplicant the ladder to the stains
    of unbounded gestures
fire barking forth streams of regrets beyond hypocritical
    suggestions of the possible
fire fleeing from the muscular seas where man's escapes
    linger

a man who quivers at the vague presumptions of the labyrinths
    of fire

a fire that weaves the massed surging swell of characters
    —submits
harmony—let this word be banished from the feverish world
    I visit
savage affinities undermined by emptiness covered
    with murders
crying out at the impenetrable impasse sobbing
    with tattered flamingos
for the fire of anger varies the flickering of the subtle remains
according to the mumbling modulations of hell
that your heart strains to hear among the giddy salvos
    of stars
and stony in my garments of schist
I have pledged my waiting to the oxidized desert of torment
to the unshakable advent of its flame

Marianne Van Hirtum

Euthanasia—A Cat Kidnapped—Thirty Francs—the Veterinarian

This was very simple, really. At noon, the Lady from the fourth floor, meeting the little young woman from the sixth in the hallway, asked her to be kind enough to come up with her, for she had a favor to ask. "It's this way," she said, "It's very simple. I'd like you to agree to take my cat to be put to sleep. That poor animal is suffering. She's seventy-two years old now. I don't have the strength to take her down there." Little Emie agreed at once, because of her usual willingness to help. The appointment was set for two the following afternoon. "There's five francs in it for you," added the Lady with a gracious smile.

At two o'clock, then, the next day, Emie rang the bell on the fourth floor. The other side of the door there was a commotion, then a fairly long silence reigned. "Well," Emie said to herself, "they're in no hurry." At last the door opened and the Lady exclaimed with a bewitching smile, "Oh! Poor little Emie, you've chosen a very bad moment: it had completely slipped my mind that we were baptising our little boy today, could you come back tomorrow at five o'clock?" Emie acquiesced—what else could she do?—and went away. Back in her own room, she took off her pretty red hat and her gloves, and, rather listlessly, went back to work.

The following morning, returning from an errand in town, Emie met the Lady from the fourth floor in the hallway. "Oh my dear girl," said the Lady, "would you be so sweet as to kindly do me a big favor. It's this way: our dog isn't at all well. He's over a hundred fifty years old, would you be so very good as to take him down there for me, to have him put to sleep: we don't have the heart for the job, ourselves." Emie, who was kind, said yes. The appointment was set for the following day at three o'clock. When, the following day at three, Emie rang the bell on the fourth floor, the Lady joyfully opened the door and at once cried, "Oh you poor child! You've come at such a bad time! I'd quite forgotten we were celebrating today our hundredth wedding anniversary, my husband and I. Would you be so kind, please, as to come back tomorrow evening at six o'clock?" Emie answered that she would be there. The door closed quietly. Emie had to go out that day: so she did not take off her pretty red hat.

Ithell Colquhoun, *Tepid Waters,* 1939; oil on wood, 35⁷/₈ × 24 inches, Southampton City Art Gallery, United Kingdom/Bridgeman Art Library. © VAGA.

When she came back from town, at the front door of her house she met the Lady from the fourth floor who tugged sweetly at her sleeve, saying, "My little child, I find it hard to ask you to do me a very big favor. This is what it's all about: our horse Robert is sick. He's just over three hundred thirty-two years old. Would it please you, to spare us that hateful trip, to take him tomorrow down there where they put animals to sleep? Let me add—without wanting to hurt your feelings—that there's five francs waiting for you, Emie." Emie, kindhearted as always, replied that such a favor did not bother her. As early as five o'clock in the morning she put on her pretty red hat. Then, as she still had a little time left, according to her alarm clock, she prepared herself tea with milk and drank it very thoughtfully. Then she shut her door and went down to the fourth floor. She waited a while after ringing the bell. The Lady cautiously opened the door a crack. "Oh!" she said, upon seeing little Emie, "my dear child, what a bad time you've chosen. Just imagine, today—my Goodness! I'd completely forgotten, scatterbrain that I am—we have to celebrate our last little boy's solemn communion. Couldn't you come back tonight at ten o'clock?" Emie, with her customary graciousness, replied that, indeed, there was no problem, she herself had so much to do that morning, anyway, and went off, her pretty red hat a little askew.

At ten that evening, Emie courteously rang the bell on the fourth floor. The door remained closed, but the Lady's voice reached her, muffled, from behind the door: "Do please excuse me, gracious child, we're celebrating such a great event, you understand: tonight's the marriage of our grownup daughter to her best friend from school, I can't allow myself . . .": the rest was so unintelligible that little Emie went off on tiptoe.

A few weeks went by. Emie was ill in the meantime. She went to the best specialists for treatment. When she was better, on sick leave, one fine morning she was very happy to go to the milliner's to treat herself to a new little hat, which she chose in red, this time. Just for a change, she said to herself, filled with joy. Returning from that happy errand, she ran right into the Lady from the fourth floor.

The Lady had put on a considerable amount of weight, so Emie did not recognize her right off. When she had got over her surprise and greeted the Lady in a friendly fashion, the Lady took her hand and asked her in a low voice if she would consent to come up with her to her apartment for a few moments, since she had a little favor to ask. She added in Emie's ear that if three francs would be welcome. . . . Very happy with her pretty red hat, Emie accepted at once and went up behind the Lady. The latter, because of her new corporeal opulence, walked more slowly, so the climb was long and difficult. Emie was dreaming of meeting a mirror in which she could admire herself at her leisure.

When they had reached the fourth floor the Lady collapsed in a chair. Feeling tired, Emie did the same. A moment went by, each getting her wind back.

Then the Lady spoke to Emie in a low voice. "It's nothing," she said, "Nothing, or nothing much, anyway. My poor husband has just had his five hundredth birthday. He's at the end of his tether. Between you and me, whatever you do, don't repeat this to anyone: he smells these days. Would you have the civility, Mademoiselle, to take him, with the usual precautions, to those people to have him put to sleep? That would save us all sorts of worries . . . " "When?" asked Emie. "Well, right away, if you like. I'll go into the toilet, for the sight of all that business would be too painful for me, you understand. My husband is hidden in the kitchen closet. His basket is on the chair, all you have to do is get him into it: that won't take but a moment.—Oh, please don't forget to wash out his dish as you go through.—Thank you."

Emie carefully closed the front door and went off toward the kitchen, while the Lady took care to shut herself in the toilet. The whole business took a little more time, though, than it takes to put an old man of five hundred in a basket.

Nevertheless, the following morning, Emie, wild with joy, was able to buy a new little hat, in red this time. When she went home, joyfully, she had a shock, seeing a great crowd standing in front of her house. The firemen were there in full uniform, nothing was missing. Emie went up and questioned the neighbors. "Oh my poor girl," was the response, "a very painful thing has happened.

"There's been a huge leak on the third floor. A real flood, you know. It didn't do any good to ring the doorbell on the fourth floor, no one answered. Then the Concierge had the marvelous idea of calling in the firemen; they broke the door down: oh! what a smell! Just imagine, there wasn't anyone there. But the Fire Chief had the wonderful idea of forcing the toilet door that seemed to be jammed from the inside.—You know . . . they found Madame so swollen and dead in there that the doorway had to be widened to be able to pull her out, an while the firemen were dragging her over the rug in the entrance hall, her stomach burst under too much pressure and you know out of it came . . . a little dog, a very big cat, a tiny horse . . oh, Mademoiselle! Is her husband going to be flabbergasted when he gets home from work! . . . Madame loved him so . . . he loved Madame so. Times are bad, Mademoiselle!"

The next week, Emie decided that red hats did not suit her any more so well as before. With the three francs from the Lady on the fourth floor she bought herself a pretty black hat.

William Carlos Williams

Theessentialroar

First the roar first brilliantly overdone THEN the plug in the pipe that takes them home with a ROAR and a cigarette and a belly full of sweet sugar and the roar of the film or to sit at the busy hour in the polished window of Union Club at the northeast corner of fifty-first street across the street from St. Patrick's (so to speak) neat gray catholic cathedral and feel the roar pleasantly pricking the face but they're all face as the Indian said to Ben Franklin who also knew French women like the New York Journal which knows that unless it roars it does not do the trick and that's the trick that you have to have the money for like Weissmuller when he slaps the water with his hands, quick, the way they talk and THAT's what makes them WIN, it just HAPPENS but when a baby drops a ball of twine and it rolllllllls unwinding about their feet neatly semicolon placed in rows while the cigar train is sucked at by the throat of the tube and it rolls without WITHOUT any roar at all along among the feet everybody smiles because it DOES something to everybody it SURPRISES them all because it SHOWS UP the roar and nice colored men smile and a nice fat man picks it up and a very nice lady smiles like the translation of a norse saga that the sea has left when the plug slips through the pipe, the toss and danger of the cold sea is dead in English keeps them kidded so the emptiness of the continent has been filled, that's the crowd at the door jamming and pushing both ways, YOUNG hit a ball with a stick stick to it roar out around the middle its the brush hedge on which the vine leans hell with booze who can't invent noise that carries a rock drill in its breeches WHOOP it up and we'll ride the bronk with the hands tied ka plunk ka plunk opens up the old clam under your ribs till the whisky of it tickles the capillaries around the fissure of Sylvius and the milky way weigh spits out a drop or two of fire to you? I'm just too lazy like when he got the capsicum vaseline on the finger of his glove when he was making the regional examination and the result was SURPRISING.

Joseph Cornell, *Yellow Sand Box,* 1960. © Joseph and Robert Cornell Memorial Foundation.

OTHER WORKS

René Magritte, *Le Balcon de Manet (Manet's Balcony),* 1950; from *Le Peintre de l'imaginaire,* no. 137, Giraudon/Art Resource. © ARS.

COLLECTIVE WORKS

ANDRÉ BRETON AND PAUL ELUARD

INTRA-UTERINE LIFE

To be nothing. Of all the ways the sunflower has of loving the light, regret is the most beautiful shadow on the sundial. Crossbones, crossword puzzles, volumes and volumes of ignorance and knowledge. Where is one to begin? The fish is born from a thorn, the monkey from a walnut. The shadow of Christopher Columbus itself turns on Tierra del Fuego: it is no more difficult than the egg.

A great self-assurance—and great without term of comparison—enables the ghost to deny the reality of the forms that enchain it. But we have not yet reached that point. The disconcerted gestures of statues in their moulds produced those imperfect, ghostly figures: the Venuses whose absent hands caress the poet's hair.

From one bank of the river to the other, washerwomen shout at each other the name of a fantastic personage who wanders over the earth feigning hatred for everything he embraces. Their songs are everything that carries me away and is nevertheless carried itself, as carrier pigeons photograph the enemy camp without wanting to. Their eyes are less far from me than the vulture from its prey. I understand now that a woman's face is visible only during sleep. It is in vertigo, among the even grasses of heaven. Seen from within or without, it is the pearl a thousand times more valuable than the diver's death. From without, it is the admirable slingshot; from within, it is the bird. The brambles tear it and the mulberries stain it black, but it bestows on the bushes the strange source of its seething light. Impossible to find out what has become of it since I discovered it.

The doe between two leaps likes to look at me. I keep her company in the clearing. I fall slowly from the heights, I still weigh only the weight you lose at thirty thousand feet. The extinguished chandelier that lights me bares its teeth when I caress the breasts I didn't choose. Great dead branches pierce them. The valves that open and close in a heart which is not mine and which is my heart are everything useless that will be sung in two-four time: I cry, no one hears me, I dream.

This desert is false. The shadows I dig enable the colours to appear like so many useless secrets.

I shall, they say, see. I shall, they see, hear. Silence as far as the eye can see is the keyboard that begins with those twenty fingers that are not. My mother is a spinning top whose whip is my father.

For seducing the weather I have shivers for adornment, and the return of my body back into itself. Ah, to take a bath, a bath of the Romans, a sand bath, an ass's milk sand bath. *To live* as one must know how to knot one's veins in a bath! To travel on the back of a jellyfish, on the surface of the water, then to sink into the depths to get the appetite of blind fish, of blind fish that have the appetite of the birds that howl at life. Has anyone ever seen birds sing around four in the afternoon in April? Those birds are mad. It is I. Has anyone ever before seen the sun cover the night with its dead weight, as the fire covers the ashes? For suns I have flame becoming smoke, the wild moan of a hunted animal, and the first waterdrop of a shower.

Be careful! They are expecting me. Day and night are going to be at the station. I shall never recognise them if I burden myself with the suitcases of justice.

SIMULATION OF GENERAL PARALYSIS

Thou my great one whom I adore beautiful as the whole earth and in the most beautiful stars of the earth that I adore thou my great woman adored by all the powers of the stars beautiful with the beauty of the thousands of millions of queens who adorn the earth the adoration that I have for thy beauty brings me to my knees to beg thee to think of me I am brought to my knees I adore thy beauty think of me thou my adorable beauty my great beauty whom I adore I roll the diamonds in the moss loftier than the forest whose most lofty hail of thine think of me—forget me not my little woman when possible at inglenook on the sand of emerald—look at thyself in my hand that keeps me stead-fast on the whole world so that thou mayest recognise me for what I am my dark-fair woman my beautiful one my foolish one think of me in paradises my head in my hands.

They were not enough for me the hundred and twenty castles where we were going to love one another tomorrow they shall build me a hundred thousand more I have hunted forests of baobabs from thine eyes peacocks panthers and lyre-birds I will shut them up in

Antonin Artaud, *L'Immaculée conception (The Immaculate Conception),* ca. January 1945; graphite and wax crayon, 24 × 18¾ inches, private collection. © ARS.

Antonin Artaud, *La Maladresse sexuelle de Dieu (The Sexual Awkwardness of God)*, ca. February 1946; 24⁷/₈ × 19¹/₂ inches, private collection. © ARS.

my strongholds and we will go and walk together in the forests of Asia Europe Africa America that surround our castles in the admirable forests of thine eyes that are used to my splendour.

Thou hast not to wait for the surprise that I want to give thee for thine anniversary that falls today the same day as mine—I give it to thee at once since I have waited fifteen times for the year one thousand before giving thee the surprise of asking thee to think of me in hide-and-seek—I want thee laughing to think of me my young eternal woman. Before falling to sleep I have counted clouds and clouds of chariots full of beets for the sun and I want to bring thee to the astrakhan shore that is being built on two horizons for thine eyes of gasoline to wage war I will lead thee by paths of diamonds paved with primroses with emeralds and the cloak of ermine that I want to cover thee with is a bird of prey the diamonds that thy feet shall tread I got them cut in the shape of a butterfly.

Think of me whose only thought is the glory wherein the dazzling wealth of an earth and all the skies that I have conquered for thee slumber I adore thee and I adore thine eyes and I have opened thine eyes open to all those whom they have seen and I will give to all the beings whom thine eyes have seen raiment of gold and crystal raiment that they must cast away when thine eyes have tarnished them with their disdain. I bleed in my heart at the very initials of thy name that are all the letters beginning with z in the infinity of alphabets and civilisations where I will love thee still since thou art willing to be my woman and to think of me in the countries where there is no man.

My heart bleeds on thy mouth and closes on thy mouth on all the red chestnut-trees of the avenue of thy mouth where we are on our way through the shining dust to lie us down amidst the meteors of thy beauty that I adore my great one who art so beautiful that I am happy to adorn my treasures with thy presence with thy thought and with thy name that multiplies the facets of the ecstasy of my treasures with thy name that I adore because it wakes an echo in all the mirrors of beauty of my splendour my original woman my scaffolding of rosewood thou art the fault of my fault of my very great fault as Jesus Christ is the woman of my cross—twelve times twelve thousand one hundred and forty-nine times I have loved thee with passion on the way and I am crucified to north east west and north for thy kiss of radium and I want thee and in my mirror of pearls thou art the breath of him who shall not rise again to the surface and who loves thee in adoration my woman lying upright when thou art seated combing thyself.

Thou art coming thou thinkest of me thou art coming on thy thirteen full legs and on all thine empty legs that beat the air with the swaying of thine arms a multitude of arms that want to clasp me kneeling between thy legs and thine arms to clasp me without fear lest my locomotives should prevent thee from coming to me and I am thou and I am before thee to stop thee to give thee all the stars of the sky in one kiss on thine eyes all the kisses of the world in one star on thy mouth.

Thine in flames.

PS.—I would like a Street Directory for mass a Street Directory with a knotted cord to mark the place. Bring also a Franco-German flag that I may plant it in No Man's Land. And a pound of that chocolate with the little girl who sticks the placards (I forget). And then again nine of those little girls with their lawyers and their judges and come in the special train with the speed of light and the outlaws of the Far West to distract me for a moment who am popping here unfortunately like champagne corks. The left strap of my braces has just broken I was lifting the world as though it were a feather. Canst thou do something for me buy a tank I want to see thee coming like fairies.

SIMULATION OF DELIRIUM OF INTERPRETATION

When that love was over, I felt as homeless *as the bird on the branch*. I was no longer fit for anything. Nevertheless I observed that the patches of oil on the water reflected my image and I noticed that the *Pont-au-Change,* near the bird market, was becoming more and more arclike in form.

And that is how, one fine day, I crossed over forever to the other side of the rainbow through looking at the iridescent birds. Now there is nothing for me to do on earth. No more than other birds do I say that I no longer have to commit myself to earth, *to put in a winged appearance on earth*. I refuse to repeat with you the slang song: 'We die for the little birds, come and feast your little birds.'

The shower's dazzling colours speak parrot language. They hatch the wind that emerges from its shell with seeds in its eyes. The sun's double eyelid rises and falls on life. The birds' feet on the windowpane of the sky are what I used to call the stars. The earth itself, whose motion seems so inexplicable as long as one remains beneath the vault, the earth with its *webfeet* of deserts is itself obedient to the laws of migration.

Feather summer is not yet over. The trapdoors have been opened, and the harvest of down is being thrust inside. The weather is *moulting*.

The cock on the steeple ornaments the smoke from the guns while the orange-breasted widow hies herself to the cemetery whose crosses are tiny flashes of diamonds of the Southern Cross, and man continues to *imagine himself* on earth like the blackbird on the buffalo's back, on the sea like the gulf on the crest of the waves: the solid blackbird and the liquid seagull.

Horus, finger at lips, is the avalanche. I hadn't before seen those birdcatchers who hunt for men in the sky and drive themselves from their nests with the stones they toss in the air.

The phoenixes come, bringing me my ration of glowworms, and their wings which they constantly dip in the gold of the earth are the sea and the sky which glow only on stormy days and which hide their lightning-tufted heads in their feathers when they fall asleep on the air's one foot.

The lightning mills have broken out of their shells and are flying swiftly away. The sand consumes the dunes. The horizon tries to avoid the clouds.

You must admit that your *bed-cages,* and your twisted bars, and your gnawed floors, and your nutmegs, and your latest-style scarecrows, and your train trips in a pigeonhole compartment, and your *hedgerow races* in the twilight of robins flying away, and the hours and the minutes and the seconds in your woodpecker heads, and your glorious conquests— what about them, your glorious conquests of cuckoos! All those traps of grace were never there for any other purpose than to get me past the barriers of danger, the barriers that separate fear from courage. Don't count anymore on me to help you forget that your phantoms wear the bustles of birds of paradise.

In the beginning was the song. Everybody to the windows! From one side to the other you can see nothing but Leda. My whirling wings are the doors through which she enters the swan's neck, on the enormous deserted square which is the heart of the bird of night.

FORCE OF HABIT

The table is placed in the dining room; the taps give out clear water, soft water, tepid water, scented water. The bed is as large for two as for one. After the bud will come the leaf, and after the leaf the flower, and after rain fine weather. Because it is time, the eyes open, the body stands up, the hand stretches out, the fire is lit, the smile contends with night's wrinkles for their unmalicious curve. And they are the clock's hands that open, that stand up, that stretch out, that set light to themselves and mark the hour of the smile. The sun's ray goes about the house in a white blouse. It's going to snow again, a few drops of blood are going to fall again at about five o'clock, but that'll be nothing. Oh! I was frightened, I suddenly thought there was no longer any street outside the window, but it is there just the same as ever. The druggist is even raising his metal shutters. There soon will be more people at the wheel than at the mill. Work is sharpened, hammered, thinned down, reckoned out. Once more the hand takes pleasure in finding the security of sleep in the familiar implement.

Provided it lasts!

The mirror is a marvellous witness, changing all the time. It gives evidence calmly and with power, but when it has finished speaking you can see that it has been caught out again over everything. It is the current personification of truth.

On the hairpin-bend road obstinately tied to the legs of him who assesses today as he will assess tomorrow, on the light bearings of insouciance, a thousand steps each day espouse the steps of the vigil. They have come already, and they will come again without being invited. Each one has passed that way, going from his joy to his sorrow. It is a little refuge with an enormous gas jet. You put one foot in front of the other, and then you are gone.

The walls cover themselves with pictures, the holidays sift themselves with bouquets, the mirror covers itself with vapour. As many lighthouses on a stream, and the stream is in the vessel of the river. Two eyes the same, for the use of your single face—two eyes covered with the same ants. Green is almost uniformly spread over the plants, the wind follows the birds, no one risks seeing the stones die. The result is not a trained animal but an animal trainer. Bah! It is the indefeasible order of a ceremony already, on the whole, so very gorgeous! It is the repeating pistol which makes flowers appear in vases and smoke in the mouth.

Love, in the end, is well satisfied with seeing night clearly.

When you are no longer there, your perfume is there to search for me. I come only to get back the oracle of your weakness. My hand in your hand is so little like your hand in mine. Unhappiness, you see, unhappiness itself profits from being known. I let you share my lot, you cannot not be there, you are the proof that I exist. And everything conforms with the life which I have made to assure myself of you.

—What are you thinking about?
—Nothing

The Original Judgment

Don't read. Look at the designs created by the spaces between the words of several lines in a book and draw inspiration from them.

Give your hand to the others to keep.

Don't lie down on the ramparts.

Take back the armour that you took off when you reached the age of discretion.

Put order in its place, disturb the stones of the road.

If you bleed and if you are a man, erase the last word on the slate.

Form your eyes by closing them.

Let the dreams you have forgotten equal the value of what you do not know.

I have known a railway signalman, five female gatekeepers, and one male gatekeeper. And you?

Don't prepare the words you cry out.

Live in abandoned houses. They have been lived in only by you.

Make a bed of caresses for your caresses.

If they come knocking at the door, write your last will and testament with the key.

Rob sound of its sense; even light-coloured dresses can hide muffled drums.

Sing of the enormous pity of monsters. Evoke all the women standing on the Trojan horse.

Don't drink water.

As with the letter *l* and the letter *m,* you'll find the wing and the serpent near the middle.

Speak according to the madness that has seduced you.

Wear sparkling colours, it's not usual.

What you find belongs to you only as long as you hold out your hand.

Lie as you bite the judges' ermine.

You are the pruner of your life.

Hand yourself, brave Crillon, they'll unhang you with their *That depends.*

Bind faithless legs.

Let the dawn stir the fire of the rust of your dreams.

Learn to wait, with your feet in front of you. That's the way you will soon go out, all covered up.

Light up the perspectives of fatigue.

Sell what you eat, buy what you need to die of starvation.

Surprise them by not confusing the future of the verb 'to have' with the past of the verb 'to be'.

Be the glazier for the stone set in the new windowpane.

When they ask to see the inside of your hand, show them the veiled planets in the sky.

On the appointed day, you will calculate the lovely dimensions of the insect-leaf.

To expose the nakedness of the woman you love, look at her hands. She has lowered her face.

Separate the chalk from the coal, the poppies from the blood.

Do me the favour of entering and leaving on tiptoe.

Semicolons; you see how amazing they are, even in punctuation.

Lie down, get up, and now lie down.

Until further *orders,* until further religious orders, that is until the most beautiful girls adopt the cross-shaped decolleté: the horizontal beam showing the breasts, the foot of the cross revealing the belly, whose base is slightly russet-brown in colour.

Forgo that which has a head on its shoulders.

Adjust your gait to that of the storms.

Never kill a nightbird.

Look at the convolvulus blossom: it does not allow one to hear.

Miss the obvious goal when you are supposed to pierce your heart with the arrow.

Perform miracles so as to deny them.

Be the age of the raven who says: Twenty years.

Beware of wagondrivers with good taste.

Sketch the disinterested games of your boredom in the dust.

Don't seize the time to begin again.

Argue that your head, unlike a horse chestnut, is absolutely weightless, because it has not yet fallen.

Gild with the spark the otherwise black pill of the anvil.

Without wincing, imagine swallows.

Write the imperishable in sand.

Correct your parents.

Do not keep on your person anything that would wound common sense.

Imagine that that woman can be summed up in three words and that that hill is a chasm.

Seal the real love letters you write with a profaned host.

Don't forget to say to the revolver: Delighted but it seems to me I've met you somewhere before.

The outside butterflies are trying only to rejoin the inside butterflies: don't replace, in yourself, a single pane of the street lamp if it should happen to get broken.

Damn what is pure—purity is damned in you.

Observe the light in the mirrors of the blind.

Do you want to own the smallest and the most alarming book in the world? Have the stamps on your love letters bound and then weep—you have good reason to, in spite of it all.

Never wait for yourself.

Look closely at these two houses: in one you are dead and in the other you are dead.

Think of me who am speaking to you; put yourself in my place when you answer.

Be afraid of passing too near the tapestries when you are alone and hear someone calling.

Wring out with your own hands your body over the other bodies: accept this principle of hygiene courageously.

Eat only birds in leaf: the animal tree can stand autumn.

Your liberty with which you make me laugh till I cry is your liberty.

Make the fog flee before you.

Seeing that the mortal condition of things does not bestow on you an exceptional power of lasting, hang yourself by the root.

Leave it up to the stupid pillow to wake you.

Cut down trees if you wish, break stones too, but beware, beware of the livid light of utility.

If you look at yourself with one eye, close the other.

Don't abolish the sun's red rays.

You take the third street on the right, then the first on the left, you come to the square, you turn near that café you know, you take the first street on the left, then the third on the right, you throw your statue to the ground and you stay there.

Without knowing what you will do with it, pick up the fan that that woman dropped.

Knock on the door and cry, 'Come in'—and don't go in.

You have nothing to do before dying.

FROM "BARRIERS"

"Don't forget, gentlemen, that you aren't the masters here. Let's keep our distance. My best wishes to you.

    —I prefer those lovely shops where the cashier lady is enthroned. You can scarcely believe your eyes. But since you prefer, just go on by on the opposite sidewalk, we will be less of a bother to you.

    —Any return to beginnings presupposes a noble soul, just what we happen not to have. It only takes place in the presence of policemen.

    —Have you forgotten that policemen are neutral and that they have never been able to stop the sun?

    —No, thanks, I know what time it is. Have you been stuck in that cage for long? The address of your tailor is exactly what I need.

    —Let me give you a good piece of advice: Go straight to the avenue du Bois and offer a little coin to one of the renters in any of those buildings whose totally terrible taste arouses our passions.

    —After which we will be able to make the dead generals retreat and give them back again those battles they lost. Otherwise, we shall have to protest against the most equitable judgements in the world and the palace of justice is done for.

    —*It's nice enough weather on this side of your voice, but I assure you we should watch out for those distances I was speaking of.*

    —I'm not as sure as you are. A lamppost I love brought me to understand that army generals and nuns know how to value the loss of the very least dream.

    —It's nice enough weather on this side of your voice, but I assure you we should watch out for the distances I was speaking of.

Luis Buñuel and Salvador Dalí

Scenario for *L'Age d'or*

A surrealist film by Luis Buñuel

Scenario by Luis Buñuel and Salvador Dalí
with Gaston Modot and Lya Lys

> My general idea in writing the scenario for *L'Age d'or* with Buñuel has been to present the straight and pure course of 'conduct' of a human being pursuing love contrary to the ignoble ideals of humanity, patriotism, and all the miserable mechanisms of reality.
>
> —*Salvador Dalí*

The early scenes, which constitute a prologue, are of such ordinary and indescribable monotony that they begin to engender an almost morbid fascination proving a valuable contrast of mood when the main action develops. In a dreary landscape of arid rocks, scorpions are living. A discouraged and ineffectual bandit, who is climbing about the rocks, notices a group of archbishops who have arrived to hold Mass in this mineral setting. Running back to inform his comrades of the presence of the Church, the bandit finds his friends in a strange state of weakness and depression, but they seize their weapons and advance, excepting the youngest of them all who cannot even rise. They stumble across the rocks. One after another they fall exhausted. Their leader falls too, just within sight of the archbishops who, as the pall of desolation falls over the entire island, are now mere skeletons disposed with their vestments among the stones.

A great maritime expedition comes in sight of this coast. The expedition consists of priests, nuns, the military, statesmen, and several civilians. They are assembled for the founding of imperial Rome. Suddenly piercing cries attract the attention of all. In the mud, nearby, a man and a woman are engaged in an amorous struggle. This man, so oblivious of the spectacle which he makes, represents the individual in revolt against an established

Salvador Dalí, *Portrait of Luis Buñuel*. 1924; oil painting. L. Buñuel Collection, Mexico, Giraudon/Art Resource. © ARS.

world with which there can be no compromise. The pair is separated by force, the man arrested by the police.

Dragged through the streets of a modern city this man, who is the protagonist of the film, struggles to escape, as each object he sees transforms itself into reminders of his beloved. Finally he is released, when his identity is revealed by a document describing his high position and the importance of a patriotic and humanitarian mission confided to him by the Government. Meanwhile the woman has been invited to a party given by the Marquis de X. It should be noted that this modern party offers a parallel with the era of the "*Ancien Régime*" just preceding the French Revolution. The guests, solely concerned with the incidents of the party, are completely blind to nearby events not of their own world. A serving girl is thrown in flames from the kitchen, a tumbril is driven across the ballroom floor, a boy is shot by his father for not much reason, whereas the one event to profoundly disturb the guests is the upsetting of a teacup.

The protagonist arrives at the party and perceives his beloved across the room. From this moment all his activity is directed towards love. The body of the film is concerned with successive love scenes, dominated by acts of violence and frustration.

In the course of a final ineffectual episode the protagonist is summoned by the authorities and accused of having failed in his mission; that in consequence thousands of old people and innocent children have perished. He answers with foul insults and returns determinedly to the woman he loves. At this very moment an inexplicable accident separates them forever, and the man is last seen throwing a burning tree out of the window, a large agricultural implement, an archbishop, a giraffe, feathers.

As an epilogue the survivors of the Château de Selligny are seen, after the criminal orgies of the Marquis de Sade, crossing the drawbridge covered with snow. This last incident is accompanied by a paso-doble.

PAUL ELUARD AND BENJAMIN PÉRET

FROM *152 PROVERBS MIS AU GOÛT DU JOUR*

One good mistress deserves another.

Elephants are contagious.

A crab, by any other name, would not forget the sea.

Spare the cradle and spoil the child.

I came, I sat, I departed.

The further the urn the longer the beard.

Never sew an animal.

He who bestirs himself is lost.

Beat your mother while she's young.

When the reason is away, the smiles will play.

A little more than green and less than blond.

Cold meat lights no fire.

A shadow is a shadow all the same.

Grasp the eye by the monocle.

Who hears but me hears all.

A corset in July is worth a horde of rats.

Make two o'clock with one clock.

Better to die of love than to love without regret.

Breaking two stones with one mosquito.

RENAUD, MARIANNE VAN HIRTUM, VINCENT BOUNOURE,
MICHELINE BOUNOURE, AND JEAN-LOUIS BÉDOUIN

THE DOG: PARALLEL STORY

The hunter's dog was *worth*less and the worried hunter would sniff the air in place of his dog. But to *sniff* is not to hunt. And so one can inhale *camomile* or *smell* the scent of infusions but this is to *reject* forever the chance of finding the *coral* whose *gleam* shines only behind the *closing* of enchanted bushes that only greyhounds can open with the first *finger* of their forefeet. Showing the velvet finger. The hunter ran an ad in the *newspaper* and hung in the *subway* a notice that *Negresses* could *read*—but they had never *tamed* greyhounds. In spite of his *weekly* notices the hunter's requests *made off*. He decided to hunt no more and became a *head surgeon* operating on *cigarette-lighters* on the banks of the *Marne* in a *brick* hospital, of course. All this scarcely roused him to enthusiasm. He had the feeling he was working on *garbage* and with the *balance* of the possible this was hardly reassuring. Singing *ritornelles,* he went into courtyards to harvest *stoppers* instead of *coal* to put in his fireplace. That didn't do either. He became a *lighthouse keeper.*

One *dog* doesn't make a spring, the concierge at the Orangerie Museum used to say with *force* busy *sniff*ing that December morning air. She brewed herself *camomile* tea and began to *smell* her middle finger to know if it was time to *reject* the *coral* that was obscuring its *gleam* in an army dressing-station candle. *Closing* time having rung, she rapidly set the table before the eyes of a petrified Goya that immediately dipped its *finger* in the camomile tea and finding it too salty mopped its brow on the *subway's newspaper* just given it by the Negress playing the *tame lyre.* This Negress laid a few *weeklies* on Voltaire's armchair and her evening *made off* in that way. But the *head surgeon* made his appearance and demanded the reopening of the Museum, content to use *cigarette-lighters* instead of lighting. *The Marne* had never had so many of them. A few *bricks* all but decorated the façade of the Marne opera house which was having the première of "*Garbage.*" The *balance* marked five o'clock and the *ritornelles* were becoming blurred to the sound of *stoppers* that took the place of char*coal,* for times are difficult and it isn't easy to heat a museum in the care of a *lighthouse keeper* like the one who occults the Eiffel Tower.

What a *dog*! what a dirty trick, what a *worth*less fellow! you've seen him, it's my grandfather stretched out in the sun on the roses to *sniff* them. He smells the *camomile* too, he goes down next toward the river bank, *smells* the feet of the willows and sometimes he drowns himself until the water *throws* him *back* on the *coral* cliff, on that gentle dying *gleam*. The dog, though, doesn't die, he gets into his *zipper*, he holds himself aloof, he moves one *finger*, two fingers, he dozes, and spits into the air, he gets up and pulls a *newspaper* from his pocket, he can't find the spectacles he lost twelve years ago in the *subway*, losing track of time too with a *Negress* and plucking the strings of his *lyre*, but without going so far as to *tame* that person. But his *weekly* has not returned. He gets up with a movement that *makes off*, like the clumsy saurian and then at last he grabs his *head surgeon*'s cap which always remains for this circumstance on the beach laid on his *cigarette-lighter* but remains marked with *marl* and raw *bricks* where he, the dog, has fallen down during the drinking bouts. *Garbage*! he's going to get up now on his boots like great weights on the *scales* of the earth, those whose *ritornelle* makes you think of the *stopper*, of *coal*, of the burnt cork with which they make up circus funny men to give them a thrashing as the *lighthouse keepers* beat the revolving lens of our misery.

I bought a fine rifle at the flea market, nothing but the *dog* has colossal *value*, therefore I pulled it out to go sell it at a jeweler's on the Rue des Rosiers. Taking off his beard and his spectacles the old man *sniff*ed the dog, treated himself to a glass of *camomile* tea, *smelled*, *threw* the dog *back* behind his counter, and insulted me. The dog having broken, a great *coral* flower came out of it, as big as a palm tree I went to plant near St. Paul. There emanated from it a great *gleam* that alerted the caretakers of Viviani Square who decided its *closing*. My left middle *finger* having got caught between two *newspaper* pages I then was rushing into the *subway*, a *Negress* with large breasts put my finger between her breasts to make a *lyre* out of them. My *tamed* finger began again to live and to quiver according to its *weekly* rhythm but everything, all of a sudden, *made off*. The *head surgeon* from the Pitié Hospital, by accident in a second-class compartment, having sensed a strange tale, took out his *cigarette-lighter* and told us in a very loud voice, "I who was one of those in the taxis of the *Marne*! I'll give you a *brick* if you'll kindly come home immediately with me!"—*Garbage*! we reply, my Negress and I, I don't give a rap for your brick, I know the *old story*, it's a bribe you want to give us, a *stopper*, and I've got enough *coal* in my pocket to end my days as a *lighthouse keeper*."

"*Dog*," he said and the alpha star of the Centaur dreamed. Its *value* the relationship between the lion's tooth and the thirty-two teeth that chew it in a salad, *sniff*ing the sailing-ship's saltpeter, when the sons of *camomile* awake *smell*ing the whale's spray that *rejects* the sons and daughters of coral. A *gleam* to starboard, cries the swallow. The sea is a *zipper.* Its *fingers* turn over the pages of a *newspaper* whose columns are *subway* trains. The *Negress* at gone five in the morning takes herself for a *lyre* whose *tame* goat fires accents that make the rails sob. But the steel is *weekly* like the catastrophes the stories of which *make off*! The *head surgeons* are handicapped in the larynx, this is why they leave it to their *cigarette-lighters* to call the taxis of the *Marne,* why they'll pay three *bricks* to go get beaten up, between three ashtrays of *garbage* . . .

GAMES AND QUESTIONNAIRES

Roy Dowell, Tom Knechtel, Megan Williams, and Lari Pittman, *Cadavre exquis (Exquisite Corpse),* 1992; Drawing Center.

Surrealist Game

Do you want to hear the great voice of the oracle?

The breaking voice of life?

Sit around a table. Take a sheet of paper and write down immediately what you want to know. *What is.* . . . Fold the paper, pass it to your neighbor who will put down an answer right away, without reading your question. And so on . . .

Unfold the paper and read. You will hear echoes coming from far off, from farther off than you; and you will finally have the most beautiful conversation that you ever had with the world and yourself.

See.

What Is . . .

QUESTION: WHAT IS THE NIGHT?
ANSWER: It's breaking the same heart eternally.

Q: WHAT IS HATING?
A: Staying far behind your face, far behind.

Q: WHAT IS POETRY?
A: It's the bell tolling through all the great wind of the sky.

Q: WHAT IS DESPAIRING?
A: It's taking out the magisterial thorn.

Q: WHAT DO YOU DESIRE?
A: It's hearing the romance of romance.

Q: WHAT IS DEATH?
A: Traveling throughout the world with your eyes closed.

Q: WHAT IS DREAMING?
A: A great burst of light right in the heart.

Q: WHAT IS DESIRE?
A: A wonderful catastrophe.

Q: WHAT AM I?
A: Scrupulously separating day from night.

Q: WHAT IS LOVING?
A: Being able to sleep peacefully.

Q: WHAT IS THOUGHT THEN?
A: To walk on tiptoe dangerously over the firing line.

Q: WHAT IS BOREDOM?
A: It's a terrible sea monster.

Q: WHAT IS SPEAKING?
A: It's flying off into the great mist.

Q: WHAT IS HARMONY?
A: It's what sees the eye.

Q: WHAT IS A CHILD?
A: It's motion.

Q: WHAT'S LIFE?
A: It's desire eating the world.

Etc. . . . Etc. . . .

Answers to Questionnaires

About de Chirico's *Enigma of a Day*

WHERE IS THE SEA?

ANDRÉ BRETON: Behind the statue.

RENÉ CHAR: Everywhere in the conversation of the two personages.[1]

PAUL ELUARD: In the porticoes.

ALBERTO GIACOMETTI: Very near, behind the first arcades.

MAURICE HENRY: On the spectator's side.

BENJAMIN PÉRET: On our side, but we turn our backs to it.

TRISTAN TZARA: Ten miles away behind the chimneys.

WHERE WOULD A PHANTOM APPEAR?

A.B.:   In the second arcade. It is the gory phantom of a woman.

J.M. MONNEROT: It would be seen perhaps at the window above the porticoes.

B.P.:   It would appear suddenly from under the stone behind the statue.

DESCRIBE THE LANDSCAPE AROUND THE TOWN.

A.B.:   Villas, the richest ones covered with snow. Very far away, woman-shaped derricks. Artificial storms are blowing over shacks made of rags with windows of yellow reeds. Deserted squares are encircled with a beautiful leather belt, thirty feet high, with an obscene glass buckle.

R.C.:   A landscape in the Vosges, or in Sardinia. A few swamps, a dead sea. Immediately behind the chimneys, a chocolate factory. Under the roof, horsehair stocks. Volcanic ground. It's a beach. It's Devil's Island. In the distance and sometimes in the folds of the flag, the phantom of Hannibal. The statue is made of earth. Underground pipes drain it in order to keep it fresh. Sulfur emanations in the air.

P.E.:   The town is on a plateau. Sheer walls on all sides. Then, at the foot of the walls, the same square, then other walls, other squares, etc.

A.G.:   Around the town, a circle of sand with a stretched canvas bordering it.

YOLANDE OLIVIERO: There is no town, only the square at the top of a high mountain. Leaning over the railings, one sees only water and smoke.

T.T.:   Abandoned vineyards, a tangle of guillotines, here and there gravel shaped like swallows' eggs. A carpet made of dead butterflies starts from the sea in a straight line and ends between the chimneys. It is sprinkled with red wine and goats' excrement.

Giorgio de Chirico, *L'Enigme de la fatalité (The Enigma of Fate),* 1914; oil on canvas. Kunstmuseum, Basel. © ARS.

WHERE WOULD ONE MAKE LOVE?

A.B.:   Inside the plinth of the statue.

P.E.:   On the plinth of the statue.

A.G.:   Under the porticoes at right.

B.P.:   Standing, in the middle of the square, regardless of the two personages, who are dead.

T.T.:   The painting being blind, love would be made in the sun.

WHERE WOULD ONE MASTURBATE?

A.B.:   Behind the moving van, out of sight of the chimneys and always changing place to watch the locomotive advancing slowly.

B.P.:   Near the locomotive, between the arcades and the chimney at left, very far into the landscape.

T.T.:   Turning one's back to the painting.

WHERE WOULD ONE DEFECATE?

P.E.:   In a railway station that is outside the picture, at the right.

A.G.:   In the background, to the right of the chimney.

M.H.:   In the statue's right hand.

Y.O.:   On the stone, exactly.

B.P.:   On the statue's right foot.

T.T.:   On the stone at left.

WHOM DOES THE STATUE REPRESENT?

A.B.:   Lincoln.

P.E.:   The father.

A.G.:   A disciple of Cavour.

M.H.:   A furniture mover, famous in the country.

Y.O.:   Benjamin Franklin.

B.P.:   The inventor of decalcomania.

T.T.:   A celebrated inventor in matters of baking.

WHAT TIME IS IT?

A.B.:   Eleven p.m.

P.E.:   Noon.

A.G.:   Three a.m. The sun is false.

M.H.:   Noon.

CÉSAR MORO: Four-thirty p.m.

Y.O.:   Five p.m. in summer.

B.P.:   Between six and seven p.m. in June.

T.T.:   The midnight sun.

WHAT ADVERTISEMENT SHOULD BE PUT UP ON THE BUILDING AT THE LEFT?

P.E.:   Spend your honeymoon in Detroit.

A.G.:   The word *soap* above each arcade.

M.H.:   Paramount.

Y.O.:   Dubonnet.

T.T.:   Bovril or Bowling.

About Paris

WOULD YOU KEEP, DISPLACE, MODIFY, TRANSFORM, OR SUPPRESS THE OBELISK?

ANDRÉ BRETON: Install it at the entrance of the slaughterhouses, where it will be held by an immense gloved hand.

PAUL ELUARD: Insert it delicately into the steeple of the Sainte Chapelle.

TRISTAN TZARA: Make it round, and place, at the top, a steel pen of a suitable size.

THE LION OF BELFORT[2]

A.B.: Give it a bone to gnaw and turn it westward.

P.E.: Place on its back a diver in a diving suit, holding in his right hand a pot with a hen dipping in it.

T.T.: Pierce it with an enormous rod and roast it to flames of bronze.

THE OPERA?

A.B.: Change it into a fountain of perfumes. Rebuild the staircase with bones of prehistoric animals.

T.T.: The Zoo, the section with monkeys and kangaroos, should be installed in it. Replace the exterior decoration with skeletons. On the stairway outside, install the steel reproduction of a bicycle as high as the whole facade.

THE LAW COURTS?

A.B.: Raze them. A magnificent graffito should be traced on the site, to be seen from the air.

P.E.: Raze them. A bathing pool should take their place.

BENJAMIN PÉRET: Destroy them and replace them with a bathing pool to which only beautiful nude women would be admitted.

NOTRE DAME?

A.B.: Replace the towers with an immense oil-and-vinegar cruet, one flask filled with blood, the other with sperm. The building would be used as a school for the sexual education of virgins.

THE STATUE OF CLEMENCEAU?

T.T.: Place around the statue thousands of sheep in bronze, including one in camembert.

Notes

[1] The two small figures standing in the middle of the square in Chirico's picture.—M.J.

[2] This animal commemorates in bronze, at the Place Denfert-Rochereau in Paris, the siege of the town of Belfort during the Franco-Prussian War of 1870–71.—M.J.

TRANCE EVENT

Trance Event

I remember a waterfall at the bottom of grottoes. Someone I knew, a friend, called Robert Desnos, spoke. He had discovered, by the help of a strange sleep, several secrets lost by all. He spoke as nobody speaks. The great common sea was now at last in the room, which was any room with its wondering utensils. (Louis Aragon)

(Desnos, *spontaneously writing*): the Tower.

Q.: Who is the Tower? A woman?
A.: Yes, of course.

Q.: Do you know her?
A.: Yes (*he leans on the pencil, the lead breaks*).

Q.: Is she beautiful?
A.: I don't know.

Q.: Has she other qualities?
A.: I don't like her.

Q.: Is she here?
A.: Yes (*broken pencil lead*).
A.: (*in English*) If you want.

Q.: What will you do in five years?
A.: The River (*from the final letter starts a drawing: wave, small boat, smoke. Written with much care*). She is called Bergamote.

Q.: What will Breton do in five years?
A.: (*Drawing of a circle with its diameter*):
Picabia Gulf Stream Picabia.

Q.: Do you like Breton?
A.: Yes (*the lead breaks, then, legibly*): Yes.

Q.: What will Eluard do in five years?
A.: 1,000,000 francs.

Man Ray, *Nude with Shells,* ca. 1925–1929; gelatin silver print, 4⁷/₈ × 6⁷/₈ inches. Courtesy of the J. Paul Getty Museum. © ARS.

Q.: What will he do with this money?
A.: War to the fleet.

Q.: Who is Max Ernst?
A.: The deep river and the Spanish grammar.

Q.: What do you think of Simone Breton?
(*No answer.*)

Q.: Who is she? What do you see for her?
A.: I (*crossed out*) convolvulus (*drawing of an eye with an arrow*) the beautiful loved one (*a drawing, above which is written*): the horse.

Q.: It's Gala Eluard who holds your hand.
A.: (*A drawing.*)

Q.: What do you see for her?
A.: The fatal hour that you will see.

Q.: What will she do?
A.: (*Drawing of a G clef.*)

Q.: Will she die soon?

A.: Opera opera.

Q.: Is that all for Gala Eluard?

A.: Oh, there will be matches in three colors (*drawing of a hand leaning on a curve*), a hand against the moon.

Q.: What do you know about Max Ernst?

A.: Fraenkel's white smock at the lunatics' hospital.

Q.: Who is Max Ernst?

A.: F sharp.

(*Desnos wakes up.*)

DREAMS

Kay Sage, *All Soundings Are Referred to High Water,* 1947; oil on canvas. Photo: Charlotte Phil. Davison Art Center, Wesleyan University. © ARS.

ANTONIN ARTAUD

DREAM

I

He was an aerial photographer. From the height of an immutable airplane, he was taking a picture of the flight of precise mechanics who knew what the plane was doing. The air was filled with a lapidary murmur like the light all around. But the lighthouse sometimes failed to light up the apparatus.

Finally we were only two or three on the wings of the machine. The airplane was hanging from the sky. I felt myself in an odious equilibrium. But as the mechanical system reversed itself, we had to turn around in the emptiness, getting our footing on some rings. Finally the operation succeeded, but my friends had left; there were only the repair mechanics who were turning their braces and bits in the emptiness.

Just then, one of the two wires broke:

—Stop work! I yelled at them, I'm falling! We were five hundred meters from the ground.

—Patience, they replied, you were born to fall.

We had to avoid walking on the wings of the machine. I felt them, though, resisting under me.

—But if I fall, I cried, I knew I couldn't fly.

And I felt that everything was cracking.

A cry: "Send the lancets!"

And immediately *I imagined* my legs sliced by the lasso, the airpane leaving my feet and myself suspended in the emptiness, with my feet on the ceiling.

I never knew if *it had happened.*

Antonin Artaud, *Sort/Spell,* May 22, 1939; violet pencil and watercolor on burnt paper. Dedicated to Roger Blin, the entire text (recto and verso) says: "All those who have gotten together to keep me from taking HEROIN all those who have touched Anne Manson because of that Sunday May 1939 I will have them pierced alive in a Paris square and I will have them perforated and their intestines burned. I am in a Mental Asylum but this dream of a Madness will be enacted and enacted by ME.— Antonin Artaud." In Paule Thévenin and Jacques Derrida, eds., *Antonin Artaud: Dessins et portraits* (Paris: Gallimard, 1986). © ARS.

II

And immediately, I arrived at the expected wedding ceremony. It was a marriage where only virgins were getting married, but there were also actresses, and prostitutes; and to reach the virgin, you had to pass over a little stream, a water all prickly with rushes. The husbands shut themselves in with the virgins and dealt with them immediately.

One of them, more virgin than the others, was wearing a dress with bright squares, her hair curly. She was being possessed by a well-known actor. She was small and rather plump. I was sorry she didn't love me.

The room where they put her had a door that didn't close altogether, and through the crack of the door I witnessed her succumbing. I was rather far from the crack, but among all the people who were in the room, no one but me was paying any attention to what was happening in the room. I saw her already naked and standing, and I admired how her brazenness was surrounded with freshness and a kind of resolute decision. She was perfectly aware of her sex, but as of something absolutely natural and normal at that moment: she was with a young husband. And so we went after her in a boat.

III

The three of us were dressed like monks, and as a sequel to the monk's robes, Max Jacob arrived in a little coat. He wanted to reconcile me with life, with life or himself, and felt before me the dead mass of his reasoning.

Before that we had pursued a few women. We took them on tables, in chairs, in the stairs and one of them was my sister.

The walls were black, the doors stood out clearly, and you could see the lighting of the caves. The whole decor was a purposeful *analogy* and a *created* one. My sister was lying on a table, she was already pregnant and had on many coats. But she was on another level from me in another milieu.

There were tables and shiny doors, staircases. I felt that it was all ugly. And we had put on long robes to hide our sin.

Then my mother arrived dressed like an abbess. I was afraid she would come. But Max Jacob's short coat shows he had nothing to hide.

He had two coats, a green and a yellow, and the green was longer than the yellow. They appeared after each other. We inspected our papers.

ANDRÉ BRETON

DREAM

I

The first part of this dream is devoted to the creation and presentation of a costume. The face of the woman for whom it was made should play the role of a simple ornamental motif, like those that are often used in the ironwork of a balcony or a cashmere shawl. The parts of the face (eyes, hair, ear, nose, mouth, and the various wrinkles) are subtly sketched out by light-tinted lines: like certain masks from New Guinea, but more delicate in execution. The human truth of these features is not diminished, and the repetition several times in the costume, particularly in the hat, of this purely decorative element prevents it from being considered alone or as any more alive than a formation of veins in a regularly veined piece of marble. The form of the costume is such that it does not leave out anything of the human silhouette. It's like an equilateral triangle, for example.

    I am lost in my contemplation.

Finally I go up the street of Aubervilliers in Pantin, towards the Town Hall when, in front of a house I used to live in, I meet a burial procession which, to my great surprise, is going in the opposite direction from the Parisian cemetery. Soon I have caught up with the hearse. On the coffin a rather old man, extremely pale and in great mourning, wearing a high hat, is seated. He can only be the deadman; turning to the right and left, he is greeting the passersby. The procession enters the match factory.

II

I arrive in Paris and go down the staircase of a station similar to the Gare de l'Est. I have to urinate, and get ready to cross the square, on the other side of which I can relieve myself, when a few steps from me on the same sidewalk, I find a little urinal, a new model, very small, rather elegant. No sooner have I entered it than I notice it moving; since I am not alone in it, I become aware of the inconvenience of this. But it's a vehicle like another, and I decide to stay on the platform. From there I see the disquieting sight of a second "flying-urinal" quite near by, and just like ours. Unable to draw the attention of my fellow-travelers to its erratic movements and the danger it represents for the pedestrians, I climb down while mine is still moving, and succeed in persuading the imprudent driver to leave his post and follow me. He's a man under thirty who, when questioned, acts extremely evasive. He presents himself as a military doctor, and has a driver's license. A stranger in the town we are in, he says he has just arrived "from the bush" without being more precise. Although he is a doctor, I try to convince him he may be very sick; however, he enumerates the symptoms of a great number of maladies, beginning by different fevers: symptoms he doesn't seem to have, of the simplest clinical kind. "At the very most I am perhaps a paralytic." When I examine his reflexes, which I do immediately, they are not conclusive (a normal kneecap, a heel weak with what I diagnose in the dream as "a tendency to tendonitis"). I forgot to say that we stopped at the threshold of a white house and that my interlocutor kept going up and down one of the stairs as steep as a whole floor. Pursuing my questioning, I try in vain to find out how he used his time "in the bush." During one of his mountings of the stairs, he finally remembered that he had assembled some sort of collection over there. I want to know what kind.

"A collection of five shrimp." He comes back down: "I confess, dear friend, that I am very hungry," and saying this, he opens a straw suitcase that I had not noticed until now. He takes advantage of the suitcase to show me his collection, indeed composed of five shrimp, of very different sizes and looking fossilized (the shells, hardened, are empty and completely transparent). But other entire shells, in great quantity, slide to the ground, when he raises the top part of the case. And as I express my astonishment: "No, there are only five: these." From the bottom of the case he takes out a piece of roasted rabbit and, without any instrument other than his hands, he starts eating it, tearing it apart with his nails. The flesh is hanging in long filaments like that of skates, and it seems to be of a pasty consistency. I can barely stand this nauseating spectacle. After a long silence my companion says to me: "You always recognize criminals by their enormous jewels. Remember that there is no death: there are only reversible meanings."

III

It is evening at my place. Picasso is standing in front of the sofa in the corner, but he is in the intermediate state between his actual one and that of his soul after his death. He is sketching distractedly in a sketchbook. Each page has only a few rapid strokes and the notice in tall letters of the price he is asking: 150 francs. He scarcely speaks and doesn't seem at all interested in the idea that I tried to find out how he spent his time at Beg-Meil, where I arrived just after he had left. Apollinaire's shadow is also in this room, standing against the door, somber and full of reservations. The shadow lets me accompany him; I don't know where he is going. As we go along, I am eager to ask him a question, a leading one, since I cannot really converse with him. But what do I want to know more than anything? Because he will doubtless not satisfy my curiosity more than once. Why should I care to find out from Apollinaire what has happened to his political opinions since his death, to ascertain that he is no longer so patriotic, and so on? After reflecting I decide to ask the shadow what he thinks of himself such as we knew him, of this more or less great poet that he was. That's the second time he's been questioned about this and I want to excuse myself for the question. Does he think his death was premature, is he at all glad about his fame? "No and no." When he thinks of Apollinaire, he admits it's like thinking about someone else, whom he likes in just a banal way. We are about to take a path laid down by the Romans, and I think I know where the shadow wants to lead me (I'm sure he won't surprise me at all, and am rather proud of that.) At the other extremity of this path there is a house which has played a considerable role in my life. A corpse is stretched out on a bed and around it, in a phosphorescent light, there are sometimes hallucinatory phenomena which I've witnessed. But we haven't yet gotten there and already the shadow is opening the two panels framed with golden buttons of a dark red door. I am right there, so far it is just a brothel. Incapable of making him change his mind, I sadly bid the shadow farewell, and retrace my steps. Soon I am faced with seven or eight young women, detaching themselves from a group I can barely make out on the left side and who, with their arms stretched out, are barring my way, *all four of them.* They are determined to make me turn around. Finally I get rid of them with many compliments and promises, each worse than the last. Now I've taken my seat in a train across from a girl in mourning who, it seems, conducted herself shamefully, and whose mother is reprimanding her. She could make amends, but she remains almost totally silent.

Giorgio de Chirico

Dream

I'm putting up a useless fight with a man whose eyes are gentle and corrupt. Every time I seize him he frees himself just by extending his incredibly strong and powerful arms; they are like irresistible levers, like all-powerful machines, those gigantic cranes lifting, far above the teeming workplaces, floating fortresses with towers as heavy as the breasts of antediluvian mammals. I'm putting up a useless fight with a man whose eyes are gentle and corrupt; from each embrace, however frenzied, he frees himself gently, smiling, just stretching out his arms a little. . . . This is my father appearing to me like this in a dream, although when I look at him he is not exactly as I used to see him during my childhood. And yet it is he; there is something *more distant* in each expression of his face, something that I used to see in him perhaps, and which now, after more than twenty years, appears to me when I see him in dreams, in his total power.

The struggle ends by my *giving up: I renounce;* then the images are confused: the river (the Pô or the Pénée) that I felt running alongside me while I was struggling now becomes darker; the images are confused as if storm clouds had descended low on the earth; there was an *intermezzo,* during which I was perhaps still dreaming, but I remember nothing except anguished quests along dark streets, when the dream cleared up again. I am in a square of great metaphysical beauty; perhaps it's the *Piazza Cavour* in Florence; or perhaps also one of those very lovely squares in Turin, or perhaps neither one nor the other; on one side you see porticos, and above them, apartments close-shuttered with their solemn balconies. On the horizon are hills with villas; over the square, the sky is very bright and storm-washed, but you feel that the sun is setting, for the shadows of the houses and of the few passersby are very long on the square. I gaze towards the hills where you can glimpse the last clouds of the fleeing storm; here and there, the villas are completely white, with something solemn and sepulchral about them, seen against the black curtain of the sky here. Suddenly I find myself under the porticos, mingling with a group of people pressing up around the door of a pastry shop, where multicolored cakes fill every floor of the shop; the crowd huddles around and keeps looking in, just as they do at the doors of pharmacies when a sick person is brought in wounded, or someone who has fallen ill in the street; but while I am looking, I see, from behind, my father standing in the middle of the pastry shop eating a cake. I don't know if it's because of him that the crowd is pressing forward; a certain anguish grips me and I feel like fleeing towards the west into a new and more hospitable country, and at the same time I am looking for a knife or a dagger under my clothes, for it seems to me that some sort of danger is menacing my father in this pastry shop, and I feel that if I go in, the knife or the dagger are indispensable, like when you enter the cave of bandits, but my anguish is increasing and suddenly the crowd presses around me tightly and draws me towards the hills; I have the impression that my father is no longer in the pastry shop, that he is fleeing, that they are going to go after him like a thief, and I awaken in the panic of this thought.

Joseph Cornell

Some Dreams, 1947–1969

dreams ever different ever varied endless voyages
endless realms ever strange ever wonderful
—*October 1961, diary entry*

Feb. 8, 1947

dreamed of vaults with all kinds of whipped cream pastries. Rich day . . . layer cake—cherry Danish—calm feeling

Night of May 11, 1947

Asleep in chair by stove—dreamed of opening window (at corresponding late hour). Window for icebox and seeing in basement of neighbors house 2 pet cockatoos in cage dimly illuminated (house dark) this from the bird cage of picture cockatoos in own cellar

Stayed up all night dozed briefly by stove (oven lit)—drowsy at breakfast but did not sleep all day. Worked through from listless to harmonious afternoon & evening. The feeling that a *definite* stage of progress had been reached.

Election Day, Nov 4, 1947

warm and rainy

one of those distant snatches of a dream that used to be recurrent (a certain locale a house that comes back from childhood)

this time in spite of its elusiveness a positive touch of grace producing a fleeting but completely happy feeling about my work too often enjoyed without this

Diary—write up dream of night of Oct 13, 1949

early morning ride on bike—getting off train with commuters in strange town—waterfall through lanes 2

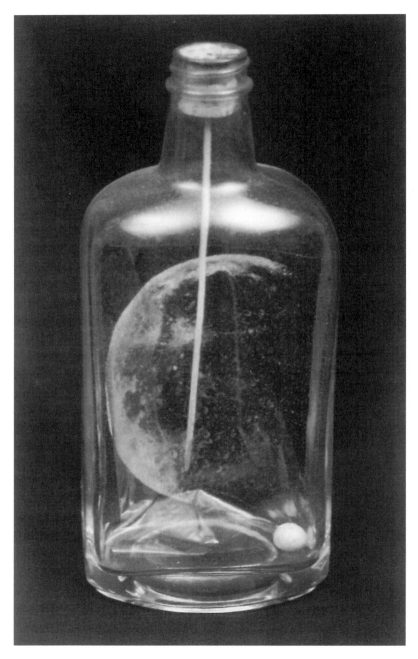

Joseph Cornell, *Song Title Lunar Bottle,* 1933. © Joseph and Robert Cornell
Memorial Foundation.

house on water circling on bike for numerous views reminiscent of Nyack childhood
on Hudson

Exalted feelings upon awakening

autumn leaves turning thorough window light on same

March 28, 1950

Diary note "Le Secret d'Eugénie—Turks finished in morning good working spurt satisfaction in craft versus difficulty of forcing—there was the additional stimulus to find
another piece of jetsam (flotsam?) in the china repository similar to the "Moutarde
Dijon" broken jar already put to use with good effect and satisfaction for the AVIARY
series—a spontaneous "lifting" above former edginess and nervousness symptomatic of jour-
neyings—

a battered jagged jar of white, once containing cold cream or cologne—like
the "Moutarde Dijon" this too from France. Left almost intact in oval frame a flying
Cupidon with Gabriel—horn white on white a bas-relief requiring from its worn contours close scrutiny to read "Le Secret d'Eugénie." It may have come from the distant
past—the golden age of the etiquette and enseigne of the Romantic Era—the link of
the "nostalgia of the sea," of the late Autumn days spent here, the expeditions that have
yielded so many former surprises, etc. The warmth of the afternoon faded quickly—on
the return there was a kind of haze with the setting sun penetrating more autumnal than
springlike—a dalmatian supplied another image & the Italian shepherd in goatskin coat
and conventional hat with arm upstretched—garden statue—conspired further toward
a dream (imaginary) hypnagogic musings before the fireplace resting from the journey—
the Empress Eugenie is escaping from the Communards—a Neapolitan boy statue holds
the reins as hitching post—the carriage under way a dalmatian trots along behind the rear
wheels

the dream deepens—a flying white cupid blasts its horn flying on ahead—Eugénie
is escaping with her secret—(Dénouement) to title caption the closing paragraph as device
to end the foregoing notes (story based thereupon)—see last section of De Quincey's
ENGLISH MAIL-COACH (tumultuousissamente)

in the morning had heard "THE CROWN DIAMONDS" Auber overture over the radio—
the link to the Second Empire in the "VIOLETTES IMPERIALES" film with Raquel Meller—
music for the above, etc. holding the jagged jar to one's ear as one hears music from a seashell

tactility of the "MOUTARDE DIJON" in the cage like a piece in a Cubist painting—on
way home candy & soda shop—"discovering" a lone copy of FLAIR with the blue cover
(same as cage panel) French number with the wonderful Supervielle story, "A Child of the

Joseph Cornell, *Hôtel,* n.d. © Joseph and Robert Cornell Memorial Foundation.

Joseph Cornell, *Untitled* (Hôtel du Nord), 1950–1951. © Joseph and Robert Cornell Memorial Foundation.

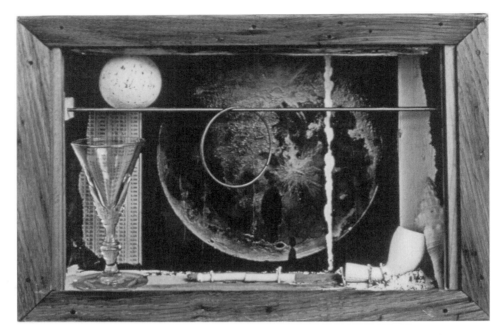

Joseph Cornell, *Soap Bubble Pipe* series, n.d. © Joseph and Robert Cornell Memorial Foundation.

High Seas"—week later coming across Dijon mentioned many times in the "Gaspard de la Nuit" section of the book of poems by that name in Aloysius Bertrand

6/7/58

PIPE DREAM again this A.M. new collage work adding measure of quiet—joy peaceful mood—working on weeks' accumulation to crystalize something coherent—poetic and reverential rather than literal

12/5/65

dreams yesterday noon on couch unable to catch segment—riding a bicycle around in a bare hard-earth terrain—some stones probably—sense of felicity agility with the vehicle— but suddenly I take cognizance of where I am up too high on a rough narrowness—giddiness dissipated with sobering I dismount before I topple off this new path suddenly became precarious, dangerous

3/3/69

milk is being poured into a blue willow-pattern cereal dish for a young girl whose Mother stands by—dust in it hadn't been noticed in time—black specks floating around on the surface—the image graphic, one speck large enough for a fly but it didn't seem to be that specific shape—the milk was powdered—we might say the type of phenomenon halfway between malignant hallucination or nightmare—& beautiful fairy-tale hallucination where dream "business" defies reasoning.

runaway hallucination that was all remembered and deemed the final picture before awakening at 4:30 A.M.—snow finally coming afer all in progress now

3/7/69

before it fades

not too hard to hold but one knows that it is going fast dream business evident.

a prominent musical director as a mailman! moving around in a shadowy atmosphere possibly even around the corner of my bed—tall wearing a fedora—comments exchanged.—detail is difficult here in spite of the quite definite character of minutiae in the mind's eye—an envelope from an artist-acquaintance: large format but this magazine collection portraits of women (?)—some element of fantasy probably cover & inside figures taking up whole sheet with ample background

The second dream after breakfast (pressure forcing me into sleep—not uncommon but not too common—supreme instance upstairs on red couch—Kentucky moving van across street quite possibly influence on dream)

And so business of gluing the dining room table while conversing with Robert behind the stair-way and invisible—as though Bill Watson's radio program were in progress—gluing the large round table like doing a 9″ × 12″ masonite board for a collage—obvious minutiae of this part lost but finally Robert was at the stair landing unshaved but of a genial countenance—stubble predominant—aspect of the whole figure vague but as though standing—cathartic

REAL—then the snow shoveled, good feelings from exchange with Bruesch girls shoveling and this spurring to make notes—insight into table—states of mind in spite of reluctance to "scribble" so much

3/16 into 17/69

DREAM   separate paper

going past a radiantly beautifully standing model as though life-class—she remained there to her pose not looking at me—coming back again same person seated fully clothed—I asked if she were so & so—no, a "Mrs. Sides"—girls clustered around her—a normal friendly atmosphere not experienced in dream too often (but only remembered dream— no telling what marvels in the unremembered—so that graphic character to everything & yet so elusive—business of leading a very portly man through the active, atmospheric place—but this too inscrutable now for any detail

    wonder of the workings of the mind the *ever-ever diversified* independence of "props." pondering the distance of things like ORLANDO—*this* if nothing else GRATITUDE

3/20/69

yesterday this time—cannot recall delving into Freud ("Interpretation of Dreams") since possibly 1964—though my state cloudy nothing at all redemptive—just misery—but this instance of fiasco should not negate prior sessions with this work & a better yield in subsequent recourse there to sparking from E.P.'s dictum, her better than average feeling for Freud's philosophy, views, etc. (i.e., that he did not overemphasize sex—her spontaneously [good] reactions to collage "fillies" [attic] Dosso Dossi "Circe")

3/31/69

Dream: balloon ascent way up dropping a few 1000 feet at my writing

    in semi-awakening something extraordinarily beautiful about Joyce though at 7:10 A.M. now first penning this sheet no image granted

6/12/69

and since 1965 the dream of Caruso—sauntering jauntily from a shop—immaculate dandy—I'd been in the shop with him he hadn't purchased—in the shadowy rear scrutinizing the glass case *completely* at a loss to remotely account for these images "out of the blue" as slightest cognizance of shred of a clue—beyond anything the brilliance & sheen of the *graphic* image—hallucinatory effect as to color *not* a disturbing experience

5/13/69

real Chopin piano pieces heard earlier in morning but listened to indifferently despite the will for better attention. a very real feeling of joy about Tina now—cancelling out feelings of "waste" before and after sleep—such a long conversation—no real importunity towards her re: "expecting." Workings of the psyche pondered offering of this detail so beautifully satisfying—genial rapport—the dream her elaboration of the gold piece. "Imagery" appreciated now—if but one "granted" clear . . . not uncommon I've noticed quite frequently— i.e., consciousness of much lost & YET the graphic, salient IMAGE . . . physiognomy of Chopin (first) more pronounced than Liszt latter much vaguer if nothing more than a general foil, pendant. . . . The mystery of this intrigues me greatly

too much should not be made of "unravelling"—*the beautiful* relaxation in the aftermath & the satisfaction of the graphic granted should suffice—

6/14/69   Saturday morning moving fast to high noon

Dream

an incomparable dream, inscrutable its instigation but marvelous—clear, graphic, breathtaking in the "merveilleux" of its *coup d'oeil*

a heroic dream, even . . . and now . . . the challenge . . . words!

this dream had to do with old photographs (such as I used to collect obsessively) in particular one showing the Tower of Pisa—some confusion about it being "actually" that— THEN an "image" a photograph showing in the distance the leaning tower in its environment very tiny in quintessentialized imagery—in the foreground a tall spire of a church, slender, and one wondered how it would have been photographed—from what prodigious vantage point could the total be snapped (presumably before the time of aerial photography) THEN, from the extravaganza of the workings of the dream state—a *close-up* of the dizzying height of (presumably) another church steeple, the one definitely, however, from which the shot was taken—the intrepid crew as though roped like Alpine climbers (literally so?) one above the other—the surmounting spire of ampler proportions than the one seen in the photograph. But now the photograph has come to life (or *is living,* there is distinct pleasure in recording this versus futility but doing it anyway—"PISA" from the white box material (*could* it be so *circuitous*)

July 16 Tues into Wed., penned 2:00–3:00 A.M.

BEWARE now . . . the rambling . . .

Portrait of Joseph Cornell in his house on Utopia Parkway, 1969. Photo: Hans Namuth. Permission by Namuth Studio.

10/19/68 8:15 a.m.

Dream

Conversing with Marcel Duchamp and telling him that Delacroix weas staying in a N.Y.C. hotel—he did not believe it but did believe it when a Parisian one was mentioned—something about wanting to obtain from Delacroix one of his handkerchiefs probably or possibly via Duchamp

Thus the fact that Delacroix was alive in our contemporary scene taken for granted in the dream and just the locale the source of any doubt?—first dream about Duchamp since his passing

10.19.68 Wed. Duchamp/Delacroix

item: a "distant cousin" of the Debussy dreaming queried in real life about Debussy seeing or knowing him Duchamp has spoken of his inaccessibility, "like Einstein."

consider the dream interpreting it (granting it significance beyond the enigmatical) in the light of the "OBJECT" ("*l'objet*") curiously observed in some kind of *perspective, tradition,* Delacroix—Redon—Duchamp—Redon had followed Delacroix one night out of hero worship (MELLERIO) Duchamp openly acknowledged Redon as an influence "*le royaume de l'objet*" surrealism

own penchant for collecting from way back leading into preoccupation with "*l'objet*"—own spontaneous outgoing admiration for Delacroix—the 3 Escholier tomes before knowing Duchamp period of cellar atelier working on the '50s Delacroix's "Journals." the Nadar reproduction on the bulletin board—the "Journal" entering into the fiber of daily life—afternoons in Flushing Main St.—snack + library pattern (the old library same site)

"Delacroix's Handkerchief"—consider as a title for a crystallized vision of the random notes as an article

12/23/69   Susan Sontag dream

difficulty of recapture
an open wooded area—this *definite*
a church scene
agony of leave-taking of S.

church scene—going back she was absent from the seat she'd occupied priorly—a sadness in the penning now—others in the same place no feeling towards them one detail though difficult seems easier more lucid—the agony of parting takes place on a path in a sparsely wooded area—there is this strong sense of mystical magnification—though apparently close to each other it is as though the head towards high above me & farther away than normal giving the impression of and the path inclined and now so intense & inscrutable the mystique while the difficulty of recording stems afresh there is immense gratitude that there *was* this dream, regardless . . . there is no mystique about erstwhile intense preoccupation with S.S.

7:00 A.M. another dim image—an open field but with a woodsy flavor (many?) people scattered about possibly as though traipsing along with some kind of common purpose

east a summery soft suffusion of pale rose-orange in the vaporous clouds & nearer horizon a sharp soft blue Redonesque

RENÉ CREVEL

I DON'T KNOW HOW TO CUT IT UP

Geologists never have any doubts, and find life really simple, for they have managed to make of the globe that concerns them just a little ball of unthreatening mosiacs you can take apart. They cut the earth in two and then offer us a mild beverage, ideal and ridiculous, of successive eras. And the trick is played—actually it seemed so easy that for centuries our psychologists have tried it out. It's useless. The elements remain fused together. The slice of life is a snatch of fog sadly bleeding, and we still have to deal with the dolorous surprises of dreams.

Yes, our dreams. This little smoke that our desire for security is always pursuing, suddenly evaporates, and everything has to start all over. And we are seeking some new fire. I am thinking of this jar in a de Chirico decor—near this house which you thought, Breton, must be sheltering a sphinx—that remains on the stage otherwise bare after the departure (finally!) of the importunate dancers. Let's try out our little symbol. The importunate dancers are the daily diversions not even offering any picturesque mediocre seduction that might help us indulge in some illusory pastime. But time doesn't pass or drift by. The dancers have left and it's a good thing. The jar is by itself on the stage. A curl of smoke is coming from it. Are you going to tell me that a little hunchback is hidden there, calmly smoking his pipe? You can call the hunchback a sexual instinct or an instinct of conservation, anyway, smoke and dreams continue to rise from the jar, from our sleep. And these dreams and this smoke aren't composed of a jar, of a hunchback, a pipe any more than a sleep, a body, an instinct.

We don't have the stupid consolation of slicing ourselves up or quartering ourselves. A real and imponderable cloud rises from my free hours. but on waking I have to admit that I remember images less than this state that arose from them. Beginning once more to lead a controlled life, I am trying with my limited waking experience to follow in reverse what our pedants call the process, and from a vague but decisive state, I am on the lookout for details which, however, won't seem incontrovertible.

As the day distances me from the nocturnal dream, and the state that resulted from it evaporates, I am constrained to run after a greater number of images and words in order to recreate it. And so the temptation of art is born. You take that jar and a hunchback. You take that body and a sex. You take a canvas and some brushes. You take paper and a pen. Alas there is no more smoke, nor dreams. A child questioned in the morning will explain its joy or its nocturnal terrors by a single fact. At noon the accessories of the dream will have been multiplied, tripled two hours later, and so on.

So we are looking for *clear* and *insufficient* sensations capable of creating a *vague* and *sufficient* state. I am dreaming of a taste of human flesh (not caressed or bitten, but eaten.) I awake with a surprise in my mouth. How did it get there? I think I have seen garlands of skin in pieces. These garlands were decorating my room, heavy with human fruits like those hanging lanterns of July 14. I suppose I must have picked one of those fruits and eaten it. But this hypothesis and the images which I'm tempted to embellish are not enough. I am sure of a taste of flesh in my mouth. The tongue is an unknown island in the geography of dreams, and yet on waking, my tongue, yes, my tongue thinks it not so difficult to become a cannibal.

That's a dream that has nothing picturesque about it. However, I am offering it as one of my stranger ones. It haunted me a whole day and the next one. Looking for this shock which made me, in my confusion, the equal of God, I am trying to build a tower that will never manage to raise me so high as this smoke with the taste of human flesh.

Our sleep cut in two, we see that the liberated spirit does not always tie itself to these so-called wonders that we enjoy in our lucid moments. More than dragons or volcanic eruptions, this clearing out by emptiness terrifies me, making me dream, for example, that I am not dreaming, with a combination of the strictest and most lucid reasonings.

Awakened abruptly, I surprise myself doing some inexorably logical task. But am I mad? For I had a dream that wasn't.

MICHEL LEIRIS

THE COUNTRY OF MY DREAMS

On the steps leading to the perspectives of emptiness, I stand upright, my hands resting on a blade of steel. A cluster of invisible lines crosses my body, linking all the intersecting points of the ribs of the edifice with the sun at its center. I walk along untouched among these wires piercing me and each particle of space breathes a new soul into me. For my spirit does not accompany my body in its turnings; like a machine taking its motor energy from the wire stretched out lengthwise, my flesh quickens at the touch of the perspectives lines that, in passing, fill its most secret cells with the aim of the monument, the fixed soul of the structure, the reflection of the curve of vaults, of the arrangement of basins and of walls intersecting at right angles.

If I trace around myself a circle with the point of my sword, the wires feeding me will be severed and I'll never be able to get out of the circular cell, having separated myself from my spatial pasture and shut myself into a little column of immutable spirit, narrower than the cisterns of the palace.

Stone and steel are the two poles of my captivity, the communicating vessels of slavery: I can only flee from one by shutting myself in the other—until the day when my blade will bring the walls down, with great bursts of stars.

Far below me there stretches a plain entirely covered by an immense flock of black sheep bumping into one another. Dogs are mounting the horizon and pressing against the sides of the flock, forming it into a rectangle less and less oblong. Now I am above a forest of birches whose dappled crests strike against each other and lose their color, while the trunks, stripping their white skin from themselves, construct a great square box, the only thing standing in the denuded plain.

In the center of the box, like a medal in its setting, there is laid the thinnest slice of the last trunk and I distinctly perceive the heart, the bark, and the sapwood.

The disk of wood with a filigree of medullar beams, is only a glass porthole, the orifice of a cone cutting into the thick wall enveloping me the unique window of my time.

The words in your note to Charles Henri Ford about " the detaining tower " in the Americana Fantastica number of VIEW are the only concrete reaction I've had so far, and they satisfy and affect me profoundly. I had felt that the whole thing was much too subtle and complex to attempt in the comparatively limited space of a magazine, and without your appreciative words I would continue to think of it as futile. Will you please accept the heartfelt thanks of both Berenice and myself? * * * The handwritten correction of a phrase in your note was especially interesting as it confirmed a suspicion formulated nine years ago when I acquired in a second-hand book shop a number of CLOSE-UP containing your review of documentary films in an article called " Fiction or Nature ". This published article was corrected like proof in handwriting of such exquisite precision and delicacy that it gave me the feeling that it belonged to it's author. Later when I came to know of Parker Tyler's obsession with Carlyle Blackwell and your work I quoted the passage to him about that actor in your article. * * * * Speaking of natural history there are a couple of volumes from the library of the tower that its little proprietress is taking the liberty of sending on to you in partial payment for your appreciation. She has marked a couple of spots that she greatly hopes will be of outstanding interest to you.

Very sincerely yours,

Joseph Cornell, *Letter to Marianne Moore,* n.d. Rosenbach Museum.
Reproduced by permission. © Joseph and Robert Cornell Memorial
Foundation.

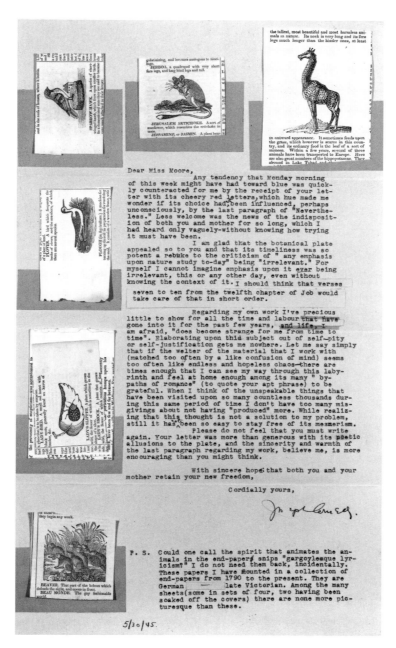

Joseph Cornell, *Letter to Marianne Moore, with Animals,* 1945. Rosenbach Museum. Reproduced by permission. © Joseph and Robert Cornell Memorial Foundation.

In the hemisphere of night I only see the solid white legs of the idol, but I know that higher up, in the eternal ice, its bust is a hole black like the nothingness of naked substance with no attributes.

Among the crowd gathered around the pedestal, someone repeats ceaselessly: "The lining of the solar sepulchre whitens the tombs . . . the lining of the solar sepulchre . . . etc. . . ."

With the angular cut of the blade, the decision was to be made. I found myself on a ploughed land, the sun on my right and to my left, the dark disk of a flight of vultures in a line parallel to the furrows, their beak toward the hollows, riveted by the magnetism of the earth.

Stars were turning over in each cell of the atmosphere. The birds' claws were cutting the air like a glass, leaving behind them incandescence in their wake. My palms were becoming painful, pierced by these lances of fire, and at times one of the vultures would slide along a lightbeam, with the light clutched between his claws. His rectilinear descent led him to my right hand that he tore into with his beak, before climbing back up to rejoin the flock drawing dizzily near the horizon.

I soon perceived that I was motionless, the earth turning under my feet and the birds beating their wings to keep at my level. I plunged into horizons like so many mirrors in succession, each of my feet placed in a furrow like a rail, staring at the wake of the vultures.

But finally they flew past me. Swelling all the cavities of their being to lighten themselves, they mingled with the sun. The earth stopped of a sudden, and I tumbled into a deep well filled with bones, an ancient oven bristling with stalagmites: rapid dissolution and petrification for kings.

Between the slumber of voices and the reign of statues, a rose enriches the blood where the corporeal blue bathes, absorbing a little at a time. The taste of the coronas coming down to the level of the closed mouths suggests a quicker calculation than that of instantaneous gestures. Sea-tangles have traced circles to wound our foreheads. I am thinking of the Roman warrior who watches over my dreams; he raises his shield to the height of my eyes and gives me two words to read:

attol   and   sépulcrons

If Pascal's wager can be pictured by the cross you can make from a gambling die, what can the decomposition of the shield teach me?

For a long time now, I have pulled off fiber by fiber the face of the warrior: first I obtained the profile of a medal, then a grassy surface and an almost limitless swamp with broken beams emerging from it. Today I have managed to put a name on each bit of flesh. The white of the eyes is called *courage*—the pink of the cheeks is written: farewell—and the curves of the helmet so exactly wed the curls of smoke that I can only name them: somnifers.

But the stomach of the child represents a hideous gorgon, whose hair forms the numbers 3 and 5 twisting together. The 8 of their sum turns upside down and I arrive at the Infinite, a snake of the sexual member swallowing itself. Then it is that the owl of lines lies down under the whip of matter. All I have left to do is to accomplish the murder in front of an endless architecture. I will shatter the statues and trace crosses on the earth with my knife. The vents will widen and caves will quietly emerge from the stars—fruits of the spheres and statues, clusters of luminous globes rising like so many transparent bubbles from a smoker of soap, across the pigments of death and the red bulb of a coal lamp.

During my life white and black, the tide of sleep obeys the motion of the planets, like the cycle of menstruation and the periodic migrations of birds. Behind the flock of birds, a delicious oarblade will lift once more: liquid night will substitute for the airy day world, feathers will change to scales and the golden fish will rise from the abysses to take the place of the bird, laid down in its nest of feathers and insect remains. Pebbles covered with words—the words themselves knocked about, faded and polished—bury themselves in the sand among the reeds and the shells of algae, when all terrestrial life pulls back and hides in its dark dwelling, those mineral orifices.

    Zenith,   Porphyry,   Péage

are the three words I read the most frequently.

They first appeared to me only partially: the Z in a zebra stripe or the zig-zag of conflict, an oblique flight towards the incidences but then persevering in a parallel path—the Y of the other-land (Elsewhere, What is there? Will we be sibYls there? What can I do if I no longer have my eYes?)—

—The A spreading ever wider its rapacious angle under which stretches a fictitious horizon, while P Pushed Open the Door of the Passions.

Then the three words formed themselves and I could make them leap into my hands with other words I already owned, reading the sentences they composed as I went along:

Are you paying, Oh Zenith, the toll of porphyry?

Which I answered, throwing up my pebbles to ricochet:

The porphyry of Zenith isn't the toll we take.

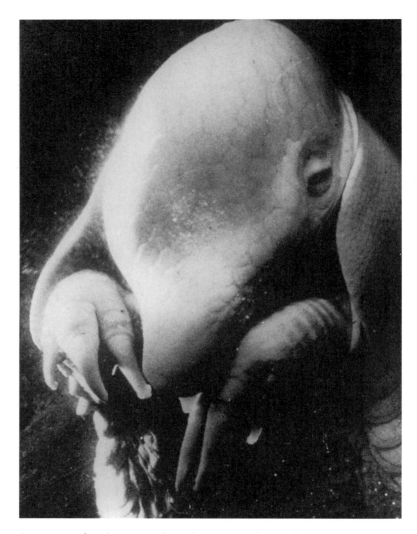

Dora Maar, *Père Ubu,* 1936; gelatin silver print, 15¹/₈ × 11¹/₂ centimeters. Gilman Paper Company collection, New York. Reproduced by permission. All rights reserved.

Dream

1. I am dead. I see the sky forming clouds of dust like the cone of air shot through, in a theatre, by a projector's rays. Many luminous globes, milky white, are lined up in the sky. From each of them protrudes a long metallic stem, one of them piercing my chest from one end to the other—but I feel no pain. I move towards the globes of light sliding gently along the stem, holding by my hand other men who are climbing like me towards the sky, each one sliding along the rail running through them. You hear nothing but the screeching of the steel in our chests.

2. I see so clearly the relation between a rectilinear displacement of a body and a paling perpendicular to the motion, that I shriek aloud.

3. I imagine the rotation of the earth in space, not in some abstract and schematic way, with the axis of the poles and the equator made tangible, but in its reality. The roughness of the earth.

4. André Masson and I are spinning in the air like gymnasts.

    A voice cries out at us: "Acrobats of the world, are you going to come down soon or not?" At these words, we somersault above the horizon and fall into a concave hemisphere.

PAUL NOUGÉ

THE DANCER'S STORY

You will see all right, this woman has so much charm she can do without a story. The moments of her life are linked together smoothly like the steps of her dance. And when she dances everything all around joins in her dance, to the point where she could then become motionless, remain suspended without our being granted the means to notice this. But now the dancer is resting, walking about through her kingdom of fine sand, ropes, nickel-plated bars, animals, and men before proving to herself, through her dancing, her dominion over this world. She pushes her bare arm between the two pieces of canvas of the tent to feel if the air is cool yet and she encounters two overhot lips. She quickly withdraws that hand, pulls herself together, and her well-directed dancer's fist strikes the importunate fellow's invisible face. Recovering her equanimity, she would like to go out a little, but a billboard, on which no doubt work is being done, completely obstructs the doorway. The dancer is patient, she is in a good humor, and anyway the billboard is sliding, moving off.

There is a young man in front of her, his face and gestures expressing a form of admiration so naïve and so pure that she really could not take offense or reply, with gestures similar to his, to a feeling she cannot even imagine being able to share. And if she smiles at him in the most gracious way possible, this is because he also has just smiled at her and if he lightly strokes her cheek with a hand trembling a little, why then would she not caress his face tenderly? Why be surprised at that marvelous dance he is doing in front of her, assuredly the most refined homage he could render the queen of dance and the most obvious sign of happiness? Why now refuse his extended hand, why not follow him, if he wants, to the ends of the earth? But for the moment it is only to the door of her dressing room, where he lets her put on traveling clothes suitable for disguising a dancer who is giving up her dominion for a purer triumph.

Now she is ready and slipping to the place of the final rendezvous. The wild animal that suddenly leaps across the passageway might frighten her. But he is there astride that dream bicycle gleaming in the crisscross beams from the spotlights as the pathetic moment during her aerial round dance. Let her go on with him them, the world lies before them. But is it a mere misfortune that causes the animal to get there before her, and the man to take off now with the beast riding behind, and to have just faded into the horizon of the plain, leaving her there, suspended in her prison of glass, in the shimmering empty kingdom of her purposeless dance?

Chronique scandaleuse des

Pays-Plats

par I. K. BONSET

TOUS CES GENS SONT DES IMBÉCILES SENTIMENTALES → Galérie des hommes célèbres ↔

Bremmer: le tjòk‹tjòk‹tjòk de la peinture.

Berlagé: arabesque romantique — maison avec closet hégelien sentimentalisme infantile.

van Deyssel: Bas‹bleu lardé de la littérature catholique.

Bolland: Diarrhée de monsieur Hégel.

van Eeden: Clown. Poire pourrie de 1880. Traître de la barbe de Jésus Christ.

Havelaar: Chemise malpropre de Tolstoï.

de Meester: Domestique de la litérature de laine. A. K. O.

Roland Holst: Dilettante en edition de luxe. (Je hais la peinture sans sexe!)

Madame Roland Holst: Le gosier hystérique de l'idiotisme socialiste.

Plaschaert: qu'est ce que c'est ça?

Querido: !—,—?—:—„ "—()—•

Willem Kloos: Le pot de chambre de Pétrarque.

Bonset: o°

Théo van Doesburg: Tempérament salpêtreux.

Rensburg: Pick‹wick‹mennike de la lune. Prêtre de l'éneuchisme sans fil.

Rooyaard: Singe innocent devant le miroir de Talma.

cottage stile cottage stile cottage stile cottage stile cottage stile cottage stile cottage stile cottage stile cottage stile cottage stile cottage stile cottage stile cottage stile cottage stile cottage stile cottage stile

---

Raoul Hausmann — Tatlin lebt zu Hause

GEORGES RIBEMONT-DESSAIGNES

SAVANTS

Celui qui mange une purée d'yeux bleus voir plus loin dans le ciel

Celui qui nourrit ses poissons rouges avec du guano de perroquet et comprend leur langage

La sueur de cheval a la vertu du beurre pour frire des gardénias

Celui qui se nourrit de verge de souteneur pour s'occuper de balistique

Les araignées et les abeilles utilisant les artistes

Les artistes modernes et les artistes modernes

Kurt Schwitters

Klublokal Zur Verbesserung der Kultur.

der andere wieder: »Knirps, Insekt, Schurke, wie sich dieser Laubfrosch blähte! — Darauf antwortete der eine: »Armselige Wage, Beutelschneider Duk — »Was?« sagte der andere plötzlich, »Du, du, du? bin ich Dein Hausknecht? Hört ihn doch, den Kalbskopf, ich platze vor Lachen!« Darauf antwortete der eine: »Elender Frahlhans!« — Plötzlich sagte der andere: »Feiger Schurke!« — Da sagte der eine: »Pardon, ich habe ganz vergessen, Sie meiner Braut vorzustellen.« — Plötzlich sagte der andere: »Dabei fällt mir ein, ich habe meinen Namen noch gar nicht genannt. Ich heiße Meier.« — Darauf sagte der eine: »Ebenfalls Meier, Vorsitzender des Vereins zur Veredlung der Hunderassen.« Plötzlich sagte der andere Meier: »Wollen Sie nicht in unseren Klub zur Verbesserung der Kultur eintreten? Sie sind unser Mann, Sie sind ein edler Mensch.« — Darauf antwortete der eine Meier: »ich schätze mich außerordentlich glücklich einen Menschen, wie Sie, kennen zu haben. Ich und mein Hund treten gern in Ihrem Klub bei.« Darauf begaben sich beide Herren mit Hund und Braut ins

---

Theo van Doesburg, *Chronique Scandaleuse des Pays-Plats (Scandalous Chronicle of the Low Countries),* including I. K. Bonset [a.k.a. Theo van Doesburg] and Kurt Schwitters, poster for the Galerie des hommes célèbres. All rights reserved. © ARS.

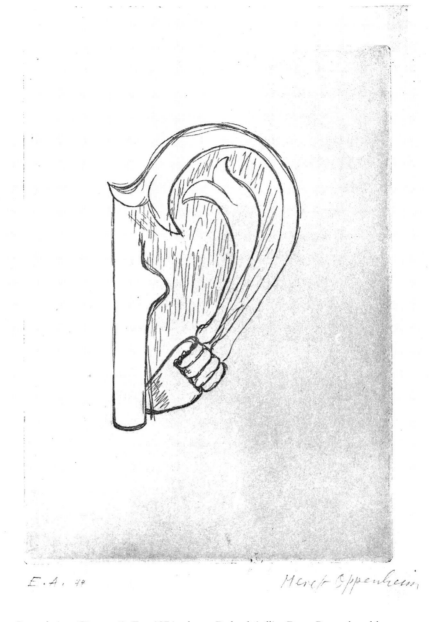

E.A. 44   Meret Oppenheim

Méret Oppenheim, *Giacometti's Ear,* 1974; photo: Roland Aellig, Bern. Reproduced by permission. © ARS.

Address to the Pope

The Confessional is not you, o Pope, it is us, but understand us and may the Catholic world understand us.

In the name of Fatherland, in the name of Family, you urge the sale of souls, the unlimited pulverizing of bodies.

We have too many paths to cross, too great a distance to go between our souls and ourselves, to let your tottering priests intervene with that heap of adventurous doctrines on which all the eunuchs of world liberalism feed.

As for your Catholic and Christian God, who, like all other Gods, has conceived of all evil:

1. You confiscated him.
2. We have nothing to do with your canons, index, sin, confessional, priests, we are thinking of another war, war to you, Pope, you cur.

Here the spirit confesses to the spirit.

From top to bottom of your Roman masquerade, the hatred of the immediate truths of the soul triumphs, the hatred of those flames burning in the spirit itself.

We are not born to this world. O Pope, confined to the world, neither earth nor God speaks through you.

The world is the abyss of the soul, warped Pope, Pope exterior to the soul, leave our souls in our souls, we do not need your knife of enlightenments.

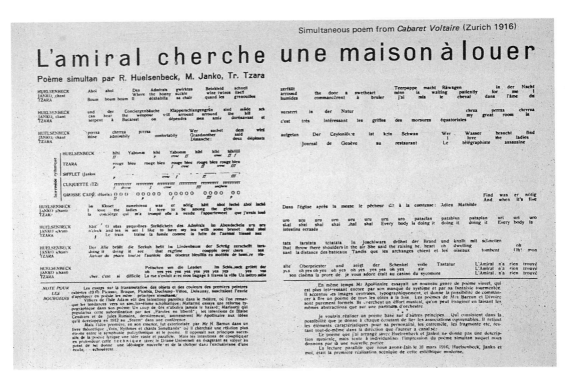

"L'amiral cherche une maison à louer (The Admiral Is Looking for a House to Rent)," a simultaneous poem recited by Richard Huelsenbeck, Marcel Janco, and Tristan Tzara, at the Cabaret Voltaire in Zurich, on March 31, 1916. Huelsenbeck recited in German ("Ahoi ahoi Des Admirals gwirktes Beinkleid schnell zerfällt"), Tzara in French ("Boum boum boum Il déshabilla sa chair quand les grenouilles humides commencèrent à brûler"), and Janco sang in English ("Where the honny [sic] suckle wine twines itself around the door a sweetheart mine is waiting patiently for me"). Tzara's note, "For the Bourgeois," which appears in the printed version, explains that Henri Barzun had been working out a relation between a polyrhythmic symphony and the poem, that Guillaume Apollinaire had been trying out the notion of a visual poem, but that he, Tzara, wanted the listeners to make the link between the diverse elements according to their own personalities. This triple reading was, he said, the "first scenic realization of this modern aesthetic." It was printed on May 15, 1916, by the Cabaret Voltaire, pp. 6–7. Tzara's words were first written in Romanian, and the French version was printed in *Cannibale* 1 (April 25, 1920), and in *Die Schammade* in Cologne in 1920, p. 13.

David Hare, André Breton, and Max Ernst

VVV

VVV

that is, V+V+V. We . . . — . . . — . . . —

that is, not only

V   as a vow—and energy—to return to a habitable and conceivable world, Victory over the forces of regression and of death unloosed at present on the earth, but also V beyond this first Victory, for this world can no more, and ought no more, be the same, V over that which tends to perpetuate the enslavement of man by man,

and beyond this

VV   of that double Victory, V again over all that is opposed to the emancipation of the spirit, of which the first indispensable condition is the liberation of man,

whence

VVV   towards the emancipation of the spirit, through these necessary stages: it is only in this that our activity can recognize its end

Or again:

one knows that to

V   which signifies the View around us, the eye turned towards the external world, the conscious surface,

some of us have not ceased to oppose

VV   the View inside us, the eye turned toward the interior world and the depths of the unconscious,

whence

VVV   towards a synthesis, in a third term, of these two Views, the first V with its axis on the EGO and the reality principle, the second VV on the SELF and the pleasure principle—the resolution of their contradiction tending only to the continual, systematic enlargement of the field of consciousness

towards a total view,

VVV

which translates all the reactions of the eternal upon the actual, of the psychic upon the physical, and takes account of the myth in process of formation beneath the VEIL of happenings.

JACQUES VACHÉ

[MANIFESTO OF UMORE]

Letter of August 18, 1917

However . . . and then, almost the whole TONE of our gestures still remains to be decided—
I want it to be dry, with no literature to it, especially not in the sense of "ART."

Moreover,

ART, doubtless, does not exist—So it is useless to sing on about it—and yet! people make
art—because that is the way it is and not any other way—Well—What can we do about
it?

So we love neither ART, nor artists (down with Apollinaire) AND how RIGHT TOGRATH IS
TO ASSASSINATE THE POET!—However since on account of that we have to spill out a bit
of acid or old lyricism, quick, let it be jerky—because locomotives go in a hurry.

So too modernity, constant and killed every night again—We have nothing to do with
MALLARMÉ, no hatred—but he's dead—But we no longer know either Apollinaire, nor
Cocteau—For—We suspect them of making art too consciously, of patching up some
romanticism with telephone wire and not knowing the engines. THE Constellations un-
hooked again!—how boring—and then sometimes don't they speak seriously! Someone
believing something is a very peculiar being.

BUT SINCE SOME ARE BORN HAM ACTORS ....

Well—I see two ways to let that take place—To form personal sensation with a flamboyant
collision of rare words—say, not too often!—or then to draw angles, or squares of feelings—
the latter, naturally, at the moment—We will let logical Honesty—the responsibility of
contradicting us—like everyone.

—OH ABSURD GOD!—for everything is a contradiction—isn't that so?—and the person who
will not let himself be caught up in the hidden and shady life of everything will be UMORE.—

O My alarm clock—eyes—and hypocritical—who detests me so frightfully! . . . and will be UMORE the person who will feel the pitiful trompe-l'owil of the universal simili-symbols.

—It's in their nature to be symbolical.

—UMORE should not produce—but what can you do?—I grant a little UMOUR to LAF-CADIO—for he doesn't read and only produces amusing experiments—like assassinations—and without any satanic lyricism—my old rotted Baudelaire!!!—He needed our dry art a bit; machinery—rotating things with stinking oils—vibrate—vibrate—vibrate—whistle!—Reverdy—amusing the pohet, and boring in prose, Max Jacob, my old faker—MARIO-NETTES—MARIONETTES—MARIONETTES—do you want some nice marionettes of colored wood?—Two eyes—dead-flame and the crystal round of a monocle—with an octopus typewriter—that's better.

SOURCE NOTES

Please note that asterisks in the sources below indicate that the writing or translation was prepared for this volume.

MEMOIRS OF SURREALISM

EILEEN AGAR
"Am I a Surrealist?" from *A Look at My Life* (London: Methuen, 1988).

MARY ANN CAWS
"Remembering Jacqueline Remembering André"★

RENÉ CHAR
"The Journey Is Done," *Yale French Studies* 31 (May 1964).

GIORGIO DE CHIRICO
From *The Memoirs of Giorgio de Chirico*, trans. Margaret Crosland (New York: Da Capo Press, 1984).

RENÉ MAGRITTE
"Lifeline," *View* (December 1946; "Surrealism in Belgium"), trans. Felix Giovanelli.

MAN RAY
"At the Beginning of My Career . . . Dadamade," from *Self-Portrait* (Boston: Little, Brown, 1963).

ANDRÉ MASSON
"Painting Is a Wager," from *Le Plaisir de peindre* (Nice: La Diane française, 1950), tr. in *Yale French Studies* 31 (May 1964).

PHILIPPE SOUPAULT
"Hymn to Liberty," from *Histoire d'un blanc* (Paris: au Sans Pareil, 1927), in *transition* 10 (January 1928), trans. Maria Jolas.

TEXTS

ANONYMOUS [SCRUTATOR]
"Automatic Drawing," *The Occult Review* (April 16, 1910).

GUILLAUME APOLLINAIRE
"Oneirocriticism," trans. and ed. Roger Shattuck, in *Selected Writings of Guillaume Apollinaire* (New York: New Directions, 1971).

Louis Aragon

From *Paris Peasant*, trans. Simon Watson Taylor (London: Jonathan Cape, 1971).

From *The Fate of La Fontaine,* in *Treatise on Style*, trans. Alyson Waters (Lincoln: University of Nebraska Press, 1991).

Hans Arp

"Notes from a Diary," trans. Eugène Jolas, *transition* 21 (1932, "The Vertical Age").

Fernando Arrabal

"The Folly Stone," trans. and ed. J. H. Matthews, *The Custom-House of Desire: A Half-Century of Surrealist Stories* (Berkeley: University of California Press, 1975).

Antonin Artaud

"The Shell and the Clergyman: Film Scenario," trans. Stuart Gilbert, *transition* 19–20 (June 1930).

"The Mountain of Signs," from *Letter to the Tarahumaras*, in *The Antonin Artaud Anthology*, trans. and ed. Jack Hirschman (San Francisco: City Lights, 1965).

From "Van Gogh: The Man Suicided by Society," trans. Mary Beach, in *The Antonin Artaud Anthology*, ed. Jack Hirschman.

Georges Bataille

"The Absence of Myth" in "Le Surréalisme in 1947," trans. Mary Low, in *Arsenal: Surrealist Subversion* (Chicago: Black Sun Press, 1989).

Hans Bellmer

"What Oozed through the Staircase," in *Autobiography of Surrealism*, ed. and trans. Marcel Jean (New York: Viking, 1980).

Yves Bonnefoy

"The Anti-Plato," 1970, from *Du Mouvement et de l'Immobilité de Douve* (Paris: Gallimard, 1970), trans. Mary Ann Caws.★

Kay Boyle

"A Complaint for M and M," in *transition* 27 (May 1938).

Victor Brauner

"On the Fantastic in Painting," trans. Lucy Lippard, from "Le Fantastique en peinture and théâtre," *VVV* 2–3 (1943–1944).

André Breton

"Age," in *Poems of André Breton,* trans. and eds. Mary Ann Caws and Jean-Pierre Cauvin (Austin: University of Texas, 1982).

"Unclean Night," from *Soluble Fish*, 1924, trans. Samuel Beckett, in *Surrealism*, ed. Julien Levy.

"The Sexual Eagle Exults," from *L'air de l'eau,* 1934, in André Breton, *Oeuvres completes* II: Edition etablie par Marguerite Bonnet Avec, pour ce volume (Paris: Gallimard, 1992); trans. Mary Ann Caws.★

"Less Time," from *Soluble Fish*, 1924, trans. Mary Ann Caws and Matthew Caws, from *HarperCollins World Reader*, eds. Mary Ann Caws and Christopher Prendergast (New York: HarperCollins, 1986).

"Lethal Relief," from *The White-Haired Revolver*, 1932, trans. Samuel Beckett, in *Surrealism*, ed. Julien Levy.

"The Verb To Be," in *Poems of André Breton,* trans. and eds. Mary Ann Caws and Jean-Pierre Cauvin.

"Vigilance," from *The White-Haired Revolver*, 1932, in *Poems of André Breton,* eds. Mary Ann Caws and Jean-Pierre Cauvin; trans. Mary Ann Caws.★

"Dreaming I See You," in *Poems of André Breton,* eds. Mary Ann Caws and Jean-Pierre Cauvin; trans. Mary Ann Caws.★

"Ascendant Sign," from *Free Rein*, trans. Michel Parmentier and Jacqueline d'Amboise (Lincoln: University of Nebraska Press, 1995).

"Dear Hazel of Squirrelnut," from *Mad Love*, trans. Mary Ann Caws (Lincoln: University of Nebraska, 1987).

Claude Cahun
"I Am Still Waiting," answer to questionnaire: "What was the most important encounter of your life?" in *Minotaure* 3-4 (1933); trans. Mary Ann Caws.★

Leonora Carrington
"The House of Fear," from *The House of Fear*, trans. Kathrine Talbot with Marina Warner (New York: Dutton, 1988).

"Uncle Sam Carrington," from *The House of Fear*, trans. Kathrine Talbot with Marina Warner.

Aimé Césaire
"Serpent Sun," "The Automatic Crystal," "The Virgin Forest," and "Sentence," from *The Collected Poetry of Aimé Césaire*, trans. and eds. Clayton Eshleman and Annette Smith (Berkeley: University of California Press, 1983).

"Breaking with the Dead Sea," *Tropiques* 3 (October 1941); trans. Mary Ann Caws.★

Suzanne Césaire
"The Domain of the Marvelous," *View* 1 (1941); trans. Mary Ann Caws.★

René Char
"Artine" and other extracts from *Moulin premier (First Mill)*, trans. Mary Ann Caws, from *Selected Poems of René Char*, eds. Mary Ann Caws and Tina Jolas (New York: New Directions, 1993).

Malcolm de Chazal
From *Sens plastique*, trans. Patricia Terry.★

Arthur Cravan
"Notes" from *VVV* 1 (1942), trans. Terry Hale, in *Four Dada Suicides,* eds. Roger L. Conover, Terry Hale, and Paul Lenti (London: Atlas Press, 1997).

René Crevel
From *Babylon*, trans. Kay Boyle (San Francisco: North Point Press, 1985).

"Every One Thinks Himself Phoenix . . . ," from *Le Clavecin de Diderot*, trans. Samuel Beckett, in *Surrealism*, ed. Julien Levy.

Salvador Dalí
"The Stinking Ass," in *This Quarter* 5, no. 1 (September 1932), trans. J. Bronowski.

"The Great Masturbator," in *The Autobiography of Surrealism*, ed. and trans. Marcel Jean.

LÉON DAMAS
"No One Remembers," from *Présence africaine* 28 (1965); trans. Mary Ann Caws.★

ROBERT DESNOS
From *Deuil pour deuil (Mourning for Mourning)*, 1924, trans. and ed. Mary Ann Caws, *The Surrealist Voice of Robert Desnos* (Hanover: University of Massachusetts Press, 1982).

"Oh Pangs of Love," "I Have So Often Dreamed of You," "Sleep Spaces," "If You Knew," and "No, Love Is Not Dead," from *To the Mysterious One*, 1925; trans. Mary Ann Caws, in *The Surrealist Voice of Robert Desnos*.

"Obsession" and "Three Stars" from *Les Ténèbres*, 1927, trans. Mary Ann Caws, in *The Surrealist Voice of Robert Desnos*.

From *La Liberté ou l'amour! (Freedom or Love!)*, 1928, trans. Mary Ann Caws, in *The Surrealist Voice of Robert Desnos*.

MARCEL DUCHAMP
"The Bride," from *The Bride Stripped Bare by Her Own Bachelors*, in *Surrealism*, ed. and trans. Julien Levy.

JEAN-PIERRE DUPREY
"Nothing on Earth" from *First Poems, 1947–1949*, in *Jean-Pierre Duprey, Oeuvres complètes*, ed. François de Dio (Paris: Christian Bourgois, 1990); trans. Mary Ann Caws.★

ELSA BARONESS VON FREYTAG-LORINGHOVEN
"Café du Dôme" and "X-Ray," in *transition* 7 (October 1927).

PAUL ELUARD
"Lady Love," "Second Nature," and "Queen of Diamonds," trans. Samuel Beckett, in *Surrealism*, ed. Julien Levy.

"Identities" and "The Victory at Guernica," from *Cours Naturel (Natural Course)* (Paris: Gallimard, 1938); trans. Mary Ann Caws.★

"Dawn," from *Les Nécessités de la vie (The Necessities of Life)* (Paris: Gallimard, 1932); trans. Mary Ann Caws.★

From *Nuits partagées (Shared Nights)*, Paul Eluard, *Oeuvres complètes* (Paris: Gallimard, 1968); trans. Mary Ann Caws.★

MAX ERNST
"The Hundred-Headless Woman," *View* 7-8 (June 1941, poetry supplement).

JEAN FERRY
"Kafka or 'The Secret Society,'" from *The Custom-House*, ed. and trans. J. H. Matthews.

ALBERTO GIACOMETTI
"Poem in Seven Spaces," "The Brown Curtain," "Grass Coal," and "Yesterday, the Quicksands," from *Le Surréalisme au service de la Révolution* 5 (1933); trans. Mary Ann Caws.★

JULIEN GRACQ
"Ross' Barrier," *View* VI, nos. 2–3 (March–April 1946).

GEORGES HENEIN
"Healthy Remedies," *VVV* 1 (1942); trans. Mary Ann Caws.★

Radovan Ivsic
"The Fool's Speech," from Act I, scene 3, and Act V, scene 1, "The Fool," from *King Gordogain*, trans. Roger Cardinal (Zagreb: Croation P.E.N. Centre & Most/The Bridge, 1993).

Frida Kahlo
Letter to Jacqueline Lamba, from *The Diary of Frida Kahlo*, ed. Sarah M. Lowe (New York: Abrams, 1996); tr. slightly altered, Mary Ann Caws.★

Comte de Lautréamont (Isidore Ducasse)
From "Chant III," from *Chants de Maldoror*, 1868, in *Surrealism*, ed. and trans. Julien Levy.

Annie Le Brun
"Twelfth Ring" and "About Fashion," from *Sur-le-Champ (Right Away)*, in *Tout Près, Les Nomades (The Nomads So Near)*, 1967; trans. Mary Ann Caws.★

Michel Leiris
"From the Heart to the Absolute," *transition* 16–17, trans. Eugène Jolas.

Georges Limbour
"In the Heat of Inspiration," *transition* 49, no. 5, trans. John Weightman.

Mina Loy
"Oh Marcel. . . . Otherwise I Also Have Been to Louise's," from *The Last Lunar Baedeker*, ed. and trans. Roger L. Conover (London: Carcenet, 1985).

"Auto-Facial-Construction," from *The Last Lunar Baedeker*, ed. and trans. Roger L. Conover (New York: Farrar, Straus, and Giroux, 1996).

Pierre Mabille
"The Realm of the Marvelous," from *The Mirror of the Marvelous*, in *Tropiques* 4 (January 1942); trans. Mary Ann Caws.★

"The Destruction of the World," from *The Mirror of the Marvelous*, in *View* I, nos. 9–10 (December 1941–January 1942), trans. Charles Henri Ford.

René Magritte
"Continuous Experience," from *Surrealism in Broad Daylight*, Manifesto no. 1 (October 1946); trans. Mary Ann Caws.★

André Pieyre de Mandiargues
"The Passageway of Judiciary Pleasures," from *Dans les années sordides* (Monaco, 1943), in *View* VI, nos. 2–3 (March–April 1946), trans. Paul Bowles.

Joyce Mansour
"The Vices of Men," from *Cris*, 1953, "They Have Weighed," from *Déchirures (Tearings)*, 1955, "Pericoloso Sporgersi," from *Rapaces (Rapacious)*, 1960, and "Your Figure or the War against Fat," from *The Only Defense against the Iron Curtain*, in *Bief* 5 (1959), from *Prose et poésie: Oeuvres complètes*, ed. Hubert Nyssen (Paris: Actes Sud, 1991); trans. Mary Ann Caws.★

Marcel Mariën
"Psychological Aspects of the Fourth Dimension," from *Poids et Mesures*, in *View* (December 1946, "Surrealism in Belgium"), trans. Felix Giovanelli.

André Masson
"The Bed of Plato," from *View* I, nos. 7–8 (June 1941), trans. Clark Mills.

MATTA

"Sensitive Mathematics—The Architecture of Time," in *Minotaure* 11 (Spring 1938), in *Surrealists on Art,* ed. and trans. Lucy Lippard (New York: Prentice-Hall, 1970).

RENÉ MÉNIL

"Colors of Childhood, Colors of Blood," *Tropiques* 5 (1942); trans. Mary Ann Caws.★

"Poem," *Tropiques* 10 (February 1944); trans. Mary Ann Caws.★

JOAN MIRÓ

"Harlequin's Carnival," from *Verve* I, no. 4 (January-March 1939), in *Surrealists on Art*, ed. and trans. Lucy Lippard.

"Each Speck of Dust," from *VVV* 2-3 (1941); trans. Mary Ann Caws.★

PAUL NOUGÉ

"Nothing" and "Sketch of the Human Body," from Paul Nougé, *L'Experience continue* (Brussels: Editions de la *Revue Les Lèvres nues*, 1966); originally in *Les Lèvres nues* 4 (1955); trans. Mary Ann Caws.★

MÉRET OPPENHEIM

"My Friend's Dog," "Round the World," "Without Me Anyway," and "Finally," from Méret Oppenheim, *Defiance in the Face of Freedom*, ed. Bice Curiger (Cambridge, Mass.: MIT Press and New York: Parkett Publishers, 1989), trans. Catherine Schelbert.

WOLFGANG PAALEN

"The Volcano-Pyramid: A Mythological Hypothesis Suggested by the Appearance of a New Volcano," 1943, from Wolfgang Paalen, *Form and Sense* (New York: Wittenborn and Co., 1945).

VALENTINE PENROSE

"May—1941," from *VVV* 1 (1942); trans. Mary Ann Caws.★

BENJAMIN PÉRET

Poems "Listen" and "Where Are You" and stories "One to One," and "The Four Elements," 1945, from Benjamin Peret, *Death to the Pigs*, trans. Rachel Stella (Lincoln: University of Nebraska Press, 1988).

FRANCIS PICABIA

"Aphorisms," from *Littérature*, in *Autobiography of Surrealism*, trans. and ed. Marcel Jean.

PABLO PICASSO

"In the Corner a Violet Sword," *transition* 21 (1934), trans. Eugène Jolas.

"Give and Take Twist and Kill," from *Cahiers d'Art 7–10*, in *Surrealism*, ed. and trans. Julien Levy.

GISÈLE PRASSINOS

"The Wool Dress," in *The Custom-House*, ed. and trans. J. H. Matthews.

RAYMOND QUENEAU

"Surprises," "Dream," "The Rainbow," and "Interjections" from *Exercises du style*, trans. Barbara Wright (New York: New Directions, 1981).

ALICE RAHON

"Despair," from *A Même la terre* (Paris: Editions surréalistes, 1936); trans. Myrna Bell Rochester, in *Surrealist Women: An International Anthology*, ed. Penelope Rosemont (Austin: University of Texas Press, 1998).

Jacques Rigaut

From *Lord Patchogue*, trans. Terry Hale, in *Four Dada Suicides*, eds. Roger L. Conover, Terry Hale, and Paul Lenti (London: Atlas Press, 1997).

Harold Rosenberg

"Life and Death of the Amorous Umbrella," *VVV* I (June 1942).

Raymond Roussel

"Bertha the Child-Flower," trans. Mary Ann Caws.★ This piece is from a discarded manuscript passage from *Locus Solus*. Permission from *Revue de la Bibliothèque Nationale* 43 (1992).

Kurt Schwitters

"Quadrangle," from *Causes and Outbreak of the Great and Glorious Revolution in Revon*, in *transition* 3 (June 1927), trans. Eugène Jolas.

"priimiitiitiii," *transition* 3 (June 1927), trans. Eugène Jolas.

"Lanke Tr Gl (skerzoo aux meiner soonate in uurlauten)," *transition* 21 (1932, "The Vertical Age").

Marcel Schwob

"Paolo Uccello," in *transition* 49, no. 5 (1949), trans. J. G. Weightman.

Louis Scutenaire

"Entries in a Journal," *View* (December 1946, "Surrealism in Belgium"), trans. Felix Giovanelli.

Rrose Sélavy

[Robert Desnos, personage borrowed from Marcel Duchamp] "Rrose Sélavy demande," *View* V, no. 1.

Kurt Seligmann

"Magic and the Arts," in *View* I, nos. 7–8 (December 1941), trans. Martin James.

Léopold Sédar Senghor

"Speech and Image: An African Tradition of the Surreal," trans. John Reed and Clive Wake, in *Poems for the Millennium*, ed. Jerome Rothenberg and Pierre Joris (Berkeley: University of California Press, 1994).

Philippe Soupault

"The Silent House," *transition* 3 (June 1927), trans. Elliot Paul.

"Twilight," "One Two or Three," "Georgia," "Tristan Tzara," and "André Breton," from *Epitaphs*, 1919, and "To Drink," from *Songs*, 1921, in Philippe Soupault, *Georgia, Épitaphes, Chansons* (Paris: Gallimard, 1984); trans. Mary Ann Caws and Patricia Terry.★

Dorothea Tanning

From "Blind Date," *VVV* 2–3 (1942); trans. Mary Ann Caws.★

Tristan Tzara

"Note on Art," "Note on Poetry," "Before Night," and "Part XIX," trans. Mary Ann Caws, in *Tristan Tzara: "Approximate Man" and Other Writings*, ed. Mary Ann Caws (Detroit: Wayne State University Press, 1973).

Marianne van Hirtum

"Euthanasia—a Cat Kidnapped—Thirty Francs—The Veterinarian" in *The Custom-House*, ed. and trans. J. H. Matthews

William Carlos Williams
"Theessentialroar" in *transition Workshop*, ed. Eugène Jolas (New York: Vanguard Press, 1949).

Other Works

Collective Works

André Breton and Paul Eluard
"Intra-Uterine Life," "Simulation of General Paralysis," "Simulation of Delirium of Interpretation," "Force of Habit," and "The Original Judgment," trans. John Ashbery, from *L'Immaculée conception (The Immaculate Conception)* in *What Is Surrealism?,* ed. Franklin Rosemont (New York: Monad, 1978).

André Breton and Philippe Soupault
From "Barriers," extract from *The Magnetic Fields*, 1919 (repr. Paris: Lachenal and Ritter, 1988); trans. Mary Ann Caws.★

Luis Buñuel and Salvador Dalí
Scenario for *L'Age d'or*, in *Surrealism*, ed. and trans. Julien Levy.

Paul Eluard and Benjamin Péret
152 Proverbes Mis au Goût du Jour, 1925, in *Surrealism*, ed. and trans. Julien Levy.

Renaud, Marianne van Hirtum, Vincent Bounoure, Micheline Bounoure, and Jean-Louis Bédouin
"The Dog: Parallel Story," by Renaud, Marianne van Hirtum, Vincent Bounoure, Micheline Bounoure, and Jean-Louis Bédouin in *The Custom-House*, ed. and trans. J. H. Matthews.

Games and Questionnaires

Anonymous
"Surrealist Game," in *Tropiques* 5 (April 1942); trans. Mary Ann Caws.★

Answers to Questionnaires
"About Giorgio de Chirico's *Enigma of a Day*" (André Breton, René Char, Paul Eluard, Alberto Giacometti, Maurice Henry, Benjamin Péret, and Tristan Tzara), and "About Paris" (André Breton, Paul Eluard, and Tristan Tzara), from *Le Surréalisme au service de la Révolution* 6 (May 16, 1933), in *The Autobiography of Surrealism*, ed. and trans. Marcel Jean.

Trance Event

Robert Desnos with Louis Aragon
"Trance Event," in *The Autobiography of Surrealism*, ed. and trans. Marcel Jean.

Dreams

Antonin Artaud
"Dream," from *La Révolution surréaliste* 3 (April 13, 1925); trans. Mary Ann Caws.★

André Breton
"Dream," from *La Révolution surréaliste* 1 (December 1924); trans. Mary Ann Caws.★

Giorgio de Chirico
"Dream," from *La Révolution surréaliste* 1 (December 1924); trans. Mary Ann Caws.★

JOSEPH CORNELL

Some dreams, 1947–1969, from his *Diaries* (unpub., from Archives of American Art); trans. Mary Ann Caws.★

RENÉ CREVEL

"I Don't Know How to Cut It Up," from *La Révolution surréaliste* 2 (January 15, 1925); trans. Mary Ann Caws.★

MICHEL LEIRIS

"The Country of My Dreams," from *La Révolution surréaliste* 1 (December 1924); trans. Mary Ann Caws.★

"Dream," from *La Révolution surréaliste* 4 (July 15, 1925); trans. Mary Ann Caws.★

PAUL NOUGÉ

"The Dancer's Story," in *The Custom-House,* trans. and ed. J. H. Matthews.

CHANTS AND MANIFESTOES

ANONYMOUS

"Address to the Pope," in *The Autobiography of Surrealism*, trans. and ed. Marcel Jean.

DAVID HARE, ANDRÉ BRETON, AND MAX ERNST

VVV (June 1942); announcement

JACQUES VACHÉ

"Manifesto of UMORE," an extract from letter to André Breton, August 18, 1917. From Jacques Vaché, *Lettres de Guerre de Jacques Vaché* (Paris: K éditeur, 1949); trans. Mary Ann Caws.★

Index

Page numbers in *italics* indicate a photograph of a work of art. An asterisk (★) after a page number indicates a photograph of the subject.